About the Author

Marcel Lewinski is an Assistant Adjunct Professor of History Education at Illinois State University. Previously, he was an award-winning high school social studies teacher. He taught a wide range of subjects including geography, world history, economics, political science, sociology, and contemporary problems. Lewinski is professionally active in many organizations and has given presentations at many state, regional, and national conferences. He has conducted numerous workshops for social studies teachers and has traveled all over the world. As author of several textbooks in the social studies, Mr. Lewinski acts as a consultant to school systems and has often contributed to educational publications.

Reading Consultant

Timothy Shanahan, Ph.D., Professor of Urban Education, Director of the Center for Literacy, University of Illinois at Chicago; Author, AMP Reading System

Reviewers

The publisher wishes to thank the following educators for their helpful comments during the review process for *World Geography and Cultures.* Their assistance has been invaluable.

Nelson Acevedo, Curriculum Instructional Specialist, New York City Alternative Schools and Programs, Jamaica, NY; **Sylvia Berger,** Special Education Resource Teacher, Markham District High School, Markham, Ontario, Canada; **Justin Delfosse,** Special Education Teacher, West High School, Green Bay, WI; **Mary Glover,** Senior Director, San Diego County Office of Education, Juvenile Court and Community Schools, San Diego, CA; **Debora Hartzell,** Lead Teacher for Special Education, Lakeside High School, Atlanta, GA; **Lenore Heino Hoyt,** Social Studies Teacher, Centennial High School, Circle Pines, MN; **Robert Johnston,** Supervisor of Social Studies, Waterbury Public Schools, Waterbury, CT; **Daniel Kingery,** Special Education Department Chair, Golden Valley High School, Santa Clarita, CA; **Eleanor White,** Special Education Director, Rochester Community Schools, Rochester, MI; **J. B. Whitten,** Exceptional Student Education Teacher, Lennard High School, Ruskin, FL; **Sara Yanoush,** Special Education Teacher, Pace High School, Brownsville, TX

Acknowledgments appear on pages 613–614, which constitutes an extension of this copyright page.

ISBN-13: 978-0-7854-6383-2

ISBN-10: 0-7854-6383-6

3 4 5 6 7 8 9 10   11 10 09

World Geography and Cultures

by
Marcel Lewinski

PEARSON

AGS Globe

Shoreview, Minnesota

Contents

Biography

Spotlight Story

Geography in Your Life

Graph Study/Chart Study

Reading Strategy

Map Skills/Map Study

Writing About Geography

Geography in Today's World

Celebrations

Everyday Life

How to Use This Book: A Study Guide

Welcome to the study of world geography. You may be asking yourself, "Why do I need to know about people and places other than the United States?" When we study geography of the world, we learn more about how the world is today. Many countries are very important to the United States. They provide us with goods and services. In turn, the United States sells its goods and services to other nations. It is important that we know about our world and about the people who live in it. Everyone can help make the world a better place to live.

As you read the units, chapters, and lessons of this book, you will learn about the places and people of our world.

Before you start to read this book, you need to understand how to use it. You also need to know how to be successful in this course. Information in this first section can help you achieve these things.

How to Study

These tips can help you study more effectively:

- Plan a regular time to study.

- Choose a desk or table in a quiet place where you will not be distracted. Find a spot that has good lighting.

- Gather all the books, pencils, paper, and other equipment you will need to complete your assignments.

- Decide on a goal. For example: "I will finish reading and taking notes on Chapter 1, Lesson 1, by 8:00."

- Take a five- to ten-minute break every hour to keep alert.

- If you start to feel sleepy, take a break and get some fresh air.

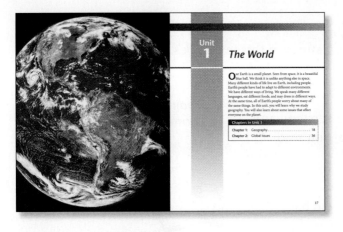

Before Beginning Each Unit

Read the unit title and study the photograph. Do you recognize anything in the photo?

◆ Read the opening paragraphs.

◆ Read the titles of the chapters in the unit.

◆ Read the Chapter Summaries and Unit Summary to help you identify key ideas.

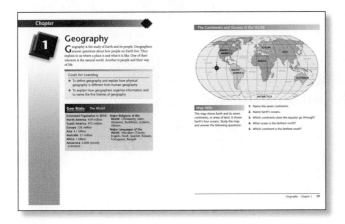

Before Beginning Each Chapter

◆ Read the chapter title.

◆ Read the opening paragraphs.

◆ Study the Goals for Learning. The Chapter Review and tests will ask questions related to these goals.

◆ Study the Geo-Stats. They give you information about the place or places in the chapter.

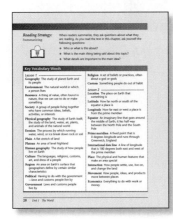

◆ Read the paragraph and bullets on the Reading Strategy page. The strategy will help you become a better reader. Reading Strategy notes in each lesson will help you apply the strategy as you read.

◆ Read the words and definitions in the Key Vocabulary Words box. The words in this list are important vocabulary words in the chapter.

◆ Read the Chapter Summary to help you identify key issues.

◆ Look at the Chapter Review. The questions cover the most important information in the chapter.

Note These Features

You can find complete listings of these features in this textbook's table of contents.

Reading Strategy
Tips to help you understand and make sense of what you read

Reading Strategy:
Summarizing

Biography
Highlights people who have made contributions to the world

Geography in Your Life
Relates geography to the modern world

Everyday Life
Tells about the daily life of a teen who lives in the area featured in the chapter

Spotlight Story
Tells about an important part of history related to the geography unit

Spotlight Story

Writing About Geography
Provides geography topics to write about in each chapter

Writing About Geography

Geography in Today's World
Discusses current concerns around the world, such as ways to help the environment, world famine, and world literacy

Celebrations
Describes festivals and other ceremonies in different parts of the world

Before Beginning Each Lesson

Read the lesson title and restate it in the form of a question. For example, write: *What is Geography?*

Look over the entire lesson, noting the following:

◆ bold words

◆ text organization

◆ photos

◆ maps

◆ graphs and charts

◆ Lesson Review questions

As You Read the Lesson

◆ Read the major headings.

◆ Read the subheads and paragraphs that follow.

◆ Study the maps, graphs, and charts.

◆ Before moving on to the next lesson, see if you understand the concepts you read. If you do not, reread the lesson. If you are still unsure, ask for help.

◆ Practice what you have learned by completing the Lesson Reviews.

Using the Bold Words

Knowing the meaning of all the boxed words in the left column will help you understand what you read.

Geography

The study of planet Earth and its people

These **vocabulary words** appear in **bold type** the first time they appear in the text and are often defined in the paragraph.

    Geography is the study of the planet Earth and its people.

All of the words in the left column are also defined in the **Glossary.**

    Geography (jē og′ rə fē) The study of planet Earth and its people (p. 21)

Word Study Tips

◆ Start a vocabulary file with index cards to use for review.

◆ Write one term on the front of each card. Write the chapter number, lesson number, and definition on the back.

◆ You can use these cards as flash cards by yourself or with a study partner to test your knowledge.

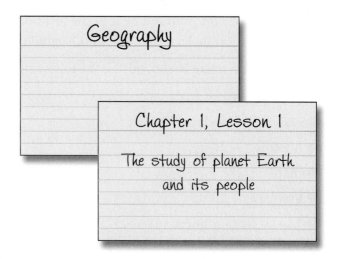

Geography

Chapter 1, Lesson 1

The study of planet Earth and its people

Taking Notes in Class

◆ Outline each lesson using the subheads as the main points.

◆ Always write the main ideas and supporting details.

◆ Keep your notes brief.

◆ Write down important information only.

◆ Use your own words.

◆ Do not be concerned about writing in complete sentences. Use phrases.

◆ Do not try to write everything the teacher says.

◆ Use the same method all the time. Then when you study for a test, you will know where to go to find the information you need to review.

◆ Review your notes to fill in possible gaps as soon as you can after class.

Using a Three-Column Chart

One good way to take notes is to use a three-column chart. Make your own three-column chart by dividing a sheet of notebook paper into three parts. In Column 1, write the topic you are reading about or studying. In Column 2, write what you learned about this topic as you read or listened to your teacher. In Column 3, write questions, observations, or opinions about the topic, or write a detail that will help you remember the topic. Here are some examples of different ways to take notes using the three-column chart.

The topic I am studying	What I learned from reading the text or class discussion	Questions, observations, or ideas I have about the topic
Geography	• physical geography studies landforms and physical features • human geography studies how people live on Earth	• Is there a chart of landforms? • I wonder what I will learn about people in other countries.

Vocabulary Word	Definition	Sentence with Vocabulary Word
Plateau	an area of level highland	The field is located on a plateau.

Country	Facts about this country	Page Number
Canada	located north of the United States	p. 93
	Hudson Bay is largest body of water	p. 98
	most of Canada has subarctic climate	p. 99
	most people live in urban areas	p. 102

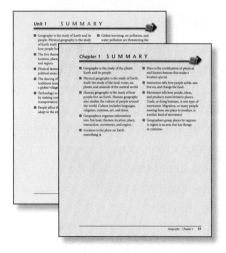

Using the Summaries

◆ Read each Chapter Summary to be sure you understand the chapter's main ideas.

◆ Review your notes and test yourself on vocabulary words and key ideas.

◆ Practice writing about some of the main events from the chapter.

◆ At the end of each unit, read the Unit Summary to be sure you understand the unit's main ideas.

Using the Reviews

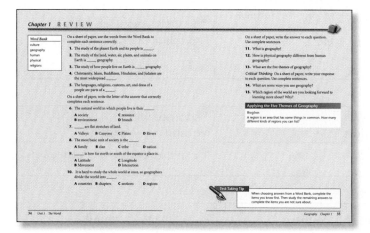

◆ Answer the questions in the Lesson Reviews.

◆ In the Chapter Reviews, answer each fill-in-the-blank, multiple choice, short-answer, and critical-thinking question.

◆ Write an answer to the Applying the Five Themes of Geography question.

◆ Review the Test-Taking Tips.

Preparing for Tests

◆ Complete the Lesson Reviews and Chapter Reviews. Make up similar questions to practice what you have learned. You may want to do this with a classmate and share your questions.

◆ Review your answers to Lesson Reviews and Chapter Reviews.

◆ Reread the Chapter Summaries.

◆ Test yourself on vocabulary words and key ideas.

Reading Checklist

Good readers do not just read with their eyes. They read with their brains turned on. In other words, they are active readers. Good readers use strategies as they read to keep them on their toes. The following strategies will help you to check your understanding of what you read. A strategy appears at the beginning of each chapter of this book.

- **Summarizing** To summarize a text, stop often as you read. Notice these things: the topic, the main thing being said about the topic, important details that support the main idea. Try to sum up the author's message using your own words.

- **Questioning** Ask yourself questions about the text and read to answer them. Here are some useful questions to ask: Why did the author include this information? Is this like anything I have experienced? Am I learning what I hoped I would learn?

- **Predicting** As you read, think about what might come next. Add in what you already know about the topic. Predict what the text will say. Then, as you read, notice whether your prediction is right. If not, change your prediction.

- **Text Structure** Pay attention to how a text is organized. Find parts that stand out. They are probably the most important ideas or facts. Think about why the author organized ideas this way. Is the author showing a sequence of events? Is the author explaining a solution or the effect of something?

- **Visualizing** Picture what is happening in a text or what is being described. Make a movie out of it in your mind. If you can picture it clearly, then you know you understand it. Visualizing what you read will also help you remember it later.

- **Inferencing** The meaning of a text may not be stated. Instead, the author may give clues and hints. It is up to you to put them together with what you already know about the topic. Then you make an inference—you conclude what the author means.

- **Metacognition** Think about your thinking patterns as you read. Before reading a text, preview it. Think about what you can do to get the most out of it. Think about what you already know about the topic. Write down any questions you have. After you read, ask yourself: Did that make sense? If not, read it again.

Using Globes and Maps

A globe is a model of Earth. Looking at the globe, you can see that Earth is round. You can see Earth's features and surfaces. A globe is the best way to show Earth. However, how do you show the round features of a globe on a flat page? You use a map.

You also can see that geographers divide Earth into halves or **hemispheres**. The **equator** divides Earth into the Northern Hemisphere and the Southern Hemisphere. The equator is an imaginary line that circles the middle of Earth.

The **prime meridian** and the **international date line** divide Earth into the Eastern Hemisphere and the Western Hemisphere. The prime meridian is an imaginary line that circles Earth from the North Pole to the South Pole. The international date line is on the side of Earth you cannot see here. It is directly opposite the prime meridian.

Geographers measure distances from the equator and the prime meridian. These distances are imaginary lines called **latitude** and **longitude**.

The Hemispheres

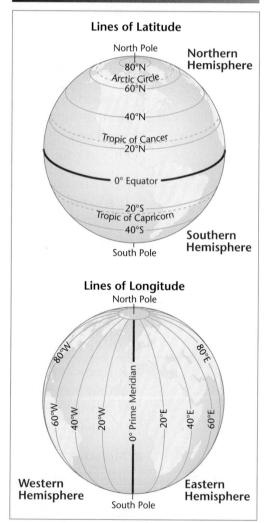

Lines of Latitude

North Pole
Northern Hemisphere
80°N
Arctic Circle
60°N
40°N
Tropic of Cancer
20°N
0° Equator
20°S
Tropic of Capricorn
40°S
Southern Hemisphere
South Pole

Lines of Longitude
North Pole
80°W
60°W
40°W
20°W
0° Prime Meridian
20°E
40°E
60°E
80°E
Western Hemisphere
Eastern Hemisphere
South Pole

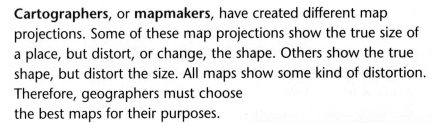

Cartographers, or mapmakers, have created different map projections. Some of these map projections show the true size of a place, but distort, or change, the shape. Others show the true shape, but distort the size. All maps show some kind of distortion. Therefore, geographers must choose the best maps for their purposes.

A **Mercator projection** stretches the lines of latitude apart. It does not show the true size of landmasses. A Mercator projection does show true shape, however.

Landmasses in a **Robinson projection** are not as distorted as in a Mercator projection. However, there is some distortion in the size of the landmasses.

Mercator Projection

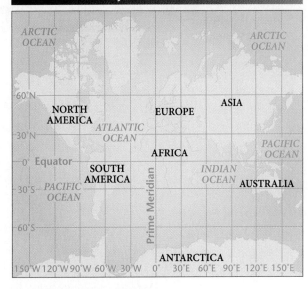

Robinson Projection

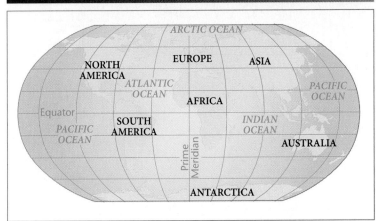

Critical Thinking

Why would a mapmaker choose to use a Robinson projection instead of a Mercator projection?

Reading a Map

To understand geography, you need to know how to read maps. To read a map, you need to understand its parts. The main parts of a map are a title, a key, a compass rose, and a scale. Many of the maps you see are **general purpose maps**. These are political maps and physical maps. A **political map** shows features that people determine, such as country boundaries, cities, and capitals.

The **title** of a map tells the area the map covers. →

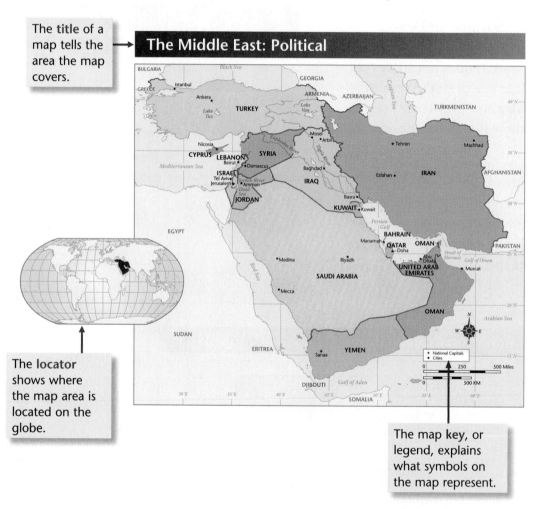

The **locator** shows where the map area is located on the globe.

The map **key**, or legend, explains what symbols on the map represent.

A **physical map** shows how high a landmass is. It also shows natural features such as rivers and oceans. Some of the maps you see show specific kinds of information. These maps are called **special purpose maps**. There are many types of special purpose maps. For example, a climate map is a special purpose map. It shows the typical weather in a place. Look at the World Climate Zones map on page 15.

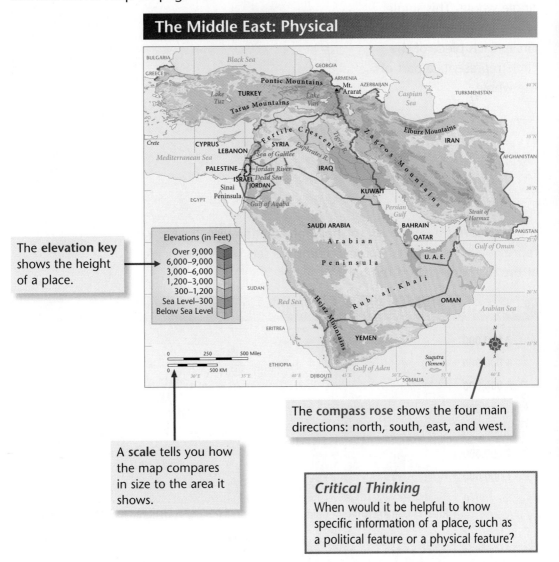

The Middle East: Physical

The **elevation key** shows the height of a place.

Elevations (in Feet)
Over 9,000
6,000–9,000
3,000–6,000
1,200–3,000
300–1,200
Sea Level–300
Below Sea Level

A **scale** tells you how the map compares in size to the area it shows.

The **compass rose** shows the four main directions: north, south, east, and west.

Critical Thinking

When would it be helpful to know specific information of a place, such as a political feature or a physical feature?

Reading Graphs and Charts

Graphs and charts organize and present information in a visual way. There are different types of graphs and charts.

A **circle graph** is sometimes called a pie graph. It is a good way to show the sizes of parts as compared to a single whole. This single whole is represented as a circle. Each piece of the circle represents a part of the whole.

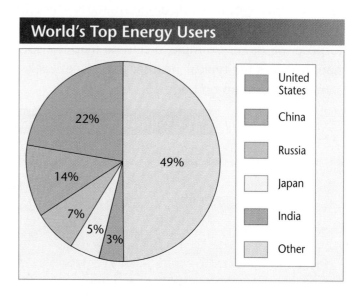

World's Top Energy Users

- United States
- China
- Russia
- Japan
- India
- Other

49%
22%
14%
7%
5%
3%

A **bar graph** is a good way to show information visually. Each bar represents a set of facts. You can compare sets of facts by looking at the different sizes of the bars.

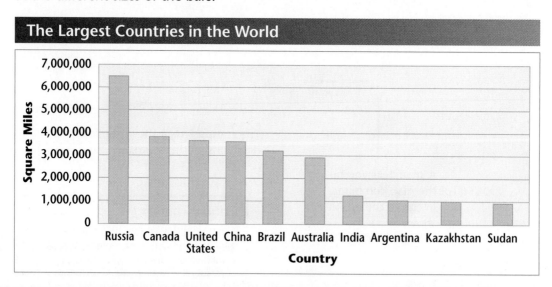

The Largest Countries in the World

Square Miles

7,000,000
6,000,000
5,000,000
4,000,000
3,000,000
2,000,000
1,000,000
0

Russia Canada United States China Brazil Australia India Argentina Kazakhstan Sudan

Country

World Facts

Fact	Place	Location	Size
Highest Mountain	Mount Everest	Nepal and China	29,035 feet high
Longest River	Nile	North and East Africa	4,160 miles long
Largest Island	Greenland	North Atlantic	840,000 square miles
Largest Body of Water	Pacific Ocean	From west of North and South America to east of Asia and Australia	63,800,000 square miles

A **chart** can also be called a table. Charts are organized into rows and columns. Charts can help you to compare information.

A **line graph** shows the relationship between two sets of information. A point is placed at the intersection of every fact. When all the points are on the graph, a line is drawn to connect them. You can get a quick idea as to the trend, or direction, of information by looking at the ups and downs of the line.

World Population Growth: Historical

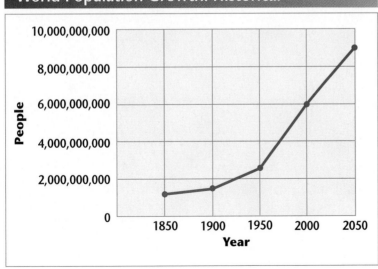

Critical Thinking
If you were to organize information about your classmates into categories such as age and gender, would you use a chart or a graph? Explain.

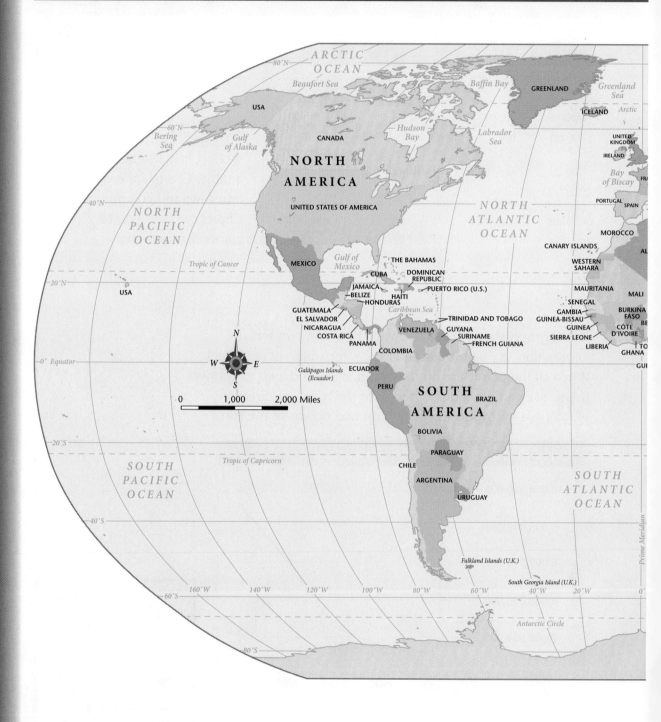

ARCTIC OCEAN

Beaufort Sea

Baffin Bay

GREENLAND

Greenland Sea

ICELAND

Arctic

USA

Bering Sea

Gulf of Alaska

CANADA

Hudson Bay

Labrador Sea

UNITED KINGDOM

IRELAND

Bay of Biscay

FRA

NORTH AMERICA

NORTH ATLANTIC OCEAN

PORTUGAL

SPAIN

NORTH PACIFIC OCEAN

UNITED STATES OF AMERICA

MOROCCO

CANARY ISLANDS

AL

Tropic of Cancer

MEXICO

Gulf of Mexico

THE BAHAMAS

WESTERN SAHARA

USA

CUBA

DOMINICAN REPUBLIC

MAURITANIA

MALI

JAMAICA

HAITI

PUERTO RICO (U.S.)

SENEGAL

BELIZE

GAMBIA

BURKINA FASO

HONDURAS

GUINEA-BISSAU

GUATEMALA

Caribbean Sea

TRINIDAD AND TOBAGO

GUINEA

BE

EL SALVADOR

CÔTE D'IVOIRE

NICARAGUA

VENEZUELA

GUYANA

SIERRA LEONE

COSTA RICA

SURINAME

LIBERIA

TO

PANAMA

FRENCH GUIANA

GHANA

COLOMBIA

Galápagos Islands (Ecuador)

ECUADOR

GUI

N

W   E

S

PERU

SOUTH AMERICA

BRAZIL

0   1,000   2,000 Miles

BOLIVIA

PARAGUAY

CHILE

Tropic of Capricorn

ARGENTINA

SOUTH PACIFIC OCEAN

URUGUAY

SOUTH ATLANTIC OCEAN

Falkland Islands (U.K.)

South Georgia Island (U.K.)

Prime Meridian

160°W   140°W   120°W   100°W   80°W   60°W   40°W   20°W   0

Antarctic Circle

80°S

80°N

60°N

40°N

20°N

0° Equator

20°S

40°S

60°S

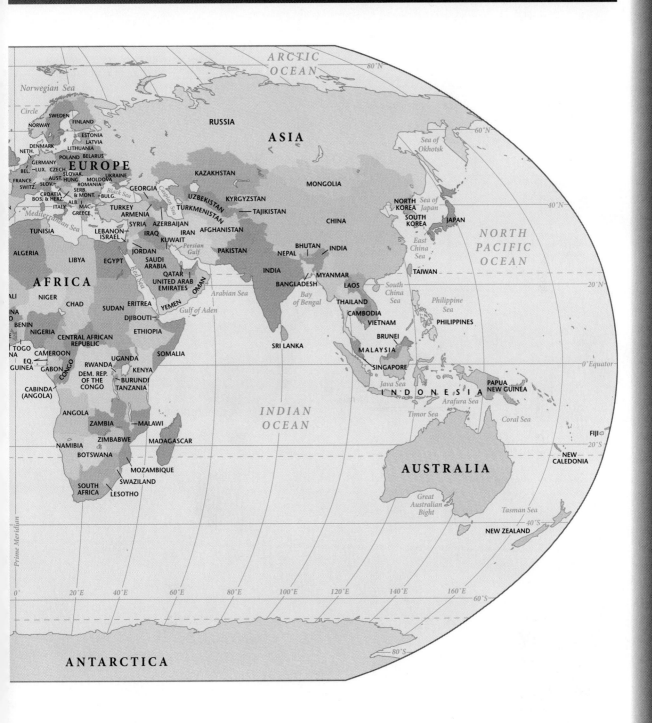

ARCTIC OCEAN

80°N

Norwegian Sea

Circle

SWEDEN

NORWAY

FINLAND

RUSSIA

ASIA

60°N

Sea of Okhotsk

DENMARK

ESTONIA

LATVIA

LITHUANIA

NETH.

GERMANY

POLAND BELARUS

BEL.

LUX. CZECH

SLOVAK.

EUROPE

KAZAKHSTAN

MONGOLIA

NORTH KOREA

Sea of Japan

40°N

FRANCE

SWITZ.

AUST. HUNG.

SLOV.

MOLDOVA

UKRAINE

SOUTH KOREA

JAPAN

CROATIA

BOS. & HERZ.

SERB. & MONT.

ROMANIA

Black Sea

GEORGIA

UZBEKISTAN

KYRGYZSTAN

CHINA

ITALY

ALB.

MAC.

GREECE

BULG.

TURKEY

ARMENIA

Caspian Sea

TURKMENISTAN

TAJIKISTAN

NORTH PACIFIC OCEAN

Mediterranean Sea

SYRIA

AZERBAIJAN

East China Sea

TUNISIA

LEBANON

ISRAEL

IRAQ

IRAN

AFGHANISTAN

TAIWAN

20°N

ALGERIA

LIBYA

EGYPT

JORDAN

KUWAIT

Persian Gulf

SAUDI ARABIA

PAKISTAN

BHUTAN

NEPAL

INDIA

MYANMAR

LAOS

South China Sea

AFRICA

QATAR

UNITED ARAB EMIRATES

OMAN

Red Sea

Arabian Sea

INDIA

BANGLADESH

THAILAND

Philippine Sea

MALI

NIGER

CHAD

SUDAN

ERITREA

DJIBOUTI

YEMEN

Gulf of Aden

CAMBODIA

VIETNAM

PHILIPPINES

BENIN

NIGERIA

CENTRAL AFRICAN REPUBLIC

ETHIOPIA

BRUNEI

TOGO

CAMEROON

EQ.

GUINEA

GABON

CONGO

SOMALIA

SRI LANKA

MALAYSIA

SINGAPORE

0° Equator

RWANDA

DEM. REP. OF THE CONGO

UGANDA

BURUNDI

KENYA

TANZANIA

INDONESIA

Java Sea

PAPUA NEW GUINEA

CABINDA (ANGOLA)

Arafura Sea

ANGOLA

ZAMBIA

MALAWI

INDIAN OCEAN

Timor Sea

Coral Sea

FIJI

NAMIBIA

ZIMBABWE

BOTSWANA

MADAGASCAR

20°S

NEW CALEDONIA

MOZAMBIQUE

SWAZILAND

AUSTRALIA

SOUTH AFRICA

LESOTHO

Great Australian Bight

Tasman Sea

40°S

NEW ZEALAND

Prime Meridian

0°

20°E

40°E

60°E

80°E

100°E

120°E

140°E

160°E

60°S

ANTARCTICA

80°S

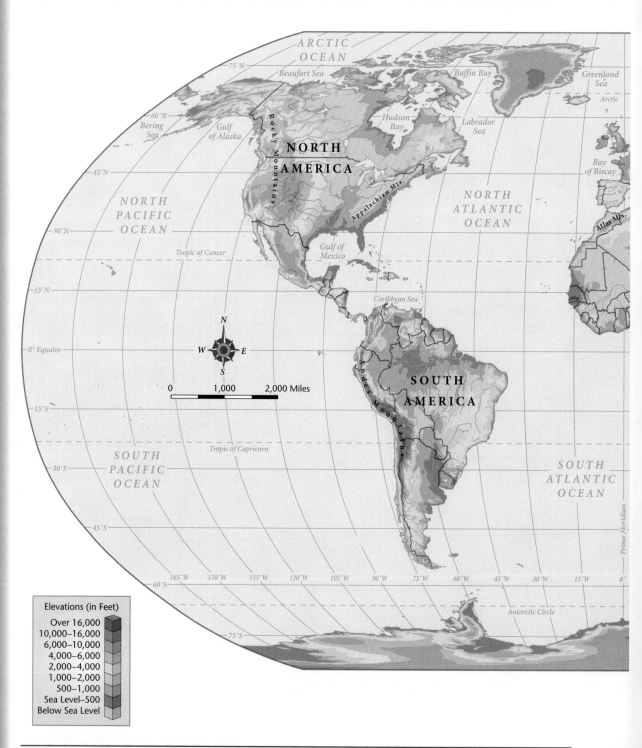

ARCTIC
OCEAN

Beaufort Sea

Baffin Bay

Greenland
Sea

Arctic

75°N

60°N

Bering
Sea

Gulf
of Alaska

Hudson
Bay

Labrador
Sea

Rocky Mountains

NORTH
AMERICA

45°N

Bay
of Biscay

NORTH
PACIFIC
OCEAN

30°N

Appalachian Mts.

NORTH
ATLANTIC
OCEAN

Atlas Mts.

Tropic of Cancer

Gulf of
Mexico

15°N

Caribbean Sea

N

0° Equator

W   E

S

SOUTH
AMERICA

Andes Mountains

0   1,000   2,000 Miles

15°S

SOUTH
PACIFIC
OCEAN

Tropic of Capricorn

30°S

SOUTH
ATLANTIC
OCEAN

Prime Meridian

45°S

60°S

165°W 150°W 135°W 120°W 105°W 90°W 75°W 60°W 45°W 30°W 15°W 0°

Antarctic Circle

Elevations (in Feet)

Over 16,000
10,000–16,000
6,000–10,000
4,000–6,000
2,000–4,000
1,000–2,000
500–1,000
Sea Level–500
Below Sea Level

75°S

ARCTIC
OCEAN

Norwegian Sea

Circle

S i b e r i a

ASIA

Sea of
Okhotsk

Ural Mts.

75°N

60°N

EUROPE

Alps

Black Sea

Caucasus

Caspian Sea

Sea of
Japan

45°N

NORTH
PACIFIC
OCEAN

30°N

Mediterranean Sea

s.

Gobi Desert

Plateau of Tibet

AFRICA

Persian
Gulf

H i m a l a y a

East
China
Sea

S a h a r a
D e s e r t

Red Sea

Arabian Sea

Gulf of Aden

Bay
of Bengal

South
China
Sea

15°N

Philippine
Sea

0° Equator

Java Sea

Arafura Sea

INDIAN
OCEAN

Timor Sea

Coral Sea

15°S

Kalahari
Desert

AUSTRALIA

Victoria Desert

30°S

Great
Australian
Bight

Tasman Sea

45°S

Prime Meridian

0°   15°E   30°E   45°E   60°E   75°E   90°E   105°E   120°E   135°E   150°E   165°E

60°S

75°S

ANTARCTICA

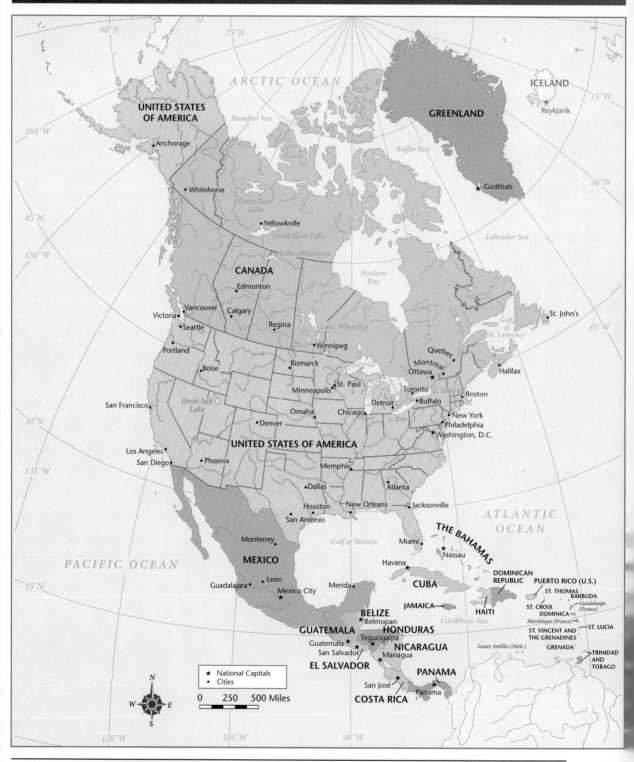

ARCTIC OCEAN

UNITED STATES OF AMERICA

Beaufort Sea

GREENLAND

ICELAND

Reykjavik

15°W

60°N

75°N

165°W

Anchorage

Baffin Bay

30°W

Whitehorse

Great Bear Lake

Godthab

45°N

150°W

Yellowknife

Great Slave Lake

Lake Athabasca

Labrador Sea

Hudson Bay

CANADA

Edmonton

Vancouver   Calgary

Victoria

Seattle

Regina

Lake Winnipeg

Gulf of St. Lawrence

St. John's

45°W

Portland

Winnipeg

Quebec

Boise

Bismarck

Superior

Montreal

Ottawa

Halifax

30°N

San Francisco

Great Salt Lake

Minneapolis   St. Paul

Omaha

Denver

Chicago

Detroit

Toronto   Buffalo   Boston

L. Ontario

L. Erie

New York

Philadelphia

Washington, D.C.

UNITED STATES OF AMERICA

135°W

Los Angeles

San Diego

Phoenix

Memphis

Dallas

Houston

San Antonio

New Orleans

Atlanta

Jacksonville

ATLANTIC OCEAN

THE BAHAMAS

15°N

PACIFIC OCEAN

Monterrey

Gulf of Mexico

Miami

Nassau

MEXICO

Guadalajara   Leon

Mexico City

Merida

Havana

CUBA

DOMINICAN REPUBLIC

PUERTO RICO (U.S.)

ST. THOMAS

BARBUDA

JAMAICA

HAITI

ST. CROIX

DOMINICA

Guadeloupe (France)

Martinique (France)

ST. LUCIA

BELIZE

Belmopan

GUATEMALA   HONDURAS

Tegucigalpa

Guatemala

San Salvador

EL SALVADOR

NICARAGUA

Managua

Caribbean Sea

Lesser Antilles (Neth.)

ST. VINCENT AND THE GRENADINES

GRENADA

TRINIDAD AND TOBAGO

PANAMA

San José

COSTA RICA

Panama

N

W   E

S

★ National Capitals
• Cities

0   250   500 Miles

120°W

105°W

90°W

Caribbean Sea

Managua ★

San José ★

Panama

10°N

Barranquilla

Caracas

Valencia

VENEZUELA

TRINIDAD AND TOBAGO

Cúcuta

Medellín

Bogotá ★

COLOMBIA

Georgetown ★

GUYANA

Paramaribo ★

SURINAME

Cayenne ★

FRENCH GUIANA

Mitú

0°
Equator

Quito ★

ECUADOR

Guayaquil

Galápagos
Islands
(Ecuador)

Talara

PERU

Manaus

Belém

Fortaleza

Trujillo

Huánuco

Pôrto Velho

BRAZIL

Recife

10°S

Lima ★

Ica

Cuzco

BOLIVIA

La Paz ★

Salvador

★ Brásilia

Goiânia

Santa Cruz

Sucre ★

20°S

Iquique

PACIFIC OCEAN

Antofagasta

PARAGUAY

Rio de Janeiro

São Paulo

30°S

CHILE

Asunción ★

Córdoba

Rosario

Santiago ★

Buenos Aires ★

URUGUAY

Montevideo

ATLANTIC OCEAN

Concepción

ARGENTINA

Valdivia

40°S

Puerto Montt

N

W ● E

S

Comodoro Rivadavia

★ National Capitals
● Cities

50°S

0   250   500 Miles

Falkland Islands
(U.K.)

South Georgia Island
(U.K.)

90°W   80°W   70°W   60°W   50°W   40°W

Europe

15°W · 0° · 15°E · 45°E

60°N · 45°N

ICELAND
Reykjavik ★

Norwegian Sea

Faroe
Islands
(Denmark)

NORTH
ATLANTIC
OCEAN

FINLAND
SWEDEN
NORWAY
Oslo ★
Stockholm ★
Helsinki ★

Gulf of Bothnia

RUSSIA
Moscow ★

Tallinn ★
ESTONIA
Baltic Sea
Riga ★ LATVIA
LITHUANIA
Vilnius ★
Minsk ★
BELARUS

North Sea

IRELAND
Belfast ★
Dublin ★

UNITED
KINGDOM
London ★

DENMARK
Copenhagen ★

RUSSIA

English Channel

NETHERLANDS
Amsterdam ★

Berlin ★
GERMANY

Warsaw ★
POLAND

Kiev ★
UKRAINE

Brussels ★
BELGIUM

Prague ★
CZECH
REP.

Paris ★
LUXEMBOURG

LIECHTENSTEIN
Bern ★

Vienna ★ ★ Bratislava
AUSTRIA
SLOVAKIA
Budapest ★
HUNGARY

MOLDOVA
Chisinau ★

FRANCE

SWITZERLAND
Ljubljana ★
SLOVENIA
★ Zagreb
CROATIA

Belgrade ★
SERBIA
AND
MONTENEGRO

Bucharest ★
ROMANIA

Bay of Biscay

MONACO ★
ITALY

BOSNIA AND
HERZEGOVINA
Sarajevo ★
Sofia ★
BULGARIA

Black Sea

PORTUGAL
Madrid ★
ANDORRA

Corsica

Adriatic Sea
Tirana ★
Skopje ★
MACEDONIA

Ankara ★

Lisbon ★
SPAIN
Gibraltar (U.K.) ★

Sardinia

Rome ★

ALBANIA

TURKEY

Balearic Islands

Tyrrhenian Sea

Aegean Sea

Algiers ★

N
W · E
S

Tunis ★

Sicily

GREECE
Athens ★

Ionian Sea

Rabat ★

AFRICA

Valletta ★
MALTA

Crete

★ National Capitals

Tripoli ★

Mediterranean Sea

Alexandria ★

0 200 400 Miles

Red Sea

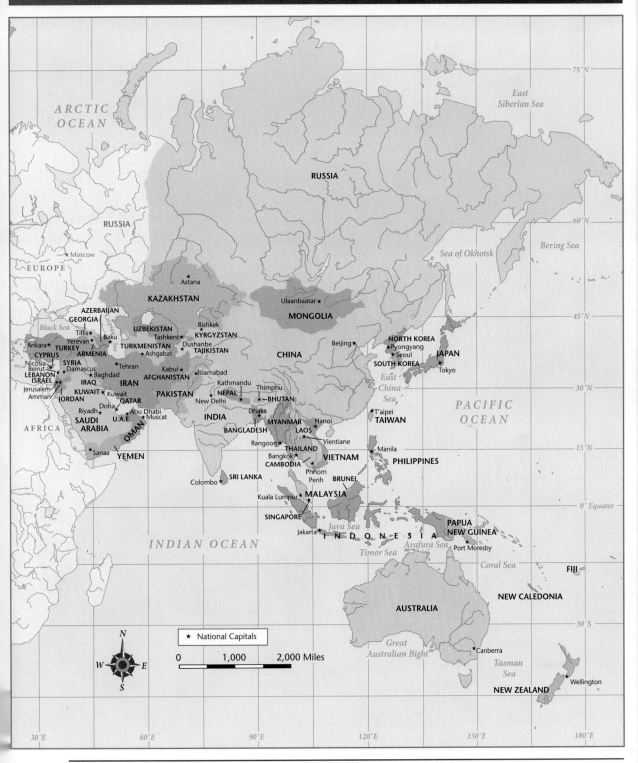

ARCTIC OCEAN

East Siberian Sea

75°N

RUSSIA

60°N

Bering Sea

RUSSIA

EUROPE

★ Moscow

Sea of Okhotsk

★ Astana

KAZAKHSTAN

Ulaanbaatar ★

MONGOLIA

45°N

AZERBAIJAN
GEORGIA
Tiflis★
Ankara★ Yerevan★ Baku
TURKEY
CYPRUS ARMENIA
Nicosia★
Beirut★
LEBANON SYRIA
ISRAEL Damascus
Jerusalem★★ IRAQ
Amman JORDAN

UZBEKISTAN
Tashkent★
TURKMENISTAN
Ashgabat★
Tehran★

Bishkek
★
KYRGYZSTAN
Dushanbe★
TAJIKISTAN

CHINA

Beijing ★

NORTH KOREA
Pyongyang
★Seoul
SOUTH KOREA

JAPAN
★
Tokyo

East China Sea

PACIFIC OCEAN

Black Sea

Kabul ★
AFGHANISTAN

Islamabad

Kathmandu

Thimphu
★

★

30°N

Kuwait
KUWAIT
QATAR
Riyadh★ Doha
U.A.E.★ Abu Dhabi
SAUDI ★ Muscat
ARABIA

IRAN

PAKISTAN

New Delhi
INDIA

NEPAL
★
★BHUTAN

Dhaka
★

MYANMAR Hanoi

★T'aipei

TAIWAN

OMAN

BANGLADESH
Rangoon★
LAOS
THAILAND

Vientiane
★

★ Manila

AFRICA

★ Sanaa

YEMEN

Red Sea

Colombo★

SRI LANKA

Bangkok★
CAMBODIA

VIETNAM
Phnom
Penh

PHILIPPINES

15°N

BRUNEI

Kuala Lumpur★
SINGAPORE

MALAYSIA
★

0° Equator

Jakarta★ I N D O N E S I A

Java Sea

PAPUA
NEW GUINEA
Port Moresby

INDIAN OCEAN

Timor Sea

Arafura Sea

FIJI

Coral Sea

NEW CALEDONIA

30°S

AUSTRALIA

Great
Australian Bight

★Canberra

Tasman
Sea

Wellington

NEW ZEALAND

30°E   60°E   90°E   120°E   150°E   180°E

Africa

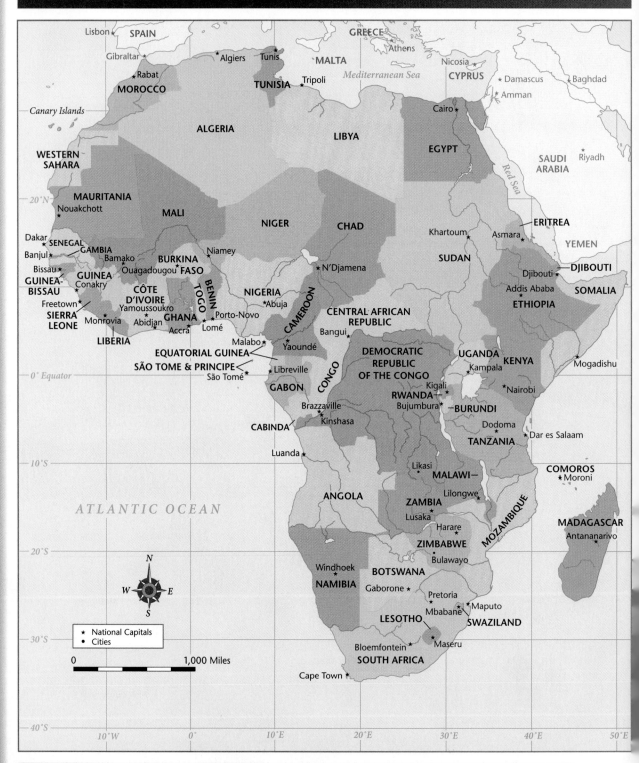

National Capitals
★ National Capitals
● Cities

0   1,000 Miles

Lisbon ★ SPAIN
GREECE
Athens ★
Gibraltar ★ ★ Algiers ★ Tunis
MALTA
Nicosia ★
CYPRUS
★ Rabat
MOROCCO
TUNISIA
★ Tripoli
Mediterranean Sea
Cairo ★
Damascus ★
Amman ★
Baghdad ★

Canary Islands

ALGERIA
LIBYA
EGYPT
SAUDI ARABIA
Riyadh ★

WESTERN SAHARA

Red Sea

20°N
MAURITANIA
★ Nouakchott
MALI
NIGER
CHAD
ERITREA
Khartoum ★
Asmara ★
YEMEN

Dakar ★ SENEGAL
Banjul ★ GAMBIA
Bamako ★
Niamey ★
SUDAN
Djibouti ★ DJIBOUTI
Bissau ★
GUINEA-BISSAU
BURKINA FASO
Ouagadougou ★
Addis Ababa ★
SOMALIA
Conakry ★
GUINEA
CÔTE D'IVOIRE
NIGERIA
★ N'Djamena
ETHIOPIA
Freetown ★
Yamoussoukro ★
TOGO
BENIN
CAMEROON
CENTRAL AFRICAN REPUBLIC
SIERRA LEONE
Monrovia ★
Abidjan ★
GHANA
Accra ★
Porto-Novo ★
★ Abuja
Bangui ★
LIBERIA
Lomé ★
Malabo ★
Yaoundé ★
UGANDA
KENYA
Mogadishu ★

EQUATORIAL GUINEA
SÃO TOMÉ & PRINCIPE
Libreville ★
DEMOCRATIC REPUBLIC OF THE CONGO
Kampala ★
São Tomé ★
CONGO
Kigali ★
RWANDA
Nairobi ★
0° Equator
GABON
Brazzaville ★
Bujumbura ★ BURUNDI
CABINDA
Kinshasa ★
Dodoma ●
Dar es Salaam ●
TANZANIA
Luanda ★

Likasi ●
COMOROS
Moroni ★
10°S
MALAWI
ANGOLA
ZAMBIA
Lilongwe ★
Lusaka ★
ATLANTIC OCEAN
MOZAMBIQUE
MADAGASCAR
Antananarivo ★
Harare ★
20°S
ZIMBABWE
Bulawayo ●
Windhoek ★
BOTSWANA
NAMIBIA
Gaborone ★
Pretoria ★
Mbabane ★ ★ Maputo
LESOTHO
SWAZILAND
30°S
Maseru ●
Bloemfontein ●
SOUTH AFRICA
Cape Town ★

N
W   E
S

40°S
10°W   0°   10°E   20°E   30°E   40°E   50°E

World Climate Zones

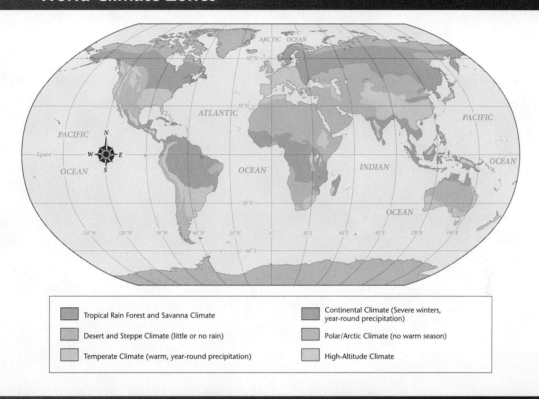

■	Tropical Rain Forest and Savanna Climate	■	Continental Climate (Severe winters, year-round precipitation)
■	Desert and Steppe Climate (little or no rain)	■	Polar/Arctic Climate (no warm season)
■	Temperate Climate (warm, year-round precipitation)	■	High-Altitude Climate

World Time Zones

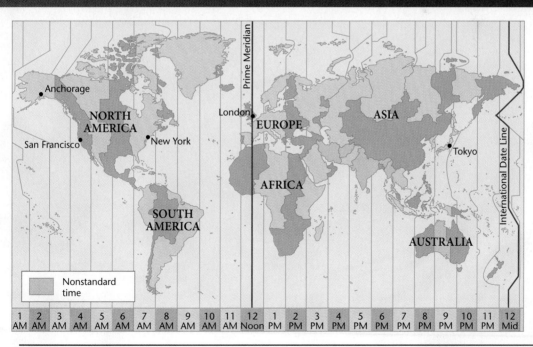

Unit 1

The World

Our Earth is a small planet. Seen from space, it is a beautiful blue ball. We think it is unlike anything else in space. Many different kinds of life live on Earth, including people. Earth's people have had to adapt to different environments. We have different ways of living. We speak many different languages, eat different foods, and may dress in different ways. At the same time, all of Earth's people worry about many of the same things. In this unit, you will learn why we study geography. You will also learn about some issues that affect everyone on the planet.

Geography

Geography is the study of Earth and its people. Geographers answer questions about how people on Earth live. They explain to us where a place is and what it is like. One of their interests is the natural world. Another is people and their way of life.

Goals for Learning

◆ To define geography and explain how physical geography is different from human geography

◆ To explain how geographers organize information and to name the five themes of geography

Geo-Stats The World

Estimated Population in 2010:
North America 459 million
South America 475 million
Europe 726 million
Asia 4.1 billion
Australia 21 million
Africa 1 billion
Antarctica 5,000 (mostly scientists)

Major Religions of the World: Christianity, Islam, Hinduism, Buddhism, Judaism, Sikhism

Major Languages of the World: Mandarin Chinese, English, Hindi, Spanish, Russian, Portuguese, Bengali

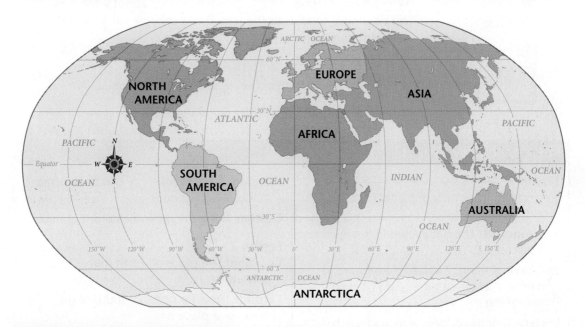

Map Skills

This map shows Earth and its seven continents, or areas of land. It shows Earth's oceans.

Study the map and answer the following questions:

1. Name the seven continents.

2. Name Earth's oceans.

3. Which continents does the equator go through?

4. What ocean is the farthest north?

5. Which continent is the farthest south?

Reading Strategy:
Summarizing

When readers summarize, they ask questions about what they are reading. As you read the text in this chapter, ask yourself the following questions:

◆ Who or what is this about?

◆ What is the main thing being said about this topic?

◆ What details are important to the main idea?

Key Vocabulary Words

Lesson 1

Geography The study of planet Earth and its people

Environment The natural world in which a person lives

Resource A thing of value, often found in nature, that we can use to do or make something

Society A group of people living together who have common ideas, beliefs, activities, or interests

Physical geography The study of Earth itself; the study of the land, water, air, plants, and animals of the natural world

Erosion The process by which running water, wind, or ice break down rock or soil

Plain A flat stretch of land

Plateau An area of level highland

Human geography The study of how people live on Earth

Culture The languages, religions, customs, art, and dress of a people

Region An area on Earth's surface that geographers define by certain similar characteristics

Political Having to do with the government —laws and customs people live by

Government Laws and customs people live by

Religion A set of beliefs or practices, often about a god or gods

Custom Something people do out of habit

Lesson 2

Location The place on Earth that something is

Latitude How far north or south of the equator a place is

Longitude How far east or west a place is from the prime meridian

Equator An imaginary line that goes around the middle of Earth; it lies half way between the North Pole and the South Pole

Prime meridian A fixed point that is 0 degrees longitude and runs through Greenwich, England

International date line A line of longitude that is 180 degrees both east and west of the prime meridian

Place The physical and human features that make an area special

Interaction How people settle, use, live on, and change the land

Movement How people, ideas, and products move between places

Economics Everything to do with work or money

Objectives

- ◆ To define geography
- ◆ To describe the two main branches of geography

Geography

The study of planet Earth and its people

Environment

The natural world in which a person lives

Resource

A thing of value, often found in nature, that we can use to do or make something

Society

A group of people living together who have common ideas, beliefs, activities, or interests

Reading Strategy:
Summarizing

What does the study of geography include?

What Is the Study of Geography?

Geography is the study of the planet Earth and its people. As you study geography, you will learn about the world around us. You will learn answers to many questions: What form does the land have? Is it, or was it, covered with forests or grasses? Is the weather hot or cold, dry or rainy?

You will also learn answers to questions about the people of the world: Where did they come from? Why did they settle in some places and not in others? What do they eat? How do they dress? What languages do they speak? How have they changed their physical **environment,** or the natural world in which they live?

You use geography every day. When you look at a map to find a shopping mall, you are using geography. When you read about events taking place in other countries, you are using geography. Geography affects what you do and what you eat.

How Does Geography Link People?

Today the people of the world are linked more closely than at any other time in history. The United States ships products and services to many parts of the world. For example, Americans sell farm products all over the world. People in the United States buy products from many other countries. Workers in other countries make most clothes, shoes, televisions, and DVD players sold in the United States. Much of the way we live depends on energy **resources** from around the world. A resource is something of value, like oil, that we use to make something.

Probably the biggest change of the last 100 years has been the development of a global **society.** We are all members of this society—people who have things in common. We share the same home—Earth. In the future, we may be more and more dependent upon each other.

What Is the First Branch of Geography?

Geography has two main branches. One branch studies physical features of Earth, such as mountains, valleys, oceans, lakes, and rivers. This branch is called **physical geography.**

Physical geography looks at Earth itself. What does the land look like? Is it flat? Does it have mountains? What is the weather like? What plants and animals live on the land? Physical geography looks at the natural features of Earth. These are features made by nature and not by people.

What Are Some Landforms on Earth's Surface?

Only about 30 percent of Earth's surface is land. Water covers most of Earth. The water is in oceans, lakes, rivers, and **glaciers.** A glacier is a large, slow-moving sheet of ice. Water is also found under ground.

The oceans and seas hold most of the water on our planet. This water is salty and we cannot drink it or use it for farming. However, ocean water evaporates and turns into clouds, leaving the salt behind. Wind carries the clouds over land. Then, the water may drop back to Earth as rain or snow. In time, water flows back to the sea. This process is called the water cycle.

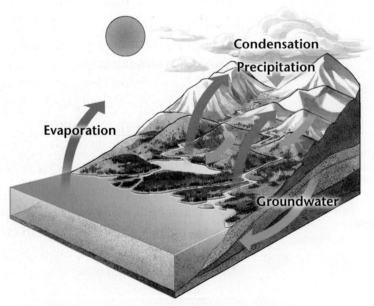

This is an illustration of how the water cycle works.

Erosion

The process by which running water, wind, or ice break down rock or soil

Plain

A flat stretch of land

Plateau

An area of level highland

Water and air are always changing the surface of Earth. Wind, ice, and flowing water break down rocks. Wind and water erode Earth's surface. **Erosion** is the process of gradually wearing away. Erosion shapes Earth's surface. It wears mountains down to hills and creates valleys and canyons. It creates flatlands called **plains** and the high, flat areas known as **plateaus.** We call these physical features landforms.

Geography in Your Life

Meteorologists Predict the Weather

Since ancient times, people have tried to predict the weather. Predict means to tell beforehand what the weather will do. Farmers want to know if the sun will shine on their crops. Travelers want to know if they need to pack a heavy winter coat. Meteorologists on the radio and television help both the hopeful farmer and the worried traveler. A meteorologist is a weather forecaster.

Since 1960, modern meteorologists have used satellites that circle Earth to collect weather information. These satellites provide a view of cloud patterns. Meteorologists use this information to help predict natural disasters such as floods before they happen. Then they can warn people to move to safety.

Meteorology is the study of Earth's atmosphere. Meteorology students in colleges around the world study computer models, graphs, charts, satellites, and weather balloons. They study pressure patterns to predict storms. They also study the interaction between Earth's ocean and its atmosphere.

They study them to help people and to learn about the formation of Earth.

Satellites help predict weather.

What Is the Second Branch of Geography?

The other main branch of geography is **human geography.** Human geography studies how people live on Earth. It looks at everything people do. Do they live in cities, farms, or small villages? Are their homes made of wood or brick? What jobs do people have? How do they earn a living?

Human geography also studies the **culture** of people around the world. Culture is everything that people make, build, think, believe, and do. Culture includes languages, religions, customs, art, and dress. Geographers sometimes divide the world into cultural **regions.** They group together people who share the same way of life.

What Human Factors Do Geographers Study?

The family is the most basic unit of a society. Every culture has a family structure. Some cultures define family in different ways. For example, a family of mother, father, and their children is a **nuclear family.** A family that also includes aunts, uncles, cousins, and grandparents is an **extended family.**

Human geography

The study of how people live on Earth

Culture

The languages, religions, customs, art, and dress of a people

Region

An area on Earth's surface that geographers define by certain similar characteristics

Nuclear family

A mother, father, and their children

Extended family

A mother, father, children, aunts, uncles, cousins, and grandparents

A nuclear family includes a mother, father, and their children.

An extended family also includes aunts, uncles, cousins, and grandparents.

Clan

A large group of related families

Tribe

A group of people sharing the same habits, language, and ancestors

Political

Having to do with the government—laws and customs people live by

Government

Laws and customs people live by

Religion

A set of beliefs or practices, often about a god or gods

In some cultures, the family can be a whole **clan,** a large group of related families. A clan can include hundreds of people. Some cultures have **tribes** as well. A tribe is a group of people sharing the same customs, language, and ancestors.

Human geography also studies **political** factors, such as countries and **governments.** Every culture has a government, which makes rules and tries to bring order to people's lives.

Why Do Geographers Study Languages?

Language is one of the most important features of a culture. People who share a language can share ideas and beliefs. Language helps tie people together. Thousands of languages are spoken around the world. In fact, people in Africa speak more than 1,000 languages. There are 13 major language families in the world. The largest is the Indo-European language group, used by nearly two billion people. This language group has more than 75 different languages. English, German, Polish, and Russian belong to this family. The languages in the same family are related. They may have some words in common. They may have the same alphabet and grammar. You will learn more about languages in other chapters.

What Is Religion?

Religion is an organized set of beliefs, often about a god or gods. Most religions have rules about how people should behave. Religious beliefs and practices can shape family life, influence art, and mold a culture's form of government. In fact, religion often affects an entire culture.

Most people in the world belong to one of the five major religions. Christianity, Islam, Buddhism, Hinduism, and Judaism are the most widespread religions. You will learn more about each of these religions in future chapters.

Custom

Something people do out of habit

Reading Strategy:
Summarizing

What are customs?

Word Bank

environment 2

geography 3

region 4

religion 5

resource 1

Writing About Geography

Write a paragraph telling how geography affects the way you live.

What Are Customs?

A **custom** is something people do out of habit. Every culture has its own set of customs. In some cultures, people eat using chopsticks. In other cultures, people use silverware. Habits like this are called customs. Customs are very important parts of a culture.

Customs include what clothes people wear and how they style their hair. These customs are often affected by physical geography. For example, in cold areas, people may wear fur. In warm areas, people may wear fewer clothes.

Celebrations and ceremonies are also customs. Different cultures often celebrate the same event, such as a wedding or a funeral. But the celebrations may look very different. A wedding in Africa is quite unlike a wedding in Japan.

Lesson 1 Review On a sheet of paper, use the words from the Word Bank to complete each sentence correctly.

1. The _____ is the natural world in which we live.

2. A _____ is a thing of value, often found in nature, that we can use to do or make something.

3. Human _____ studies how people live on Earth.

4. An area of Earth's surface that geographers define by certain similar characteristics is a _____.

5. A set of beliefs, often about a god or gods, is called _____.

What do you think ?

Which branch of geography do you think is most important?

Objectives
- To learn how latitude and longitude determine location
- To know what a region is
- To learn the five themes of geography

Location
The place on Earth that something is

Relative
How one place compares to another place

Absolute
The exact spot or area of a place

Latitude
How far north or south of the equator a place is

Longitude
How far east or west a place is from the prime meridian

Equator
An imaginary line that goes around the middle of Earth; it lies half way between the North Pole and the South Pole

How Do Geographers Organize Information?

Organizing geographic information is not easy. To help organize it, geographers developed five basic themes. A theme is a broad idea—a different way of looking at Earth and its people. The five themes of geography are location, place, interaction, movement, and region.

What Is Location?

Location answers the question "where?" Location is the place on Earth where something is. Locations can be described in relation to other things. For example, we might describe Mexico as a country located south of the United States. This is **relative** location.

An address tells you an exact or **absolute** location of a spot or place. Geographers also use **latitude** and **longitude** to describe location on Earth. Latitude explains how far north or south of the **equator** a place is. The equator is an imaginary line that goes around the middle of Earth. The North Pole is located at 90 degrees north of the equator. The South Pole is located at 90 degrees south of the equator.

Lines of Longitude and Latitude

Lines of Latitude
North Pole
80°N
Arctic Circle
60°N
40°N
Tropic of Cancer
20°N
0° Equator
20°S
Tropic of Capricorn
40°S
South Pole

Lines of Longitude
North Pole
80°W
60°W
40°W
20°W
0° Prime Meridian
20°E
40°E
60°E
80°E
South Pole

Map Study Degrees of latitude and longitude can be broken down for accuracy. For instance, an exact location in New York City is 40° 41' 51" N, 74° 0' 23" W. What is the latitude measurement of the equator? What is the longitude measurement of the prime meridian?

Prime meridian

A fixed point that is 0 degrees longitude and runs through Greenwich, England

International date line

A line of longitude that is 180 degrees both east and west of the prime meridian

Place

The physical and human features that make an area special

Interaction

How people settle, use, live on, and change the land

Longitude explains how far east or west a place is from a fixed point at 0 degrees longitude. The fixed point is called the **prime meridian.** It runs through the town of Greenwich, England. On the opposite side of Earth from the prime meridian is another line of longitude called the **international date line.** It is about 180 degrees both east and west of the prime meridian in the Pacific Ocean.

What Is Place?

Place is another theme. All places have special features that make them different from other places. Geographers describe places by both their physical and human features. Is a place hilly? Does it have cliffs? What is the weather like? What kinds of plants and animals are found there? These are all questions about physical features. But a place also has human features. A city could be described by its special buildings, music, and food. Questions about human features answer such questions as: "How many people live there? Who are they? What language do they speak? What customs do they follow?"

What Is Interaction?

A third theme is **interaction** between people and their environment. Interaction examines what people have done to the place where they live. Human activities often change what a place is like. This theme answers questions such as: "How do people use this land?" "How do they live in this place?" "How have people changed this place?" People interact with their environment, and they are also affected by it. For example, early colonists in the United States cut down trees to build homes. In areas with few trees, they built houses of stone or sod, which is soil covered with grass. They started farming. They grew plants that they brought from Europe.

Movement

How people, ideas, and products move between places

Migration

A large movement of people from one place to another

People migrate to escape wars, or to find freedom, food, a better job, or better weather.

What Is Movement?

Most people move several times in their lives. **Movement** is a theme that geographers use to organize information about these changes in location. The key question it answers is, "Why and how do people, products, and ideas move between places?"

Geographers are interested in two types of movement. One type is trade. People go from one place to another to do business. Trade is needed because people usually do not have everything they need in their own area. They must trade what they have in order to get what they need. Trade helps to spread goods around the world. It also helps to spread ideas. While people are trading, they learn about other lands and other ways of life.

Another type of movement is **migration.** Migration is the movement of people from one place to another. Every place on Earth has advantages and disadvantages. People often move to take advantage of what a place might offer. When people migrate, they move to new places to live. Like trade, migrations also help to spread ideas. Usually, people take their customs, beliefs, and way of life with them.

These people are using boats on a river to move their goods. They trade their goods to get what other things they need.

Why Divide the World Into Regions?

Reading Strategy:
Summarizing

What is the main idea of this paragraph?

It is hard to study the whole world at once, so geographers divide the world into regions. Region is the final of geography's five themes. Region answers the question, "How are places on Earth alike and different?"

There are many different types of regions. One way to define a region is by its physical features. Physical features include mountains, rivers, deserts, and lakes. Sometimes even a common feature made by humans sets a region apart from other areas. An example would be the Cotton Belt of southern United States, where cotton is the main crop grown.

The Sahara Desert and Rocky Mountains are regions.

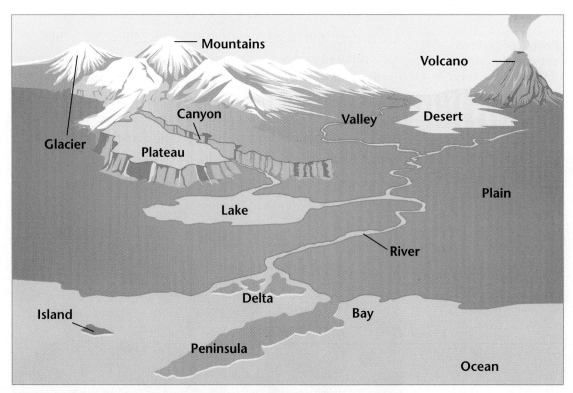

This is an illustration of many landforms, or physical features.

Climate

The average weather conditions over a period of time

Economics

Everything to do with work or money

Climate is another way of defining regions. Climate is the average of weather conditions over a period of time. Climate controls what kinds of plants and animals can live in a region. For example, there are plants and animals in Australia that exist nowhere else on Earth.

Another way of looking at regions is historical. For example, a geographer might study the history of the six states that were among the first places in the United States settled by Europeans. This region is called New England.

Economics is everything that has to do with work and money. It is another way of defining regions. For example, geographers might group together countries where most people make their living by herding animals or farming.

This book uses political regions most of the time. Political regions have set boundaries and a common system of government. The United States is an example of a political region. Each state is another.

These five themes—location, place, interaction, movement, and region—will help you study Earth and its people. Enjoy your study of world geography and cultures.

Reading Strategy: Summarizing

This paragraph summarizes the five themes of geography

Lesson 2 Review On a sheet of paper, write the answer to each question. Use complete sentences.

1. What are the five themes of geography?

2. What are two tools a geographer uses to locate the exact location of a place?

3. What are two ways the early colonists in the United States changed their environment?

4. What are two types of movement?

5. Why do geographers divide the world into regions?

What do you think ?

How do the five themes of geography help geographers organize information?

World Literacy

Literacy is the ability to read and write. Countries that ship products and services to many parts of the world are called developed countries. Usually, people who live in developed countries like the United States have more people who can read and write. Some countries have many people who only grow enough food for their family to eat. These countries often have fewer people who can read and write.

Wrap-Up

1. How developed would you say the countries of Sweden and the United States are?

2. What other factors may affect literacy?

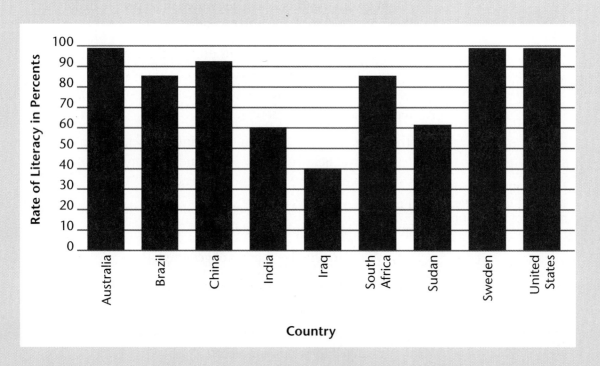

Make a Difference

Reading aloud to children could help make them better readers. Choose a book you enjoyed as a young child. Read it aloud to a younger brother, sister, or neighbor.

Chapter 1 SUMMARY

- Geography is the study of the planet Earth and its people.

- Physical geography is the study of Earth itself; the study of the land, water, air, plants, and animals of the natural world.

- Human geography is the study of how people live on Earth. Human geography also studies the culture of people around the world. Culture includes languages, religions, customs, art, and dress.

- Geographers organize information into five basic themes: location, place, interaction, movement, and region.

- Location is the place on Earth something is.

- Place is the combination of physical and human features that make a location special.

- Interaction tells how people settle, use, live on, and change the land.

- Movement tells how people, ideas, and products move between places. Trade, or doing business, is one type of movement. Migration, or many people moving from one place to another, is another kind of movement.

- Geographers group places by regions. A region is an area that has things in common.

Chapter 1 R E V I E W

Word Bank

culture
geography
human
physical
religions

On a sheet of paper, use the words from the Word Bank to complete each sentence correctly.

1. The study of the planet Earth and its people is _____.

2. The study of the land, water, air, plants, and animals on Earth is _____ geography.

3. The study of how people live on Earth is _____ geography.

4. Christianity, Islam, Buddhism, Hinduism, and Judaism are the most widespread _____.

5. The languages, religions, customs, art, and dress of a people are parts of a _____.

On a sheet of paper, write the letter of the answer that correctly completes each sentence.

6. The natural world in which people live is their ___B___.

    A society   **C** resource
    B environment   **D** branch

7. ___C___ are flat stretches of land.

    A Valleys   **B** Canyons   **C** Plains   **D** Rivers

8. The most basic unit of society is the ___A___.

    A family   **B** clan   **C** tribe   **D** nation

9. ___A___ is how far north or south of the equator a place is.

    A Latitude   **C** Longitude
    B Movement   **D** Interaction

10. It is hard to study the whole world at once, so geographers divide the world into ___D___.

    A countries   **B** chapters   **C** sections   **D** regions

On a sheet of paper, write the answer to each question. Use complete sentences.

11. What is geography?

12. How is physical geography different from human geography?

13. What are the five themes of geography?

Critical Thinking On a sheet of paper, write your response to each question. Use complete sentences.

14. What are some ways you use geography?

15. Which region of the world are you looking forward to learning more about? Why?

Applying the Five Themes of Geography

Region

A region is an area that has some things in common. How many different kinds of regions can you list?

Test-Taking Tip

When choosing answers from a Word Bank, complete the items you know first. Then study the remaining answers to complete the items you are not sure about.

2

Global Issues

Today, the countries of the world are more closely linked than ever before in history. People and goods move easily from country to country. Resources from far away places help us to live well. New forms of technology and communication bring us closer together. At the same time, conflicts caused by different beliefs, religions, and politics seem to be growing. Economic development is not equal. Some countries are getting richer while others are getting poorer.

Goals for Learning

◆ To describe how the world is a global village, and explain how technology is changing the world

◆ To identify environmental problems in the world, and explain how humans interact with the environment

◆ To identify war, disease, and too many people as world problems

◆ To describe the global economy

Geo-Stats   The World Today

Population: Almost 7 billion

Estimated World Population by 2050: More than 9 billion

Most Populated Country: China (1.3 billion)

Largest Country: Russia (over 6 million square miles)

Average World Life Expectancy: 63 years old for males, 66 years old for females

Highest Divorce Rate: United States (3.7 per 1,000 married couples per year)

Use of Cellular Phones: Over 2 billion worldwide

People Using the Internet: Over 1 billion

Number of Languages: 3,000–6,000

Population of the World

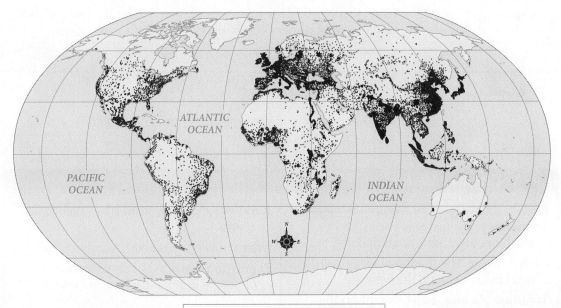

World Population Distribution
• Each dot represents 100,000 people

Map Skills

Perhaps one of the greatest challenges the world will face in the new century is controlling population. The world's population is increasing by 77 million people each year. Experts believe that over 9 billion people will live on Earth by the year 2042. Unfortunately, the land may not be able to support that many people. This map shows where in the world people live. Cities are the most crowded areas. Each dot on the map represents 100,000 people. The areas with the most red on this map are the most crowded.

Study the map and answer the following questions:

1. What does this map tell you about the world's population?

2. On what continent does the population appear to be highest?

3. On what continent does the urban population appear to be lowest?

4. What do you think life would be like if everyone in the world lived in crowded areas?

5. Where do you think most people will live in the future? Explain why you think so.

Reading Strategy:
Questioning

Asking questions as you read will help you understand and remember more of the information. Questioning the text will also help you to be a more active reader. As you read, ask yourself:

◆ What is my reason for reading this text?

◆ What decisions can I make about the facts and details in this text?

◆ What connections can I make between this text and my own life?

Key Vocabulary Words

Lesson 1

Technology The use of science and machines to improve ways of doing things

Global village The sharing of ideas, cultures, and customs around the world

Tradition An idea, belief, or custom that people pass down to their decendants

Lesson 2

Global warming The heating up of Earth from burning oil and gas

Pollution Something dirty, impure, or unhealthy

Irrigate To bring water to farmland by pipes or channels

Developing country A country in which people are poor and earn their living mostly by farming

Developed country A country that has money to provide services for its people

Natural resource A raw material from the earth

Lesson 3

Human rights Freedoms that all people enjoy, no matter where they live or who they are

Rural An area away from cities, such as a farm

Urban Having to do with a city

Population density The average number of people living in each square mile of an area

Urbanization Developing more cities or having more people moving into cities

Slum A rundown, poor, overcrowded part of a city

Lesson 4

Import A product from another country; to bring a product from another country into one's own country

Export Something sent to another country; to sell something to another country

Economy A system of building, using, and distributing wealth and resources

Service industry A business that does not make a product

Globalization The steady bringing together of all the world's economies into one

Multinational Companies that do business in many countries

Free trade Trade between countries without taxes or other limits

Objectives

♦ To describe how the world is a global village

♦ To describe the effects of technology on geography

Technology

The use of science and machines to improve ways of doing things

Global village

The sharing of ideas, cultures, and customs around the world

Tradition

An idea, belief, or custom that people pass down to their descendants

How Is the World a Global Village?

The world seems smaller than it used to be. We know that its size has not changed. So what has? Today, people around the world share ideas, art, music, and different ways of living. This has happened because of advances in **technology.** Technology is the use of science and machines to improve the ways of doing things. Because of this technology, the world is changing into a **global village.**

A village is a place where a few people live and work together. Villagers know each other and share ideas, customs, and lives. A global village is a term for the sharing of ideas, cultures, and **traditions** around the world. A tradition is an idea, belief, or custom that people pass on to their children and grandchildren.

The global village is interdependent—what happens in one nation affects other nations. For example, when the price of oil from the Middle East goes up, manufacturers in the United States have to spend more to produce goods. People then pay more when they buy these goods. If storms damage the coffee crop in Colombia and Brazil, it affects coffee drinkers in other parts of the world.

Technology links the whole world together. Technology makes the globe we live on one village—a global village. Improving communication and transportation connects our village. This allows us to share our cultures around the world.

How Has Technology Affected Geography?

Technology has changed how we collect and use information. Geographers today collect information from many sources, including outer space. Hundreds of satellites provide geographers with lots of information. Satellites are objects built to orbit Earth. Satellites send us pictures of different parts of the world. Photos show huge dust storms over Africa and large chunks of ice floating in the ocean. Pictures from space can show seas, lakes, and rivers in detail.

NASA is the National Aeronautics and Space Administration. NASA has launched hundreds of satellites.

Satellites also help forecast weather. They help us observe the weather and track storms. They track changes in the air and gasses above Earth.

Computer technology allows geographers to use the information satellites collect. Computers store information, see trends and patterns, and do complex math problems. Then geographers can predict changes in climate, crop failures, storms, and periods of dry weather. They can see if the glaciers are growing or melting and predict what the effects may be.

What Else Has Technology Affected?

Reading Strategy: Questioning

What details are important for you to understand what this paragraph is about?

Satellites have also changed communication. They have changed business, politics, and leisure in important ways. Today we can see events in remote parts of the world "live via satellite." Some people have satellite TV services that allow them to view hundreds of stations. People around the world use cellular phones. Telecommunications, or communicating electronically, is becoming an important way of doing business. The Internet is an international computer network that connects millions of people all over the world. E-mail lets us write messages to people anywhere in the world. In 2006, there were over one billion Internet users in the world. The largest number of users is in the United States, but there are millions of Internet users everywhere.

One hundred years ago, most goods traveled on railroads, on rivers or oceans, or on dirt roads.

New technologies have also changed transportation. Long ago, nearly all goods were shipped on boats. Railroads became the most important form of transportation in the 1800s. Railroads provided a fast and inexpensive way to move materials and products. The United States still ships many goods by rail. Japan and France have developed high-speed trains that can travel at speeds over 100 miles per hour.

After cars were invented, people did not have to rely as much on waterways and railroads. People built roads to connect places. The airplane let us reach once-remote places, like the islands of the Pacific. Airplanes connect cities and people around the world.

Geography in Your Life

GPS Technology

The development of the global positioning system (GPS) uses a network of 24 satellites to help travelers understand their location. The military developed the GPS for their use. In the 1980s, the government made the system available for everyone. Now, some people have a GPS unit in their car that gives them directions to where they are going. GPS satellites circle Earth twice a day and transmit signal information to Earth.

Word Bank

cars   5

global village   2

Internet   4

satellites   3

technology   1

Lesson 1 Review On a sheet of paper, use the words from the Word Bank to complete each sentence correctly.

1. The world seems a smaller place because of _____.

2. The _____ is a term used to describe the sharing of ideas, cultures, and traditions around the world.

3. As objects that are built to orbit Earth, _____ provide geographers with a great deal of information.

4. The _____ is an international computer network that connects millions of people all over the world.

5. The invention of _____ gave people more freedom, because they no longer had to rely on waterways and railroads.

What do you think ?

How have computers changed your life?

Global warming

The heating up of Earth from burning oil and gas

Pollution

Something dirty, impure, or unhealthy

What Is Global Warming?

Since the 1980s, scientists have warned us about **global warming**. They believe that gases from cars and factories are heating up Earth. This could cause many problems for the world. Find out more about global warming by reading the Geography in Today's World feature on page 56.

What About Air Pollution?

The burning of wood, oil, coal, and natural gas causes most air pollution. Worldwide **pollution** levels are increasing. Pollution is something that is dirty, impure, or unhealthy. Cars that burn gasoline are a major source of pollution. The number of cars worldwide is growing. Pollution is a global problem because the air and the ocean water are always moving. Heat, moisture, and pollution move around the world.

Air pollution might change Earth's climate forever. A high layer of gas called the ozone layer protects Earth. It filters out the sun's harmful rays. Scientists believe the ozone layer may

be thinning. They have discovered a "hole" over Antarctica. They believe that the gases found in spray cans and refrigeration systems cause the damage. Harming the ozone layer could lead to higher rates of skin cancer and crop failure.

A major source of air pollution is cars that burn gasoline.

What About Water Pollution and Erosion?

Water covers 70 percent of Earth. Like air, water is something people often take for granted. However, oceans, lakes, and rivers are in serious trouble. The oceans have been damaged by man-made pollution. Farming and industrial waste products have poisoned major lakes and rivers. In poor countries, many people do not have clean water to drink.

Another growing problem is soil erosion, or the wearing away of soil. People around the world depend on soil to grow their food. However, millions of tons of topsoil are blowing or washing away. Cutting down the forests, having too many animals, and using poor farm methods cause this.

How Do People and Environment Interact?

People affect the environment in both good and bad ways. They build dams to bring water to dry areas. Farmers have used **irrigation** for thousands of years. To irrigate is to bring water to the fields. People cleared land for living space, farmland, and mining. The changes we have made on the physical environment have affected wildlife, plants, and culture. These changes have created garbage, air pollution, and water pollution.

People have always had to adapt to the environment they live in. For example, people who live in Arctic climates build shelters made of snow. Europeans brought horses to America, and the native people learned to use them to hunt buffalo. In places where the climate is very hot, people have adapted by taking a midday rest. Daylight saving time is another way we have adapted. We set clocks ahead one hour in the spring to enjoy more daylight in the evenings. In the fall, we set the clocks back again.

This terrace farm in Asia is an example of how people adapt to their surroundings. Terrace farming lets the farmers grow crops where they otherwise could not.

What Will Improve the Environment?

Recently, representatives from almost all of the world's countries met to discuss environmental concerns. Some countries passed laws to control the amount of pollution that can be released into the air. Many countries have banned the use of a chemical that destroys the ozone layer. Some countries punish businesses that cause water pollution. Some of these efforts have improved the quality of the air and water.

What Are Developing Countries Doing?

Every nation wants to improve the environment. **Developing countries** face problems that richer countries may not have. A developing country's people are poor and usually earn their living from farming. They export wood, coal, and oil to earn money. They cut down trees to make land for farming. The population in many developing countries is growing. These developing countries need money. Because of this, they rely on richer countries for money to help clean up the environment. However, many of the richer nations are giving less money to the poorer countries.

Developed countries are richer and their people live better. Many people in these countries want to save forests. They want to reduce pollution by cutting down on the use of coal, oil, and natural gas. All this may help the environment, but it hurts developing countries that want to sell their **natural resources**. A natural resource is a raw material, such as oil, that comes from the earth.

How Can People Protect the Environment?

You and your family can help the environment by reducing, reusing, and recycling. Each of us creates a lot of trash—an average American creates four pounds of trash each day. Over half of everything we throw away ends up buried in a landfill. We should all try to reduce the amount of goods, water, and energy we use. We can reuse things instead of throwing them away or buying something new.

Recycled plastic is used to make some playground equipment. Recycled paper products are used to make other paper products.

We can recycle things that we can no longer reuse. Most cities now collect aluminum cans, plastic containers, glass, and paper. They sell these things to businesses that make new products out of them.

In a global village, we all share the problems. We depend on Earth to supply us with our needs. The challenge for the future is to improve the quality of life for all people without destroying Earth's environment.

Lesson 2 Review On a sheet of paper, write the answer to each question. Use complete sentences.

1. What is global warming?

2. What causes most air pollution?

3. Why is soil erosion a problem?

4. What is one example of how people affect the environment?

5. What have countries done to help the environment?

What do you think ?

What are some ways you can reduce, reuse, or recycle to help the environment?

Celebrations

Earth Day

The first Earth Day was April 22, 1970. Senator Gaylord Nelson organized it. His idea was that everyone would take one day to learn about taking care of Earth. About 20 million Americans celebrated the first Earth Day.

By the year 2000, 30 years later, there were 5,000 environmental groups in 184 countries. Now, we celebrate Earth Day around the world each April 22.

Celebrations vary from place to place. Some people plant trees on Earth Day. Others recycle trash or clean up lakes or rivers. Musicians and others often come together on Earth Day to celebrate and help people learn about saving Earth from harm.

Critical Thinking How does your community celebrate Earth Day?

Objectives

◆ To define the global culture

◆ To describe some problems the world's people face

Reading Strategy:
Questioning
_____

Think beyond the words. Consider your own thoughts and experiences as you read.

What Is the Global Culture?

Culture includes languages, religions, art, food, traditions, customs, and housing. It reflects how people live. As the global village becomes more connected, different culture groups come into more contact with one another. People must understand how other groups use the land, organize and lay out cities, treat women, educate their children, and observe customs and holidays.

The United States influences the new global culture. American television, movies, music, fast food, and clothing styles influence people all over the world. The global culture has also changed the United States. Music from Asia, Africa, and Latin America has become part of American popular music. Americans enjoy foods from all over the world.

People can buy food grown in other places of the world.

Some companies do business and hire workers all over the world. People need a common language so they can talk with other people. Almost 25 percent of the world's population now speaks English. It is becoming a global language. English is the official language of more than 75 countries. It is the language of international business, science, and government. However, the most popular language spoken is Mandarin Chinese. English is the second most popular language spoken. Hindi, Spanish, Russian, and Arabic are also popular languages. Many people speak more than one language. However, business people know that speaking the same language is not enough. They must also know about the cultures of the people with whom they want to do business.

What Problems Affect the World?

For some people, the new century promises peace, wealth, easy travel, and instant communication. For most, it offers little hope. Most of the world's people live in poverty around big cities. Millions of people cannot find jobs.

Religious beliefs and love for one's country are causes of many conflicts.

War is one of the worst problems affecting the people of our global village. War affects thousands of people in Africa and Asia. Wars have many causes. Conflict develops when one group of people believes it is better than another. People are sometimes unhappy with their government. Religion can also cause conflicts. Sometimes a group is eager to spread its beliefs and even force them on others. Competition for the same resources also causes conflict.

Germs spread diseases, usually from one person to another.

Disease is another global problem. Poor people in developing countries are often the victims of disease. Their housing and food are poor, making them more likely to become sick. When they do get sick, they often cannot afford to see a doctor. AIDS affects people in almost every country, especially those in Africa. Millions of Africans have died from AIDS, and many more millions have the disease. Poor people in developing countries also die of many diseases that could easily be cured with proper treatment. In developing countries, 55 percent of deaths are from diseases passed from one person to another. However, in developed countries these diseases cause only 14 percent of deaths.

What About World Population?

Reading Strategy:
Questioning

What do you think you will learn by reading this section?

According to the United Nations, the world's population will be 9.3 billion in 2050. Population is growing fastest in the developing countries. The increased number of people makes it difficult for many of these countries to improve their quality of life. At the same time, most of the developed countries will have fewer people.

Migration affects population. Each year, nearly 3 million people move from poor countries to richer ones. Many people come to the United States from poor countries in Latin America. Most European countries and some Asian nations have a shrinking population. But most Asian countries have fast-growing populations.

What Are Some Human Rights Problems?

Human rights mean that all people have the same rights. It does not matter where people live, what nationality they are, or whether they are men or women. The United Nations is concerned about human rights. Some basic human rights are:

- The right to life, liberty, property, and safety
- The right to an education
- The right to have a job
- Freedom of thought including religion
- Freedom of expression and opinion

Who Helps Solve Global Problems?

The United Nations (UN) is an important international organization. It was formed in 1945. Today, almost all of the countries of the world are members. The United Nations tries to settle disagreements, improve the way people live, and keep peace around the world. By 2015, the United Nations wants to reduce poverty worldwide, halt the spread of AIDS, and provide worldwide primary education.

Here are some UN agencies that provide special services:

- The United Nations International Children's Emergency Fund (UNICEF) cares for sick, starving, and homeless children.
- The Food and Agricultural Organization (FAO) helps poor farmers grow more food.
- The World Health Organization (WHO) focuses on improving people's health.

The United Nations also provides troops to act as peacekeepers in troubled areas. The UN member nations provide the troops. Their goal is to keep the peace. UN peacekeepers have been used in Korea, the Middle East, Eastern Europe, and in Africa. However, the United Nations has not always been successful in solving problems.

What About Overcrowding?

People live all over the world. Most people live in the middle latitudes. This is an area between 30 degrees and 60 degrees north latitude. This area has the best conditions for people to live. The climate is warm and rainy enough to grow food.

For thousands of years, most people lived in **rural** areas. Rural areas are places away from the city, such as farms or small villages. Farming was the main activity. People who live in **urban** areas live in or around cities. Cities are the center of government, business, learning, and religion. In 1900, only 14 out of every 100 people lived in cities. Now, about half the world's people live in cities—about 50 of every 100 people.

Where Are the Largest Cities?

Cities are getting larger. In 1950, there were only 83 cities in the world with more than one million people. Today, there are over 400 cities with more than one million people. Geographers say that urban areas have a high **population density**, or the number of people in a certain space. Cities have a high population density. The population density of rural areas is smaller.

Some areas of the world are very crowded. Areas with mountains, deserts, or extreme cold have few people.

Biography

Bill and Melinda Gates

Bill Gates made millions of dollars with his computer company. In 2000, Bill and Melinda Gates, his wife, created a foundation. It is not a government foundation; it is a private organization. The foundation gives money and other things to help people around the world. One goal of the Bill and Melinda Gates Foundation is to prevent deaths from diseases worldwide. In the world's poorest countries, it provides vaccines, or shots to stop diseases. The foundation also hopes to help African farmers produce more farm crops. It wants to provide more and better food to children in developing countries. Bill and Melinda Gates believe that every human life has an equal value.

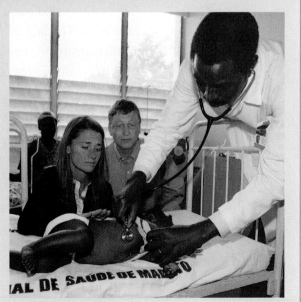

This picture of Earth from space shows urban areas that have lights. Notice that you can see the shapes of some continents.

Urbanization

Developing more cities or having more people moving into cities

Slum

A run-down, poor, overcrowded part of a city

A city with over 10 million people is sometimes called megacity or megalopolis.

Europe and North America used to have the largest cities. Now, most city people live in Asia. The largest city in the world is Tokyo, Japan, which has about 35 million people. Seoul, Korea; Mumbai, India; Delhi, India; and Shanghai, China, are other huge cities in Asia. Two of the largest cities in the world are in Latin America—Mexico City, Mexico, and Sao Paulo, Brazil. Each has more than 20 million people.

Why Do People Move to Cities?

Cities offer jobs, education, and hope. Most people move to cities to try to improve their lives. It is usually easier to find work and schools in cities. Medical care is usually better. The movement of people from rural to urban areas is called **urbanization.**

What Are the Effects of Urbanization?

Life in cities also has a bad side. Cities often have many problems. The lack of jobs is a big urban problem. Poverty is another problem. People without money or jobs sometimes turn to crime. Cities often have a lot of crime and violence.

The number of people moving to cities is so great that cities cannot keep up. Cities, especially in developing countries, cannot build roads and sewers, or provide garbage collection, electricity, or transportation fast enough. Many of these countries are too poor to provide all the services needed.

Poor housing or not enough housing is also a problem. Many of the people moving to cities live in **slums.** A slum is a run-down, poor, overcrowded part of a city. In developing countries, many people live in shantytowns. A shanty is a small, roughly built shack or hut. Most shanties do not have heat, running water, electricity, or even toilets.

Percentage of Urban Populations

	World	Africa	Asia	Australia	Europe	North America	South America
	49%	40%	40%	92%	73%	81%	78%

Chart Study Which continent has the largest urban population?

Growing cities also have environmental problems. Many have a lot of air and water pollution. Cars and trucks cause a lot of the air pollution. Cutting down trees for new housing may cause flooding and mudslides.

Lesson 3 Review On a sheet of paper, write the answer to each question. Use complete sentences.

1. Name one problem that affects the world.

2. What is the belief that all people have the same rights called?

3. Name an important international organization.

4. What are urban areas?

5. List three reasons why people move to cities.

What do you think ?

Do you think New York or North Dakota has a higher population density? Explain.

Objectives

◆ To know how trade affects the world economy

◆ To compare and contrast developed and developing countries

Import

A product from another country; to bring a product from another country into one's own country

Export

Something sent to another country; to sell something to another country

Specialize

To work on what one does the best

Economy

A system of building, using, and distributing wealth and resources

An average American makes about $44,000 per year. In some parts of Africa, an average person makes less than $1,000 per year.

How Does Trade Affect the Global Economy?

The world has always been a place where countries both work together and compete. People need to trade because they want or need things that they cannot get in their own countries. Most countries **import** and **export** goods. Imports are products brought in from a different country. The United States depends on other countries for much of its oil, cars, natural resources, and other goods. Other countries depend on the United States for food products, computers, and machines. Exports are products made in one country and sold to other countries.

International trade is growing. This allows countries to **specialize**; that is, they work on what they do best. For example, U.S. farmers can grow bananas, but it is expensive to do so. Other countries can grow them easier and cheaper. But farmers in the United States can grow crops like wheat more easily. One country can specialize in growing bananas; another country can specialize in growing wheat.

Trade has a bad side too. For example, many Americans buy clothes made in other countries. Because of this, U.S. factories may close down and workers might lose jobs. In the same way, the United States can grow some crops more cheaply than farmers in other countries. Selling that food at lower cost may mean that farmers in other countries cannot sell theirs. Those farmers may lose their farms and their way of life.

The global **economy** is causing a growing gap between rich and poor countries. Economy is a system of building, using, and distributing wealth and resources. Most developing countries depend on the developed nations for trade, investment, money, and food. Sometimes people move from poorer countries to richer ones in search of a better life for themselves and their children.

Service industry

A business that does not make a product

What Do Developed Countries Have in Common?

Most people in developed countries live quite well. They usually do not have to worry about food, clothing, and shelter. They usually live longer, are able to read and write, and are skilled. Developed countries have good transportation and communication systems. Farmers in these countries use machines. Large farms produce all the food people need. Because of this, most people live in urban areas and work in factories, offices, and businesses. These businesses have the money to train workers on computers and other technology. The largest part of most developed economies is **service industries.** Service industries pay for work done for other people, not work to make a product.

What Do Developing Countries Have in Common?

Developing countries are usually much poorer than developed countries. The basic needs people have use up most of what they earn. There is little money left over. Often, people do not get enough to eat or good medical care. They do not live as long as people in developed countries. Many people do not know how to read or write. In rural areas, children must work the fields, so they go to school for only a few years. Many people are farmers or live in small villages. If villagers move to cities, many cannot find work. Most manufactured goods in developing countries have to be imported. However, most people cannot afford to buy them. Communication is often poor. Farmers and workers cannot get products to markets because of poor transportation.

Reading Strategy:
Questioning

Study the photo. Ask yourself how it relates to what you are reading.

People in developing countries sometimes use oxen instead of machines to help with farm work.

Reading Strategy:
Questioning

What do you
already know about
economics?

Globalization

The steady bringing
together of all the
world's economies
into one

Multinational

Companies that do
business in many
countries

Free trade

Trade between
countries without
taxes or other limits

What Are the Economic Trends in the World?

A trend is a general direction something is taking. One
economic trend, particularly in developed countries, is
globalization. It refers to the gradual bringing together of
all the world's economies into one. You can see the trend in
the United States. The U.S. economy was not greatly affected
by events outside its borders until about 30 years ago. The
economy was self-contained, or complete in itself. Now, the
U.S. economy is international. Both imports and exports are
increasing. **Multinational** corporations now account for at
least half of U.S. exports and more than half of U.S. imports.
Multinational companies do business in many countries. World
events affect the American economy more than ever before.

Because the international marketplace is interdependent, many
countries have joined the World Trade Organization (WTO).
The 150 members of this global organization deal with rules of
trade among nations. The WTO oversees trade agreements. It
also handles trade disputes and checks on the trading practices
of its members. The WTO also provides technical help and
training for developing countries.

Many nations have created **free trade** agreements to trade more
easily with one another. Free trade means trading between
countries without taxes or other limits. Probably the best-
known example of a free trade
agreement is the North American
Free Trade Agreement (NAFTA).
NAFTA is a trade agreement
between the United States,
Canada, and Mexico. However,
free trade agreements also exist in
the European Union, Africa, Asia,
South America, Central Europe,
Central America, the Caribbean,
and among some Arab states.

Some people who live in developed countries work in
offices for a service industry.

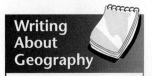
Who Helps Poorer Nations?

Many of the world's poorer nations need help from developed countries. The developed countries give **foreign aid.** They give money, medicine, tools, or machinery to help less developed countries. Sometimes the aid is a gift and does not have to be paid back. Other times, the aid is a loan that the poorer country must repay.

Developed countries send much of their aid through two international organizations—the World Bank and the International Monetary Fund (IMF). The World Bank loans money to developing countries at low interest rates. The countries use the money to build bridges, dams, roads, and schools and to improve health care and the environment. The IMF collects money from its 184 members to help countries in need.

Lesson 4 Review On a sheet of paper, write the answer to each question. Use complete sentences.

1. What term means *work on what they do best?*

2. Name one benefit and one harmful effect of international trade.

3. What are some things that developed countries have in common?

4. What are some things less developed countries have in common?

5. What is globalization?

What do you think ?

Do you think it would be a good idea for people in the rich, developed countries to be taxed to provide money to improve life for people in developing countries?

Global Warming

The average global temperature has risen 1°F over the past 100 years. Scientists think it will rise another 2° to 4°F in the next 100 years. This is called global warming.

Over millions of years, Earth's climate has changed many times. There have been great ice ages when snow and ice covered much of Earth. There have also been periods of warm, wet weather, such as when there were dinosaurs on Earth. Some scientists wonder if the warming trend is part of the natural cycle. Many scientists believe it is something else. They say that part of the warming is due to human activity.

When more carbon dioxide stays in the air, it makes it possible for the air temperature to rise. Common activities such as burning wood, coal, oil, or natural gas release carbon dioxide and other gases. Some carbon dioxide is absorbed by forests. In many parts of the world, however, people are cutting down forests and jungles for farmland and firewood. But most carbon dioxide is absorbed by the oceans. The ocean currents seem to be warming along with the air temperature. As they warm, oceans cannot hold as much carbon dioxide.

The effects of global warming could be terrible. As the world warms, the ice caps at both poles would melt. Glaciers would melt. The rise in the sea level could flood low-lying lands. Many cities and islands could be under water. If this happens, two billion people around the world would have to move inland. The global oceans have risen 6 to 8 inches over the past 100 years.

Wrap-Up

1. What do some scientists believe is causing Earth to warm?

2. What would happen if the ice caps melt?

Make a Difference

Look into ways of reducing the amount of gasoline or electricity your family uses. Do you turn off lights and appliances when you are not using them? Could you carpool or combine trips to reduce the amount of gasoline your family uses?

- Global village is a term used to describe the sharing of ideas, cultures, and traditions around the world.

- Technology has affected how information is collected. Satellites provide much of this information.

- Cellular phones, communicating electronically, the Internet, and e-mail are types of technology that are changing how companies do business.

- Global warming is a problem caused by gases produced from burning fuels. This could cause many problems for Earth.

- People have changed the environment. Air pollution, water pollution, and erosion are problems people have created.

- People can work to improve the environment. They can reduce waste, reuse things, recycle, and reduce pollution.

- The world is developing a global culture. People need a common language to communicate.

- War, disease, and overpopulation are global problems.

- The United Nations is an international organization that deals with world problems. The United Nations helps protect human rights, settle disagreements, and tries to improve the lives of poor people throughout the world.

- About half the people in the world live in cities. Many cities around the world have more than one million people. Growing cities cause environmental problems.

- Developed countries are creating a global economy. International trade is growing.

- Developing countries are poorer than developed countries.

- The World Trade Organization and free trade agreements deal with trade between countries.

Chapter 2 REVIEW

Word Bank

global warming 2
interdependent 1
recycle 3
United Nations 4
World Trade
   Organization 5

On a sheet of paper, use the words from the Word Bank to complete each sentence correctly.

1. The global village is _____ because what happens in one nation affects every other nation.

2. Some scientists believe gasses from cars and factories cause _____.

3. To help the environment, people can reduce, reuse, and _____.

4. An important international organization is the _____.

5. The _____ deals with the rules of trade between nations.

On a sheet of paper, write the letter of the answer that correctly completes each sentence.

6. The world seems smaller than it used to be because of advances in ___B___.

   A geography   **C** industry
   B technology   **D** medicine

7. ___C___ gather information about weather, storms, and changes on Earth.

   A Villagers   **B** Cars   **C** Satellites   **D** Railroads

8. In ___C___ countries, most people are poor and earn their living from farming.

   A industrial   **C** developing
   B developed   **D** United Nations

9. Burning wood, oil, coal, and natural gas causes most ___D___.

   A diseases   **C** communication
   B erosion   **D** air pollution

10. Population is affected by ___A___.

   A migration   **C** communication
   B satellites   **D** erosion

On a sheet of paper, write the answer to each question. Use complete sentences.

11. Why do people sometimes describe the world as a global village?

12. What are two environmental issues that will affect the world in the future?

13. What are two economic trends in the world today?

Critical Thinking On a sheet of paper, write your response to each question. Use complete sentences.

14. How do you think communication will change in the next ten years?

15. What do you think is the greatest threat to the future of the world—war, disease, overpopulation, pollution, or something else? Explain your choice.

Applying the Five Themes of Geography

Interaction

How do you affect the geographical environment you live in? How does your geographical environment affect you?

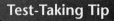

Test-Taking Tip

When studying for a test, review any worksheets, tests, quizzes, Lesson Reviews, or Chapter Reviews you completed that cover the same information.

The 100-Person World

Imagine that we could shrink Earth's population to a village of exactly 100 people. Those people would still represent how the world population is today. What would the village be like? Here are some facts that would describe such a village.

- There would be 57 people from Asia, 21 from Europe, 14 from North America and South America, and 8 from Africa.

- There would be 52 females and 48 males.

- There would be 30 white people and 70 non-white people.

- There would be 30 Christians, the other 70 would be non-Christians, including 15 Muslims, 10 Hindus, and 5 Buddhists.

- Over half of all the wealth in the village would be in the hands of six people. All six would be Americans.

- Half would not have enough food to eat.

- Only one person of the 100 would own a computer.

- Only one person out of the 100 would have a college education.

Wrap-Up

1. On what continent do most of the world's people live?

2. Are most of the world's people white?

3. What country is the richest country in the world?

4. What shows that most people in the world are poor?

5. How do we know that most people in the world do not receive a good education?

The facts on this page are for an imaginary world of 100 people, but Earth actually has almost 7 billion people.

- Geography is the study of Earth and its people. Physical geography is the study of Earth itself; human geography studies how people live on Earth.

- The five themes of geography are location, place, interaction, movement, and region.

- Physical features, climate, economics, or political areas can determine regions.

- The sharing of ideas, cultures, and traditions around the world is creating a global village.

- Technology is changing the world by making communication and transportation easier.

- People affect their environment, and adapt to the environment they live in.

- Global warming, air pollution, and water pollution are threatening the world environment.

- Overpopulation, war, disease, and urbanization are global problems.

- The United Nations is an important international organization striving to solve some of the world's problems.

- International trade is growing, creating a global economy.

- People in developed countries live quite well. People in developing countries often do not get enough to eat or good medical care. Some organizations help people in developing countries.

The United States and Canada

Canada and the United States have many things in common. They make up the northern part of the continent of North America. This photograph is of Banff National Park in the Canadian Rockies. It is Canada's oldest national park, and has glaciers, mountains, lakes, and pine forests.

In the next two chapters, you will discover what makes the United States and Canada leaders in the world. You will discover why they are wealthy nations. You will also learn about the problems they face.

3

The United States

As we begin a new century, the United States is the world's richest and most powerful country. It also has many beautiful physical features. The United States is a nation that has many natural resources. It also has many different people from many different countries.

In this chapter, you will learn how geography helped make the United States a great nation.

Goals for Learning

◆ To describe where the United States is located

◆ To identify the mountain ranges, plains, rivers, and climate of the United States

◆ To describe the many cultures and religions of the United States

◆ To describe the natural resources, industries, and environmental challenges of the United States

Geo-Stats   The United States of America

Population: 300,000,000

Area: 3,717,796 square miles

Length of Coastline: 12,373 miles

Length of Roads: 4.08 million miles

Longest River: Mississippi River system (3,710 miles)

Highest Mountain: Mount McKinley (20,320 feet) in Alaska

Major Cities: Washington DC (national capital); New York City, Los Angeles, Chicago, Houston

Major Religions: Christianity, Judaism, Islam, Buddhism

Major Languages: English, Spanish

Official Currency: U.S. Dollar

Workforce: 149.3 million

Number of Daily Newspapers: 1,500

Number of Television Sets: 2.75 per household

Map Skills

The United States has 50 states and four basic regions. The Pacific Ocean separates Hawaii from the rest of the states. Canada separates Alaska from the 48 states that border one another. Canada is north of the United States, and Mexico is south of the United States. The United States is part of North America.

Find a state that you know about or live in. To what region does it belong? What states border it? Continue studying the map and answer the following questions:

1. What are the four regions on this map?

2. What oceans border the United States?

3. What is its national capital?

4. Which countries border the United States?

5. Why do you think that most of the states in the West are large and most in the Northeast are small?

Reading Strategy:
Predicting

Previewing a text helps readers think about what they already know about a subject. It also prepares readers to look for new information—to predict what will come next. Keep this in mind as you make predictions:

◆ Preview text features to predict what you will be reading about.

◆ Use what you know to predict what will be next.

◆ Check your predictions. You may have to change your predictions as you learn more information.

Key Vocabulary Words

Lesson 1

Continent One of the seven large areas of land on Earth

Industry Any form of business, trade, or making things by machines

Lesson 2

Basin A low area of land surrounded by higher land, often mountains

Sea level The level at the surface of the ocean

River system A group of rivers that join together

Tributary A smaller river that flows into a larger one

Hydroelectric Power created by running water

Tropics The area between the Tropic of Cancer and the Tropic of Capricorn

Humid continental climate A climate with long, cold winters and hot, wet summers; a climate with four different seasons

Steppe climate A climate with very hot summers and very cold winters, with little precipitation

Subtropical climate A climate with hot and humid summers and mild winters

Highland climate The varying climate of a mountainous area

Marine West Coast climate A climate from southeast Alaska to northern California that has mild, cloudy summers and wet winters

Mediterranean climate A climate like that of countries near the Mediterranean Sea: mild, wet winters and hot, dry summers

Lesson 3

Multiculturalism A blend of many cultures

Christian A person who accepts the teachings of Jesus

Roman Catholic A Christian who is part of the largest branch of Christianity, led by the pope

Protestant A Christian who does not belong to the Roman Catholic branch of Christianity

Immigrant A person who leaves one country to live in another

Metropolitan A city and its suburbs

Lesson 4

Renewable resource A natural resource that can be replaced as it is used up

Objectives

◆ To describe the location of the United States

◆ To identify its four geographical regions

Continent

One of the seven large areas of land on Earth

Industry

Any form of business, trade, or making of things by machines

Where Is the United States Located?

The United States is located south of Canada and north of Mexico. These three countries make up most of what geographers call North America. North America is a **continent.** It is one of seven large areas of land on Earth. The United States lies between two oceans. The Atlantic Ocean forms the east coast of the United States. The Pacific Ocean forms the west coast.

The United States is located in the middle latitudes. Its climate is neither too hot nor too cold. Being in the middle latitudes also means that people can earn a living in many different ways.

What Are the Four U.S. Regions?

The United States government collects a lot of information about the way Americans live. It collects facts about their jobs, what they do with their free time, and where they live. The government groups the nation into four regions: the Northeast, the South, the Midwest, and the West. Geographers define these regions according to their physical, economic, and historic features. They also divide each of these four regions into smaller ones called subregions.

What Is the Northeast Region?

The Northeast has many people and large cities, but it is the smallest region of the United States. It extends westward from the Atlantic Ocean and includes 11 states and Washington DC. It is the center of banking and **industry** in the United States. Industry is any form of business or trade, or making things with machines. It was the first region to build factories where products were made using machines. It has some of the oldest factories in the United States. These factories took advantage of the region's many rivers, which supplied power to run machines.

New York City is the nation's biggest city. Over 20 million people live in the New York City area. Many of the nation's biggest and most important businesses have headquarters there. Boston, Massachusetts; Philadelphia, Pennsylvania; and Baltimore, Maryland, are other important cities in the Northeast region.

The Northeast is home to many cultures. Originally, people who came from Europe settled in the Northeast. In recent times, people have come from Latin America and Asia.

What Is the Southern Region?

South and west of the Northeast region lies the region geographers call the South. It contains 14 states. Its broad, coastal plain borders the Atlantic Ocean and the Gulf of Mexico. Further inland, the land becomes hilly. Forests cover much of this land. The South has many port cities. New Orleans in Louisiana, and Houston and Beaumont in Texas are the biggest.

The South today differs from what it once was. At one time, it was a mostly rural cotton-growing area. Today, farming remains, but other industries are more important. The region is a major source of lumber. The wood is used to make paper and furniture. The South has major factories where workers put cars together. The South attracts factories because of its mild climate and its low cost of labor. Its sunny weather makes it popular with tourists and retired people.

The new industries have attracted many new people to the South. Many have come from other parts of the United States. Hispanics or Latinos, Spanish-speaking people, make up most of the newcomers. In southern Florida, they make up the majority of people.

New York City has over 20 million people.

Reading Strategy: Predicting

Based on what you have read so far, predict what you think the next paragraphs will include.

Reading Strategy:
Predicting

Think about what you predicted earlier. Was your prediction right, or did you need to change it?

What Is the Midwest Region?

The Midwest region borders all three of the other regions. It contains 12 states and is a large plain. Its rich soil is good for growing grain. Bakers use grain to make bread, so it is sometimes called America's "breadbasket." Most of the grain and corn in the United States comes from the Midwest. The Midwest is also the "dairy belt" of the United States. It produces a lot of milk, cheese, and butter.

The Midwest has several large cities. Many are located on the shores of the Great Lakes. Chicago—the third largest city in the United States—is an important manufacturing, business, and transportation center in Illinois. Cleveland and Toledo in Ohio; Milwaukee, Wisconsin; and Detroit, Michigan, are other cities located on the Great Lakes. Many of these cities are important centers of industry. Minneapolis, Minnesota, and St. Louis, Missouri, are important cities located on the Mississippi River.

What Is the Western Region?

The largest of the four regions in area is the West. It also has the fewest people. It has 13 states, including Alaska, the largest of the 50 states. Alaska has large stretches of land on which no trees can grow. Only grasses and mosses grow on some of this land. The West also includes the Rocky Mountains and part of the Great Plains. There is so much wheat grown in the Great Plains that it is named the "wheat belt." The biggest and driest deserts of the United States cover large parts of the West. A desert is a dry area in which few or no people live.

The Great Plains have large fields to grow crops.

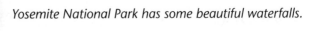

Yosemite National Park has some beautiful waterfalls.

Many people live in the coastal area of California. In fact, most of the people who live in the West live in California. It has more people than any other state. But huge areas of the West have few people. The natural beauty of the West attracts many visitors. The region has many beautiful national parks such as Yellowstone and Yosemite National Park.

Los Angeles, California, is the second largest city in the United States. Other big cities of the West are the port cities of Seattle, Washington, and San Diego and San Francisco, California. Two of the fastest-growing cities are Phoenix, Arizona, and Las Vegas, Nevada. Denver, Colorado, is a key transportation center.

Word Bank

Midwest 1

Northeast 4

regions 2

South 5

West 3

Lesson 1 Review On a sheet of paper, use the words from the Word Bank to complete each sentence correctly.

1. The region that borders the other three regions is the _____.

2. To study areas better, geographers divide them into _____.

3. The largest of the four regions of the United States is the _____.

4. The region with the largest city in the United States is the _____.

5. The region with a mild climate and low cost of labor is the _____.

What do you think ?

If you had a choice, in which region of the United States would you like to live? Why? Give three reasons with your answer.

Continental Divide

Highest mountain peaks in the Rockies that divide the rivers flowing to the east and to the west

Basin

A low area of land surrounded by higher land, often mountains

Sea level

The level at the surface of the ocean

Crater

A bowl-shaped hole

River system

A group of rivers that join together

Tributary

A smaller river that flows into a larger one

What Are the Main Physical Features?

In the United States, the Appalachian Mountains stretch from Maine to Alabama. The Rocky Mountains stretch from Alaska to Mexico. These two mountain ranges are on either side of the Central Plains.

There are two large mountain systems along the Pacific coast, the Sierra Nevada and the Cascade Range. These mountains have some of the highest peaks in the United States. The highest peaks are in Alaska. The tallest mountain in North America is Denali, also known as Mount McKinley, in Alaska.

The **Continental Divide** is the line of highest peaks in the Rockies. It divides rivers flowing to the east and to the west. Between the Rockies and the Sierra Nevada lies the Great **Basin.** A basin is a low area of land surrounded by higher land, often mountains. The Great Basin contains Death Valley—the lowest place in North America. This California valley lies 282 feet below **sea level.** Sea level is the level at the surface of the ocean.

What Did the Ice Age Do?

North America has more lakes than any other continent. During the last ice age thousands of years ago, huge glaciers covered much of the land. As these ice sheets moved, they dug deep **craters** in the earth. A crater is a bowl-shaped hole. When the ice melted, lakes formed in these holes. The last ice age created the five Great Lakes. Together they hold the largest freshwater supply in the world.

How Did the Ice Age Create the Mississippi?

When the glaciers melted, water ran off in large streams that became great rivers. These rivers formed the Mississippi **River system.** A river system is a group of rivers that join together. The Mississippi River, with its many **tributaries,** drains the plains in the middle of the United States. A tributary is a smaller river that flows into a larger one.

The Mississippi is one of the chief rivers in the United States— it is almost 2,500 miles long. The Missouri and Ohio Rivers are large tributaries. The Mississippi empties into the Gulf of Mexico near New Orleans, Louisiana. There, the Mississippi has created a **delta.** A delta is an area of rich land at the mouth of a river. A river carries dirt downstream to form the delta.

What Else Does Water Affect?

The United States has many lakes and rivers. They are important sources of freshwater. Sometimes workers dam rivers to create **hydroelectric** power, or power created by running water. Rivers are important for trade and transportation.

The oceans on both coasts are important for shipping and fishing. Many of the goods the United States buys from other countries come on ships that travel across the ocean. The oceans supply fish, lobsters, crabs, and other seafood. Oceans are also responsible for much of our weather.

The United States

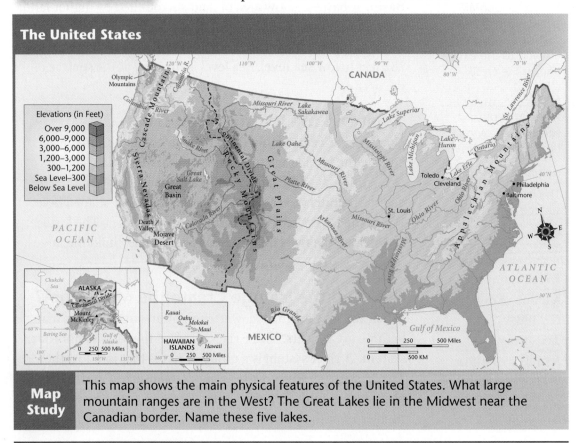

Map Study

This map shows the main physical features of the United States. What large mountain ranges are in the West? The Great Lakes lie in the Midwest near the Canadian border. Name these five lakes.

Tropic of Cancer

An imaginary line that lies 23.5 degrees north of the equator

Tropic of Capricorn

An imaginary line that lies 23.5 degrees south of the equator

Tropics

The area between the Tropic of Cancer and the Tropic of Capricorn

Weather is the condition of the air at a given time or place.

What Influences Climate?

Climate is the average of weather conditions over a period of time. Earth is tilted as it rotates in space. Its position to the sun determines climate. The equator lies halfway between the North Pole and the South Pole. The **Tropic of Cancer,** an imaginary line, lies 23.5 degrees north of the equator. The **Tropic of Capricorn** lies 23.5 degrees south of the equator.

Oceans, latitude, elevation, and landforms influence climate. Oceans have areas of warm and cold water. Winds blowing across warm ocean water can carry heat to the land. Oceans are the main source of precipitation.

Precipitation and temperature affect the climate. Precipitation is rain or snow that falls from the sky. A region can be warm or cold, wet or dry. Being near to or far from an ocean or lake affects the climate. Water can keep an area cool in the summer and warmer in the winter.

The latitude of a place affects its climate. The **Tropics** is the area between the Tropic of Cancer and the Tropic of Capricorn. The Tropics receive the most direct rays of sunlight. They are warm year around. Areas north of the Tropic of Cancer and south of the Tropic of Capricorn sometimes get only indirect sunlight. These areas usually have colder climates and four seasons.

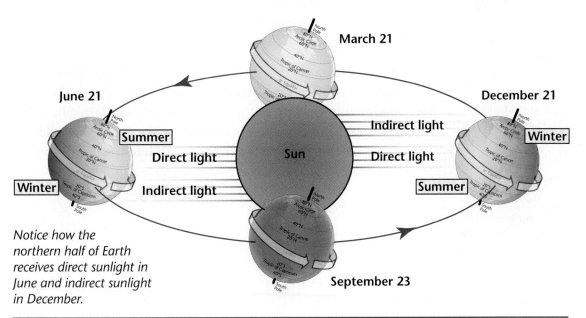

Notice how the northern half of Earth receives direct sunlight in June and indirect sunlight in December.

Elevation or height above sea level also affects climate. Places with higher elevations are usually colder.

Landforms such as mountains influence climate, too. Winds carrying clouds rise when they reach mountains. The air cools, and rain falls. When winds reach the other side of the mountains, the winds become warm and dry.

What Climates Are in the United States?

The United States has many climates. The Northeast and Midwest regions have a **humid continental climate.** They have four seasons, with long, cold winters and hot, wet summers. The area between the western edge of the Midwest and the mountains has a **steppe climate.** It has very hot summers and very cold winters, with little precipitation. The land is covered with wild grasses and few trees.

The South has a **subtropical climate.** Subtropical areas border on the Tropics. Summers are hot and humid, with lots of moisture in the air. Winters are mild.

The West has many climates. In mountain areas there is a **highland climate,** in which temperatures vary greatly. The **windward** side of the mountains—the side from which the wind is blowing—receives larger amounts of rain or snow. The **leeward** side—the side away from the wind—receives less rain. In the West, the windward side is the west side, which is closest to the ocean.

The coast from southeast Alaska to northern California has a **marine West Coast climate.** This area has mild and often cloudy summers with wet winters. Southern California has a **Mediterranean climate.** This climate is like that of countries near the Mediterranean Sea in Europe. It has mild, wet winters and hot, dry summers.

Reading Strategy:
Predicting

Before you read this paragraph, predict how you think geography affects the way people live. Then see if you are right.

How Does Geography Affect People?

People adapt to the conditions around them. For example, people in hot climates such as Florida do not need winter coats. People in cold climates such as North Dakota do. The Northeast has thin, rocky soil and a short growing season, so few people farm. But the Midwest has good farmland and good growing conditions, so more people farm. People fish in the North Atlantic. Where many trees grow, workers use wood to make paper and furniture.

From early in U.S. history, people changed the environments in which they lived. They cut forests, plowed fields, dammed rivers, and built cities.

Lesson 2 Review On a sheet of paper, write the answer to each question. Use complete sentences.

1. What are the names of three mountain ranges located in the United States?

2. How did the Great Lakes form?

3. What river system drains the middle of the United States?

4. What are important sources of freshwater?

5. What factors influence climate?

What do you think

What effect do you think a large lake like Lake Michigan would have on the weather of that region?

Geography in Your Life

Acid Rain

Scientists use the term acid rain for rain or snow that contains harmful acids. Factories, power plants, and automobiles burn coal, gasoline, and oil. That causes sulfur dioxide and nitrogen oxide to pollute the air. When these oxides mix with water vapor in the air, it creates sulfuric acid and nitric acid. This creates acid rain.

Acid rain pollutes lakes and rivers. Fish and wildlife die. It damages buildings, statues, and bridges. It harms land and forests. It can get into human drinking water and affect food.

Acid rain affects Canada, the United States, and western Europe. In 1990, the U.S. Congress set standards to reduce the amount of acid rain in the United States and Canada.

Multiculturalism

A blend of many cultures

Cultural diffusion

The borrowing of language, customs, and religion from other cultures

Christian

A person who accepts the teachings of Jesus

Christianity

The religion of Christians

Roman Catholic

A Christian who is part of the largest branch of Christianity, led by the pope

Protestant

A Christian who does not belong to the Roman Catholic branch of Christianity

What Cultures Are in the United States?

Culture is the way of life of a group of people. The United States blends many cultures. This is called **multiculturalism.** Some parts of this culture are like Europe because about 70 percent of Americans have European backgrounds. About 12 percent of Americans have African roots. In recent years, many people have come from Asia and Latin America. Latinos make up about 13 percent of the population. There are also many American Indian cultures. All these people had their own language, religion, and customs.

Sometimes cultures change. They do this by borrowing from one another. This is called **cultural diffusion.** For example, today most Americans enjoy foods like pizza, tacos, and egg rolls. Different cultures brought all these foods to the United States. Music played in the United States also comes from many different cultures. Jazz came from African American music. Salsa comes from Latin America. Rap and hip-hop reflect both African American and Latin American cultures.

More than 300 million people live in the United States. About 77 percent are **Christians.** They believe in the teachings of Jesus.

Christianity, the religion of Christians, has many branches. The largest branch is the **Roman Catholic** Church. The head of this branch is the pope. All other Christians are **Protestants.** More than half of Americans are Protestants. They have many of the same beliefs as Catholics.

Other religions in the United States include Judaism, Islam, and Buddhism.

Immigrant

A person who leaves one country to live in another

Reading Strategy:
Predicting

Look at the picture below. Can you predict what the text will be about?

What Languages Do the People Speak?

Most people in the United States speak English. However, nearly one of five people speak a language other than English at home. About 10 percent—almost 30 million people—use Spanish as their first language. The number of people coming to the United States from Spanish-speaking countries, especially Mexico, is increasing.

Throughout most of its history, the United States has welcomed **immigrants**—people from other countries. They have adopted the culture and language of the majority Americans. But many immigrants keep their native culture and language. Because of this, some cities have immigrants who do not speak English. Instead, they speak the language of their native countries.

Celebrations

Powwows

The first people to live in North America were American Indians. A powwow is a celebration of American Indian culture. At a powwow, dancers, singers, musicians, artists, and families gather to celebrate their traditions.

Powwows are usually outdoors. Vendors sell food and goods. There are singing and dancing contests. Sometimes, people who are not American Indians are welcomed. But, visitors usually cannot attend the religious ceremonies that are often part of such powwows.

Long ago, powwows were a special custom of the Plains Indians. Today the custom has spread to other groups. The powwow has become one feature of an ever more unified American Indian culture.

Critical Thinking How do powwows help to unify American Indian culture?

Metropolitan

A city and its suburbs

Suburb

An area next to a city

Megalopolis

A vast city made up of many cities, one right next to another

Many American Indians live on reservations. A reservation is an area that has been set aside for them. There are about 300 reservations in the United States.

Where Do Most People Live?

In the past, most Americans lived in small farm communities. Today, the United States is a nation of cities. Nearly 80 percent of Americans live in **metropolitan** areas. A metropolitan area includes a city and its **suburbs.** The suburbs are areas next to a city.

The 40 largest metropolitan areas in the United States have more than one million people each. Most of these people live in suburbs. The automobile and a well-developed transportation system helped the growth of suburbs. Some cities and their suburbs have grown so large that they have absorbed nearby cities. All together, they create one large city. For example, a person can drive from Boston, Massachusetts, to Washington DC and never leave an urban, or city, area. In the 1960s, geographers began to use the name **megalopolis** to describe that type of area. The word means "a very large city."

Many cities in the United States developed because of changes in transportation. The first cities to develop were all located on the Atlantic Ocean. They were all port cities: Boston, Philadelphia, New York, and Baltimore. Soon, however, the country expanded westward. Settlers used rivers as early highways. Many cities developed along these rivers or where two rivers met. New Orleans, located at the mouth of the Mississippi River in Louisiana, is one example. In Missouri, St. Louis grew where the Missouri and Mississippi Rivers come together. The coming of the railroads also helped the growth of other cities. Chicago is near the center of the United States. This Illinois city became a railroad center.

St. Louis grew into a city where two rivers come together.

Reading Strategy:
Predicting

What do you know about what is happening in the United States? Predict what these paragraphs may tell you.

What Trends Are Affecting the United States?

A trend is a general movement. Three important trends affect the United States today. First, the population is changing. At one time, most people in the United States were alike. They were mostly white and Christian. They spoke English and shared the same culture. Over time the United States has attracted many immigrants from other countries. They have their own religions, languages, and cultures.

Second, the population of the South and Southwest are growing faster than the rest of the country. The Sunbelt states—California, Arizona, Texas, and Florida—are the fastest growing states. The Rust Belt states—older, industrial northern states—are growing more slowly or losing population. The Rust Belt starts around Lake Michigan and continues into upstate New York.

Third, the economy of the United States is changing. In the past, most Americans were farmers. Others worked in factories. Today, over 70 percent of working Americans work in service industries doing things for other people. Some examples of service workers are teachers, salespeople, entertainers, and nurses.

Celebrations

Kwanzaa

Kwanzaa is a harvest holiday. It celebrates family, community, and the values of African ancestors. It features candle lighting, gift giving, and eating.

Kwanzaa started in the 1960s. It runs from December 26 to January 1. African Americans of any religion can celebrate Kwanzaa. Each day honors a certain principle, such as creativity, faith, unity, working together, and purpose.

Critical Thinking What are some other ways to honor the values celebrated at Kwanzaa?

Biography

Willis Carrier: 1876–1950

In 1915, American engineer Willis Carrier discovered how to control humidity in a print shop. This allowed the books to print properly. Then Carrier invented modern air conditioning. At first, only businesses such as hotels and movie theaters used it. But after World War II, people began installing air conditioning in their offices and homes.

Today, Carrier's invention cools people in their homes, cars, and work places. Air conditioning makes it possible for people in hot climates to live comfortably.

Lesson 3 Review On a sheet of paper, write the word in parenthesis that makes each statement true.

1. American (culture, trend) is a blend of American Indian cultures and cultures from Europe, Africa, Asia, and Latin America.

2. Cultures (never, sometimes) change.

3. Most people in the United States are (Protestants, Catholics).

4. Most people in America live in (metropolitan, rural) areas.

5. In the United States, people are moving to the (Rust Belt, Sunbelt).

Writing About Geography

A brochure is a small, folded advertisement for something. Choose a place in the United States that many tourists visit each year. Research this place. Then write your own brochure about it. Explain why people would want to visit it.

What do you think ?

Do you think cities in the United States will continue to grow, or will more people choose to live in smaller towns? Give two or three reasons for your answer.

What Are Two Important Natural Resources?

The United States is the richest country and the third largest country in the world. Why do Americans live better than people in many other countries do? One reason is the country's rich natural resources, which are raw materials produced by nature.

One such resource is its rich farmland. U.S. farmers produce enough food for everyone in the United States with a lot left over to sell to other countries. Water is a second important natural resource. The United States has water for crops and hydroelectric power. Its many rivers serve as highways for transporting goods. Ocean water provides seafood.

What Are Other Important Natural Resources?

Forests are a third natural resource. Forests cover much of the United States. If managed properly, they are a **renewable resource.** In other words, they can be replaced as they are used up. In the Southeast, logging is an important industry. Workers in the huge forests of the Pacific Northwest make lumber and pulp from wood. Pulp is a wood product used to make paper.

This hydroelectric dam in Tennessee produces electricity.

Coal, natural gas, and oil are natural resources. Huge deposits of coal lie deep in the earth. In fact, the United States owns about one-third of all the known coal deposits on Earth. Coal is located in Pennsylvania, West Virginia, Kentucky, Tennessee, Ohio, and Alabama. There is oil and natural gas in Alaska, California, and the Texas and Louisiana coasts of the Gulf of Mexico. There are many other minerals, especially copper and lead, in the mountains of western United States.

What Resources Helped Build Industries?

Many natural resources helped the United States build its industries. Using natural resources was cheaper than using goods from another country. One important product for an industrialized country is steel. Workers used iron ore from Minnesota and coal from the Appalachian Mountains to make steel. Huge steel mills developed around Pittsburgh, Pennsylvania; Cleveland, Ohio; and near Chicago, Illinois. These mills helped the United States become an industrial giant in the late 1800s. In the 1980s, many older factories closed because foreign countries were able to produce better steel at lower cost. Many workers lost their jobs.

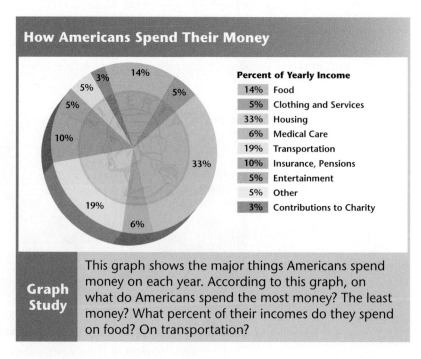

How Americans Spend Their Money

Percent of Yearly Income

14%	Food
5%	Clothing and Services
33%	Housing
6%	Medical Care
19%	Transportation
10%	Insurance, Pensions
5%	Entertainment
5%	Other
3%	Contributions to Charity

Graph Study

This graph shows the major things Americans spend money on each year. According to this graph, on what do Americans spend the most money? The least money? What percent of their incomes do they spend on food? On transportation?

What Are Some U.S. Industries?

The United States has the world's largest economy. It is a world leader in the production of food and manufactured goods. Only 2 percent of Americans are farmers. Yet, they produce enough food to feed all Americans, and also feed many people in the rest of the world.

Only about 13 percent of Americans work in manufacturing jobs. The United States is the world's largest aircraft maker. It also makes automobiles, transportation equipment, electronics, and other products that people use every day. Manufacturing jobs are being moved to other countries to cut labor costs.

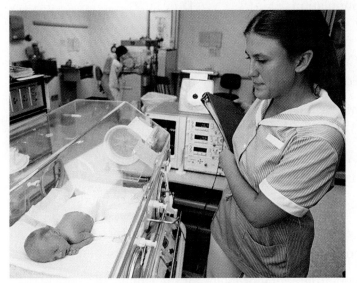

This nurse is an example of someone who works in a service industry.

Reading Strategy:
Predicting

Can you predict what environmental challenges the United States faces?

What Are Some Service Industries?

Today, nearly 75 percent of Americans work in service industries. A service industry does not make a product, it provides a service. Doctors, lawyers, teachers, and bankers are all service workers. One of the fastest-growing service industries is health care.

What Environmental Challenges Exist?

Americans produce more garbage than any other people on Earth. It costs over $30 billion to get rid of the over 200 million tons of waste produced each year. This garbage hurts the environment. Recycling is one answer to this problem. However, the United States recycles only a small percentage of what it uses.

Air pollution—or impure and unhealthy air—is another big environmental problem. Pollution can cause serious diseases like asthma. Air pollution is a bigger problem around cities than in rural areas. However, winds can carry pollution from one area to another.

Sometimes chemicals end up in rivers and lakes, causing water pollution. Industries are often the source of this pollution. Sometimes cities dump untreated human waste into the oceans. Then pollution makes seafood unsafe to eat. Water pollution can also cause serious health problems in people and animals.

Lesson 4 Review On a sheet of paper, write the letter of the answer that correctly completes each sentence.

1. One reason Americans live better than people in other countries is its rich _____.

   A rivers   **C** natural resources
   B population   **D** oceans

2. _____ can be renewable resources.

   A Coal mines   **C** Natural gas
   B Forests   **D** Oil fields

3. Pennsylvania, West Virginia, Kentucky, Tennessee, Ohio, and Alabama have rich deposits of __C__.

   A oil   **C** coal
   B natural gas   **D** iron ore

4. Today, _____ employ most Americans.

   A service industries   **C** paper plants
   B coal mines   **D** steel plants

5. An environmental problem for the United States is _____.

   A air pollution   **C** too much garbage
   B water pollution   **D** all of the above

What do you think ?

Why might water be a more valuable resource in the future?

Old-Growth Forests

About 10 percent of the trees in the United States are in old-growth forests. The trees in those forests are hundreds of years old. No one has ever logged them. Today, people are fighting over these trees. Logging companies want to start cutting them down. Old-growth trees provide the best and cheapest wood. By cutting them down, logging companies say they can provide jobs.

On the other side are people who work to protect the natural environment. These people are called environmentalists. They want to stop all logging in old-growth forests. They point out that when the trees are gone, the jobs will be lost anyway. And the trees will be gone forever.

Recently, scientists have noticed that a bird called the spotted owl is dying out. Spotted owls live in old-growth forests. Most scientists agree that the vanishing owls are a warning sign. If they are dying out, many other animals who live in forests must be dying, too. Many people believe that saving the forests could help save these animals.

Wrap-Up

1. What is an old-growth forest?

2. What are the arguments for logging old-growth forests?

Make a Difference

How much old-growth forest is in your state? Find out from the Department of Natural Resources. Ask what the state's policy is on old-growth forests. Then write a paragraph explaining your position on what you learned.

A Time to Decide

My name is Jakob. I am 17 years old and live in Stratsburg, Pennsylvania. I live in an Amish community. Does that make me Amish? Not really, at least not yet. I'm still trying to decide whether to accept the teachings of my church or not.

Being Amish means obeying the teachings in the Bible. We believe this means avoiding modern conveniences. On my family's farm, we get our water from a well. We use oil lamps for light. We travel by horse and buggy and grow most of our own food. Doing these things lets us have our own community, without help from other people.

Some Amish groups are stricter than others. But almost all communities have the tradition of *rumspringa.* This is the period after we turn 16. It's the time when we choose whether to become baptized into the church or not. *Rumspringa* means "running around." We spend time away from our Amish community, going into town, seeing what teens who are not Amish do. For some, *rumspringa* lasts a short time. For others, it takes years.

The first thing I did was buy a pair of blue jeans. I'd been saving for a long time. I never wear them on our farm, though. Most of us change out of our Amish clothes at a gas station once we are out for the night.

At first, all of the new things seemed so strange. Riding in cars, going to movies, and parties were all new. I was startled when I first saw makeup on my friend Anna's face.

Many of my friends have tried other new things—like smoking—but not me.

Our parents know the things we do, but they try to ignore them. They know it is our time to choose. And since we are not yet baptized, we are not breaking church rules.

I sometimes feel tired by the things I am doing. I stay out late but get up early to help with farm chores. Some kids don't live at home during *rumspringa.* They get jobs and find apartments with friends. Others live at home but come and go as they please.

I think I'm close to making my decision. I will miss the video games the most.

Wrap-Up

1. What are some ways the Amish avoid modern conveniences?

2. Why do you think Amish parents let their teenagers have extra freedom?

- The United States, Canada, and Mexico are the three largest countries in North America.

- Geographers use regions to study different areas. They define regions according to physical features, their history, and their economy.

- Geographers usually divide the United States into four regions: the Northeast, the South, the Midwest, and the West.

- The United States has a varied landscape. It is relatively flat along the Atlantic coast. A large mountain range in the East is the Appalachian range. The middle of the United States is also relatively flat. The West has many high mountains, including the Cascade and Rocky Mountains.

- Huge, slow-moving sheets of ice called glaciers formed many lakes and rivers when they melted. Among these were the five Great Lakes and the Mississippi River system.

- Average weather is called climate. The United States has many climates. The Northeast and Midwest regions have four seasons, with long, cold winters and hot, wet summers. The South has a subtropical climate with hot and humid summers and mild winters. Because of its mountains and coastline, the West has several climates.

- U.S. culture blends cultures from many other lands. The cultures of American Indians and people from Europe, Africa, Latin America, and Asia have influenced U.S. culture.

- The people of the United States follow almost all major religions of the world, but most Americans are Christians.

- Nearly 80 percent of Americans live in metropolitan areas. It is a very urbanized country.

- The United States is rich in natural resources including farmland, water, forests, and minerals.

- Some people in the United States work in manufacturing industries, such as steel, computers, and electronics. But most people work in service industries such as restaurants, schools, repair shops, and stores.

- The United States faces several environmental problems, such as air and water pollution and too much garbage.

Chapter 3 REVIEW

Word Bank

culture 5
glaciers 3
North America 1
Tropic of Cancer 4
West 2

On a sheet of paper, use the words from the Word Bank to complete each sentence correctly.

1. The United States, Canada, and Mexico are the three largest countries in the continent of _____.

2. The largest region in the United States is the _____.

3. The five Great Lakes and many of the rivers in the United States formed when _____ melted.

4. The imaginary line 23.5 degrees north of the equator is called the _____.

5. Language and religion are two parts of _____.

On a sheet of paper, write the letter of the answer that correctly completes each sentence.

6. _A_ is a measure of how far north or south of the equator a place is.

   A Location   **C** Longitude
   B Latitude   **D** Distance

7. The region with the largest city in the United States is the _A_.

   A Northeast   **C** Midwest
   B South   **D** West

8. Borrowing things from other cultures and making them a part of your own is cultural _B_.

   A stealing   **C** acquisition
   B diffusion   **D** birth

9. Nearly 80 percent of the people of the United States live in _C_ areas.

   A country   **C** metropolitan
   B small town   **D** mountain

10. Coal, water, forests, natural gas, and oil are examples of _____ D .

A manufacturing   **C** service industries
B imports   **D** natural resources

On a sheet of paper, write the answer to each question. Use complete sentences.

11. What is the climate like in each of the four regions of the United States?

12. Why does the United States have so many cultures?

13. What are some environmental challenges the United States faces?

Critical Thinking On a sheet of paper, write your response to each question. Use complete sentences.

14. Imagine you have the task of locating a new manufacturing plant somewhere in the United States. In what region would you build the plant? Give two or three reasons.

15. How have Americans changed their physical environment? Give two or three examples.

Applying the Five Themes of Geography

Location
How did the location of the Northeast region affect its growth?

Test-Taking Tip

Prepare for a test by making a set of flash cards. Write a word on the front of each card. Write the definition on the back. Use the flash cards in a game by yourself or with a partner to test your knowledge.

4

Canada

Canada is the second largest country in the world. It has many things in common with its neighbor to the south, the United States. It has much land and open space. Canada has many industries, and its people live well. Canada has far fewer people than the United States. However, the two countries share a similar culture and economy.

Goals for Learning

◆ To describe where Canada is located and its regions

◆ To describe how glaciers changed Canada and the climates of Canada

◆ To describe the diversity of Canada and how most people in Canada live

◆ To describe the economy of Canada and its environmental challenges

Geo-Stats Canada

Population:
33,000,000

Area: 3,849,670
square miles

Length of Coastline:
151,394 miles

Length of Roads:
870,000 miles

Longest River:
Mackenzie (2,635 miles)

Highest Mountain:
Mount Logan (19,551 feet)

Major Cities: Ottawa (capital),
Toronto, Montreal, Vancouver,
Edmonton, Calgary

Major Religion: Christianity

Major Languages:
English, French

Official Currency:
Canadian Dollar

Workforce: 17.6 million

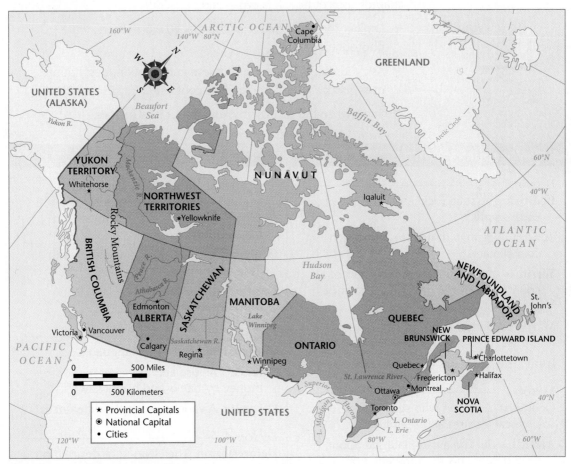

Map Skills

Canada is a large nation north of the United States. Like the United States, it is part of North America. It has ten large provinces, or states, and three territories—Yukon Territory, Northwest Territories, and Nunavut. It is a nation with a wide range of temperatures and many prairies, lakes, and mountains.

Study the map and answer the following questions:

1. What is the largest territory in Canada?

2. What large body of water is near the center of Canada?

3. What territory and province border Alaska?

4. What is Canada's capital?

5. Why do you think Canada is a cold place to live?

Reading Strategy:
Text Structure

Understanding how text is organized helps you decide which information is most important. Before you begin reading this chapter, look at how it is organized.

◆ Look at the titles, headings, boldfaced words, and photographs.

◆ Ask yourself: Is the text a problem and solution, description, or sequence? Is it compare and contrast or cause and effect?

◆ Summarize the text by thinking about its structure.

Key Vocabulary Words

Lesson 1

Bedrock The solid rock under the soil of Earth's surface

Tundra A plain with no trees located in cold climates

Territory An area of land that is part of a country, but is not officially a province or state of a country

Maritime Bordering on or being near the sea

Inuit The native people of Canada

Lesson 2

Geologist A person who studies Earth's physical features and their history

Arctic Circle The area of latitude about 66.5 degrees north of the equator

Permafrost Ground that is always frozen

Subarctic climate The cold climate that is just outside the Arctic Circle

Chinook A hot, dry wind along the eastern slopes of the Rocky Mountains

Continental climate The climate in landlocked areas far from oceans; a climate of short, warm summers and long winters

Drought A long period of weather with little rain

Landlocked Surrounded by land far from oceans

Lesson 3

Bilingual Speaking two languages

Finance The use and management of money by banks and businesses

Diversity A variety of people; differences

Lesson 4

Deforestation The clearing or destruction of forests

Clear cutting Cutting down and removing every tree in an area

Wetland Land covered by water some or most of the time, but where plants continue to grow

Bedrock

The solid rock under the soil of Earth's surface

Tundra

A plain with no trees located in a cold climate

Reading Strategy:
Text Structure

As you read, look for the words *first, second, third,* and so on. These words help you understand the order of things in the paragraphs.

Remember that a plain is a low-lying flat area.

Where Is Canada Located?

Canada, the largest country in North America and the second largest in the world, stretches 3,426 miles from east to west. This is almost one-quarter of the way around the world. The Atlantic Ocean borders Canada on the east, and the Pacific Ocean borders it on the west.

Canada has the longest coastline of any country in the world. Its northern-most point is Cape Columbia on Ellesmere Island, which is only 477 miles from the North Pole. From this point to Canada's farthest point south is over 2,000 miles. Canada's border with the United States is the longest border in the world that is not protected by an army.

What Physical Regions Exist?

Canada has six physical regions. The Canadian Shield is the first and largest physical region. Located in eastern Canada, it covers nearly half of the nation. Its name came from the hard **bedrock** beneath the soil. Bedrock refers to the solid rock under the soil of Earth's surface.

West of the Canadian Shield lies the second physical region, the Interior Plains. A huge range of mountains in the far west makes up a third region. The Arctic region is the fourth physical region. It lies in the far north and has hundreds of islands in the Arctic Ocean. This area also has a very large area of **tundra.** Tundra is a plain with no trees.

In eastern Canada, the Appalachian Mountains make up its fifth physical region. Ancient glaciers wore down these old mountains. Today the area has gently rolling hills with fertile valleys in between. The sixth and smallest physical region in Canada is the Great Lakes-St. Lawrence lowlands. This region is between the Appalachian Mountain region and the Canadian Shield region.

What Political Regions Exist?

Geographers divide Canada into six political regions. These include ten provinces, or states, and three territories. A **territory** is an area of land that is part of a country, but is not officially a province or state of that country.

What Are the Maritime Provinces?

The smallest political region includes the four **Maritime** Provinces. Maritime means bordering on or near the sea. New Brunswick, Newfoundland and Labrador, Nova Scotia, and Prince Edward Island make up the Maritime Provinces. They border the Atlantic Ocean. These were the first places that Europeans settled in Canada.

The Maritime Provinces are a rugged area of low, forested mountains. Only Prince Edward Island has any large areas of flat farmland. Geographers call the shallow waters off the eastern shore of Newfoundland the Grand Banks.

What Is Quebec?

To the west and north of the Maritime Provinces is Quebec. It is Canada's largest province. About one out of every four Canadians lives in Quebec. Its most famous cities are Montreal and Quebec City. Both cities are located on the St. Lawrence River. Montreal is the largest inland port in the world.

Toronto is a large city in Ontario. It is farther south than some cities in the northern United States.

Inuit

The native people of Canada

Remember that another name for farming is agriculture.

This Inuit is dressed for winter weather.

What Is Ontario?

West of Quebec is the industrial heartland of Canada, the province of Ontario. It is the third political region. Great forests cover northern Ontario. Most of the region's people live in southern Ontario. Ontario is one of the fastest growing business centers in the world. Toronto, the biggest city in Canada, is located in Ontario. Canada's capital city of Ottawa is also in Ontario.

What Are the Prairie Provinces?

At one time, the Prairie Provinces region was a large prairie covered with tall grasses. European settlers plowed the grasses under and planted grain crops. Today, the Prairie Provinces produce much of the world's wheat. Manitoba, Saskatchewan, and Alberta make up the Prairie Provinces. The chief industries are manufacturing, agriculture, and fertilizer production. Alberta produces natural gas and oil. The mountains are beautiful, so tourism is also important. Some of the main cities in this region are Winnipeg in Manitoba, and Calgary and Edmonton in Alberta.

What Is British Columbia?

The fifth political region in Canada is British Columbia. The Coast Mountains and the Canadian Rockies separate it from the rest of the country. There are thick forests for logging and salmon-rich waters for fishing in British Columbia. The largest city in British Columbia is Vancouver, the third largest city in Canada. It is Canada's major port city on the Pacific Ocean.

What Is the Arctic North?

The sixth political region in Canada is the Arctic North. It covers more than a third of the country. The Arctic North includes the Yukon Territory, the Northwest Territories, and Nunavut. The Canadian government created the new territory of Nunavut for the **Inuit,** the native people who live there. People once called them Eskimos. The Arctic North region is cold and dry. Geographers predict that life will soon change in the Arctic North. That is because miners have discovered huge mineral deposits there.

Provinces and Territories of Canada

Province/Territory	Area in Square Miles	Population
Alberta	255,287	3,256,800
British Columbia	365,948	4,254,500
Manitoba	250,947	1,177,600
New Brunswick	28,355	752,000
Newfoundland and Labrador	156,649	516,000
Nova Scotia	21,425	937,900
Ontario	412,581	12,541,400
Prince Edward Island	2,185	138,100
Quebec	594,860	7,598,100
Saskatchewan	251,866	994,100
Northwest Territories	503,951	42,800
Yukon Territory	186,661	31,200
Nunavut	818,959	28,300

Chart Study This chart lists information about Canada's provinces and territories. Which has the highest population? The lowest? How many square miles is Quebec? Alberta?

Word Bank

Canada 1

Canadian Shield 2

Nunavut 5

territories 3

Toronto 4

Lesson 1 Review On a sheet of paper, use the words from the Word Bank to complete each sentence correctly.

1. _____ is the second largest country in the world.

2. The largest physical region of Canada is the _____.

3. Canada has ten provinces and three _____.

4. Canada's biggest city is _____.

5. Canada created the territory of _____ for the Inuits.

What do you think ?

Why is it good that Canada and the United States are good friends and trading partners? What is it that has made them this way?

◆ To understand how glaciers shaped the physical regions of Canada

◆ To identify Canada's subarctic and other climates

◆ To understand how geography affects Canadians

Geologist

A person who studies Earth's physical features and their history

Remember that a glacier is a large, slow-moving sheet of ice.

Reading Strategy:
Text Structure

As you read this lesson, look at the map on the next page to find things that are mentioned in the lesson.

What Are Some Physical Features of Canada?

Glaciers once covered much of Canada. They shaped its land. Glaciers also wore down the high mountains that once stood in eastern Canada.

Geologists study physical features of Earth. They say that these eastern Canadian mountains formed about 280 million years ago. As time passed, glaciers, wind, and water wore them down. Today, these old mountains range in height from 500 feet to about 4,000 feet. These give the Maritime Provinces gently rolling land.

The melting glaciers left behind many lakes and rivers. In fact, Canada has over 2 million lakes, more lakes than any other country in the world. About 30 percent of the world's freshwater is located in Canada.

What Else Did Glaciers Do?

Glaciers also affected the central plains. Melting glaciers left behind rich topsoil for growing crops. To the west of the central plains rise the peaks of the *cordillera*. This Spanish word means mountain range.

The Canadian Rocky Mountains are a part of the same range as the Rocky Mountains found in the United States. Some of these mountains reach 12,000 feet. The western *cordillera* includes the Coast Mountains in British Columbia and the St. Elias Mountains in the Yukon. The tallest mountain in Canada is Mount Logan in the St. Elias Mountains. It is over 19,550 feet tall. Even today, glaciers cover much of these mountains. The western *cordillera* is rich in minerals and timber.

Glaciers also created Canada's 50,000 islands. No people live on many of the islands. The four largest islands are Baffin, Victoria, Ellesmere, and Newfoundland. Newfoundland has the most people, nearly 500,000. Some of these islands are larger than many European countries.

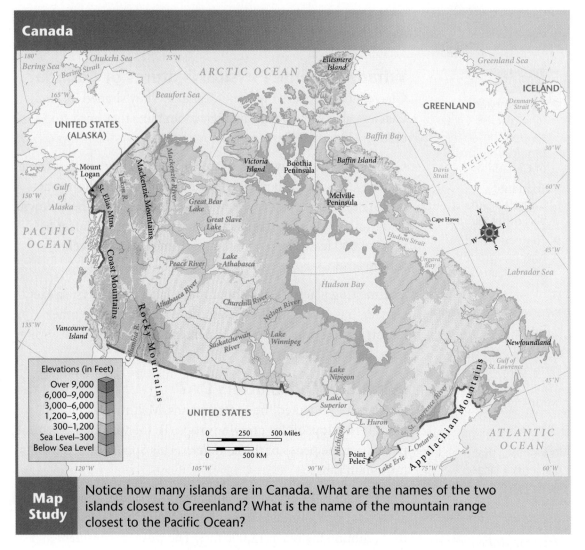

Map Study

Notice how many islands are in Canada. What are the names of the two islands closest to Greenland? What is the name of the mountain range closest to the Pacific Ocean?

What Major Bodies of Water Are in Canada?

Canada's biggest water feature is Hudson Bay. It is bigger than the state of Texas. Few people live along the flat, swampy lowlands of its southern shore.

The St. Lawrence Seaway connects the Great Lakes with the Atlantic Ocean.

Canada's longest river is the Mackenzie. It is located in the Northwest Territories and flows 2,635 miles. Like Hudson Bay, the Mackenzie is frozen much of the year. A smaller, but more important river is the St. Lawrence. About 16 million people—more than 60 percent of Canadians—live in the St. Lawrence lowlands. Other large rivers are the Yukon and the Columbia.

Canada and the United States share four of the five Great Lakes. Lakes Superior, Huron, Erie, and Ontario border both countries. Niagara Falls is located on the border between the United States and Canada. This huge set of waterfalls is beautiful and a popular tourist site.

What Is a Subarctic Climate?

Most of Canada has a **subarctic climate.** This cold climate is the area near the **Arctic Circle,** or 66.5 degrees north of the equator. Because of this, Canada is one of the coldest countries in the world. Its average temperature is 22°F.

In the Arctic North, the ground is always frozen. Geographers call it **permafrost,** or permanently frozen ground. The Arctic North receives less snowfall than the rest of Canada. It is so cold that little of the snow ever melts. Many other parts of Canada have long and cold winters, too. However, even in the Northwest Territories and the Yukon, summer temperatures can reach 80°F, but summers are short.

What Other Climates Does Canada Have?

Canada's west and east coasts have a maritime climate. Being close to water influences this climate. Rain falls more frequently than snow even in the winter. On the windward side of the coastal mountains, some places receive about 60 inches of rain per year.

The **landlocked** Prairie Provinces have a **continental climate.** Land surrounds a landlocked area. It is far from an ocean. In a continental climate, people experience warm summers and cold winters. In Canada, there are short, warm summers because it is in the higher latitudes. The Prairie Provinces of Manitoba, Saskatchewan, and Alberta are on the side of the western mountains which does not receive much rain. Sometimes a hot, dry wind called a **chinook** blows down from the Rocky Mountains. In winter, it provides a break from the cold temperatures. If the chinook comes in summer, it can cause long periods of dry weather. This is called a **drought.**

Canada's southernmost point, Point Peele in Ontario, is about as far south as northern California. Southern Ontario has Canada's mildest climate. Most of Canada's people live in this area in the lowlands of the St. Lawrence River. They enjoy four different seasons.

How Does Geography Affect the Canadians?

The native Inuit have always lived in balance with nature. Their language reveals the respect they have for it. For example, they have many names for snow because it is important in their lives. Many of these native people lived by hunting and fishing.

Fish and other seafood are plentiful in the coastal waters of Canada. Many commercial fishermen work there. Salmon fishing is especially important on the Pacific coast. Many freshwater fish swim in Canada's rivers and lakes. These fish provide food and attract tourists who like to fish.

Agriculture is big business in Canada's fertile valleys and central plains. Canada also has vast mineral and oil deposits. Huge forests provide lumber and the raw material for paper. These resources provide work for many Canadians.

Lesson 2 Review On a sheet of paper, write the answer to each question. Use complete sentences.

1. What created most of Canada's physical features?

2. What is the highest mountain in Canada?

3. What is Canada's most important river even though it is not the longest?

4. What do geographers call ground that is permanently frozen?

5. What kind of climate does most of Canada have?

What do you think ?

If you could choose any part of Canada to live in, where would it be? Give two or three reasons.

What Was the First Canadian Culture?

The oldest Canadian cultures are those of its native peoples, like the Inuit. In 1999, the Canadian government set aside a new territory called Nunavut for the Inuit to govern themselves.

The Inuit have their own language and culture. However, their way of life is changing. In the past, many lived in ice or snow houses called igloos. They traveled with dog sleds or in small, covered canoes called kayaks. Today, many live in wooden or brick homes. They use snowmobiles and watch television. Other cultures are influencing their lives.

What Cultures Exist in Canada?

French people explored and settled along the St. Lawrence River. In 1867, Canadians won the right from Britain to govern themselves. At that time, only 3.4 million people lived in Canada. Today, Canada's population is about 33 million. Canada has always welcomed immigrants, and many came from Europe. Since the 1970s, immigrants have come from Asia. Many settled in Vancouver. People from Asia, Africa, and Arab countries now make up 6 percent of Canada's population.

In the past, many Inuits lived in igloos—dome homes made of ice or snow.

What Languages Do Canadians Speak?

Most Canadians speak English. However, in Quebec, most people speak French. Canada is a **bilingual** country because it has two official languages, English and French. In some parts of Canada, road signs and other messages appear in both languages. Besides English and French, many Canadians speak other languages.

What Religions Do Canadians Practice?

Almost 82 percent of Canadians are Christians. But many of the immigrants have brought their native religions to Canada. Most big cities have people who follow other world religions. Many Inuit people practice their own religion.

Where Do Most Canadians Live?

About 70 percent of Canadians live in urban areas. Many live in Canada's three largest cities: Toronto, Montreal, and Vancouver.

Located in Ontario, Toronto is the center of culture, industry, and **finance**. Finance is the use and management of money by banks and businesses. Toronto has Canada's largest stock exchange. People who live in Toronto come from all over the world. It is a lot like New York City in the United States.

Montreal is the second largest French-speaking city in the world—Paris, France, is first.

In Quebec, Montreal is the center of French-Canadian culture. It is the center for French-speaking theater and for French-language newspapers. Montreal has two French-Canadian universities and is a major financial and industrial center.

Vancouver is much younger than Toronto or Montreal. It developed after the completion of the Canadian Pacific railroad. Then Vancouver became the industrial, business, and financial center of British Columbia.

Calgary and Edmonton in Alberta are centers for Canada's oil industry. They are two of Canada's fastest growing cities.

Montreal has both French and English signs—these signs are in French.

What Trends Affect Canada Today?

Three important trends affect Canada today: **diversity**, its ties to the United States, and cultural clashes. Diversity is a variety of people living in one place. Immigrants are moving to Canada. Its government has passed laws that recognize their different and varied cultures.

Canada and the United States have close ties. Three out of four Canadians live within 200 miles of Canada's border with the United States. The United States has a big influence on Canada's culture. It produces much of what Canadians read and see on television. The economic ties between the two countries are very strong. The United States buys more than 85 percent of all Canadian exports. Canada is the largest supplier of oil and gas for the United States. American businesses have invested billions of dollars in Canadian industries.

Cultural clashes between French-speaking and English-speaking Canadians is a problem. Some French Canadians are afraid of losing their culture and language. The Quebec government insists that all business be conducted in the French language. Some people even want to make Quebec an independent nation from Canada. Canada's future may depend on its ability to join these two groups into one.

Quebec

Since the 1950s, some people in Quebec have called for independence from the rest of Canada. The people of Quebec have voted on independence several times. The political party that governs Quebec favors independence. So far, the voters have voted against it. Many Canadians are afraid that if Quebec separates from the rest of Canada, other provinces might want their independence too.

Lesson 3 Review On a sheet of paper, write the word in parenthesis that makes each statement true.

1. Canada is a country of (immigrants, drought).

2. Canada has two official languages: English and (French, Italian).

3. Canada is a mostly (urban, rural) country.

4. The largest city in Canada is (Toronto, Vancouver).

5. The French-speaking people in (Quebec, Ottawa) want to keep their language and culture.

What do you think ?

The United States has a large Spanish-speaking population in some places. Should the United States recognize Spanish as an official language like Canada recognizes French? Why or why not?

Objectives

◆ To explain the value of Canada's water and mineral resources to their economy

◆ To explain the importance of manufacturing forest and mineral products

◆ To identify environmental problems that affect Canada

Reading Strategy:
Text Structure

Preview this lesson. Read the section heads, boldfaced words, and preview the photo.

What Are Some Natural Resources?

Canada is rich in natural resources. It has rich farmland. Water is another important resource. Its rivers provide hydroelectricity, or electricity created by running water. Its lakes and rivers provide seafood. Commercial fishing is one of Canada's biggest industries. Canada has about 10 percent of the world's forests. These cover almost one-quarter of the country.

Canada is one of the world's largest exporters of minerals. Minerals make up 12 percent of Canada's total exports. Canada leads the world in the production of uranium. It also produces aluminum, zinc, and gypsum. British Columbia contains some of North America's largest coal deposits. Huge reserves of oil and natural gas are in Alberta, the Northwest Territories, and off the coast of Newfoundland. Canada has the world's second-largest amount of oil. It is the largest foreign supplier of energy to the United States, including oil, gas, uranium, and electric power. Over half of its imports come from the United States. U.S. businesses have invested in Canadian industries.

What Are Some Major Canadian Industries?

Mining is another industry tied to Canada's great resources. Few people work in mining, but it plays an important role in the economy. For example, many people sell and distribute Canadian minerals.

Canada is one of the world's biggest wheat producers. Farmers also produce oats, barley, and dairy products. A typical farm in Canada is large and uses lots of farm machinery. However, few people work in agriculture.

As in most developed countries, most Canadians work in service industries. About 70 percent of Canadians work in industries such as tourism, banking, and restaurants. Today, it is more likely that Canadians work in an office, store, or warehouse than on a farm, in a mine, or in a factory.

Manufacturing is important to Canada's economy, especially in Ontario and Quebec. Every major U.S. automaker operates factories in Canada. Canada is also a big producer of machinery and equipment.

Forest products are one of Canada's largest exports. Canada sells paper products all over the world. Canadian trees provide about one-fourth of all the paper used for newspaper around the world. Pulp, the raw material used in making paper, is another big export. Canada exports large amounts of its lumber to other countries.

What Are Canada's Environmental Problems?

Canada's environmental problems are similar to those of the United States. Canadians produce a lot of garbage. Burying or burning garbage is expensive. Air and water pollution are also problems. Air pollution has decreased in Canada, but it is still a big problem. The paper industry is a major source of water pollution.

Soil erosion is a problem in Canada's central plains because of poor farming methods.

Deforestation, the cutting and clearing of forests, is another problem in Canada. Loggers have destroyed many valuable forests. Logging companies often practice **clear cutting**, which means cutting down every tree in a given area. Clear cutting an area makes it difficult for animals to live there and it lets the soil wash away, which pollutes the water.

A similar problem is the destruction of **wetlands**. A wetland is land covered with water some or most of the time, but where plants continue to grow. Wetlands absorb water. When people destroy wetlands, flooding becomes a problem in the area. Also, many birds live in wetlands. Draining wetlands to create farmland threatens the lives of birds.

This forest was clear-cut; that is, every tree in the area was cut down.

Lesson 4 Review On a sheet of paper, write the letter of the answer that correctly completes each sentence.

1. Canada has about 10 percent of the world's ____.

   A forests   **C** mining
   B electricity   **D** farms

2. Canada is the world's leading producer of _____.

   A gold and silver   **C** oil and natural gas
   B copper   **D** uranium

3. Most Canadian workers work in _____.

   A manufacturing   **C** banking
   B service industries **D** mining

4. An important forest product is _____.

   A manufactured   **C** oil
   B pulp   **D** erosion

5. Logging companies practice _____, which is bad for the environment.

   A exporting   **C** clear cutting
   B farming   **D** erosion control

What do you think ?

Do you think Canada's close ties with the United States are good or bad for each country? Explain.

A Girl Tending Goal

My name is Simone. I am 16, and I live in Toronto, Canada.

You've probably heard about how big hockey is in Canada. It's true. Most kids at least try it when they're little. And everyone knows the details of every recent game: high school, college, or professional. When teachers and parents try to make a point, they use hockey terms. The pastor at my church has even compared heaven to the frame of the goal net!

For me, the goal crease is heaven. See, I'm the goaltender on my high school girls' team. The goal crease is the area right in front of the net. Only a goalie can be in this zone. This is where I do some of my best defensive work.

I've been playing hockey since I was four years old. Sometimes my mom complains that the equipment is too expensive. Sometimes she worries too much about my safety. I just remind her that the goalie is the safest player on the ice. Forget about the flying puck, the sharp blades, and the whooshing sticks, Mom! The equipment for goalies is far more protective than that for other players.

I love the extremes I experience when goaltending. We goalies are sometimes the reason a game is won. It's awesome to stop a goal that could have lost us the game. When my teammates pile up on me, those are some of the best moments of my life.

It isn't all about the winning, obviously. I've had plenty of times when I've been the reason for a loss. I don't let it get me too down, though. After all, that's part of the package. I can't stop every goal, but I can try to learn from each game.

My days are pretty full, mostly with hockey. I weight train at the gym each morning before school, working on different muscle groups. After school I hit the ice for several hours before going home to eat and do some homework. Afterwards, if it's not too late, I head back to the ice rink. I keep my grades up because I want to play in college. I hope I can get a scholarship.

I can't imagine not playing hockey. It's in my blood.

Wrap-Up

1. Why do you think hockey is so popular in Canada?

2. What is the goal crease?

Chapter 4   S U M M A R Y

- Canada is the second largest country in the world.

- Like the United States, Canada has lots of industries.

- Canada has six physical regions: the Canadian Shield, the Interior Plains, the western mountainous region, the Arctic, the Appalachian Mountain region of the east, and the Great Lakes-St. Lawrence lowlands.

- Canada has six political regions: the Maritime Provinces, Quebec, Ontario, the Prairie Provinces, British Columbia, and the Arctic North.

- Canada has a varied landscape. Glaciers wore down mountains in the east. The Maritime Provinces have gently rolling hills. The middle of Canada is relatively flat with rich farmland. The west has many high mountains, including the Canadian Rocky Mountains.

- Glaciers also left behind many islands. The islands of Ellesmere, Baffin, Victoria, and Newfoundland are larger than many countries of Europe. Canada has more lakes than any other country in the world. About 30 percent of the world's freshwater is located there.

- Most of Canada has a subarctic climate. It is one of the coldest countries in the world. Its west coast has a maritime climate; the Prairie Provinces have a continental climate.

- The Inuit, the native people of Canada, have their own language and culture. Immigrants from Europe have influenced Canada. Immigrants from Asia, Africa, and Arab countries now make up 6 percent of Canada's population.

- Almost all major religions of the world are represented in Canada. Most Canadians are Christians.

- Canada has two official languages: English and French.

- Most of the Canadian population lives in urban areas, and within 200 miles of the United States.

- Canada is rich in natural resources including farmland, water, forests, and minerals.

- Most people work in Canadian service industries. Some work in manufacturing industries. Forest products, mining, and farming are tied to Canada's great natural resources.

- Canada has several environmental problems similar to those in the United States: air and water pollution, too much garbage, farmland erosion, deforestation, and the destruction of wetlands.

Chapter 4 REVIEW

Word Bank

Canadian Shield 1
forest 5
subarctic 3
United States 2
urban 4

On a sheet of paper, use the words from the Word Bank to complete each sentence correctly.

1. The largest physical region in Canada is the _____.

2. Canada is north of the _____.

3. Most of Canada has a _____ climate.

4. Most Canadian people live in _____ areas.

5. Pulp and other _____ products are important Canadian exports.

On a sheet of paper, write the letter of the answer that correctly completes each sentence.

6. A ___A___ is a plain with no trees located in a cold climate.

   A tundra   **C** desert
   B continent   **D** savanna

7. Canada is the ___A___ largest country in the world.

   A second   **C** third
   B fourth   **D** fifth

8. Canada's two official languages are English and ___B___.

   A Greek   **C** Inuit
   B French   **D** Spanish

9. Canada and ___C___ have very close economic and cultural ties.

   A Great Britain   **C** the United States
   B France   **D** Russia

10. Most Canadians work in ___D___ industries.

    A manufacturing   **C** mining
    B fishing   **D** service

On a sheet of paper, write the answer to each question. Use complete sentences.

11. What physical features of Canada help make it a major trading nation?

12. What are Canada's natural resources and what is their importance to its economy?

13. What are the major industries of Canada?

Critical Thinking On a sheet of paper, write your response to each question. Use complete sentences.

14. Is Canada's cultural diversity a strength or a weakness? Explain your answer.

15. Why do you think Canadians chose Ottawa as their capital instead of Toronto or Montreal?

Applying the Five Themes of Geography

Interaction
Find magazine or newspaper pictures or draw a series of pictures that show the effects of human interaction and environment in Canada.

Test-Taking Tip
When studying for a test, write your own test based on the chapter goals for learning. Have a partner do the same. Then complete each other's test. Double-check your answers together.

The St. Lawrence Seaway

It was a dream for a long time to bring ocean-going ships to inland ports. The dream came true in 1959 when the St. Lawrence Seaway was built. The seaway is a system of canals, dams and locks. It is over 450 miles long, from the eastern end of Lake Erie to Montreal. The seaway was needed because the Great Lakes are much higher than the Atlantic Ocean. Workers built a series of locks. A lock is an enclosure in a waterway with gates at each end. It "locks in" water between the gates.

Ships heading up the St. Lawrence River from the Atlantic Ocean have to be raised. The ship enters the lock, and workers fill the lock with water from upstream. This raises the ship to the level of the next waterway. A ship traveling the seaway goes through 15 locks to reach Lake Superior. By then, the locks have raised a ship almost 600 feet above sea level. To help ships get back to the Atlantic Ocean, workers let the water out of the locks.

The seaway was a joint United States and Canadian project. Construction began in 1954 and ended in 1959. Now ships from the Atlantic can travel thousands of miles into the interior of North America. Ships from Europe can reach over 50 port cities on the Great Lakes. Toronto, Windsor, and Thunder Bay— port cities in Ontario, Canada—get a lot of business. The port cities of Detroit, Michigan; Toledo, Ohio; Chicago, Illinois; and Duluth, Minnesota, in the United States do, too.

But the seaway disappointed everyone. Shipping did not increase as much as expected. The seaway was out of date almost by the time it was completed. New technology changed ocean-going ships. They became so big they did not fit in the locks.

For three months a year, the waterway is frozen over. No ships can travel through its locks during these months. Today, ships use the seaway mostly to carry raw materials like coal, iron ore, and wheat. Another disappointment was that new forms of sea life were introduced to the Great Lakes. The sea lamprey and zebra mussels cause a lot of damage to native fish.

Wrap-Up

1. What was the dream of Canadian and U.S. port cities along the Great Lakes?

2. How long did it take to build the St. Lawrence Seaway?

3. What does a lock in a waterway do?

4. How many locks are in the St. Lawrence Seaway?

5. Why did the seaway disappoint people?

- The United States, Canada, and Mexico are the three largest countries in North America. Canada is the second largest country in the world.

- The United States has four physical regions. Canada has six.

- Both Canada and the United States have high mountains, vast prairies, long rivers, and big lakes.

- When the glaciers melted, they formed many lakes and rivers. Among these were the Mississippi River system in the United States and the Great Lakes. Canada shares four of the Great Lakes with the United States. Canada has more lakes than any other country in the world.

- The United States has many climates. The Northeast and Midwest regions have four seasons, with long, cold winters and hot, wet summers. The South has a humid subtropical climate. Because of its mountains and coastline, the West has several climates.

- Most of Canada has a subarctic climate, making it one of the coldest countries in the world.

- Both the United States and Canada blend cultures from many other lands. The American Indian cultures and cultures of Europe, Africa, Latin America, and Asia have influenced U.S. culture. The Inuit, who are the native people of Canada, along with Europeans and Asians, have influenced the Canadian culture.

- English and French are the two official languages of Canada. English is the language of the United States.

- People in Canada and the United States practice almost all the major religions of the world. Most people in these countries are Christians.

- Most people in both the United States and Canada live in urban areas.

- Both Canada and the United States are rich in natural resources including farmland, water, forests, and minerals.

- In both the United States and Canada, most people work in service industries. Many people also work in manufacturing industries.

- Both Canada and the United States face air and water pollution and produce too much garbage. The destruction of wetlands and deforestation challenge Canada.

Unit 3

Latin America

In this unit, you will learn about Latin America, which is south of the United States. You will study Mexico and the many countries of Central America, the Caribbean, and South America.

Latin America got its name because the main languages spoken there are Spanish and Portuguese. Both of these languages grew out of Latin, the language of the ancient Romans.

These nations have many things in common. Some of the earliest cities were founded thousands of years ago. These countries have many important rivers, deserts, rain forests, and mountains. In this unit, you will see how Latin America is very different from the United States and Canada.

This is a photo of Machu Picchu. It is an ancient Incan city in Peru. People visiting Peru can tour the ruins.

5

Mexico

The country of Mexico has a long and interesting history. Over 500 years ago, people from Europe sailed to Mexico. Long before that, however, it had some of the world's greatest civilizations. Today, Mexico is a country that has many industries. It is also an important trade partner of its northern neighbor, the United States.

Goals for Learning

◆ To describe the country of Mexico and its regions

◆ To identify Mexico's most important physical features and climate

◆ To describe the diverse cultures of Mexico and where and how people in Mexico live

◆ To describe the economy and the environmental challenges Mexico faces

Geo-Stats Mexico

Population: 107,450,000

Area: 754,120 square miles

Length of Coastline: 5,794 miles

Length of Roads: 155,250 miles

Longest River: Río Grande/Río Bravo del Norte (1,900 miles)

Highest Mountain: Pico de Orizaba (18,700 feet)

Major Cities: Mexico City (capital), Guadalajara, Monterrey, Puebla

Major Religions: Roman Catholic, Protestant Christian

Major Languages: Spanish, native languages

Official Currency: New Mexican nuevo peso

Workforce: 38 million

Number of Daily Newspapers: 309

Number of Television Sets: 25 million

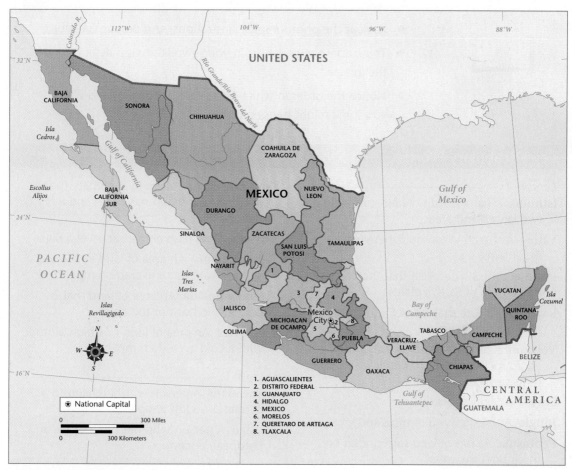

Map Skills

Mexico lies south of the United States in North America and north of Central America. This beautiful country has 31 states and a growing economy.

Study the map and answer the following questions:

1. Which ocean, gulfs, and bay surround Mexico?

2. What is the capital of Mexico?

3. Which river separates much of Mexico from the United States?

4. Which Mexican states border the United States?

5. What countries does Mexico border on the south?

Reading Strategy:
Visualizing

Visualizing is another strategy that helps readers understand what they are reading. It is like creating a movie in your mind. Use the following ways to visualize text:

◆ Look at the photographs, illustrations, and descriptive words.

◆ Think about experiences in your own life that may add to the images.

◆ Notice the order in which things are happening and what you think might happen next.

Key Vocabulary Words

Lesson 1
Isthmus A narrow strip of land connecting two larger land areas

Valley A stretch of lowlands between mountains

Plate tectonics The belief that there is slow movement of Earth's plates

Earthquake The shaking of Earth's surface from plate movement

Volcano A mountain formed when hot liquid rock comes from deep within Earth to its surface

Lava Hot, liquid rock

Jungle A thick growth of trees and vines

Peninsula A strip of land surrounded on three sides by water

Lesson 2
Rain forest A thick area of trees in the Tropics where a great deal of rain falls

Tropical savanna climate A climate that is hot year-round and has a wet and a dry season

Altitude How high above sea level a place is

Tierra caliente An area of land in a low altitude with a hot average temperature

Tierra templada An area of land that is neither too hot nor too cold

Tierra fría An area of land in a high altitude with a cold average temperature

Lesson 3
Descendant A person who is related to a certain group of people

Mestizo A person who has both native and European ancestors

Lesson 4
Offshore Off or away from land in water

Trade barrier A law or act that limits imports or puts special taxes on them

Isthmus

A narrow strip of land connecting two larger land areas

Valley

A stretch of lowlands between mountains

Plate tectonics

The belief that there is slow movement of Earth's plates

Remember, to irrigate means to bring water to fields rather than depend on natural rainfall. People use pipes to channel the water.

Where Is Mexico Located?

Mexico, the nation just south of the United States, is shaped like a triangle. It is widest in the north where it borders the United States. This border is about 1,900 miles long. In the south, Mexico borders the Central American countries of Belize and Guatemala.

The Pacific Ocean borders Mexico on the west. The Gulf of Mexico borders it on the east. The narrowest part of Mexico, the **Isthmus** of Tehuantepec, is only 134 miles wide. An isthmus is a narrow strip of land connecting two larger land areas.

Where Is Mexico's Central Plateau Region?

Mexico has four physical regions. The Central Plateau is its largest region. Like all plateaus, the Central Plateau is an area of level highland. This plateau has two parts. The northern half is generally dry. Farmers must irrigate to raise crops there.

The southern half of the Central Plateau is higher than the northern half. Because the southern half gets more rain, farmers can grow more crops there than in the northern half. They often grow corn, which is Mexico's most important crop. Geographers describe this part of the Central Plateau as Mexico's heartland.

The heartland of the Central Plateau has the richest farmland in Mexico. Most of Mexico's people live in this area. Within it is the **Valley** of Mexico. It is a stretch of lowlands between Mexico's mountains. The Valley of Mexico is almost 50 miles long and 40 miles wide. Mexico City, the capital of Mexico, sits in this large valley.

Scientists believe that Earth's crust is broken up into several huge slabs called plates. These plates move slowly beneath Earth's surface. Physical geographers call their movement **plate tectonics.** Sometimes these plates crash into one another. Then the edge of one plate may slide beneath that of another. This is one way in which mountains form.

Earthquake

The shaking of Earth's surface from plate movement

Volcano

A mountain formed when hot liquid rock comes from deep within Earth to its surface

Lava

Hot, liquid rock

The Central Plateau region has many **earthquakes.** They happen whenever Earth's plates shift. Four important tectonic plates come together in Mexico. This creates a great deal of shifting, which causes earthquakes. These earthquakes have killed many people and destroyed property.

Mountains can also form from hot liquid rock that comes from deep within the earth. It rises to Earth's surface and forms **volcanoes.** Geographers call this liquid rock **lava.** Mexico has many active volcanoes.

Volcanoes can destroy property and kill people, but they also can bring silver, gold, copper, and lead close to the surface. Then it is easier to mine these minerals.

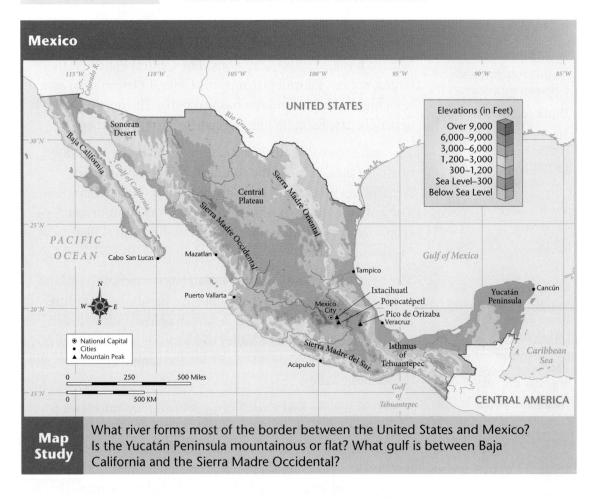

Mexico

Map Study What river forms most of the border between the United States and Mexico? Is the Yucatán Peninsula mountainous or flat? What gulf is between Baja California and the Sierra Madre Occidental?

Where Is Mexico's Coastal Plains Region?

Coastal plains form a rim around Mexico's great central region of plateau and mountains. The eastern coastal plain runs along the Gulf of Mexico. The plain runs from the Texas border to the Yucatán Peninsula. The western coastal plain along the Pacific is more narrow and dry than the gulf coastal plain. Farmers there use irrigation to grow cotton, wheat, and other crops.

Geographers divide the coastal plains into two subregions. The northern half of the plain is warm, but receives little rainfall. **Jungle,** a thick growth of trees and vines, covers the rainy south.

Where Is the Desert Region in Mexico?

The northwestern part of Mexico is a desert region. The Sonoran Desert is Mexico's largest desert. The most western part of Mexico is a peninsula called Baja California. A **peninsula** is a strip of land surrounded on three sides by water. Few people live in this region, but it is popular for tourists.

Where Is the Yucatán Peninsula Region?

The Yucatán Peninsula is the fourth region of Mexico. Because this region is part of the eastern coastal plain, it is somewhat flat. The Yucatán Peninsula is formed mostly of limestone, which is a soft rock that dissolves in water. Sometimes this creates huge underground caves. The Yucatán Peninsula is not very good for farming, so few people live there.

Lesson 1 Review On a sheet of paper, use the words from the Word Bank to complete each sentence correctly.

1. The country on Mexico's northern border is the _____.

2. Mexico's largest region is the _____.

3. Farmers in Mexico use _____ to bring water to their crops.

4. Many mountains form because of _____.

5. The largest desert in Mexico is the _____.

Word Bank

Central Plateau 2

irrigation 3

plate tectonics 4

Sonoran 5

United States 1

What do you think ?

How might Mexico's geography help explain why many Mexicans come to the United States to live?

Objectives

◆ To identify Mexico's most important physical features

◆ To describe the climates of Mexico

Rain forest

A thick area of trees in the Tropics where a great deal of rain falls

What Mountains Are in Mexico?

Mexico's main physical feature is its mountains. High mountain ranges rise on the east, west, and south of the Central Plateau. Geographers call all these mountain ranges the Sierra Madre.

The Sierra Madre Occidental is the southern part of the same mountain range that makes up the Rocky Mountains in the United States. The Sierra Madre Oriental continues as the Sierra Nevada range. Deciduous forests cover the dry northern part of the Sierra Madre Oriental. Deciduous trees are trees that drop their leaves in autumn. The Sierra Madre del Sur extend down to the Isthmus of Tehuantepec. A narrow plain there separates these mountains from the Pacific Ocean. Tropical **rain forests** cover the southern Sierras. This type of dense forest grows in the Tropics where a great deal of rain falls.

What Are Mexico's Tallest Mountains?

Mexico's tallest mountain is Pico de Orizaba, which is an old volcano. It is 18,700 feet high. The people of Mexico City can see two other tall snow-covered mountains from their homes. One is Popocatépetl, which means "Smoking Mountain." The other is Ixtacihuatl, also known as "Sleeping Woman."

This active volcano's name—Popocatépetl— means "smoking mountain."

Active Volcanoes in Mexico		
Volcano	**Last Eruption Date**	**Height of Volcano**
Pico de Orizaba	1846	18,619 ft.
Popocatépetl	2007	17,883 ft.
Colima	2007	12,361 ft.
El Chichón	1982	3,773 ft.

Chart Study This chart shows active volcanoes in Mexico. An active volcano may erupt, or overflow with lava, at any time. What is the tallest active volcano? Which two volcanoes erupted in 2007? Which one erupted in 1982?

What Are Some Famous Resorts in Mexico?

Mexico has a long coastline with some of the world's most beautiful beaches. The government has developed some beaches into resorts. On the eastern coast, the government created Cancún out of a part of the Yucatán Peninsula. Acapulco, Puerto Vallarta, and Mazatlán lie on the western, or Pacific, coast. Cabo San Lucas is on the southern tip of Baja California. All of these cities have beautiful scenery and beaches.

What Major Bodies of Water Are in Mexico?

In some places the Río Grande is so shallow that people can walk across it.

Mexico is mountainous, and many parts of it have little rain. Because of this, no major river systems cross Mexico. Most of its rivers are short. They drop quickly from the high mountains to the coast. Sometimes they flow into large lakes.

The largest lakes in Mexico are Lake Chapala in the state of Jalisco and Lake Pátzcuaro in Michoacán. The Río Bravo del Norte forms part of the border between Mexico and the United States. People in the United States call this river the Río Grande.

What Is the Climate Like in Mexico?

Juarez, on Mexico's northern border, can be below 32°F in the winter and above 90°F in the summer.

Much of Mexico has a steppe climate, a dry climate usually found near deserts. The Mexican deserts have a little more rain than many deserts in other parts of the world. Some parts of these deserts receive little rain because of the high mountains beside them. The steppe can get both very hot and very cold.

Some of Mexico's coastal areas have a **tropical savanna climate.** They are hot all year. These coastal areas receive a lot of rain but have a drier season during the winter. Common savanna plants include tall grasses with a few trees.

This photo of the Church of La Valenciana shows some of Mexico's natural beauty.

How Do Mountains Affect Mexico's Climate?

Without mountains, Mexico would be hot most of the time. Temperatures usually get hotter the closer a place is to the equator. However, **altitude**, the height a place is above sea level, affects climate. A high altitude has cooler temperatures. Rainfall also usually increases at high altitudes. Because mountains cover Mexico, its climate can be both hot and cold.

What Are Mexico's Three Altitudinal Zones?

The European country of Spain ruled Mexico for 300 years. The Spanish recognized how the mountains influenced Mexico's climate. They picked out three altitudinal zones to show this. Geographers still use the Spanish names for these zones. They call the hot areas at lower altitudes **tierra caliente,** or hot land.

Higher altitudes of about 3,000 to 6,000 feet are **tierra templada,** or temperate land. These areas are neither too hot nor too cold. Much of the Central Plateau, where most of Mexico's people live, is tierra templada. Mexico City's average high temperature in January is 66°F. Its average high temperature in July is 73°F.

Mexico's higher altitudes of over 6,000 feet are **tierra fría,** or cold lands. Temperatures are colder there and frost may form. Few people live above 10,000 feet.

Lesson 2 Review On a sheet of paper, write the answer to each question. Use complete sentences.

1. What is the main physical feature of Mexico?

2. Why doesn't Mexico have long rivers?

3. What climate does much of Mexico have?

4. Which climate is hot all year around?

5. Generally, what happens to temperatures at higher altitudes?

What do you think ?

If you lived in Mexico, would you prefer to live in tierra templada? Why or why not?

Objectives

- ◆ To describe the cultures of Mexico
- ◆ To explain the role of Spain in Mexican history and culture
- ◆ To describe where most people live in Mexico

Descendant

A person who is related to a certain group of people

Mestizo

A person who has both native and European ancestors

Before Europeans came to Mexico, many native groups lived there. Some groups were small. They lived in villages and farmed the land. Others developed large empires. An empire is a nation that rules a large area of land. The Mayas built a great empire in Yucatán and Guatemala. The Toltecs, Zapotecs, and Aztecs formed empires in the Valley of Mexico.

At one time, millions of native people lived in Mexico. When the Europeans came, they brought diseases, such as measles and smallpox. These diseases killed many native people. By the end of the 1500s, about 90 percent of the natives died. **Descendants** are people related to a certain group of people. Descendants of native people still make up about 30 percent of Mexico's population. Many towns in Mexico are rural. Some are isolated, or separated from other areas. Native people there have kept much of their culture, such as religious beliefs and languages.

Who Are the Mestizos?

In 1519, a Spanish man named Hernando Cortés sailed to Mexico. There he met the Aztecs, the native people of the area. Cortés also met some smaller native groups. Some of these smaller groups were unhappy with Aztec rule. They helped Cortés defeat the Aztecs.

Soon more men that were Spanish arrived in Mexico. Some had children with native women. Historians call their descendants **mestizos.** They are people of mixed native and European ancestry. About half of the Mexican people are mestizos. Their culture is a blend of native and European people. However, their beliefs and values are often more European than native. Great differences exist among them. Some mestizos are wealthy landowners. Others are poor.

About 15 percent of the Mexican people are white. Many of them are descendents of the early Spanish settlers. Some Mexicans are immigrants. Most of them came from Central America. They came to find better jobs or to escape political trouble in their native countries. People from Japan, Canada, Spain, and the United States also live in Mexico. Some are retired people, but most of them are business people who work for Mexico's trading partners.

Reading Strategy:
Visualizing

How does the photo below tie in with this section on languages?

What Languages Do the People Speak?

Because Spain ruled Mexico for many years, Spanish is its official language. The government, businesses, and schools use Spanish. Many native people, however, speak their native languages. A visitor to Mexico may hear many native languages in different parts of the country.

Over a million native people speak only their native languages. They do not speak Spanish. Mexicans have given the world words such as *tortilla* and *tamales*. These words come from the language of the Aztec people.

These native Otomí women in central Mexico are cooking tortillas and a stew made of squash flowers.

What Is the Main Religion in Mexico?

The Spanish brought both their language and their religion to Mexico. Almost 90 percent of Mexicans are Roman Catholic. Some of the poor, however, have turned away from Catholicism and become Protestant Christians. In some rural areas, up to one-third of the population is Protestant.

What Are the Population Trends in Mexico?

In the last 100 years, Mexico's population has increased suddenly. In 1900, Mexico had about 13 million people. Today its population is over 100 million. Over one-third of the people are under 15 years of age. That is an important fact. The more people under 15, the more likely the population will continue to grow.

Reading Strategy:
Visualizing

Can you picture a country where one-third of the people are under 15?

The big increase in Mexico's population has caused problems. Many people do not have jobs. The government does not have enough money for schools and medical care for all people. To slow the rate of population growth, the government teaches people about limiting the number of children they have. However, the Catholic Church is against this.

Where Do Most Mexicans Live?

In 1900, most Mexicans lived in small farming villages. Today, over three fourths of Mexico's people live in urban areas. People have moved from villages to cities, since farming in parts of Mexico is hard. Many *campesinos,* or poor farmers, thought they could find a better and easier life in the cities. This migration of people from rural areas to cities is occurring all over the world.

An urban area is a city area rather than a village or farm.

Mexico City is one of the biggest cities in the world. Its metropolitan area has over 20 million people. About one out of every five Mexicans lives in Mexico City. The Mexican people built this city on the ruins of the old Aztec capital of Tenochtitlán.

Remember, slums are poor, overcrowded areas.

Mexico's capital is a city of differences. For example, it has beautiful tree-lined streets and tall buildings. It also has some of the worst slums in the world. Mexico City has fine places to shop. It also has noisy city markets. A visitor to Mexico City may see people traveling on horseback. That same visitor might also experience traffic jams that are worse than in U.S. cities.

Guadalajara is Mexico's second largest city. Like Mexico City, it is located on the Central Plateau. It is an important and growing industrial center. Monterrey is the largest city in northern Mexico. Its workers produce most of Mexico's steel and iron.

Tampico and Veracruz are Mexico's two biggest ports. Both are on the Gulf side of Mexico. Veracruz is a major railroad center. Trains from there carry products to and from southern Mexico. Acapulco, on the Pacific coast, is also an important port.

Lesson 3 Review On a sheet of paper, write the word in parenthesis that makes each statement true.

1. (Native people, Mestizos) make up about half of the Mexican people.

2. (Mestizos, Descendants) are people of mixed native and European ancestry.

3. (Spanish, Mexican) is the official language of Mexico.

4. More than three fourths of the Mexican people live in (rural, urban) areas.

5. (Acapulco, Veracruz) is an important railroad center that links southern Mexico and the Central Plateau.

What do you think ?

How is the migration of many Mexicans to the United States affecting both Mexico and the United States?

Our Lady of Guadalupe

December 12 is a holiday in Mexico. More than 400 years ago, Juan Diego—a Catholic American Indian—saw a vision of the Virgin Mary, whom Catholics believe is the mother of Jesus. She spoke to him in his native language. She asked that a church be built where she stood. The church leaders did not believe Juan Diego. When he went back, Mary told him to go gather some roses. Juan Diego gathered them into his *tilma,* a long cloak worn by Mexican Indians. Mary told him to take the roses directly to the priests. As Juan Diego unfolded his cloak, the roses fell out. But on the *tilma* was a figure of the Virgin Mother, just as he had described her.

For the first time, American Indians and mestizos saw the Catholic Church as their own. They called the vision "Our Lady of Guadalupe." She became an important symbol of the Mexican nation. Church leaders built a church in her honor. Juan Diego's *tilma* is still on display there today. Each year, people come to Mexico City from all parts of Mexico to celebrate this religious holiday. Some of them walk several days to get there. Many groups of dancers and musicians perform.

Critical Thinking Why do you think Juan Diego's vision changed the way American Indians and mestizos thought about the Catholic Church?

Objectives

◆ To list the natural resources Mexico has

◆ To identify the industries of Mexico

◆ To describe some of the problems Mexico faces

Offshore

Off or away from land in water

How Important Is Oil to Mexico?

Mexico is rich in natural resources; its most important resource is oil. Workers first discovered oil on the coast of the Gulf of Mexico in 1901. Mexico soon became a leading oil exporter.

In the 1970s, workers discovered large oil and natural gas fields. Most of these are located **offshore,** which means they are in water rather than on land. Oil is near Veracruz, Tabasco, Chiapas, and Baja California. Mexico's economy depends on oil. Money from oil pays for more than 40 percent of what the Mexican government spends each year. Mexico supplies gas and oil for itself and exports the rest. Its best customer is the United States.

What Are Mexico's Other Natural Resources?

Besides oil and natural gas, Mexico has many other mineral resources. Workers mine silver, copper, gold, lead, and zinc. Mexico is the world's leading producer of silver. Mexico also has large forest resources.

How Did Land Reform Change Mexico?

People can farm only about 13 percent of Mexico's total land. However, nearly one fifth of Mexicans are farmers. At one time, a few rich landowners owned almost all the land. This changed in 1910 when Mexico had a revolution. A revolution is a complete change of the government by using force.

One important result of the revolution was land reform. The government took land from the rich and gave it to poor farmers. New technology, better seeds, irrigation, and training have increased crop growth. Irrigation in northern Mexico has made it an important cotton-growing region. Mexico's other major crops are corn, wheat, soybeans, coffee, and fruit.

However, land reform and technology have created a problem for Mexico. Machines have decreased the need for workers. Many workers have left the country to find work in cities.

What Are Some Industries in Mexico?

The Mexican government hopes those farmers will find manufacturing jobs to make the economy stronger. Today, nearly one of every six workers works in manufacturing. The largest industry is metal products. Other important industrial products are cars, clothing, chemicals, food products, electrical goods, glass, and paper.

A growing part of the Mexican economy is the *maquiladoras.* These are foreign-owned assembly plants. Most of them are located near the border of Mexico and the United States. Mexican workers assemble products in these plants. American companies then sell the products using their own brand names.

The plants make cars, electrical goods, clothing, and chemicals in Mexico. *Maquiladoras* have their headquarters in the United States. However, they build plants in Mexico because labor is cheaper there than in the United States. The *maquiladoras* help U.S. companies and provide jobs for Mexican workers.

What Is Mexico's Biggest Service Industry?

Service industries are a big part of Mexico's economy. Service industries provide jobs for more than half the workers. The biggest service industries are tourism, banking, and insurance. Tourists come to Mexico for its sunshine, beautiful beaches, and scenery. They also visit the remains of Mexico's ancient cultures.

What Is NAFTA?

Mexico, the United States, and Canada signed the North American Free Trade Agreement (NAFTA). It took effect in 1994. It created one large free-trade area in North America. This means that the three countries got rid of **trade barriers.** A barrier divides one thing from another. Trade barriers divide countries because they limit imports or put special taxes on them.

Now products from the three NAFTA countries easily cross each other's borders. Mexico's biggest trade partner is the United States. The United States supplies about 50 percent of Mexico's imports and buys about 85 percent of its exports.

How Does Poverty Challenge Mexico?

Mexico faces several important challenges today. One is the growing gap between wealthy and poor people. One in four Mexicans cannot afford enough food. New reforms like NAFTA have helped some people live better. However, areas in southern Mexico do not benefit from NAFTA. Millions of peasants, Mexico's small farmers, and farmworkers remain poor. Many of them live in houses with no electricity or running water. Many children do not get enough to eat. Many are forced to drop out of school to begin earning money for their families.

A peasant is a poor farmer or farm worker.

To feed their families, some poor Mexican people have turned to crime. The illegal drug trade has become a big business. The Mexican and U.S. governments have tried to stop the flow of drugs. This is not easy. These illegal drugs—those that are against the law—provide some poor people with their income. Drug abuse is a big problem, especially in the cities.

Foreign debt is the money a country owes to other governments. Mexico, like many developing countries, borrowed money from other countries to industrialize. The United States offered a plan to help them pay it back, but Mexico still owes millions of dollars to other countries. Because of this, the government has cut back on medical care, education, and care for old people.

What Are Some Environmental Problems?

Reading Strategy: Visualizing

Can you visualize what Mexico's environmental problems look like?

Air pollution and smog are serious problems in Mexico City. The smog hanging in the air causes health problems. Water pollution is a huge problem. Millions of tons of untreated human waste flow into the rivers each year. Industry and agriculture dump chemicals into Mexico's rivers. Because of this, the city has to pump huge amounts of clean water from underground. This has caused the ground to settle and buildings to sink. Garbage is also a problem. Mexico City produces 12,000 tons of solid waste per day. Deforestation and soil erosion are big problems in other parts of Mexico.

Geography in Your Life

Pollution in Mexico City

Big cities all over the world have smog. Smog is a mixture of fog and pollution. The chemicals in smog can be harmful to breathe. Mexico City is one of the smoggiest cities in the world.

Smoke from factories, oil refineries, and three million cars pollute the air. On summer days, the skies over Mexico City can be so smoggy that you can see only two blocks, and it is difficult to breathe the air.

Writing About Geography

Why do you think the economy of Mexico is so important to the United States? Write a paragraph about this. Include details from this lesson to support your opinion.

Lesson 4 Review On a sheet of paper, write the letter of the answer that correctly completes each sentence.

1. Mexico's most important natural resource is _____.

   A coal   **B** uranium   **C** oil   **D** copper

2. Mexico is the world's leading producer of _____.

   A silver   **B** mercury   **C** gold   **D** oil

3. _____ refers to a government taking land from large landowners and giving it to those who work on it.

   A *Maquiladora*   **B** Peasant   **C** Land reform   **D** Smog

4. _____ is the free-trade agreement that took effect in 1994 among Mexico, Canada, and the United States.

   A NATO   **B** NAFTA   **C** NFL   **D** U.S.

5. Foreign _____ is the money a country owes to other governments.

   A debt   **B** smog   **C** peasants   **D** trade

What do you think ?

To reduce air pollution in Mexico City, the government has told car owners that they cannot drive one day a week. Do you think this is an effective way to reduce pollution? Why or why not?

Juan's Day

My name is Juan. I am 13 years old. I live in a small house in Mexico City. Every morning, I awaken at 4:30 to sell newspapers. My *mamá* is also awake, getting ready for her shift at the soap factory. Most often we have *atole* for breakfast. *Atole* is a warm drink thickened with corn dough, milk, and sugar.

It's cold and dark when I pick up my papers from the vendor. I hurry to a busy intersection in the city. There, I sell the papers to people walking by and to drivers sitting at the stoplight. My *mamá* worries, but I am careful around the traffic.

To attract buyers, I yell out headlines. Whether I make money or not depends on whether the news is interesting. I make only a small part of the total price of each sold paper, but I feel lucky to have something to offer my parents.

I always hope for sunshine. No people stop in the rain, and drivers do not want to roll down their windows. I also lose customers when a traffic light is broken.

At noon I go home, my clothes covered in ink from the newspapers. I wash up quickly, change into my school uniform, and have lunch before going to school. There are two school sessions—morning and afternoon. Because of my work, I attend school in the afternoon.

I do not see my 14-year-old brother at school because he attends the morning session. Pedro is a performer. He spends his afternoons in parks and on city buses, juggling, miming, or playing his guitar for tips.

After school, I do my homework and then play soccer in a nearby vacant lot. Usually, I watch TV in the evenings. I go to bed early so that I am not too tired selling my papers in the morning.

Wrap-Up

1. How does Juan get the attention of people walking or driving by?

2. Juan's job is dangerous. Do you think his brother's job is dangerous? Why or why not?

Chapter 5 S U M M A R Y

- Mexico has four physical regions: the Central Plateau, the coastal plains, the desert, and the Yucatán Peninsula.

- Mexico's main physical feature is its mountains, the Sierra Madres. Because of them, Mexico has no major river system. Mexico's long coastline features some beautiful beaches.

- Much of Mexico has a steppe climate, which is the dry climate found near deserts. Some coastal areas have a tropical savanna climate.

- Before the arrival of Europeans, Mexico had many native groups, such as the Maya, Toltecs, and Aztecs. Descendants of these native people make up 30 percent of Mexico's population. Spanish men had children with native women. Their descendants, the mestizos, make up about 60 percent of the Mexican people.

- Roman Catholicism is Mexico's main religion. However, in Mexico's rural areas, up to one-third of the people are Protestant Christians.

- Mexico's official language is Spanish.

- Over three fourths of Mexico's people live in urban areas. Mexico City is one of the biggest cities in the world.

- Mexico's main natural resources are oil and natural gas. Workers also mine silver, copper, gold, lead, and zinc. Mexico is the world's leading producer of silver.

- Because of land reform after the 1910 revolution, nearly one fifth of Mexico's people work on farms. However, manufacturing adds more to the national economy than farming. The largest industry in Mexico is metal products. Other important industrial products are cars, clothing, chemicals, food products, and electrical goods. Some big car producers from other countries operate *maquiladoras*, or assembly plants, in Mexico.

- Service industries provide jobs for more than half the workers. The biggest service industry is tourism.

- Because of the North American Free Trade Agreement (NAFTA), Mexico now conducts most of its trade with the United States.

- Mexico faces several problems: poverty; the gap between the poor and the wealthy; illegal drug trade; and the environment challenges of air and water pollution, solid waste, deforestation, and soil erosion.

Chapter 5   R E V I E W

Word Bank

irrigation *2*
mestizos *4*
mountains *3*
plateau *1*
Spanish *5*

On a sheet of paper, use the words from the Word Bank to complete each sentence correctly.

1. A _____, such as the one that covers much of Mexico, is an area of level highland.

2. In areas that do not receive enough rainfall, farmers often use _____.

3. Mexico's main physical feature is its _____.

4. The largest percentage of the Mexican people are the _____.

5. The official language of Mexico is _____.

On a sheet of paper, write the letter of the answer that correctly completes each sentence.

6. The largest physical region of Mexico is the ___B___.

   A Yucatán Peninsula   C Sonoran Desert
   B Central Plateau   D coastal plains

7. The steppe climate is usually found near ___A___.

   A deserts   C lakes
   B mountains   D oceans

8. Some native people living in Mexico have been able to keep their own culture because they live in ___D___.

   A Mexico City   C urban areas
   B the Sierra Madre   D small rural communities

9. Over ___B___ of Mexico's people live in urban areas.

   A one quarter   C two thirds
   B three fourths   D one half

10. ___A___ are foreign-owned assembly plants built close to the border between Mexico and the United States.

   A Maquiladoras   C Campesinos
   B Zapatistas   D Mestizos

On a sheet of paper, write the answer to each question. Use complete sentences.

11. What are three of the industries on which Mexico's economy depends?

12. What are some environmental problems that face Mexico today?

13. What are two ways in which Spain's long rule influenced Mexican culture?

Critical Thinking On a sheet of paper, write your response to each question. Use complete sentences.

14. Should the United States make it easier for Mexican workers to come to the United States? Why or why not?

15. What is the connection between rapid population growth and poverty?

Applying the Five Themes of Geography

Movement

Give at least two examples of the theme of movement as it applies to Mexico and the United States.

Test-Taking Tip

When a teacher announces a test, listen carefully. Write down the topics that the teacher will include on the test. Write down the items that the teacher says to review. Ask any questions you have about what the test will include.

6

Central America and the Caribbean

Many small countries make up Central America and the Caribbean. There is much natural beauty in this region. Most of the land has a tropical climate, so lots of tourists visit. The United States has played an important role in the region.

Goals for Learning

◆ To describe Central America and the Caribbean and how Spain influenced the area

◆ To identify the mainland of Central America and the rimland of the Caribbean and their climates

◆ To describe the people of Central America and the Caribbean and how they live

◆ To describe the resources, industries, and challenges of this area

Geo-Stats Key Nations of Central America and the Caribbean

Nation: Cuba
Population: 11,383,000
Area: 42,804 square miles
Capital: Havana

Nation: Haiti
Population: 8,309,000
Area: 10,714 square miles
Capital: Port-au-Prince

Nation: Puerto Rico, commonwealth of the United States
Population: 3,927,000
Area: 5,324 square miles
Capital: San Juan

Nation: Panama
Population: 3,191,000
Area: 29,157 square miles
Capital: Panama City

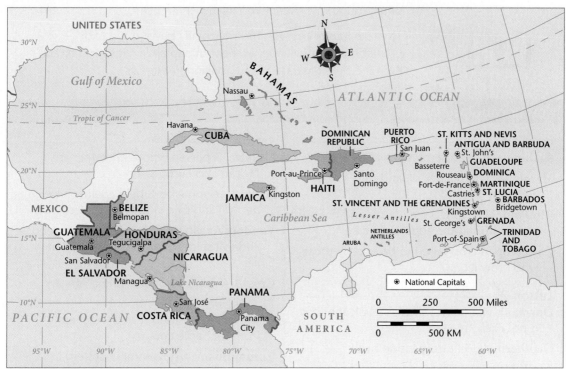

Map Skills

This map shows Central America and the Caribbean. Central America is a region between Mexico and South America. It includes seven countries. The Caribbean is a group of islands in the Caribbean Sea. The islands stretch over 2,000 miles from Mexico to South America. The largest island is Cuba, which lies just off the southern tip of Florida in the United States. Puerto Rico is a territory of the United States.

Study the map and answer the following questions:

1. Which ocean and sea touch Central America?

2. What Central American country touches South America?

3. What is the capital of Honduras? Puerto Rico? Haiti? Cuba?

4. What island is directly south of Cuba?

5. Which two countries in Central America are the farthest north?

Reading Strategy:
Inferencing

Sometimes the meaning of a text is not directly stated. You have to make an inference to figure out what the text means.

What You Know + What You Read = Inference

To make inferences, you have to think "beyond the text." Try predicting what will happen next or explain a cause and effect. Both are helpful strategies for making inferences.

Key Vocabulary Words

Lesson 1

Archipelago A chain of islands

Mainland A large area of land that is not an island

Rimland The land, often islands and coastal plains, around the edge of an area

Cash crop A crop raised to be sold by those who grow it

Lesson 2

Dormant Not active, such as a volcano that is not likely to erupt

Geothermal Heat from inside Earth

Atoll A chain of islands made up of coral

Navigable A body of water that is deep and wide enough for ships to sail on

Hurricane A tropical storm with strong winds, heavy rainfall, and huge waves

Lesson 3

Mulatto A person whose ancestors are African and European

Slave A person who is held against his or her will and forced to work for free

Voodoo A religion that believes that good and evil spirits influence a person's daily life

Creole A mixture of French and African languages

Civil war A war fought between people from the same country

Communism A government system in which there is no private property; the government owns and controls the land and goods

Lesson 4

Subsistence farming Growing crops mainly to meet the needs of one family

Overdevelopment Building an area too quickly, without paying attention to the harmful effects

Archipelago

A chain of islands

Mainland

A large area of land that is not an island

Reading Strategy:
Inferencing

What do you already know about Central America and the Caribbean islands?

Remember, the Tropics lie between the Tropic of Cancer and the Tropic of Capricorn.

Where Is Central America Located?

Central America is part of the North American continent. The northern part of Central America borders Mexico, with which it has much in common. The southern part of Central America borders Colombia in South America.

Where Are the Caribbean Islands Located?

The Caribbean Sea lies east of Central America. In this sea are hundreds of islands. Geographers call a chain of islands an **archipelago.** Many of the islands in the Caribbean archipelago are actually the tops of a mountain range on the bottom of the sea. Geographers call this archipelago the Antilles.

The four big islands of Jamaica, Cuba, Hispaniola, and Puerto Rico make up the Greater Antilles. The Dominican Republic and Haiti share the island of Hispaniola. East and south of Puerto Rico are many small islands, including the Virgin Islands, Martinique, Barbados, Grenada, and Trinidad. These smaller islands make up the Lesser Antilles. They form the eastern boundary of the Caribbean Sea. Geographers often call the Greater and Lesser Antilles the West Indies.

A third island group is the Bahamas. They lie farther north than the rest of the Caribbean islands. There are more than 700 islands in the Bahamas. Some are so small that no people live on them.

Most of the Caribbean islands, except for the Bahamas, lie in the Tropics.

What Two Subregions Exist?

Geographers usually divide Central America and the Caribbean into two subregions. The first is the **mainland.** A mainland is a large area of land that is not an island. The mainland of Central America includes its seven countries. They are Guatemala, Belize, Honduras, El Salvador, Nicaragua, Costa Rica, and Panama.

Until 1981, Belize was a British colony. It was the last colony in Central America to gain its independence.

Geographers call the second subregion the **rimland.** The rim of something is its edge. A rimland is the land, often islands and coastal plains, around the edge of an area. The islands and the coastal plains of Central America are its rimland. The largest rimland countries are Cuba, Jamaica, the Dominican Republic, and Haiti.

Important geographical and cultural differences exist between the two subregions. Most mainland people are mestizos. Like most Mexicans, they have both Spanish and native ancestors. People of the mainland live mostly in the highlands rather than on the coast.

Most rimland people have both Spanish and African ancestors. Until recently, European countries ruled many of the Caribbean islands. On some islands, the way people live and the language they speak show this European influence.

How Did Geography Shape the Area's History?

Spanish soldiers ruled Central America and the Caribbean hundreds of years ago. On the mainland, they divided the land into large farms called haciendas. Spanish people owned the land. The native people and mestizos did most of the work to make money for the Spanish.

Many plantations grew sugarcane. Sugarcane grows in warm climates. This man is working in a sugarcane field.

Cash crop

A crop raised to be sold by those who grow it

Reading Strategy:
Inferencing

What can you infer about how the people live on these islands?

Haciendas were often self-sufficient. This means that the people living and working there took care of most of their needs without outside help. The haciendas could be self-sufficient because they grew many different types of crops. They grew their own food, made their own clothing, and made their own tools.

The Spanish took the best land for their haciendas. The people who did not work for the Spanish had only poor land to farm. This pattern continues today. A small number of rich families and foreign companies own the best land, while most of the people remain poor and do not own land.

On the islands, the Spanish introduced a different use of land. They divided it into large plantations. The plantations grew only one crop; the haciendas grew many. Many plantations grew only sugarcane or bananas. Instead of eating or using these crops, the plantation owners sold them. Crops grown to sell are **cash crops.**

Lesson 1 Review On a sheet of paper, write the word in parenthesis that makes each statement true.

1. Cuba is part of the (Lesser, Greater) Antilles.

2. (The Bahamas, Dominican Republic) is the only country in this area that is not located in the Tropics.

3. The countries of Central America are part of the (rimland, mainland) subregion.

4. (Haciendas, Plantations) are large, self-sufficient farms.

5. (Plantations, Haciendas) are large farms that usually grow only one crop.

What do you think ?

How do you think having a few rich people own the best land affects the rest of the people who live on the islands?

Dormant

Not active, such as a volcano that is not likely to erupt

What Are the Mainland's Physical Features?

Like Mexico, the mainland area of Central America has high mountains. Some are more than 13,000 feet tall. Many of the mountains were probably formed when two tectonic plates crashed together. Some of the mountains are active volcanoes. Others are **dormant,** which means not active, or not likely to erupt.

The mountains give way to lowlands along the coasts. These coastal lowlands differ from one another. On the eastern side of Central America, thick rain forests cover the land. The heavy rainfall washes away good minerals from the soil. Without these minerals, the soil is not good for farming. Because the Pacific coastal lowlands on the western side receive less rain, its soil is rich. Farmers there grow many different crops.

How Did Volcanoes Make the Islands?

Most islands in the Caribbean are actually the mountain tops of dormant volcanoes. This is especially true of the Greater Antilles. The highest point of each volcanic island is usually near its center. At the water's edge, the land often flattens into a small, coastal plain.

Some islands in the Caribbean are still active volcanoes. The lava from them can both harm and help people. It harms by destroying life and property.

Six active volcanoes in Central America are over 10,000 feet high. Arenal Volcano in Costa Rica erupted again in 1995.

Geothermal

Heat from inside Earth

Atoll

A chain of islands made up of coral

Reading Strategy:
Inferencing

What can you infer about living near an active volcano?

It helps because it sometimes holds important minerals. When lava breaks down, it forms good soil for farming. Also, volcanoes are hot. People can use the heat from volcanoes to make electricity. This is called **geothermal** power. Costa Rica uses geothermal power.

How Does Coral Make Islands?

Some islands in the Caribbean are almost flat. Geographers call these small, low islands **atolls**. Atolls are ring-shaped islands that formed around a volcano that has sunk below the water level. Millions of tiny sea animals created these coral islands. As the sea animals die, their remains slowly build an island or reef on the sides of the underwater mountain. These atolls are usually just a few feet above sea level. The center of the atoll is a lagoon, or small lake. Though atolls are small, they provide food and safety to many forms of sea life. Most people who live on atolls earn their living by fishing.

Geography in Your Life

Building the Panama Canal

For many years, some Americans dreamed of a faster way to sail from the East Coast to the West Coast of the United States. At one time, ships had to sail around the tip of South America. The journey was long and dangerous. People knew this would change if the United States built a canal in Central America.

In 1904, the United States paid Panama $10 million, plus yearly rent, for a 10-mile wide strip of land. Panama is the most narrow country in Central America. In 1904, workers began to build a 51-mile-long canal there. They completed it in 1914. Today the waterway saves time and money. A ship traveling from New York City to San Francisco can save 8,000 miles by using the canal.

From 1914 to 1979, the United States owned the Panama Canal. Between 1979 and 2000, the United States and Panama owned it together. Now Panama owns and runs it alone. Recently, the people of Panama voted to make the canal wider. This will allow very large ships to use the canal for the first time.

Central America and the Caribbean

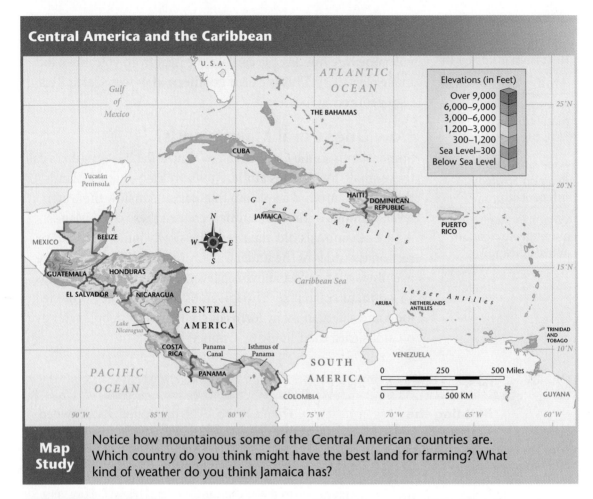

Map Study Notice how mountainous some of the Central American countries are. Which country do you think might have the best land for farming? What kind of weather do you think Jamaica has?

Navigable

A body of water that is deep and wide enough for ships to sail on

What Are the Mainland's Bodies of Water?

Most of the rivers in Central America are short and not **navigable.** This means that large ships cannot travel on them. The mainland has only a few lakes. The largest one is Lake Nicaragua. Central America has one extremely important human-made waterway. It is the Panama Canal, which connects the Atlantic Ocean with the Pacific Ocean. It makes it possible for ships to travel through Central America rather than around South America.

What Is the Climate Like?

The mountain areas of Central America have a highland climate. The area between 3,000 and 6,000 feet, the *tierra templada,* has a climate that is neither too hot nor too cold.

Most of the people live in this climate zone. The climate in the mountains is generally too cold for farming most crops.

The Caribbean lowlands have a tropical climate. Most of the time, the weather is hot and damp. As much as 100 inches of rain may fall each year. Some inland areas, like parts of Guatemala and Costa Rica, have tropical rain forests. It rains almost daily. The Pacific lowlands have a tropical savanna climate. There it is warm and sunny much of the time.

Most Caribbean islands also have tropical savanna climates. Soft winds keep the weather from getting too hot. Rain falls often, but usually not for long. However, during the **hurricane** season, this changes. These tropical storms bring heavy rainfall, strong winds, and huge waves. The hurricanes are worst from August to October. When a hurricane hits, it usually leaves behind millions of dollars of damage.

How Does the Environment Affect the People?

As in Mexico, most people in Central America choose to live in highland areas. The climate in these areas is milder than on the coasts. Farmers have cleared much of the coastal lowlands to plant cash crops like bananas and sugarcane.

The almost-constant sunshine and beautiful scenery attract millions of tourists from around the world. However, from time to time, earthquakes, volcanoes, and hurricanes remind the people of the power of nature.

Lesson 2 Review On a sheet of paper, write the answer to each question. Use complete sentences.

1. What is the main physical feature of the Central American mainland?

2. What are two ways the Caribbean islands were formed?

3. What is geothermal power?

4. In what climate zone do most people in Central America live?

5. What are hurricanes?

Mulatto

A person whose ancestors are African and European

Slave

A person who is held against his or her will and is forced to work for free

What Cultures Are in Central America?

Central America and the Caribbean have many cultures. As in Mexico, the native people have lived in the area the longest. Most of them are poor farmers. In Guatemala, about half the people are native.

Spain influenced Central American culture more than any other European country. Shortly after the Spanish came to Mexico, they traveled south into Central America. Spanish soldiers often had children with native women. As a result, many of the people in Central America are mestizos. In Honduras, about 90 percent of the people are mestizos. In Costa Rica, almost all the people have a Spanish background.

The Spanish did not take over all of Central America. Great Britain set up colonies in some parts of it. Belize, on the Caribbean coast of the Yucatán Peninsula, was a British colony. It has a large population with African ancestors. Some of them had children with Europeans. Geographers call their descendents **mulattos.**

What Cultures Are in the Caribbean?

Most people living on the Caribbean islands are also mulattos. Europeans brought millions of Africans to the islands to work as **slaves** on sugarcane plantations. A slave is a person who is held against his or her will and forced to work for free. Some African slaves had children with Europeans, so the mulatto population on the islands is high.

Great Britain used to rule some of the Caribbean islands. Britain also ruled India. Many eastern Indians, which is the name given to people from India, came to the Caribbean. They settled on islands such as Trinidad. Puerto Rico is a territory of the United States. Puerto Rico is influenced by U.S. culture.

What Are Some Signs of a Cultural Blend?

Many people migrated from the Caribbean islands to the mainland of Central America to work. The resulting culture brought together many languages. For example, in some places the language blends African languages with European ones. Music in the Caribbean blends Spanish and African music. Calypso, salsa, merengue, and reggae are forms of music that first became popular in the islands. Today, people all over the world enjoy this music.

What Religions Do the People Practice?

Usually, a place with many cultures also has many religions. Most people of Central America and the Caribbean are Christians. However, many of the native people practice their native religions. Some people of African descent believe in **voodoo.** Followers of voodoo believe in more than one god and in good and evil spirits. Voodoo is strongest in Haiti.

What Languages Do the People Speak?

A place with many cultures also has many languages. Many native people speak only their native languages. However, Spain once ruled most of Central America, so Spanish is common.

On the Caribbean islands, tourists often hear the language of the Europeans who once ruled there. For example, the British ruled Jamaica and the Bahamas, so the people there speak English. The people of Haiti, Guadeloupe, and Martinique speak mostly French. In many places, the language blends two or more languages. For example, Haitians also speak a language called **Creole.** It mixes French with African languages.

Where Do Most People Live?

Most people of Central America and the Caribbean used to live in rural areas. Today, more than half the people have migrated to urban areas. The only country in Central America with a high population density is El Salvador. Santo Domingo in the Dominican Republic and Havana in Cuba both have more than 2 million people. Other big cities are Guatemala City in Guatemala and San Salvador in El Salvador.

Reading Strategy:
Inferencing

What can you infer from this graph about living in Haiti?

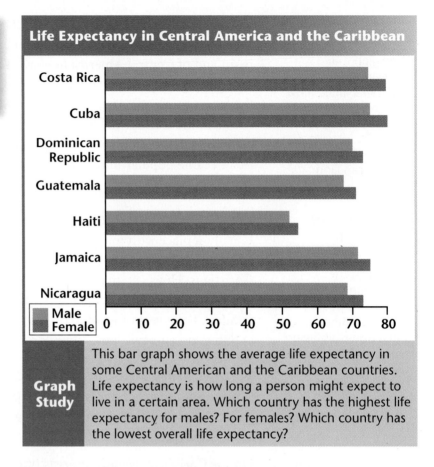

Life Expectancy in Central America and the Caribbean

Costa Rica
Cuba
Dominican Republic
Guatemala
Haiti
Jamaica
Nicaragua

Male
Female

0 10 20 30 40 50 60 70 80

Graph Study

This bar graph shows the average life expectancy in some Central American and the Caribbean countries. Life expectancy is how long a person might expect to live in a certain area. Which country has the highest life expectancy for males? For females? Which country has the lowest overall life expectancy?

Civil war

A war fought between people from the same country

What Problems Does This Area Face?

Central America faces many problems. There are great differences between the rich and the poor. Small groups of rich people control most of the wealth. However, most people are poor. Many rich people do not respect the native people.

In some countries, this unequal treatment of the poor has led to fighting. El Salvador experienced a bitter **civil war** throughout most of the 1980s. A civil war is a war fought between people from the same country. Because of this war, about 20 percent of the people left their homeland and moved to the United States.

Communism

A government system in which there is no private property; the government owns and controls the land and goods

For over 30 years, Guatemala fought its own civil war. It ended in 1995. Nicaragua had a revolution in 1979 and set up a government based on **Communism.** There is no private property in Communist countries. The government controls and owns the land and goods. The United States did not like this new government. The U.S. government supplied weapons and training to people in Nicaragua to try to overthrow the Communist government.

Another problem in Central America is lack of industries. The region still depends mostly on farming. Many countries grow the same crops. Farmers compete rather than cooperate. To live better, the countries must develop new industries. Recently, countries like the United States have built manufacturing plants there. These companies pay the workers less than they pay workers in the United States. However, workers still earn more than they did before.

Population growth is also a problem. The population of the Caribbean has more than doubled since 1960. More people mean more homes, more schools—more of everything is needed. Poor countries like those of the region have limited money. Many people do not have jobs. People have destroyed rain forests to make farmland. Many have been forced to go to other countries to improve their lives.

These farm products are for sale at markets.

The biggest challenge for the area may be how to get along with the United States. The United States has great power in the area. Its government has often sent soldiers to Cuba, Haiti, and Nicaragua. United States relations with Cuba have been especially bad.

The people who live in the Commonwealth of Puerto Rico are U.S. citizens. Some live well, but many are poor. Puerto Ricans have voted many times on whether to remain a territory, become a U.S. state, or become a free nation. So far they have decided to remain a territory.

Lesson 3 Review On a sheet of paper, write the letter of the answer that correctly completes each sentence.

1. ___*B*___ is the country that most strongly influenced Central America.

   A Great Britain   **C** France
   B Spain   **D** India

2. Africans were brought to the Caribbean as ___*D*___.

   A explorers   **C** rulers
   B soldiers   **D** slaves

3. Descendants of European and African parents are ___*A*___.

   A mulattos   **C** mestizos
   B Creoles   **D** voodoo

4. The language that is a mixture of the French and African languages is called ___*D*___.

   A English   **C** French
   B Spanish   **D** Creole

5. ___*A*___ is a territory of the United States.

   A Puerto Rico   **C** Costa Rica
   B Nicaragua   **D** Cuba

What do you think ?

Why do you think this region does not have many large cities?

Objectives

◆ To identify weather and forests as natural resources of the area
◆ To identify agriculture as a major industry
◆ To describe the environmental challenges the area faces

Subsistence farming

Growing crops mainly to meet the needs of one family

What Are the Natural Resources in This Area?

Good weather and much sunshine are the major resources of both the Caribbean islands and Central America. Because of this, many tourists visit the beautiful beaches and clear waters of the Caribbean islands. They scuba dive, snorkel, fish, and sail in these waters. Cruise ships often stop at the islands. Many people also travel to Costa Rica to enjoy the country's natural beauty. Some people come to see animals that live only in the Caribbean.

Forests are a great resource of Central America. Once they covered more than half of its land. Tropical woods like teak, balsa, and mahogany grow in these forests. One special tree provides chicle, the basic part of chewing gum.

Central America and the Caribbean do not have many mineral resources. However, workers have mined some gold, silver, and other minerals in the mountains of Nicaragua. Also, Jamaica has a large supply of the mineral bauxite, which is used to make aluminum.

What Are Some Central American Industries?

The economies of most Central American countries depend on farming. More than half the people of Guatemala and Honduras farm. Most of them do **subsistence farming**. That means the farmers mainly grow crops for their families, not to earn money. If a crop fails, the health and the lives of the family members may be in danger.

A small group of rich people and foreign businesses own much of the land in Central America. They have divided this land into huge plantations that grow bananas, cotton, or coffee. The landowners export most of these cash crops to either the United States or Europe. The crops account for most of Central America's export income.

Some American companies have built clothing factories here.

These cruise ships are docked on St. Thomas, which is near Puerto Rico in the West Indies. Tourism is an important industry in the Caribbean.

What Are Some Industries in the Caribbean?

Reading Strategy:
Inferencing

What can you infer about people who work on a plantation in the Caribbean islands?

Most people on the Caribbean islands also work in agriculture. Some work on plantations that grow sugarcane, coconuts, cacao, and bananas. Others work in plants that process the crops. For example, some factories turn sugarcane into table sugar. Some island people work on ships or on the docks. There, people package farm goods and prepare them to sell.

A big part of the economy, especially in the Caribbean, is tourism. Tourism brings in millions of dollars every year. Tourism provides many jobs. Many people work as guides and in the many hotels and restaurants that have been built. Most of these jobs require little skill or education. Because of this, the foreign owners do not pay the workers much money.

The first important export of Guatemala in the 1800s was dye made from insects. Then coffee became the most important export. Guatemalan coffee is still shipped around the world.

Many American companies have developed businesses in Puerto Rico. Many U.S. pharmaceutical companies, which make legal drugs, are located there.

Overdevelopment

Building an area
too quickly, without
paying attention to
the harmful effects

What Are the Environmental Challenges?

Overdevelopment is the biggest challenge to this area of the world. People from other countries have built tourist hotels and other things with little thought for the natural environment. They cut down native trees and plants. They often build resorts and hotels in areas where local people lived. Many people are forced out of their homes. Few of the local people share in the wealth that comes from the resorts and hotels. Also, tourism creates more traffic and pollution. Local governments are forced to spend a lot of money building roads, airports, and shopping centers for the tourists rather than helping their own people.

Another serious problem in Central America is that the rain forests are being destroyed. Many animals and plants found only in Central America live in these rain forests.

Lesson 4 Review On a sheet of paper, use the words from the Word Bank to complete each sentence correctly.

1. Good _____ is one of the major natural resources in Central America and the Caribbean.

2. At one time, more than half of the land was covered by _____.

3. In _____ farming, a farmer grows only those crops for one family.

4. A big part of the economy on the Caribbean islands is _____.

5. The rain forests support many _____ and plants found only in Central America.

Word Bank

animals 5

forests 2

subsistence 3

tourism 4

weather 1

Writing About Geography

Imagine you are a scientist making a speech. Explain why people must protect the rain forests of Central America. Write a speech that expresses your feelings. Read the speech to yourself, and then present it to the class or a partner.

What do you think ?

Do you think tourism is good for the region or bad? Give several reasons for your opinion.

Life Without School

My name is Daniela. I am 15 years old and live with my family at the base of the San Vicente volcano in El Salvador. I have not been to school for many years. That's because in 2001 an earthquake destroyed the entire village where I attended school. Many people died. And we've never rebuilt the school.

My father works on a coffee plantation. He is what they call a seasonal worker; he only works part of the year. I know from listening to my parents that most plantation owners do not want permanent workers. The owners are afraid permanent workers would organize to demand more money and more rights. Most men here work on the coffee or sugarcane plantations even though the wages are low. There is no other choice.

We need the money my father earns in order to pay rent on the small bit of land where we live. We use the land to grow most of our own food. The steep slope makes it hard to farm. But we do the best we can to grow all the rice, corn, and beans our family needs. My mother sells what is left over at the village market.

I spend my days helping around the house. I cook and serve breakfast to the entire family. This includes my parents, my four younger brothers and sisters, and my grandfather. I wash all the dishes by hand, dry them, and put them away. After that, I sweep the dirt floors. Then I do whatever my mother needs me to do. I usually care for the little ones and clean the house.

I often am in charge of the household because my mother tends to our crops with my 13-year-old brother. Sometimes she hires herself out to help neighboring farmers. I always have our noon meal ready when she comes in. While she eats, I bring my father lunch in the fields. He is always happy to see me. This quiet meal, shared with my father, is my favorite part of the day.

Wrap-Up

1. Why do plantation owners not want to hire permanent help?

2. Why do you think sharing the meal with her father is Daniela's favorite part of the day?

Chapter 6   S U M M A R Y

- Central America is part of the North American continent. The Caribbean islands, or West Indies, are in the Caribbean Sea. Except for the Bahamas, the entire area is located in the Tropics.

- Central America and the Caribbean have two subregions: the mainland and the rimland. The mainland includes the Central American countries. The rimland includes the Caribbean islands and Central America's coastal plains.

- The mainland has high mountains. Thick rain forests cover the eastern side of Central America. The Pacific coastal lowland has rich soil. Most Caribbean islands are inactive volcanic mountains.

- Most rivers in Central America are short and ships cannot use them. The Panama Canal, a waterway made by people, is its main water feature.

- The mountain areas of the mainland of Central America have a highland climate. The Caribbean lowlands have a tropical climate. The Pacific lowlands and the Caribbean islands have a tropical savanna climate.

- Descendants of native people live in Central America and the Caribbean. Many countries have a large population of mestizos, descendants of the Spanish and the native people. Belize has a large population whose ancestors came from Africa. The children of Africans and Europeans are called mulattos.

- Christianity is the main religion of the area. However, many native people have kept their own religions. Some people of African descent practice voodoo.

- Most people speak Spanish because Spain once controlled most of the area. In countries that England controlled, the people speak English. People also speak their native languages, French, and Creole.

- More than half the people have migrated from rural to urban areas. The largest cities of Central America and the Caribbean are Santo Domingo in the Dominican Republic and Havana in Cuba.

- The main natural resources are forests, good weather, sunshine, and beaches. The area has few mineral resources. The economies of Central America and the Caribbean depend on farming.

- Central America and the Caribbean face the environmental problems of overdevelopment, pollution, and the destruction of rain forests.

- The nations of this region also face the social problems of poverty, economic development, a rising birthrate, and the task of getting along with the United States.

Chapter 6 R E V I E W

Word Bank

Central America 1

Panama Canal 3

Spanish 5

urban 4

volcanic 2

On a sheet of paper, use the words from the Word Bank to complete each sentence correctly.

1. _____ is part of North America.

2. Most of the Caribbean islands are really _____ mountain tops.

3. A water feature in Central America that was made by people is the _____.

4. More than half the people of Central America and the Caribbean live in _____ areas.

5. The language spoken most often in Central America is _____.

On a sheet of paper, write the letter of the answer that correctly completes each sentence.

6. The Caribbean islands and the coastal plains of Central America are part of the ___C___ subregion.

    A mainland   **B** archipelago **C** rimland   **D** atoll

7. The Caribbean lowlands have a ___c__ climate.

    A continental **B** highland   **C** tropical   **D** maritime

8. The heat of volcanoes creates __A__ power.

    A geothermal **B** nuclear   **C** hydroelectric **D** volcanic

9. Tropical storms called __D__ bring strong winds, heavy rainfall, and huge waves.

    A tornadoes   **C** floods

    B blizzards   **D** hurricanes

10. Among the languages spoken in Central America and the Caribbean are ____.

    A native and English   **C** Creole and Spanish

    B English and French   **D** all of the above

On a sheet of paper, write the answer to each question. Use complete sentences.

11. How do most people in Central America and the Caribbean earn a living?

12. What are the two subregions of Central America and the Caribbean?

13. What is probably the most important natural resource in Central America and the Caribbean?

Critical Thinking On a sheet of paper, write your response to each question. Use complete sentences.

14. Should businesses from other countries invest or spend money in Central America and the Caribbean? Give a reason for your opinion.

15. What would you do about the environmental problems in Central America and the Caribbean?

Applying the Five Themes of Geography

Location
Why did engineers select the location they did for the building of the Panama Canal?

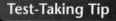

Test-Taking Tip

When studying for a test, learn the most important points. Practice writing or saying the material aloud. Have a partner listen to check to see if you are correct.

7

South America

South America is one of the world's seven continents. Much of it is covered with rain forests. South America is home to over 350 million people. In 1498, Christopher Columbus became the first European to see South America. Today, great differences exist among South America's countries and people.

Goals for Learning

◆ To describe South America

◆ To identify the most important physical features and climates of South America

◆ To describe the cultures and people who live in South America

◆ To describe the economy and environmental challenges of South America

Geo-Stats   Four Largest Nations of South America

Nation: Argentina
Population: 39,922,000
Area: 1,068,302 square miles
Major Cities: Buenos Aires (capital), Córdoba, Rosario

Nation: Colombia
Population: 43,593,000
Area: 439,737 square miles
Major Cities: Bogotá (capital), Medellín, Cali, Barranquilla

Nation: Brazil
Population: 188,076,000
Area: 3,286,488 square miles
Major Cities: Brasília (capital), São Paulo, Rio de Janeiro, Belo Horizonte

Nation: Peru
Population: 28,303,000
Area: 496,225 square miles
Capital: Lima

Map Skills

South America is the fourth largest continent in the world. It includes many small countries and one huge one.

Study the map and answer the questions:

1. What is the largest country in South America? The smallest?

2. Along which coast is Chile located?

3. Which oceans and sea surround South America?

4. What is the capital of Argentina? Uruguay? Colombia?

5. Which countries cover most of the east coast of South America?

Reading Strategy:
Metacognition

Metacognition means "thinking about your thinking." Use metacognition to become a better reader:

◆ Preview the text.

◆ Make predictions and ask yourself what you already know about the topic.

◆ Write the main idea, details, and any questions you have.

◆ Visualize what is happening in the text. If something doesn't make sense, go back and read it again.

◆ Summarize what you have read and make inferences about the meaning.

Key Vocabulary Words

Lesson 1

Pangaea The one huge piece of land that once was in Earth's ocean

Continental drift The theory that only one huge piece of land was once in Earth's ocean and that the land then drifted apart into seven continents

Lesson 2

Foothill A low hill at the base of higher hills or a mountain range

Loess A fine and fertile soil that the wind deposits on the ground

Estuary A flooded river valley at the mouth of a river where salt water from a sea mixes with freshwater from a river

Savanna climate A hot climate that has a very wet season and a very dry season

Temperate climate A climate that is neither very hot nor very cold and has warm and cool seasons

Lesson 3

Death rate The number of deaths over a given period of time

Lesson 4

Agribusiness The business of farming on large farms with many machines and chemicals

Objectives

◆ To know where South America is located

◆ To describe continental drift

◆ To identify the Caribbean, Atlantic, and Pacific regions of South America

Pangaea

The one huge piece of land that once was in Earth's ocean

Continental drift

The theory that only one huge piece of land was once in Earth's ocean and that the land then drifted apart into seven continents

Where Is South America Located?

Most people think that South America lies directly south of North America. Actually, it is quite a bit farther east. Santiago, Chile, on the western side of South America, is almost directly south of Boston, Massachusetts, on the eastern coast of North America. Much of South America is in the Tropics. The equator runs through the countries of Brazil, Colombia, and Ecuador.

South America has three long coastlines. One is on the Atlantic Ocean. Another is on the Pacific Ocean. The shortest coastline is on the Caribbean Sea. Being close to large bodies of water has affected South America's history, trade, economy, and climate.

What Is Continental Drift?

Look at the world map below. Note the shape of South America and the shape of Africa. They seem to fit together. Geographers suggest that one huge piece of land, which they call **Pangaea,** once was in Earth's ocean. Over millions of years, Pangaea broke apart. It became the seven different continents. One of these continents is South America.

Geographers give the name **continental drift** to this idea. Experts believe that some time long ago, Pangaea divided and the continents drifted apart around Earth. Fossils support this idea. Fossils are molds or remains of ancient plants or animals. Scientists have found fossils of the same plants and animals in places many thousands of miles apart. This suggests that land once connected these areas of Earth.

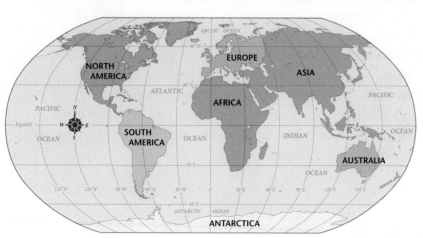

Remember to ask
yourself questions as
you read. This will
help you make sure
that you understand
what you are reading.

What Countries Are in the Caribbean Region?

Geographers divide South America into three regions based on location: Caribbean South America, Atlantic South America, and Pacific South America. Europeans first came to Caribbean South America. This region is made up of the countries that border the Caribbean Sea. It also includes the countries whose cultures are like that of the Caribbean people. The countries of Colombia, Venezuela, Guyana, Suriname, and French Guiana, which is a territory of France, are in this region.

Caribbean South America has plains and highlands. The largest plain stretches across Venezuela. Some highlands are 7,000 feet. The region has several large cities. Bogotá, Colombia, has over 7 million people. Caracas, Venezuela, has over 3 million. But most people in the region live in rural areas and small towns.

What Countries Are in the Atlantic Region?

Four countries make up this region. Uruguay and Paraguay are small; Brazil and Argentina are large. Brazil is the largest country in South America. Brazil is so large that geographers divide it into four parts.

Brazil is almost as large as the United States.

Most Brazilians live in the southeastern part of Brazil, which is its richest and most densely populated area. Its biggest cities, Rio de Janeiro and São Paulo, are there. The northeastern part of Brazil is home to about a third of Brazil's people. It is the poorest region of Brazil. Brazil's capital, Brasília, is located in its west central region. Until recently, the area around Brasília had few people. However, after it became the capital in 1960, the area quickly developed and its population is growing. The fourth part of Brazil is Amazonia. Geographers give it this name because the Amazon River flows through it. Amazonia covers 42 percent of Brazil, but it has the fewest number of people. The world's largest rain forests grow in this part of Brazil. Its thick forests and hot, damp climate make living and moving about difficult.

Writing About Geography

Choose one of the regions of South America. Imagine that you live there. Then write a personal letter to a friend in the United States. Describe the region in South America in which you live.

What Countries Are in the Pacific Region?

Pacific South America is very different from Atlantic South America. The Andes Mountains rise on the western side of South America and are the region's main feature. They are more than 20,000 feet high. That is more than 6,000 feet higher than the Rocky Mountains in the United States. The Andes make traveling in western South America difficult.

The countries in this region are Ecuador, Peru, Bolivia, and Chile. In Peru and Bolivia, a high, broad plateau sits between two mountain ranges that stretch southward. Geographers call this high plain by its Spanish name of *Altiplano.* Bolivia is the only country of the four that is landlocked; it has no seaports. Chile is shaped like a snake. It is 2,650 miles long, but only about 265 miles wide.

Sugarloaf Mountain is a landmark in Rio de Janeiro, Brazil.

Lesson 1 Review On a sheet of paper, write the word in parenthesis that makes each statement true.

1. The theory of (Altiplano, continental drift) explains how seven continents came to be on Earth.

2. Europeans first settled in the (Caribbean, Atlantic) region of South America.

3. (Brazil, Argentina) is the largest country in South America.

4. (Bolivia, Chile) is a snake-shaped country in Pacific South America.

5. The (Andes, Rocky) Mountains are on the western side of South America.

Objectives

◆ To identify the three physical regions of South America

◆ To describe the major river systems of South America

◆ To describe the climates of South America

Foothill

A low hill at the base of higher hills or a mountain range

Loess

A fine and fertile soil that the wind deposits on the ground

Remember that a plateau is an area of level highland.

Reading Strategy: Metacognition

As you read about these rivers and lakes, find them on the map. This will help you visualize the country.

What Are South America's Physical Regions?

South America has three big physical regions. The Andes Mountains form the first region. They begin at Tierra del Fuego at the southern tip of South America. The Andes stretch northward for more than 4,500 miles to Venezuela on the Caribbean coast of South America.

The Andes are the longest mountain system in the world. Some rise more than four miles above sea level. They are like a wall between the western coast and the rest of South America. In Peru and Bolivia, they are almost 300 miles wide. The few people who live in the valleys of the Andes are mostly native people. The mountains separate villages from one another.

The plains form the second physical region. They stretch from the **foothills** of the Andes eastward to the Atlantic Ocean. A foothill is a hill at the base of higher hills or a mountain range. The plains cover much of Argentina and Paraguay. In Argentina, geographers call these plains the pampas. Rich **loess** soil covers the pampas. Loess is a fine, fertile soil that is good for growing things. The wind brought loess to the plains, which are one of the richest farm areas in the world.

A large area of lowlands and plateaus in Brazil is the third physical region. The Amazon River flows through a huge area of mostly flat land. A wide coastal plain stretches along the Atlantic coast. It is here that Europeans set up the first sugarcane plantations. After they planted sugarcane year after year, the land wore out and now has poor soil.

What River Systems Exist?

Three large river systems flow through South America. The largest is the Amazon. It carries more water than the next eight largest rivers in the world. It begins in the ice-covered Andes Mountains in Peru. About 4,000 miles later, the Amazon empties into the Atlantic Ocean. The Amazon has over 1,000 tributaries. The most important of these tributaries are the Río Negro, Xingu, Putumayo, and Juruá, each over 1,000 miles long.

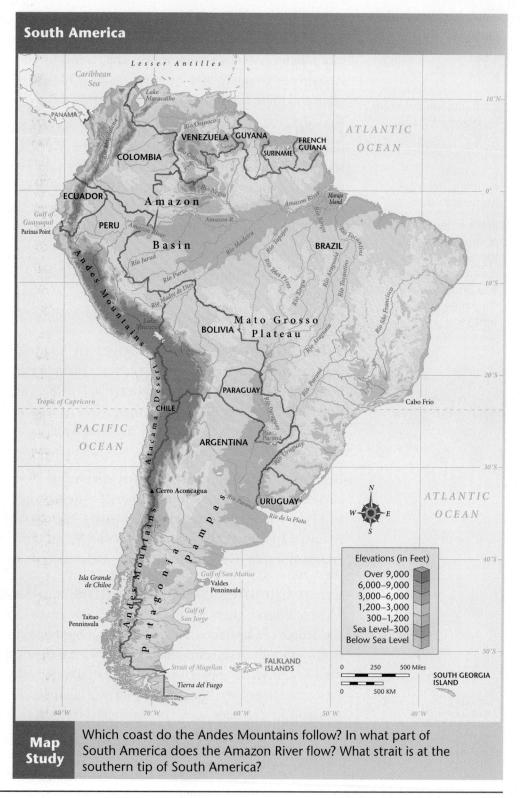

South America

Lesser Antilles

Caribbean Sea

Lake Maracaibo

PANAMA

ATLANTIC OCEAN

10°N

VENEZUELA

GUYANA

Río Orinoco

COLOMBIA

Río Orinoco

SURINAME

FRENCH GUIANA

ECUADOR

Amazon

Río Negro

Amazon River

Marajó Island

0°

Gulf of Guayaquil

Parinas Point

PERU

Amazon River

Amazon R.

Basin

Río Juruá

Río Purus

Río Madeira

Río Tapajós

Río Teles Pires

Río Xingu

BRAZIL

Río Araguaia

Río Tocantins

Río São Francisco

Andes Mountains

10°S

Río Madre de Dios

Lake Titicaca

BOLIVIA

Mato Grosso Plateau

Río Araguaia

Río Tocantins

20°S

PARAGUAY

Atacama Desert

CHILE

Tropic of Capricorn

Río Paraná

Río Paraguay

Cabo Frio

PACIFIC OCEAN

ARGENTINA

Río Paraná

Río Uruguay

30°S

▲ Cerro Aconcagua

Río Paraná

URUGUAY

Río de la Plata

ATLANTIC OCEAN

Andes Mountains

Pampas

N

W E

S

Isla Grande de Chiloe

Gulf of San Matias

Valdes Peninsula

40°S

Patagonia

Taitao Penninsula

Gulf of San Jorge

Elevations (in Feet)

Over 9,000
6,000–9,000
3,000–6,000
1,200–3,000
300–1,200
Sea Level–300
Below Sea Level

Strait of Magellan

FALKLAND ISLANDS

50°S

Tierra del Fuego

0   250   500 Miles

SOUTH GEORGIA ISLAND

0   500 KM

80°W   70°W   60°W   50°W   40°W

Map Study

Which coast do the Andes Mountains follow? In what part of South America does the Amazon River flow? What strait is at the southern tip of South America?

The second largest river system in South America is the Río de la Plata. The many rivers of this system drain an area of more than 1,500,000 square miles. The river is important to Argentina, Paraguay, and Uruguay. Because of this, geographers often call them the Río de la Plata countries.

The Río de la Plata is really a huge **estuary**. An estuary is a flooded river valley at the mouth or end of a river. There, salt water from the sea mixes with freshwater from the river. The three chief rivers that empty into the Río de la Plata estuary are the Paraná, the Paraguay, and the Uruguay. Each of these rivers is more than 1,000 miles long.

The third important river system in South America is the Orinoco. The Orinoco River drains an area of about 360,000 square miles, mostly in Venezuela. It also has many important tributaries including the Apure, the Caura, and the Caroni.

What Are Some Other Bodies of Water?

An area with many rivers is likely to have many waterfalls. A beautiful one is Angel Falls in Venezuela. It is the world's tallest waterfall. The water drops more than 3,000 feet, more than half a mile. The two biggest lakes in South America are Lake Maracaibo in Venezuela and Lake Titicaca in Peru and Bolivia.

Except for the land bridge to Central America at its northwest corner, water surrounds South America. Many people in Chile and Peru fish for a living. All three coasts—the Caribbean, the Atlantic, and the Pacific—have port cities. From these ports, companies ship many products to other parts of the world.

What Climates Does South America Have?

Most of South America falls between the Tropic of Cancer and the Tropic of Capricorn. However, high mountains stretch from north to south. As a result, South America has nearly every kind of climate. Temperature and rainfall differ greatly. The Atacama Desert of Chile is one of the world's driest deserts. The Amazon River Valley is one of the wettest tropical rain forests.

Major Rivers of the World		
River	Location	Length in Miles
Nile	Africa	4,160
Amazon	South America	4,083
Yangtze	China	3,915
Mississippi/Missouri/Red Rock	United States	3,741
Huang (Yellow)	China	3,395
Ob/Irtysh	China/Kazakhstan/Russian	3,362
Amur/Shilka	E. Asia	2,744
Lena	Russia	2,734
Congo/Zaire	Africa	2,718
Mackenzie/Peace/Finlay	Canada	2,635

Chart Study This chart shows the 10 largest rivers in the world. The Amazon is in South America. How much longer is the Nile than the Amazon? How long is the Yangtze?

Savanna climate

A hot climate that has a very wet season and a very dry season

Temperate climate

A climate that is neither very hot nor very cold and has warm and cool seasons

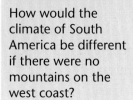
What do you think

How would the climate of South America be different if there were no mountains on the west coast?

Much of South America has tropical climates, either a rain forest climate or a **savanna climate.** Rain forests are hot and wet all year; savannas have a wet season and a dry season. In the middle latitudes of South America's Atlantic coast, people live in **temperate climates.** This means that the weather is neither very hot nor very cold, with a warm and cool season. Some areas like southern Brazil have a humid subtropical climate. Patagonia is the southern tip of South America in Chile and Argentina. It has a dry and cold climate.

Lesson 2 Review On a sheet of paper, write the answer to each question. Use complete sentences.

1. What are the three physical regions of South America?

2. What was the first plantation crop that Europeans grew on the plain of northeast Brazil?

3. What are the three great river systems of South America?

4. What is the world's tallest waterfall?

5. What are three climates in South America?

Reading Strategy: Metacognition

Before you read this lesson, think about what you can do to help you understand the lesson.

Some farmers in Peru raise alpacas.

What Are the Three Cultural Regions?

The countries of South America have much in common, but they differ, too. They can be divided into three cultural regions: Indo-America, Afro-America, and Euro-America.

Where Is the Indo-American Region?

Indo-America includes large parts of Bolivia, Peru, Ecuador, and part of Colombia. The native people who live here have influenced the region's culture. Most people still speak their own native languages. They also keep their own customs and ways of dressing.

The native people in this region are subsistence farmers. They plant the same crops and use many of the same tools that those who lived before them did. They live mainly on potatoes, corn, and a grain called *quinoa*. The people also raise sheep, llamas, and alpacas. Llamas are related to the camel. When people travel, they pack things on the llama's back. Alpacas are a type of goat. People use their silky hair to make sweaters. Most native people are the poorest people in South America. They live much as their ancestors did hundreds of years ago.

Where Is the Afro-American Region?

Afro-America includes the northern coast of South America and the east coast of Brazil. People from Africa influence this region. Years ago, Europeans came to this region and settled. They set up plantations and dug mines. Many of the native people died from European diseases. The Europeans then brought the many workers they needed from Africa.

From 1500 to the mid-1800s, European ships brought millions of African slaves to South America. Many people in this region descended from these African slaves. The music of Brazil and some popular foods show the influence of Africa.

Reading Strategy:
Metacognition

Remember to look at the photos. This will help you visualize what you are reading.

Where Is the Euro-American Region?

European influence is strongest in Euro-America. This region covers most of southern Brazil, Paraguay, Uruguay, Argentina, and Chile. In countries like Argentina, almost all of the people have European ancestry.

Today, South America still attracts many immigrants. There are many Europeans, but also people from the Middle East and Asia. They like the good weather and the rich land. They have become an important influence.

What Are Their Languages?

People from Spain settled much of South America, so Spanish is the most common language. However, people from Portugal settled in Brazil, so Portuguese is Brazil's official language. The native people speak their own languages. Immigrants often speak their native languages. Because of this, people speak Italian, German, Russian, and other languages in large cities.

Celebrations

Carnaval

An important cultural city in Brazil is Rio de Janeiro. The area around it has more than 11 million people. It is home to a world-famous festival called Carnaval, which is part of a Roman Catholic holiday. Carnaval comes just before Lent, when Catholics give up things they like. Carnaval is their last chance to have fun before Lent. People in colorful costumes ride through the streets on floats. They dance to the music of the samba. The samba came from Africa and is very popular. The same holiday is celebrated in New Orleans, where it is called Mardi Gras.

Critical Thinking Why would people have begun the celebration of Carnaval?

Reading Strategy:
Metacognition

Ask yourself questions
as you read. This will
help you make sure
that you understand
the lessons you are
reading.

Death rate

The number of deaths
over a given period of
time

What Religion Do Most People Practice?

Most people in South America are Christians, mostly Roman
Catholics. However, followers of every major world religion live
in South America. Often the native religions have blended with
Christianity. Some descendents of the African slaves still follow
their African religions.

What Are the Population Trends?

South America has one of the highest birthrates in the world.
Many babies are born each year to the people who live there.
Geographers expect its population to double in the next 25
years. In the past, South America also had a high **death rate.**
Death rate is the number of deaths over a given time. However,
today the death rate has fallen because of new medicines and
better health conditions. Most South Americans continue
to have large families. One reason is that children are extra
workers who will bring more income to the family. Another
reason is the lack of information about limiting the number
of children born. This may be because the Roman Catholic
Church is against using birth control. Many people believe
South America will lower its birthrate. If it does not do this,
too many people will continue to be poor.

Where Do Most South Americans Live?

Most South Americans live in rural areas. However, every year
thousands of poor people leave the countryside and move to
cities. They hope to find better jobs, schools, and health care.
Most of the time they do not, but they still stay.

Geography in Your Life

Plants from Rain Forests

The Amazon rain forest provides the world
with plants that people use for medicine.

Among the rain-forest medicines are ipecac,
quinine, pilocarpine, and curare. Doctors use
ipecac, which is a plant, to treat accidental
poisoning. Quinine comes from the bark
of a tree. Doctors use this drug to treat the
disease malaria.

Scientists get pilocarpine from the leaves of
a rain-forest shrub. Doctors use it to treat
glaucoma, an eye disease. Curare comes
from a rain-forest vine and relaxes a person's
muscles. Doctors also use curare to treat
some diseases of the mind.

Scientists believe that other rain-forest plants
might cure AIDS, diabetes, arthritis, cancer,
and Alzheimer's disease.

Their migration has created big problems for the cities. Many of these poor people live in slums. People often beg for food because they don't have enough to eat. Three of the largest urban areas in the world are in South America: São Paulo and Rio de Janeiro in Brazil and Buenos Aires in Argentina.

Word Bank

Afro-America ʒ

Euro-America ᒧ

Indo-America ᒋ

rural ᒧ

Spanish ᑌ

Lesson 3 Review On a sheet of paper, use the words from the Word Bank to complete each sentence correctly.

1. The influence of the native people of South America is strongest in _____.

2. The influence of the European culture in South America is strongest in _____.

3. The influence of African culture in South America is strongest in _____.

4. The language most South Americans speak is _____.

5. Most South Americans live in _____ areas.

What do you think ?

Should South American countries do more to try to keep native cultures alive? Explain your answer.

Biography

Michelle Bachelet: 1951–

In 2006, Michelle Bachelet was elected to be the president of Chile. One of the things she wanted to do during her term in office was to reduce the gap between the rich and the poor people in Chile.

Michelle Bachelet is a medical doctor. She speaks Spanish, English, German, Portuguese, and French. Her father was put into prison by the military dictator who ruled Chile from 1973 to 1990. Her father died in prison in 1974. She and her mother were also imprisoned in 1975.

Michelle Bachelet is the first woman to be elected president in Chile.

Saving the Rain Forests

Rain forests are important to the whole world. The world's biggest rain forest is in the Amazon River basin. It is a great natural resource. Some people call it "the lungs of the world." It supplies more than 20 percent of the world's oxygen. Plants take in carbon dioxide and give off oxygen. Some scientists think carbon dioxide is what causes global warming.

Rain forests contain many plants, insects, and animals. Yet the Amazon rain forest is disappearing. Some loggers would like to cut trees from the rain forest to sell for lumber. Poor native people sometimes cut down trees in the forest to create farmland. But the forest soil is very thin and not good for farming.

However, some industries are able to use the rain forest without destroying it. The rubber industry is one example. Wild rubber trees grow throughout the rain forest. Workers make thin cuts in trees, and a milky liquid called latex flows out. Workers collect this latex in containers. Factories then make latex into rubber. Though manmade rubber has replaced most natural rubber, rubber is sold all over the world for use in making tires and other items.

The rain forest has many other products that may be useful. For example, medicines are made from some of the plants. Some environmentalists encourage these uses of the rain forest. People will not cut down the rain forest if they can make more money by letting it grow.

Wrap-Up

1. How can industries use the rain forest without destroying it?

2. Why is the Amazon rain forest called "the lungs of the world"?

Make a Difference

Most paper is made from trees. The less paper we use, the fewer trees need to be cut down. Keep track of how much paper you use in a day. Work in a group to list how you could use less.

Objectives

- ◆ To define agribusiness
- ◆ To describe the economy of South America
- ◆ To name some problems Latin America is facing

Agribusiness

The business of farming on large farms with many machines and chemicals

Reading Strategy:
Metacognition

Notice the structure of this lesson. Look at the titles and features in the lesson.

What Is Agribusiness?

Agriculture is important to the economy of South America. In the mountain valleys of the Andes, native people still do subsistence farming. However, in other parts of South America, **agribusiness** has become big business. Farmers use big machines and chemicals on large farms. They grow fruits and vegetables to ship to other countries such as the United States. Sugar, bananas, coffee, and cacao are grown on plantations. Colombia and Brazil grow lots of coffee beans. Cotton, rice, corn, soy beans, wheat, and oranges are grown in Brazil. It is the world's largest exporter of oranges, orange juice, and other tropical fruits like guavas, lemons, and mangoes.

What Industries Are Important?

Brazil, Argentina, Chile, and Venezuela have many industries. This helps people in these countries live better.

Brazil's economy is one of the largest in the world. Car making is a big industry in Brazil. Car companies from other countries have spent millions of dollars building new factories there. Car companies created thousands of jobs for the people. Many people work in the factories that produce steel for the car makers. Others work in factories that put the cars together.

Today, South American factories make many kinds of goods. Their economies are growing because multinational corporations invest in them. The making of clothes and shoes are important industries. Foreign companies build plants in South America because the workers there are willing to work for less than they do in other countries.

Service industries are also growing in South America. More than one-third of the working people of Brazil work in service jobs. Many work for the government. Others work in offices, shops, or restaurants.

This is an assembly-line worker at a car factory in Brazil. Car making is an important industry in Brazil.

What Are the Natural Resources?

South America is rich in oil. Venezuela, Colombia, Brazil, Ecuador, and Argentina have oil. South America is also rich in minerals. Chile is the world's leading exporter of copper. Brazil is the second largest producer of iron ore and tin in the world. Bauxite, gold, platinum, and almost every known mineral are mined in South America.

Good weather, rich farmland, water, and rain forests are also important resources in South America. Its many rivers provide water for irrigation and hydroelectric power. Its rain forests provide lumber and useful plants. The rich farm land produces a lot of grain and livestock.

What Problems Does South America Have?

Reading Strategy:
Metacognition

Make a prediction about the problems South America has. What have you heard on the news about South America?

The biggest problem South America faces is poverty. South America has some of the most beautiful cities in the world. They have tall buildings, big hotels, and many shops. Rich people in these cities enjoy a high standard of living. But most people in South America are poor. Their lives are often very hard. If they can find work, they are usually paid very little. Many people live in homes with no electricity or running water. Many of the poor children cannot read and have little education.

Another serious problem that affects not only South America but the rest of the world is illegal drugs. Many South American farmers know that they can make more money growing plants used to make illegal drugs than from growing legal crops. Marijuana plants and the plants used to make cocaine bring farmers lots of money. These illegal drugs are shipped to the United States, Canada, and Europe. Sometimes, the police and government officials take money from drug dealers. Drug dealers use fear to continue to trade drugs for money. Columbia has lots of illegal drug problems.

A third challenge that many South American countries face is the growing power of the military. South America has a history of weak governments. Often, the military fights with the elected government. When that happens, military leaders sometimes take over. The governments of Venezuela, Ecuador, and Colombia have troubles with military force.

Lesson 4 Review On a sheet of paper, write the letter of the answer that correctly completes each sentence.

1. ___c___ is the growing of crops for money on large farms with many machines.

    A Sugarcane   **C** Agribusiness
    B Chemicals   **D** subsistence

2. The world's largest exporter of oranges is ___B___.

    A Ecuador   **C** Argentina
    B Brazil   **D** Columbia

3. One of Brazil's biggest manufacturing industries is the making of ___D___.

    A jewelry   **B** books   **C** computers   **D** cars

4. The world's leading exporter of copper is ___c___.

    A Columbia   **B** Argentina   **C** Chile   **D** Ecuador

5. The selling of illegal ___A___ is a problem that affects the whole world.

    A drugs   **B** medicine   **C** latex   **D** rubber

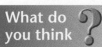

What do you think

What do you think is the best way for the United States to discourage the producing of illegal drugs in South America?

The Music of Peru

Many South American countries are affected by American culture. Fast-food chains are everywhere. Televisions show American programs. Radio stations in most countries play some music by American bands. Teenagers in many parts of South America accept this American influence. But teens in Peru have tried to keep their traditional culture. They might have fast food as a snack, for example. However, they rarely eat fast food instead of a home-cooked meal like rice with chicken and vegetables. Perhaps the most powerful sign of Peruvian teens' loyalty to their culture is their dedication to their music.

In the 1970s, Peruvians did listen to American-generated disco. But since then, large numbers of people from the rural areas have moved into cities such as Lima. And they brought their music with them.

Chica music originated in the jungle regions of Peru. It is a combination of *salsa* and *cumbia*—a dance in Columbia and Panama. Mountain music is known as *huaynas* or *huayno,* also called *música serrana.* It includes instruments such as local flutes, drums, and trumpets. Most people consider this real Peruvian music.

Chica and *música serrana* are welcome by all social classes of Peruvians. Teenagers especially love it. *Chica,* not American or other international music, continues to be at the top of the charts in Peru. The one exception to this is the influence of African music, which many teens also enjoy.

Teenagers in Peru enjoy their music together at dance clubs. Signs outside the clubs tell people which age group the club is for. And while there are no age restrictions, most people inside will be whatever the posted age suggests. One popular dance is the *zapateo,* the traditional dance to accompany *música serrana.* The *zapateo,* characterized by fast foot stomping, is enjoyed by teens throughout the country. These teens literally keep this culture alive and kicking.

Wrap-Up

1. How has the movement of people from the jungles and mountain regions influenced Peruvian musical preferences?

2. Besides music, what is another way in which Peruvian teenagers stay loyal to their own traditions?

■ South America is one of the world's seven continents. South America has three regions based on location: Caribbean South America, Atlantic South America, and Pacific South America.

■ South America has three physical regions. The Andes Mountains are a series of high mountain ranges on its western side. Plains stretch eastward from the foothills of the Andes to the Atlantic coast. Brazil has lowlands and plateaus.

■ South America has three large river systems: the Amazon, the Río de la Plata, and the Orinoco. No river in the world carries more water than the Amazon. It has over 1,000 tributaries.

■ South America has many climates. Much of it has a tropical climate that is either rain forest climate or savanna. The east coast has a temperate climate. Patagonia has a dry, cold climate.

■ South America has three cultural regions: Indo-America, Afro-America, and Euro-America. Many descendants of native people live in Bolivia, Peru, Ecuador, and Colombia (Indo-America).

Many descendants of African slaves live on the northern coast of South America and the east coast of Brazil (Afro-America). Many descendants of Europeans live in southern Brazil, Paraguay, Uruguay, Argentina, and Chile (Euro-America).

■ Christianity is South America's main religion. However, many native people have kept their own religions. Other people practice all the main religions of the world.

■ People from Spain settled in much of South America, so Spanish is the most common language. However, people also speak native and European languages. Portugal sent settlers to Brazil, so its people speak Portuguese.

■ Most South Americans live on farms or in small towns. However, many are now migrating to urban areas.

■ South America's economy depends on agriculture and industry. South America's chief natural resources are oil, minerals, rich farmland, and rain forests.

■ The cutting down of the rain forests is an environmental problem for South America. Its social problems include poverty, a rising birthrate, the selling of illegal drugs, and the growing power of the military.

Chapter 7 REVIEW

Word Bank

Amazon 3
Andes 2
Brazil 5
Pangaea 1
Spanish 4

On a sheet of paper, use the words from the Word Bank to complete each sentence correctly.

1. Geographers believe one huge land mass called _____ was in Earth's ocean.

2. The _____ Mountains are the longest mountain system in the world.

3. The _____ River carries more water than any other river in the world.

4. Many people in South America speak _____.

5. Rio de Janeiro and São Paulo are the two largest cities in _____.

On a sheet of paper, write the letter of the answer that correctly completes each sentence.

6. The largest country in South America is __D__.

    A Argentina   **B** Peru   **C** Colombia   **D** Brazil

7. Most of South America has a __A__ climate.

    A tropical   **B** steppe   **C** temperate   **D** dry, cold

8. The tallest waterfall in the world is __B__ Falls in Venezuela.

    A Andes   **B** Angel   **C** Niagara   **D** Amazon

9. Most of the Africans brought to South America came as __A__.

    A slaves   **C** immigrants
    B settlers   **D** sailors

10. The poorest people in South America are the __D__.

    A Americans   **C** Euro-Americans
    B Afro-Americans   **D** Indo-Americans

On a sheet of paper, write the answer to each question. Use complete sentences.

11. What are some main physical features of South America?

12. What are the major cash crops grown in South America?

13. Why does South America have several cultures?

Critical Thinking On a sheet of paper, write your response to each question. Use complete sentences.

14. Why do you think Brazil is the most industrialized country in Latin America?

15. Why do you think that multinational corporations like to invest in companies in South America?

Applying the Five Themes of Geography

Interaction

How did the Europeans who came to South America affect the cultures?

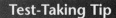

Test-Taking Tip

When studying for a test, review any worksheets, tests, quizzes, Lesson Reviews, or Chapter Reviews you completed that cover the same information.

Baseball—A Big Hit in Latin America

Americans often think of baseball as America's game. Actually, the sport is played all over the world. Many players from other countries also play baseball in the United States. Today, players from other countries play for every American major league baseball team. In 1997, 20 percent of the baseball players came from other countries. By 2006, the percentage had grown to 27 percent. In other words, more than one out of every four baseball players in the major leagues was from another country.

In 2006, these players came to the United States from 15 different countries. Many of these were Latin American countries. The small Caribbean country of the Dominican Republic sent 85 players to the United States. This was the most of any country. Venezuela had the next highest total with 43 players and Puerto Rico follows with 33. Even tiny Panama sent nine. If you add up all the Latin American players in the major leagues on the 2006 Opening Day rosters, you get a grand total of 190.

As these numbers show, baseball is popular in Central America and the Caribbean. The people do not have good playing fields and equipment, but they do have talent. Most U.S. baseball teams send scouts to these areas. These scouts search for good players who want to play ball in the United States.

The major baseball leagues in the United States have set up camps in Central America and in the Caribbean. The Dominican Republic, Puerto Rico, and Mexico all have camps. These camps develop the talent of the players in this area of the world.

The young men who reach the major leagues are lucky. Some of them become stars and earn a lot of money. A few of these players, like Carlos Zambrano and Albert Pujols, return to their homeland each year. There, they have built schools and hospitals to help their people.

Wrap-Up

1. Where is baseball played?

2. Is the percentage of baseball players from other countries increasing or decreasing?

3. Which Caribbean country had the most major league players in 2006?

4. How do the major leagues discover and develop baseball players from Central America and the Caribbean?

5. What have some players done to help their homeland countries?

- Latin America includes Mexico, Central America, the Caribbean, and South America. Mexico is south of the United States. Central America is south of Mexico. Central America and Mexico belong to the continent of North America. The Caribbean includes island nations southeast of the United States. South of Central America is South America, one of Earth's seven continents.

- Mexico has four physical regions. Central America and the Caribbean have two. South America has three physical regions.

- The main physical feature in Mexico is its mountains, the Sierra Madre. The Andes Mountains are the main physical feature in South America. Central America also has high mountains. Most Caribbean islands are inactive volcanic mountain tops.

- Much, but not all, of the climate in Latin America is tropical. Its mountain ranges have many different climates.

- Descendants of native groups make up part of the population of Latin America. The mestizos, descendants of Spaniards and native people, make up 75 percent of Mexico. Mestizos also live in Central America, the Caribbean, and South America. Descendants of native groups, European settlers, and African slaves live in South America.

- Roman Catholicism is the main religion of Mexico and South America. Christianity is practiced in Central America and the Caribbean. Many native people have kept their own religions.

- Mexico's official language is Spanish. Many people also speak Spanish in Central America, the Caribbean, and South America. However, they also speak native and European languages or a mixture of the two, such as Creole.

- Over three fourths of Mexico's people live in urban areas. Most people of Central America, the Caribbean, and South America live in rural areas.

- Mexico's chief resource is oil. Central America and the Caribbean have forests, good weather, sunshine, and beaches. South America is rich in minerals, farmland, and rain forests.

- The economies of Central America and the Caribbean depend on agriculture and tourism. However the economies of Mexico and South America depend mostly on farming and manufacturing.

- The Caribbean, Central America, Mexico, and South America face many environmental problems. Mexico faces air and water pollution and deforestation. Central America and the Caribbean also face water pollution. The cutting down of the rain forest affects both Central and South America.

Unit 4

Europe: North, West, and South

In this unit, you will learn about Europe, a continent that is a mixture of old and new ways of life. This is a photograph of Positano, Italy, in southern Europe. It was a port city and fishing village that became popular with tourists in the 1950s.

In this unit, you will learn about the British Isles, where London is located, and the mountains of Norway and Sweden. Then you will learn about the lands across the English Channel—France, and other great nations of western Europe. Finally, you will read about the ancient cities of Rome in Italy and Athens in Greece. All of these places and more make Europe a very interesting and diverse place on Earth.

8

British Isles and Northern Europe

The British Isles are made up of two large islands and many small ones. Iceland, Norway, Sweden, Denmark, and Finland make up northern Europe. They could be called the Northlands because they are so far north. The people of this region enjoy a high standard of living.

Goals for Learning

◆ To describe where the British Isles and northern Europe are located

◆ To identify the most important physical features and climate of the British Isles and northern Europe

◆ To describe the culture and the people of the British Isles and northern Europe

◆ To describe the economy of the British Isles and northern Europe and their environmental challenges

---

Geo-Stats — Key Nations of the British Isles and Northern Europe

Nation: The United Kingdom

Population: 60,609,000
Area: 94,248 square miles
Capital: London

Nation: Sweden

Population: 9,017,000
Area: 173,732 square miles
Capital: Stockholm

Nation: Republic of Ireland

Population: 4,062,000
Area: 27,137 square miles
Capital: Dublin

Nation: Denmark

Population: 5,451,000
Area: 16,638 square miles
Capital: Copenhagen

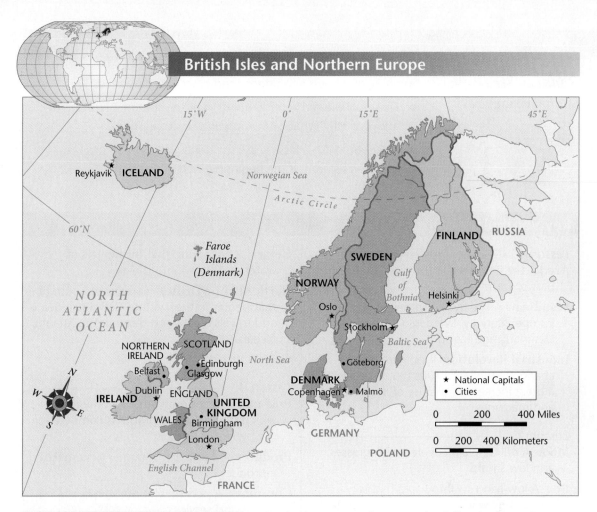

British Isles and Northern Europe

Map Skills

The British Isles include several islands off the coast of western Europe. The Republic of Ireland covers most of one of the large islands. England, Scotland, and Wales make up Great Britain, the largest island. Great Britain and Northern Ireland make up the United Kingdom. Northern Europe or Scandinavia make up the northern-most nations of Europe. Northern Europe is north and east of the British Isles and western Europe. Norway, Sweden, Finland, Denmark, and Iceland are in northern Europe.

Study the map and answer the following questions:

1. Which sea lies to the east of England?

2. Which body of water is between England and France?

3. What sea lies between Norway and Iceland?

4. Which two countries are side by side on a peninsula?

5. What is the capital of Iceland? Denmark? Finland?

Reading Strategy:
Summarizing

Summarizing helps you understand what you have read.

◆ First read the red subtitle question at the start of a lesson. Then ask yourself, "What is the answer to that question?"

◆ After you finish a lesson, ask yourself if you learned the objectives stated at the beginning of the lesson.

Key Vocabulary Words

Lesson 1

Arctic The cold area at the most northern part of Earth

Scandinavia The five countries of northern Europe: Norway, Sweden, Finland, Denmark, and Iceland

Industrial Revolution A nonviolent change in the late 1700s that included a great increase in the use of iron, steel, and machines

Lesson 2

Moor A rolling plain covered with grasses and low shrubs

Bog A low-lying swampy area that is covered by water for long periods of time

Peat Plants that have died and rotted; material burned for heat

Fjord A long, deep, narrow, U-shaped valley formed by glaciers that begins far inland and reaches the sea.

Geyser A hot spring that throws jets of water and steam into the air

North Atlantic Drift A warm ocean current that begins in the western Caribbean Sea and travels northward through the Atlantic Ocean

Gale A strong wind

Lesson 4

Free-market economy An economy in which the makers of products compete for the buyers of products

Producer A company or farmer who makes a product to sell

Consumer A person who buys and uses goods and services

Per capita income A way to measure how rich a country is by dividing total income by the number of people

Heavy industry Steel, heavy machinery, and other such industries

Objectives

◆ To know where the British Isles and Northern Europe are located

◆ To identify their physical and political regions

Where Are the British Isles and Northern Europe Located?

The British Isles are located between 50 degrees and 60 degrees north latitude. They lie off the Atlantic coast of western Europe. At one time, land connected the British Isles to the rest of Europe. A great glacier covered the continent of Europe. However, as Earth warmed, the ice melted. Then the run-off water became the North Sea and the English Channel. These two bodies of water now separate the British Isles from the European mainland.

Territories of the United Kingdom

Territory	Location	Area in Square Miles	Population
Anguilla	Caribbean Sea (Leeward Islands)	60	13,000
Bermuda	North Atlantic Ocean off of the coast of North Carolina	21	65,000
British Virgin Islands	Caribbean Sea (Greater Antilles chain)	59	22,000
Cayman Islands	Caribbean Sea	100	45,000
Channel Islands	English Channel	75	160,000
Falkland Islands	South Atlantic Ocean off of the coast of Argentina	4,700	3,000
Gibraltar	Strait of Gibraltar	2.5	28,000
Isle of Man	Irish Sea	221	73,000
Montserrat	Caribbean Sea	40	9,000
Pitcairn Island	Pacific Ocean	2	50
St. Helena	South Atlantic Ocean	47	7,000
South Georgia and South Sandwich Islands	South Atlantic Ocean	1,580	no permanent population
Turks and Caicos Islands	North Atlantic Ocean	192	26,000

Chart Study

This chart shows the many territories (not including England, Wales, Scotland, and Northern Ireland) that are part of the United Kingdom. Some are part of the British Isles, but many are not. What is the population of the Channel Islands? What is the largest territory? Where are most of the territories located?

The larger of the two main islands in the British Isles is Great Britain. Great Britain is divided into three countries—England, Wales, and Scotland. These countries, along with Northern Ireland and many smaller territories, make up the nation of the United Kingdom. The smaller of the two big islands is Ireland. It has two political parts. The Republic of Ireland, an independent country, is the southern part. Northern Ireland or Ulster is the northern part, and is part of the United Kingdom.

Northern Europe is north and east of the British Isles and western Europe. It stretches from about 55° to 73° north. Much of northern Europe is located in the cold area in the northern part of Earth called the **Arctic.** Iceland is a small island 645 miles west of Norway. The Norwegian Sea lies between Iceland and Norway. Norway shares a peninsula with Sweden. Geographers call this the **Scandinavian** Peninsula. Denmark is on its own peninsula called Jutland. The countries of northern Europe—Iceland, Norway, Sweden, Denmark, and Finland—are called the Scandinavian countries.

What Physical Regions Exist?

There are two physical regions in the British Isles. The first is the lowlands. The lowlands cover much of the southeastern half of the island of Great Britain. When the glaciers melted, the English Channel divided these lowlands from the plains that cover much of France and Germany. The second physical region is the highlands. They lie on the west and north of Great Britain. They include the old, worn-down mountains of Scotland and Wales.

Northern Europe includes four regions—the Scandinavian Peninsula, Finland, Denmark, and Iceland. These regions are both political regions and physical regions. Mountains cover much of the Scandinavian Peninsula. The Kjolen Mountains cover most of Norway. Much of northern Sweden is covered with highlands. Finland is located between the two branches of the Baltic Sea. Glaciers formed most of its land features. Most of the country is a flat plain with thousands of lakes and islands.

Denmark is another peninsula. It is one of the flattest countries in the world. Its highest point is only 568 feet. Like all the other countries in northern Europe, it has many islands. Greenland is the largest island controlled by Denmark. Most of it is covered by an ice sheet. Iceland is hundreds of miles away from the rest of northern Europe in the middle of the North Atlantic. It was formed by volcanoes millions of years ago.

What Political Regions Are in the British Isles?

The physical and political regions of northern Europe are the same. But the British Isles are divided into four political regions. The first is Ireland. The Republic of Ireland and Northern Ireland share the same island. For many years, all of Ireland was ruled by Great Britain. In 1921, the southern part of the island won its independence and became The Republic of Ireland. Northern Ireland chose to remain a part of the United Kingdom.

Reading Strategy: Summarizing

Can you now name the political regions in the British Isles?

The second political region of the British Isles is Scotland. It occupies the northern third of the island of Great Britain. Scotland is rough, yet beautiful. Few people live in some parts of Scotland. Scottish farmers have raised sheep for hundreds of years. Edinburgh, its capital, is one of Europe's banking centers. Almost 40 percent of Scotland's people live in Glasgow.

These sheep are in a field in the highlands of Scotland.

Industrial Revolution

A nonviolent change in the late 1700s that included a great increase in the use of iron, steel, and machines

The third political region of the British Isles is England. No place in England is more than 100 miles from the sea. Scotland and northern England have many beautiful lakes.

The English Midlands are in the center of the Great Britain. The **Industrial Revolution** started in these midlands. Between about 1750 and 1850, England went through a big change. New inventions like the power loom and the steam engine changed the way people worked. Britain had a lot of coal and iron ore and an excellent system of canals and railroads. Britain developed big shipbuilding, textile, and steel industries. Because of this, England became the strongest country in the world.

London, the capital of Great Britain, is located in the southern part of England. It is one of the world's greatest cities and is more than 2,000 years old.

Wales is the fourth political region of the British Isles. It lies on the western part of the island of Great Britain. Like Scotland in the north, Wales has a small population. It has rough highlands with wooded hills. Cardiff and Swansea, the two biggest cities of Wales, are located in its southern part.

Lesson 1 Review On a sheet of paper, use the words from the Word Bank to complete each sentence correctly.

Word Bank

Arctic
glaciers
Industrial Revolution
lowlands
Scandinavian

1. Much of the geography of the British Isles and northern Europe was shaped by _____.

2. The _____ is the cold area at the most northern part of Earth.

3. Norway and Sweden occupy the _____ peninsula.

4. The _____ cover much of the southern half of Great Britain.

5. The _____ was a nonviolent change in the late 1700s that included a great increase in the use of iron and steel machines.

What do you think ?

Can a country become industrialized without a good transportation system?

Moor

A rolling plain covered with grasses and low shrubs

Bog

A low-lying swampy area that is covered by water for long periods of time

Peat

Plants that have died and rotted; material burned for heat

Fjord

A long, deep, narrow, U-shaped valley formed by glaciers that begins far inland and reaches the sea

Geyser

A hot spring that throws jets of water and steam into the air

What Are Great Britain's Physical Features?

The British Isles have no tall mountains. The highest mountain is Ben Nevis. This Scottish mountain is 4,406 feet tall. The Pennines mountain range extends from Scotland into England.

The highlands area in the north of Scotland consists of **moors**. Moors are rolling plains covered with grasses and low shrubs. On the moors are **bogs**—wet, swampy areas. These low-lying areas are covered with water for long periods of time. The plants that grow there become **peat** when they die and rot. Peat can be burned for fuel. The bogs are important for wildlife, especially birds. Ireland has large areas of bogs.

What Are Northern Europe's Physical Features?

A well known physical feature of Norway and Iceland are the **fjords**. These are deep, U-shaped valleys formed by glaciers. They are long and narrow and bordered by steep cliffs.

Islands are a second feature of northern Europe. In fact, volcanoes near Iceland are still forming islands. More than 150,000 islands dot the Norwegian coast. Denmark has over 400 islands. No one lives on most of these islands. However, Stockholm, Sweden's capital, is built on 14 islands.

Mountains are a third important feature. Iceland is on the Mid-Atlantic Ridge, an underwater mountain chain. Norway has Europe's second highest mountains. They are called the Jotunheimen, or "Land of the Giants."

Geysers are a fourth important land feature. They are common in Iceland. A geyser is a hot spring that throws jets of water and steam into the air. Underground heat makes the water hot. When the pressure underground becomes too great, the hot water and steam erupt, or burst out of the ground. The people of Iceland make good use of this geothermal energy source. Most Icelandic homes and businesses have geothermal heat and hot water systems.

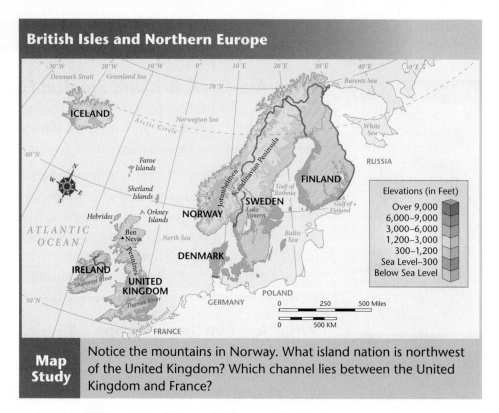

British Isles and Northern Europe

Elevations (in Feet)
Over 9,000
6,000–9,000
3,000–6,000
1,200–3,000
300–1,200
Sea Level–300
Below Sea Level

Map Study Notice the mountains in Norway. What island nation is northwest of the United Kingdom? Which channel lies between the United Kingdom and France?

Reading Strategy:
Summarizing

Why is water a big part of the history of this region?

What Bodies of Water Exist?

England's longest river is the Thames. It is short, but one of the most famous rivers in the world. It begins in the hills of southwestern England and flows to the capital city of London. The Shannon River, the longest river in the British Isles, is in Ireland. Scandinavia has many small rivers, but none that can be traveled by ships.

The British Isles and northern Europe have many lakes. Glaciers formed most of them. Lake Windermere is the largest lake in England. Northern Europe has thousands of lakes. Many are so small they have no name. Finland has large areas of marshy bogs. Lake Vanern in Sweden is northern Europe's largest lake.

The people who live in the British Isles and northern Europe have a long history of going to sea. Many explorers who traveled the world began their trip from the British Isles. Northern Europe also had great explorers, traders, and warriors. The location near the sea made fishing a good way to make a living.

North Atlantic Drift

A warm ocean current that begins in the western Caribbean Sea and travels northward through the Atlantic Ocean

Gale

A strong wind

Reading Strategy:
Summarizing

What is the climate like in northern Europe?

What Is the Climate Like?

The British Isles and northern Europe lie as far north as parts of Canada. However, the British Isles and the coastal areas of northern Europe enjoy cool to mild weather. The **North Atlantic Drift** warms the air above it. This drift is the warm ocean current that begins in the western Caribbean Sea and travels northward through the Atlantic Ocean. It brings warmth to the western shores of Great Britain. In fact, palm trees grow in some parts. This area and Norway's coastal areas have a marine West Coast climate. This climate has warm summers and cool winters. About the same amount of rain falls every month of the year.

Southern and central Sweden, where most of the people live, also has a moderate climate, as does much of southern Finland. No town in Denmark is more than 50 miles from the sea. This keeps the weather warmer than it would be if it were not close to the sea.

The weather in the Scottish highlands and Wales changes quickly. Rain falls year-round. Strong winds, called **gales**, often blow there in the winter months.

What Is the Midnight Sun?

The countries of northern Europe lie far north. Some areas are within the Arctic Circle. During the summer months, there is almost continuous daylight. However, in the winter they have mostly darkness. Northern Europe is called "the land of the midnight sun" because of its long summer days.

This beautiful fjord in Norway begins inland and continues to the sea.

The Chunnel

For over 200 years, people in England and France wanted to build a tunnel beneath the English Channel. This body of water separates the two countries. In 1986, work began. In 1994, the "Chunnel" opened. It connects Folkestone, England, with Coquelles, France.

The Chunnel is a 31-mile-long tunnel beneath the waters of the English Channel. (Channel + tunnel = Chunnel) About 24 of its 31 miles are 130 feet under water. The Chunnel has three tubes built side by side. The two outer tubes carry people and vehicles. The inner tube supplies fresh air. It also provides space for workers to do repair on the outer tubes.

Trains speed through the two outer tubes. One tube carries cars, buses, trucks, and their drivers. The second tube carries goods. The trip under the English Channel takes about 35 minutes.

Lesson 2 Review On a sheet of paper, write the answer to each question. Use complete sentences.

1. What is a bog?

2. What is a fjord?

3. What do the people of Iceland use for heat and hot water?

4. What causes the mild climate of the western shores of Great Britain and parts of northern Europe?

5. Why is northern Europe called the land of the midnight sun?

What do you think ?

What connection do you see between the United Kingdom's location and the fact that it became a world power?

Objectives

◆ To describe the cultures of Great Britain and northern Europe

◆ To identify the main religions of Great Britain and northern Europe

◆ To know the languages spoken by the British and northern European countries

What Cultures Are in the British Isles?

Like many nations, Great Britain is a mixture of different people. Many people are the descendants of people who settled there throughout history. Among the first were the Celts. Their descendants now live in Ireland, Scotland, Wales, and some parts of England. Roman armies from southern Europe sailed to England. Their ideas influenced the English language and ideas about government. When the Romans left, people from northern Europe settled in England. People from the tribes of the Anglos, Saxons, and Jutes became the English people. The Vikings and the Normans also influenced British culture.

Since the 1950s, immigrants have also come to the British Isles from countries that were once part of the British Empire. People have come from Africa, India, Pakistan, and the Caribbean.

Reading Strategy:
Summarizing

What details help you understand the culture of northern Europe?

What Cultures Does Northern Europe Have?

The Scandinavian cultures have shared a similar history for the last 1,000 years. Finland was part of Sweden for nearly 600 years; Iceland was a part of Denmark until 1944.

Most Scandinavians descended from Germanic tribes that settled in northern Europe hundreds of years ago. Denmark is the smallest country in northern Europe, but it has the highest population density. Most of Norway's people live along the narrow coastal plain. Most of Sweden's people live in southern Sweden. This is where its capital, Stockholm, is located.

Since the 1970s, Scandinavia has welcomed people from other countries. Today, people from the former Yugoslavia, Turkey, Vietnam, and the Middle East live in Scandinavia.

The Sámi are the largest minority group in Scandinavia. They were originally from Asia and are darker and shorter than most Scandinavians. About 30,000 Sámi live in Norway, Sweden, and Finland. In the past, the Sámi moved from place to place, following the herds of reindeer. Many modern Sámi now live in villages working at jobs besides reindeer herding.

The largest minority group in Scandinavia is the Sámi.

What Are the Religions in the British Isles?

Most people of the British Isles are Protestant Christians. Most people belong to either the Church of England or the Church of Scotland. Since many people have come to the United Kingdom from other countries, every major religion has followers there. Many Pakistani immigrants are Muslims. Most of the people in the Republic of Ireland are Roman Catholic Christians.

What Are the Religions in Northern Europe?

Most Scandinavians are Protestant Christians. The Lutheran Church is the official church of northern Europe. However, all Scandinavian countries give religious freedom to their citizens.

What Languages Do People Speak?

English is the official language of the British Isles. About half of the words in English come from the language of the Anglos and Saxons. The other half comes from French, Spanish, and Italian.

Most people in Ireland, Scotland, and Wales also speak English. However, some speak Celtic languages as well. Gaelic and Welsh, which about 500,000 people speak, are Celtic languages. Of course, many immigrants speak their own languages.

Icelandic, Norwegian, Swedish, and Danish are Germanic languages. In fact, a person who reads one of these languages can easily read another of these languages. English is also a Germanic language. These four northern European languages share many words with English.

The Finnish language is not like the four other languages of northern Europe. It is related to Estonian and Hungarian. Today, all Finns learn Swedish, which is Finland's second official language. In addition to their own language, all school children in northern Europe study English.

Danish is both what the people who live in Denmark are called and the language they speak.

Reading Strategy: Summarizing

Can you summarize the languages that the people in northern Europe speak and read?

Where Do People Live in the British Isles?

The island of Great Britain is crowded. Its population is about 60 million people. It has a high population density. Most of these people live in England.

Great Britain is an urbanized country; it has many big cities. Its largest and most important city is London. Other areas with many people are Birmingham, Manchester, and Leeds in England, and Glasgow in Scotland.

Where Do Northern Europeans Live?

Northern Europe has a low population density. Many big cities around the world have more people than any one of the Scandinavian countries. Most people live in urban areas. About one-third of the Swedish people live in the metropolitan areas of Stockholm, Göteborg, and Malmö. One out of every five Finns lives in the capital of Helsinki. One-fourth of all Danes live in Copenhagen. It is one of Scandinavia's biggest cities.

Celebrations

National Eisteddfod of Wales

The people of Wales, like the Irish, are proud of their Celtic roots. The Welsh have special meetings, called eisteddfodau. There, they speak Welsh, a form of Gaelic.

The National Eisteddfod is the largest of these meetings. It celebrates Welsh culture. It features contests in music, dance, arts, and crafts. The biggest contest is in poetry reading. Singing poets, or bards, have always had an important place in Welsh society.

Critical Thinking Why do you think bards have an important place in Welsh society?

Midsummer

Midnight is only half an hour away. It is Midsummer's Eve. Families are gathered on porches to wait for the sun to set. Almost everyone in Sweden has the day off because today is Midsummer.

Midsummer is a holiday celebrated throughout Scandinavia. It takes place on June 24. This holiday is a time for friends and family to get together. Often, they share a simple meal outdoors. They may have boiled, unpeeled potatoes. They may enjoy herrings, small fish from the North Sea. In some places, people decorate their homes with summer flowers.

Critical Thinking How does your community mark the beginning of summer?

Lesson 3 Review On a sheet of paper, write the letter of the answer that correctly completes each sentence.

1. The descendents of the Celts live mostly in _____.

A England and Iceland **C** Sweden and Norway
B Scotland and Ireland **D** Finland and Denmark

2. Almost all the people of northern Europe are descended from _____ tribes.

A Germanic **B** Russian **C** Estonian **D** Central Asian

3. The _____ are the largest minority group in Norway, Sweden, and Finland.

A Russians **B** Turks **C** Hungarians **D** Sámi

4. Most people of Britain and most Scandinavians are _____ Christians.

A Roman Catholic **C** Protestant
B Eastern Orthodox **D** Baptist

5. _____ is the only language in northern Europe that is not Germanic.

A Swedish **B** Norwegian **C** English **D** Finnish

What do you think

Is it a good thing to have people from other lands bring their language and religion to their new country? Explain your answer.

Objectives

◆ To describe the industries of Great Britain and northern Europe

◆ To identify the natural resources of the region

◆ To describe the problems the region faces

Free-market economy

An economy in which the makers of products compete for the buyers of products

Producer

A company or farmer who makes a product to sell

Consumer

A person who buys and uses goods and services

Per capita income

A way to measure how rich a country is by dividing total income by the number of people

Heavy industry

Heavy machinery, steel, and other industries

What Is a Free-Market Economy?

A **free-market economy** has **producers** and **consumers**. The producers are farmers and companies that make things. They compete for the business of consumers, the people who buy and use the producers' goods and services. The British Isles, northern Europe, and all the countries you have studied up to now have free-market economies.

If the free-market producers are right about what people want and need, they make money. If the producers are wrong, they may go out of business. In a free-market economy, the government usually lets producers make or grow whatever they like. However, the government may make a few rules for the producers. In this way, the government makes sure that the producers are fair.

There are several ways to tell how rich a country is. **Per capita income** is one way. This is dividing total income in a country by the number of people who live there. Based on per capita income, Great Britain and the countries of northern Europe are some of the richest countries in the world.

What Industries Are Important?

In the past, the economy of this region depended on farming and manufacturing. The largest number of workers in Britain made a living in its steel, heavy machinery, shipbuilding, and car industries. This is called **heavy industry**. Many of these heavy industries have not done well in recent years. However, several British-owned multinational corporations are among the world's largest industries.

This steel-making factory is located in Wales.

Northern Europe is still a big center of manufacturing. Sweden manufactures cars and trucks that are sold around the world. It is also a big producer of telephones. Both Sweden and Norway produce and export chemical products. Denmark makes and exports machinery and equipment. Finland produces wood products, electronics, and telephone equipment.

Shipping is a key industry in Britain and northern Europe because they are close to the sea. Norway and the United Kingdom are among the top ten shipping countries in the world. The fishing industry is very important to Norway, Denmark, and Iceland. Many people in these countries work in the fish processing industry.

Agriculture is important to the British Isles and Danish economies. Farmers are using new technology. That is, they are using science to make farming easier. With this new technology, they waste little time and energy. Because of this, the farmers of the British Isles are able to produce about two-thirds of the food the people there need. The other one-third comes from other countries. Denmark sells meat, meat products, and dairy products like cheeses and butter to other countries in Europe.

Reading Strategy:
Summarizing

Name the main industries in northern Europe.

Most jobs in Britain and northern Europe are service jobs. London has more banks than any other city in the world. It also has the largest insurance market. Great Britain is a leading developer of computer and software services. More than half of all Scandinavians work in service industries.

Sweden and Finland manufacture telephone equipment.

Many coal mines in Great Britain have closed.

How Does Trade Affect the Economy?

Trade is important to the people of the region. The countries there import and export many products and services. Major British exports include chemicals, electronics, aircraft parts, and computer-related products. London's Heathrow Airport is one of the busiest airports in the world. The United States and Germany are Great Britain's biggest trading partners. Northern European countries all export more than they import. Their biggest trading partners are the United States and other countries in Europe.

What Are Some Natural Resources?

Coal led to the rise of Great Britain as a great industrial power. It still has more coal than any other country in Europe. However, many of the coal mines have closed because they were not efficient. In 1975, workers found oil and natural gas under the North Sea near Scotland. Now, Great Britain has enough oil to meet its needs.

Northern Europe is rich in natural resources. Norway's most important resource is oil. It also gets oil and natural gas out of the North Sea. Today, Norway is Europe's largest oil producer, and exports both oil and natural gas. Most goes to other European countries.

Iron, copper, lead, and zinc have been found in northern Europe. Many of these minerals are in the far north. These minerals are hard to get to, so the countries of northern Europe don't mine as much as they could.

Forests and water are two other important resources in Scandinavia. Forests cover nearly three-fourths of Finland and half of Sweden. Both countries use their forests in large paper and pulp-making industries. Sweden is the world's third largest producer of paper products and pulp. The fast-moving rivers of the region also provide hydroelectric power.

What Are Some Environmental Problems?

The region faces the same environmental problems that other industrialized countries face. Many people worry about air and water pollution, destruction of natural areas, wasteful use of energy, and too much garbage.

In recent years some people have begun to worry about modern farming. They think that the chemicals farmers use harm the environment. The people of northern Europe are among the world leaders in protecting the environment. They recycle more aluminum, glass, and paper than most countries in the world.

What Other Problems Do They Face?

One big problem that Great Britain and northern Europe have is a low birthrate. As you know, a high birthrate can cause problems. It can keep a country from having a higher standard of living. A low birthrate is also a problem. Fewer babies are being born, but the number of older people is increasing. Many older people no longer work. The government spends money to help take care of them.

High taxes are a second problem. Many Scandinavian and British workers pay as much as 50 percent of what they earn in taxes. The governments use this tax money to help people who don't have jobs, to help older people, and for health care for everyone. This system allows all people to share their nation's wealth. But the economy may suffer if taxes are high.

Reading Strategy:
Summarizing

Summarize some problems the people in this region face.

Another problem is trying to absorb all the new immigrants moving to this region. Some people, especially the poor of the inner cities, dislike these new immigrants. Many workers fear that immigrants will take jobs away from them, because immigrants may work for less money. They think all workers may end up earning less money.

In Sweden, recycling bins are handy for people to use. Northern Europe leads the world in recycling.

Lesson 4 Review On a sheet of paper, write the word in parenthesis that makes each statement true.

1. In a (free-market, consumer) economy the maker of products competes for the buyers of products.

2. (Per capita income, Population density) is one measure of how rich a country is.

3. Most people in Great Britain and northern Europe work in (service, mining) jobs.

4. Great Britain has always had lots of (iron ore, coal), the mineral resource that helped it become an industrial power.

5. Low (birth, immigration) rate and high taxes are a concern for some Scandinavian and British people.

What do you think ?

Would a political party that makes the environment a main issue have much support in the United States? Explain your answer.

Great Graduations!

My name is Klara. I am 17 years old, and I live in Stockholm, Sweden. A few days ago, I graduated from upper secondary school. This is similar to "high school" in America. I know that Americans often have a high school graduation party. But here in Sweden, our celebrations last a little longer.

In early spring, the class agrees on a slogan or image to represent us. We have this printed on a T-shirt or a jacket. Then we wear that T-shirt or jacket often during the spring semester.

All spring, we give and attend dinner parties. These parties might be at our own homes, at restaurants, or at banquet halls. The banquet halls are more expensive, but they allow us to invite more people! Near the semester's end, we have festive breakfasts with our classmates and some teachers.

On graduation day, we wear our best suits or dresses, not graduation gowns. And we each wear a "studentmössor," which is a white cap with a black stripe and a yellow ring on the front.

After the ceremony, we move out onto the school steps to look for our families. They are easy to find. Every family holds large signs with huge photographs of us as young children. It is fun to see classmates as babies!

Graduates at nearly every Swedish school ride around on wagons decorated with birch branches.

We ride for several hours—laughing, yelling, and bragging about how great we are. It varies from school to school when this wagon-ride occurs. Sometimes the custom is to do it right after the ceremony. But at my school, we leave the ceremony with our families in a fancy vehicle. My family took me home in a rented limousine. I know one boy who rode home in a helicopter! I met my classmates later to ride around in the wagons, visiting parties.

I'm sorry to have the celebrating come to an end, but I'm excited about my future.

Wrap-Up

1. When does the celebrating begin for graduates of Swedish upper secondary schools?

2. What do Swedish graduates wear on graduation day?

- Two big islands and many small ones make up the British Isles. The largest islands are Great Britain and Ireland. Scotland, England, and Wales make up Great Britain.

- Glaciers once covered Europe. When these melted, their water formed the North Sea and the English Channel. These waterways divide the British Isles from mainland Europe.

- The British Isles have two physical regions: the lowlands and the highlands. The British Isles have many wetlands.

- The climate of the British Isles is a marine West Coast climate with mild weather. The main influence on the climate is the ocean waters and the North Atlantic Drift.

- Northern Europe or Scandinavia is five countries: Iceland, Norway, Sweden, Denmark, and Finland. Some parts are within the Arctic Circle.

- Volcanoes formed Iceland. Glaciers formed most of the land features of Norway, Sweden, Denmark, and Finland. Mountains cover much of the Scandinavian Peninsula. Denmark is one of the flattest countries in the world. Iceland has geysers, and like Norway, has fjords, islands, and mountains.

- Many people invaded the British Isles and settled there. Each influenced the culture. New immigrants have come from India, Pakistan, the Caribbean, and other places.

- The cultures of Scandinavia are alike. Most people are descended from Germanic tribes. All but the Finns speak a Germanic language. English is the official language of the British Isles. Each of the countries of northern Europe speaks their own language.

- Most people of the British Isles and northern Europe are Protestant Christians.

- Great Britain has a high population density, while northern Europe has a low population density. About 90 percent of the British people live in urban areas.

- Great Britain and the countries of northern Europe are some of the richest countries in the world.

- Great Britain has more coal than any other European country. Northern Europe is rich in natural resources, including oil and natural gas.

- Most people in Great Britain and northern Europe work in service industries. Manufacturing is important to Scandinavia.

- British Isles and northern Europe share the problems of a low birthrate, high taxes, and absorbing new immigrants. Their environmental problems such as air and water pollution are the same.

Word Bank

Arctic 2

fjords 4

Germanic 5

London 1

North Atlantic Drift 3

On a sheet of paper, use the words from the Word Bank to complete each sentence correctly.

1. The capital and leading city of the United Kingdom of Great Britain and Northern Ireland is _____.

2. The warm ocean current responsible for the mild climate of the British Isles is the _____.

3. Much of northern Europe is located in the _____.

4. The long, deep, narrow, ocean inlets that reach far inland in Iceland and Norway are _____.

5. Almost all the people of northern Europe descended from _____ tribes.

On a sheet of paper, write the letter of the answer that correctly completes each sentence.

6. The British Isles lie off the Atlantic coast of _____ Europe.

   A northern   C eastern
   B southern   D western

7. The most famous river in England is the _____.

   A Shannon   C Thames
   B Kjolen   D Avon

8. The _____ helped England become the strongest country in the world.

   A Industrial Revolution   C Northern Ireland
   B service industries   D fjords

9. _____ caused most of the physical features of northern Europe.

   A Glaciers   C Rifts
   B Aquaculture   D Plate tectonics

10. Most people in Britain and Scandinavia speak _____.

   A Celtic   B English   C Scottish   D Danish

On a sheet of paper, write the answer to each question. Use complete sentences.

11. Where are the British Isles located?

12. What are the five countries of northern Europe?

13. What are two important problems facing Great Britain and the countries of northern Europe?

Critical Thinking On a sheet of paper, write your response to each question. Use complete sentences.

14. Should the governments of the British Isles try to save languages like Welsh and Gaelic, which only a small number of people speak? Why or why not?

15. How would northern Europe be different if glaciers had not covered it during the last ice age?

Applying the Five Themes of Geography

Interaction

How is the link between England's huge deposits of coal and its rise to an industrial power an example of the theme of interaction?

Test-Taking Tip

When studying for a test, use the titles and subtitles in the chapter to help you recall the information.

9

Western Central Europe

Western central Europe has been important to world history. It has influenced world culture, religion, and industry in many ways. The countries of this region have had many wars, but are now working together instead of apart.

Goals for Learning

◆ To describe the geography of western central Europe

◆ To identify western central Europe's most important physical features and climate

◆ To describe the people and their diverse cultures

◆ To describe the economy of western central Europe and the environmental challenges it faces

---

Geo-Stats **Key Nations of Western Central Europe**

Nation: France
Population: 60,876,000
Area: 210,026 square miles
Major Cities: Paris (capital), Marseille, Lyon, Toulouse, Nice

Nation: Germany
Population: 82,423,000
Area: 137,857 square miles
Major Cities: Berlin (capital), Hamburg, Cologne, Frankfurt

Nation: Netherlands
Population: 16,491,000
Area: 16,023 square miles
Major Cities: Amsterdam (capital), Rotterdam, The Hague, Utrecht

Nation: Switzerland
Population: 7,524,000
Area: 15,941 square miles
Major Cities: Bern (capital), Zurich, Basel, Geneva, Lausanne

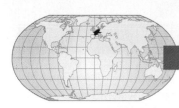
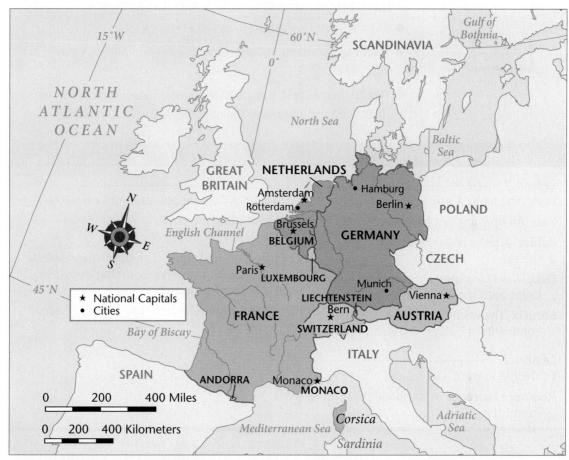

Map Skills

Western central Europe is a region of many countries. These nations have a rich history and beautiful lands. The people of this region have many cultures and speak different languages. Tourists come from all over the world to visit the many interesting countries.

Study the map and answer the following questions:

1. What is the largest country in western central Europe?

2. What is the capital of Germany? Switzerland? The Netherlands?

3. What country has Brussels as its capital?

4. What country borders both the North Sea and the Baltic Sea?

5. What countries are landlocked; that is, have no coasts on oceans or seas?

Reading Strategy:
Questioning

When you ask questions as you read a lesson, it is easier for you to understand and remember what you read. It will also help you become a more active reader. As you read, ask yourself:

◆ What can I expect to learn as I read this chapter?

◆ Can I apply anything I already know as I am reading each lesson?

◆ Are there things in this chapter about western central Europe that I can compare with the chapters I have already read?

Key Vocabulary Words

Lesson 2

Peak The highest point of a mountain

Pass An opening in a mountain range

Polder A piece of land that was once part of the sea

Dike A wall that prevents flooding and keeps back the sea

Eurasia The world's largest land mass; the continents of Europe and Asia together

Lesson 3

Dialect A form of a language

Romance language A language that comes from Latin

Lesson 4

Tariff A tax that countries put on goods they import

Currency A system of money

International trade The buying and selling of goods and services among people in different countries

Tide The regular daily rise and fall of ocean waters

Objectives

◆ To locate western central Europe on a map

◆ To identify the three physical regions of western central Europe

◆ To describe how geography shaped the region's history

Where Is Western Central Europe Located?

The countries of western central Europe include France, the Netherlands, Belgium, Luxembourg, Liechtenstein, Austria, Germany, and Switzerland. The Netherlands is sometimes called Holland. The region also includes two tiny countries. Andorra is located on the border between Spain and France. Monaco is on the coast of the Mediterranean Sea, surrounded by France. All the countries are located in the middle latitudes, between 43 degrees and 55 degrees north.

The North Sea and the English Channel are north of these countries. The countries of Poland, the Czech Republic, Slovakia, and Hungary lie to the east. The Mediterranean Sea and the countries of southern Europe are south of western central Europe. The Bay of Biscay and the Atlantic Ocean lie to the west.

Why Is the Area Important?

Western central Europe's location has helped it influence the world. It is near both Africa and some parts of Asia. For hundreds of years, people and goods have traveled to North and South America from the many ports of these countries. Explorers and settlers left these ports on long sea voyages around the world. These voyages spread European beliefs, cultures, and languages.

World War I, which was fought between 1914 and 1918, took place in western central Europe. Between 1939 and 1945, some of World War II was also fought there. These two wars were the largest that people have ever fought. Millions of people died.

The Berlin Wall divided free West Berlin from Communist East Berlin from 1961 until 1989.

What Are the Three Physical Regions?

Western central Europe has three physical regions. The largest region is the central lowlands. Geographers call it the Northern European Plain. This flat area extends from southern England to the Ural Mountains in Russia. The region is almost totally flat in the Netherlands, but somewhat hilly everywhere else. There are many rivers. Most people live in this region. It has Europe's biggest cities, such as Paris, Hamburg, and Munich.

The second physical region is the central uplands. It lies between the central lowlands and the Alps mountain range. This region stretches from the Atlantic coast of Spain to Poland. It includes central and eastern France. Most of Europe's coal is located in this area. Many industrial towns are located near the coal deposits.

Reading Strategy:
Questioning

Ask yourself, "Do I now know the three physical regions of western central Europe?"

The third physical region of western central Europe is the Alps. The Alps are Europe's highest mountains. These mountains stretch far beyond western central Europe. When people think of the Alps, they think of Switzerland. However, the Alps also cover parts of southeastern France, northern Italy, southwestern Germany, Austria, and Slovenia. Few people live there.

How Has Geography Shaped History?

Geography has played a big role in the history of western central Europe. For example, Switzerland has mountains. These high mountains allowed Switzerland to stay out of wars, because it is hard to travel through mountains. People who lived in mountain valleys developed their own culture because they were not near other people. The cultures often differed from that of the other people in their country. They often developed a different language. In fact, these people became more loyal to their region than to their country.

Having no mountains can also shape history. For example, soldiers have often marched into the plains of the central lowlands. They took over the land from the people who lived there. These armies used the many lowland rivers as highways. Of course, the people have always used these rivers to ship goods and to travel.

People who live in mountain valleys often have their own culture and their own language. Sometimes they are more loyal to their region than to their country.

Reading Strategy:
Questioning

Ask yourself, "How could geography influence history?"

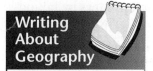

Writing About Geography

How does the geography of a place affect how people get along? Write a paragraph about your opinion.

What do you think ?

Can mountains protect countries as much today as they did in the past? Explain your answer.

How Did Geography Influence World War I?

World War I is a good example of how geography influences history. In 1914, Germany declared war against France. However, the border between the two countries kept German soldiers from attacking France directly. Thick forests covered much of the border; the rugged Vosges Mountains formed the rest of the border. This made the border hard to cross.

Belgium, a small neighbor of the two countries, wanted to stay out of the war. This was impossible, however, because of the French-German dispute. German generals decided that the best way to reach Paris, France, was to go through Belgium. They quickly took over nearly all of Belgium and the industrial area of northeastern France.

Lesson 1 Review On a sheet of paper, write the answer to each question. Use complete sentences.

1. What countries make up western central Europe?

2. How does the location of western central Europe explain why it has influenced the world?

3. What are the three physical regions?

4. In what region do most of the people live?

5. Why did Germany choose to go through Belgium to get to France in World War I?

Objectives

◆ To describe the Alps and other physical features of western central Europe

◆ To identify the region's bodies of water

◆ To describe the region's climate

Peak

The highest point of a mountain

Pass

An opening in a mountain range

Polder

A piece of land that was once part of the sea

Dike

A wall that prevents flooding and keeps back the sea

Eurasia

The world's largest land mass; the continents of Europe and Asia together

What Are the Main Physical Features?

The biggest physical feature of western central Europe is the Alps. This range of mountains is about 700 miles long and stretches across several countries. Mont Blanc is over 15,770 feet high. It has the highest **peak**, or highest point, in the Alps. Snow covers many of the peaks of the Alps. There are glaciers, waterfalls, and many streams in these mountains. There are many openings called **passes** through the mountains.

France, the largest of these countries, has other large upland areas. The Massif Central is located in the southeast-central part of France. This area of low, worn-down mountains and newer peaks covers about one-sixth of the country. France's other mountain ranges are the Vosges in the northeast; the Jura in the east; and the Pyrenees in the south on the Spanish border. Andorra is located in the Pyrenees.

Huge, sandy plains cover northern France and northern Germany. They stretch for hundreds of miles. In the Netherlands, the Dutch people have created **polders** by taking back land from the sea. For hundreds of years, they have built **dikes**, or walls to push back the sea and to prevent floods. They use huge electric pumps to keep the seawater from returning to the polders. Much of the Netherlands is polder land.

What Bodies of Water Exist?

Some people describe Europe as a giant peninsula because water surrounds it on three sides. The peninsula is on the western part of **Eurasia**, which is the world's largest piece of land. Eurasia includes the continents of Europe and Asia. Water surrounds this region on the north, the south, and the west.

The North Sea is a somewhat shallow sea that is really a part of the central lowlands region that is underwater. The Mediterranean Sea touches the southern coast of France. The Bay of Biscay forms the western shore. This bay is part of the Atlantic Ocean.

Reading Strategy:
Questioning

Do you already know some bodies of water in the area from what you have read so far?

Rivers are important to the area. People have traveled along the rivers and used them to move their products. The four most important rivers of France are the Loire, Seine, Garonne, and Rhône. The Loire is its longest river. It flows from the Massif Central to the Bay of Biscay. Paris, the capital of France, is located on the Seine, which flows into the English Channel. The Garonne flows from the Pyrenees to the Bay of Biscay. The Rhône starts in the Swiss Alps and flows into the Mediterranean Sea.

The three important rivers of Germany are the Rhine, Danube, and Elbe. The Rhine links northern and southern Europe. It is Germany's most important waterway. Every year, thousands of barges carry goods on this river. The Danube begins in Germany and flows nearly 1,800 miles eastward through nine countries in central and eastern Europe. Then it reaches the Black Sea. The Elbe flows from the southeast to the northwest. The great German harbor of Hamburg is located where the Elbe meets the North Sea.

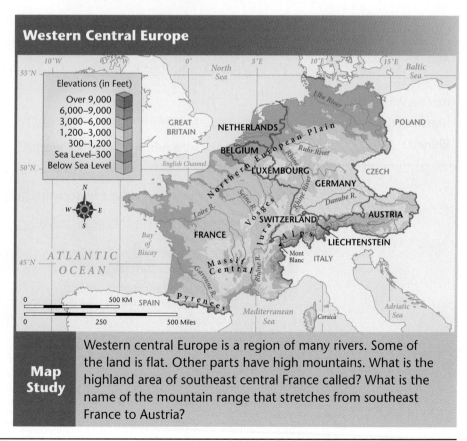

Western Central Europe

Elevations (in Feet)
Over 9,000
6,000–9,000
3,000–6,000
1,200–3,000
300–1,200
Sea Level–300
Below Sea Level

Map Study

Western central Europe is a region of many rivers. Some of the land is flat. Other parts have high mountains. What is the highland area of southeast central France called? What is the name of the mountain range that stretches from southeast France to Austria?

What Is the Climate Like?

Western central Europe has at least three climates. The main climate is marine West Coast. Northern France, Belgium, the Netherlands, Luxembourg, and Germany share this climate with the British Isles. The warm currents of the North Atlantic Drift make it neither too hot nor too cold. However, cold air from the north may cause temperatures to drop well below freezing. This is especially true in Germany.

Reading Strategy:
Questioning

Ask yourself, "Do I now know what climates are in this region?"

The area near the Mediterranean Sea has a different climate. The Mediterranean climate has mild winters and dry, hot summers. Areas like the French Riviera do not get really cold because of the mountains. The mountains block the cold winds from the north. Of course, the mountain areas have their own climate. Sometimes, strong, cold, dry winds blow down from the Alps. This wind, called the mistral, affects southern France. It can blow over 100 miles per hour and causes temperatures to drop quickly.

Lesson 2 Review On a sheet of paper, use the words from the Word Bank to complete each sentence correctly.

Word Bank

Alps (

Eurasia 3

marine West Coast 5

Massif Central 2

Rhine 4

1. The biggest physical feature of western central Europe is the _____.

2. The _____ covers about one-sixth of France.

3. Europe forms a peninsula on the western part of _____, which is the worlds' biggest piece of land.

4. Germany's most important waterway is the _____ River.

5. Most of western central Europe has a _____ climate.

What do you think ?

The Mediterranean Sea is warm. Why do you think its warmth does not affect more of western central Europe?

What Cultures Are in Western Central Europe?

Each country in western central Europe has its own rich culture. The people are proud of their language and of their influence on civilization. What is surprising about the area is how much the countries have in common. The day-to-day life of the people is similar. All the children go to school. Most parents work. Most people live in cities. The cities mix the old with the new. Some parts look the same as they did hundreds of years ago. Other parts have tall buildings and fast highways.

Europeans share an interest in music, art, and books. Most large cities have theaters, opera houses, art museums, and dance companies. In nice weather, people sit outside in sidewalk cafes where they share meals and talk. The area has a long history of making and enjoying delicious food. The people also enjoy sports. Football is a popular sport. Americans call this sport soccer. In mountain areas, skiing is popular.

Celebrations

The Salzburg Festival

Europe has been home to many great composers—people who write music. Perhaps the most well known one was Wolfgang Amadeus Mozart. Mozart was an Austrian composer born in 1756. He lived only 35 years, but he started writing music at the age of four. He created more than 600 musical works—many of them considered masterpieces.

The home in Salzburg where Mozart was born is now a museum. Every summer since 1920, the city of Salzburg celebrates Mozart's music. The Salzburg Festival brings more than 150,000 visitors to the city. At the festival, there are concerts, plays, and operas.

Critical Thinking How do festivals like this one affect a local economy?

What Languages Do They Speak?

Each country in western central Europe has its own language. Some of these languages are related. For example, German and Dutch, the language of the Netherlands, are Germanic languages. People in some parts of Switzerland, Austria, and Belgium speak a German **dialect**. That is, they speak different forms of the German language.

The people of southern Belgium, most of Luxembourg, and France speak French. This **Romance language** grew out of Latin, the language of the ancient Romans. Switzerland has four official languages. Most people there speak a German dialect. Smaller groups speak French and Italian. The fourth language is Romansh, a language also based on Latin. Many people speak several languages, including English.

What Religions Do the People Practice?

Most western central Europeans are Christians. Most are Roman Catholics. The rest are Protestants. These two groups have sometimes fought one another. The Thirty Years' War (1618–1648) was a religious war between the Catholics and the Protestants. Most European powers fought in this war.

Since the 1900s, immigrants have come to all the countries. People from northern Africa make up the largest immigrant group in France. Many people from Turkey have come to Germany. These immigrants bring with them a different culture, language, or religion. Because of this, all the major world religions can be found in western central Europe.

The people who live in the Netherlands are called Dutch. Dutch is also one of the languages they speak.

Reading Strategy:
Questioning

Ask yourself, "What do I already know about these religions?"

It took about 200 years to build Notre Dame in Paris, France. It is a landmark in Paris. Work started on the building in the 1100s and the church was completed in the 1200s.

This canal is in Amsterdam, which is the capital of the Netherlands.

Where Do Most People Live?

Most western central Europeans live in urban areas in the central lowlands. In fact, the area has one of the highest population densities in the world. People have been moving to the cities since the beginning of the Industrial Revolution. Several cities have populations of more than a million people. The largest city in western central Europe is Paris, France. In Germany, Hamburg, Berlin, and Munich have more than a million people each. Amsterdam, the capital of the Netherlands, is also large. Brussels, the capital of Belgium, is its biggest city. The Ruhr River region of Germany is a huge megalopolis of over 5 million people.

What Problems Do the People Face?

Western central Europe has an aging population. Its population is growing slowly. People are living longer. This means that more older people will need care in the future. Most governments believe that they have a duty to take care of the health and well-being of the elderly.

Reading Strategy:
Questioning

Ask yourself, "Which of these problems are the same as in other areas I've read about?"

A second problem is the economy. Economic growth in many of the countries has slowed down. France and Germany have a lot of unemployment. In the 1960s and 1970s, factories had lots of work but not enough workers. Because of this, they hired foreigners, or people from other countries. Now, some unemployed workers in France and Germany dislike these foreigners. They say that the foreigners are taking jobs away from them. Political parties in many western central European countries have spoken out against new immigration.

Geography in Your Life

Urban Planners

Since ancient times, people have planned how to make cities beautiful and easy to live in. The Industrial Revolution brought many people together in cities and led to slums. Urban planners then tried to bring a good water supply and waste system to these areas. They build parks so people have beauty in their lives. This park is in Brussels, Belgium.

Today, urban planners look at the whole city and try to make it better for everyone. They think of the flow of traffic. They set aside areas for the building of factories, tall buildings, apartments, and stores. They think of the height of buildings, which might block out the sun for the people below.

Urban planners study the needs of people. They study how people live and work in an urban area. They study how people get to work and get home. They also plan new cities.

Lesson 3 Review On a sheet of paper, write the word in parenthesis that makes each statement true.

1. The cultures of western central Europe share (much, little) in common.

2. The favorite sport of most of the countries is what Europeans call football and Americans call (soccer, baseball).

3. Switzerland has (two, four) official languages.

4. The largest city in western central Europe is (Berlin, Germany; Paris, France).

5. One big issue facing western central Europe is its (aging population, urban planners).

What do you think ?

Why is knowing and speaking more than one language a good thing?

Objectives

◆ To learn what the region's economy and trade are like

◆ To know their natural resources, industries, and environmental challenges

Tariff

A tax that countries put on goods they import

Currency

A system of money

International trade

The buying and selling of goods and services among people in different countries

Reading Strategy:
Questioning

Do you now know what international trade is? If not, reread the paragraph.

What Is the Economy Like?

All the countries of western central Europe have free-market economies and a large manufacturing base. Many of the countries have large service industries.

After World War II, France, Italy, West Germany, Belgium, the Netherlands, and Luxembourg wanted closer ties with one another. To do this, they agreed to get rid of **tariffs** and some trade barriers. A tariff is a tax that countries put on goods they import. In 1957, these countries created the European Economic Community, also known as the Common Market.

During the 1980s and 1990s the European Economic Community grew. In 1992, it became the European Union. The members agreed to reduce trade barriers even more. They also agreed to create the euro, which is a common European **currency** or system of money, for the member countries.

What Is International Trade?

Business people try to sell their goods and services for the highest price. They also try to find the cheapest way to make goods and deliver them to other countries. When they do this, they make more money. This explains why European explorers tried to find new lands. Columbus was looking for a better and faster way to get to Asia when he found the Americas. Europe could then more easily sell its goods to the people there. **International trade** is the buying and selling of goods and services among people in different countries.

People around the world want the products that are made in western central Europe. Germany exports machine tools, electrical equipment, chemical products, and cars. The world's leading maker of machinery for food and chemical processing is the Netherlands. The United States, England, Germany, and others buy these machines. Perfumes, fashions, and wines from France are world famous. France also exports machinery, transportation equipment, airplanes, chemicals and medicine.

What Natural Resources Does the Area Have?

Western central Europe has few natural resources. France, the largest western European country, has large coal and iron ore deposits, but many of its mines are closed. Importing coal from other countries is now cheaper than mining its own coal. Although France has some oil, it still has to import oil. France and Germany have fast-running rivers. Many of these rivers have dams that supply France and Germany with hydroelectric power. France built the world's first power station that depends on **tides**, the regular daily rise and fall of ocean waters.

Like France, Germany also has a lot of coal and iron ore. These resources helped to make the region an important maker of steel. Some of this coal is near the surface. Huge mines remove tons of coal at one time. Coal provides cheap energy, but it harms the environment. Like France, Germany must import oil.

The Netherlands is the only country in the area with large amounts of natural gas. The Netherlands uses about half of the natural gas it produces. It exports the rest to its European neighbors. The port of Rotterdam in the Netherlands is always busy. Many exports and imports pass through this harbor.

What Are Some of the Industries?

About one third of the region's land can be used for farming. European farmers are some of the most productive in the world. As their farms become bigger, they use more machinery. They grow many grains, especially wheat, oats, and barley. Another important crop is grapes, which they grow to make wine. France and Germany produce wine. The Netherlands is famous for its flowers and cheese. It exports flowers and dairy products around the world.

Western central Europe is one of the world's most important industrial areas. Its main industries are steel, automobiles, machines, textiles, and chemicals. The region is famous for its high-tech industries. However, most people work in service industries. Switzerland and Luxembourg are famous for banking.

Millions of people work in tourism in these European countries. Some work in hotels and restaurants; others work as guides, bus drivers, or taxi drivers. The historical places, beautiful scenery, and museums of the area appeal to many tourists. Some tourists like to hike or ski in the mountains. Others like to lie on the Mediterranean beaches.

What Environmental Challenges Exist?

Western central Europe faces the same environmental challenges as other industrialized countries. Among these are air and water pollution.

Automobile traffic causes air pollution. These countries could build more roads, but that would hurt the environment. Because of this, the countries of this region have invested a lot of money in railroads. They have some of the world's fastest and most comfortable trains. Many cities do not let people drive cars in their central business areas.

The rivers of western central Europe are badly polluted. As the population grows and river traffic increases, so does water pollution. The Rhine River is so polluted that many people do not want to eat its fish. One of Europe's biggest challenges is to stop the pollution.

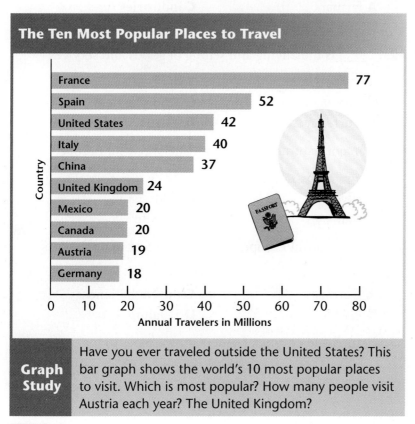

The Ten Most Popular Places to Travel

Country	Annual Travelers in Millions
France	77
Spain	52
United States	42
Italy	40
China	37
United Kingdom	24
Mexico	20
Canada	20
Austria	19
Germany	18

Graph Study

Have you ever traveled outside the United States? This bar graph shows the world's 10 most popular places to visit. Which is most popular? How many people visit Austria each year? The United Kingdom?

Skiing is a popular sport in Switzerland. These people are near the Matterhorn peak in the Alps.

Lesson 4 Review On a sheet of paper, write the letter of the answer that correctly completes each sentence.

1. The European Union is a group of _____.

   A farmers   **C** industries
   B steel workers   **D** countries

2. _____ is the buying and selling of goods and services among people in different countries.

   A International trade   **C** Trade barriers
   B Currency   **D** Tariffs

3. A major natural resource in western central Europe is _____.

   A silver   **C** gold
   B coal   **D** bauxite

4. Western central Europe's biggest producer of natural gas is _____.

   A Germany   **C** the Netherlands
   B France   **D** Belgium

Why is international trade important?

5. French and German farmers grow grapes to make _____.

   A fuel   **B** oil   **C** wine   **D** perfume

Pollution

When people think of the Mediterranean coast, they often picture clean beaches and blue water. In real life, scenes like this are fast disappearing. Rivers flowing into the Mediterranean Sea carry chemicals and industrial wastes. Countries dump garbage and sewage into the water. Oil tankers on the Mediterranean Sea have also spilled oil in the water.

The Mediterranean Sea is nearly surrounded by land. So, pollution that goes into the sea usually stays there. The pollution is also threatening the fishing industry. Some types of fish have disappeared. Many others have diseases. People who eat some fish caught in the Mediterranean Sea may get sick.

The countries around the Mediterranean can solve the problem. Sewage treatment plants could treat the waste. They can stop dumping garbage in the rivers. To solve the pollution problem, the countries that border the Mediterranean will have to cooperate, which will not be easy.

Wrap-Up

1. Why do you think countries have such a hard time cooperating to solve a common problem?

2. What is one way that the governments of the area could cooperate to reduce pollution?

Make a Difference

Most of us throw away more than we think we do. The garbage ends up in landfills. For one week, keep a list of everything you throw away. After a week, look at your list. Circle what you could recycle, reduce, or reuse.

University Bound

My name is Jantje. I am 14 years old and live in Amsterdam. I am in *groep 8* at my elementary school. *Groep 8* is like eighth grade in America. In the Netherlands, it is a very important year. My parents have told me this for as long as I can remember.

All Dutch students take a test at the end of *groep 8.* Our test scores and our teachers' recommendations determine where we go to secondary school. That is called high school in America. There are several different levels of secondary school including *VWO, HAVO,* and *VMBO.*

I am a good student. I hope my teacher recommends me for the *VWO* program. It is the hardest level to get into. After students finish *VWO,* they go to a university. University students study arts and science at a high level. No one in my family has ever attended a university. I hope to be the first.

The next hardest level of secondary school is the *HAVO* program. *HAVO* students spend their last two years studying in a certain subject area. This might be social science, natural science, culture, history, or something else. This helps prepare the student for special training at an *HBO* school. An *HBO* is not a university. *HBO's* prepare students for professional jobs in business, health care, trade, or social services. My sister attended *HAVO.* She is now in her first year at *HBO,* studying to become a social worker.

My brother is in the *VMBO* secondary program. Over half of all Dutch students are in this program. It provides general education in traditional subjects but also includes early training in the trades. My brother will study carpentry at another school when he finishes his program. Our parents were hoping he would get into *HAVO,* like my sister. But he was not accepted.

It is possible to advance to a different level of secondary school. But that takes an extra two years of schooling after finishing your program. This means it would take longer to get a job.

My parents want me to earn a good living someday. But getting there is hard.

Wrap-Up

1. What determines where a student will go to secondary school?

2. Why do you think Jantje's parents pressure him to do well in school?

- France, the Netherlands, Belgium, Luxembourg, Liechtenstein, Austria, Germany, and Switzerland make up western central Europe. These countries are south of the North Sea, east of the Atlantic Ocean, and north of the Mediterranean Sea.

- Western central Europe has three physical regions: the central lowlands, the central uplands, and the Alps.

- The main physical feature of western central Europe is the Alps. This mountain chain is about 700 miles long. It covers parts of France, Italy, Germany, Austria, Switzerland, Liechtenstein, and Slovenia.

- Northern France and Germany are areas of large plains. The people of the Netherlands have created land from the sea called polders.

- The climate of western central Europe is a marine West Coast. Cold air from the north and warm air from the North Atlantic Drift affect the climate. Areas near the Mediterranean Sea have a Mediterranean climate.

- Each country in western central Europe has its own language and culture. However, many of these languages are related because they are Germanic. Switzerland has four official languages. French is a Romance language.

- Most people of western central Europe are Christians. Most are Roman Catholics; the rest are mostly Protestants. However, immigrants continue to bring every major religion to the area.

- Most western central Europeans live in urban areas. This area has one of the highest population densities in the world.

- The countries of western central Europe have successful free-market economies. The European Union is a group of countries that work together to get rid of trade barriers and tariffs. This community of countries is uniting Europe.

- The main natural resources are coal and iron ore. Both France and Germany use their rivers for hydroelectricity. The Netherlands is the only country in western central Europe with large amounts of natural gas.

- Many people in this area farm. They raise grains, especially wheat, and grapes for wine. France and Germany produce wine. Western central Europe is one of the world's main industrial areas. However, most people work in service industries and tourism.

- Western central Europe faces the environmental problems of air and water pollution.

Word Bank

Alps ✓
Bay of Biscay ①
Germanic ⑤
Paris ③
Polders ④

On a sheet of paper, use the words from the Word Bank to complete each sentence correctly.

1. The _____ is part of the Atlantic Ocean.

2. The _____ are the highest mountains in western central Europe.

3. The largest city in western central Europe is _____.

4. _____ are lands that the people of the Netherlands made by pushing back the sea with walls.

5. Except for the French, most people of western central Europe speak a _____ language.

On a sheet of paper, write the letter of the answer that correctly completes each sentence.

6. The largest country in western central Europe is _____.

   A Germany   **C** Belgium
   B France   **D** Switzerland

7. The _____ River flows through Germany and links northern and southern Europe.

   A Rhône   **C** Rhine
   B Seine   **D** Loire

8. Most of western central Europe has a _____ climate.

   A marine West Coast   **C** continental
   B tropical   **D** highland

9. Most western central Europeans are _____.

   A Muslims   **C** Christians
   B Jewish   **D** Buddhists

10. The buying and selling of goods and services among countries is called _____.

   A bartering   **C** foreign policy
   B tariffs   **D** international trade

On a sheet of paper, write the answer to each question. Use complete sentences.

11. What are the three main physical regions of western central Europe?

12. Why do geographers think of western central Europe as a peninsula?

13. Where do most western central Europeans live?

Critical Thinking On a sheet of paper, write your response to each question. Use complete sentences.

14. Imagine that you work for a U.S. company involved in international trade. Why might knowing the French or German language help you in your work?

15. Why might some western central European countries be unwilling to join the European Union?

Applying the Five Themes of Geography

Region

Why might the European Union be considered a region?

Test-Taking Tip

Look over a test before you begin answering questions. See how many parts there are. Skim through the whole test to find out what is expected of you. Try to set aside enough time to complete each section.

Southern Europe

Southern Europe is small, but it is an important area. It contains the countries of Portugal, Spain, Italy, and Greece. Spain and Portugal once had great empires. Millions of people around the world speak their languages. Ancient Greece gave the world many ideas about government. Rome, the capital of Italy, gave the world ideas about laws.

Goals for Learning

◆ To describe where southern Europe is located

◆ To identify southern Europe's most important physical features and climate

◆ To describe the cultures of southern Europe and where most people live

◆ To describe the economy of southern Europe and the environmental challenges it faces

Geo-Stats   Southern Europe

Nation: Greece
Population: 11,130,000
Area: 50,962 square miles
Major Cities: Athens (capital), Thessaloníki, Piraeus, Patras

Nation: Portugal
Population: 10,606,000
Area: 35,672 square miles
Major Cities: Lisbon (capital), Porto, Amadora

Nation: Italy
Population: 58,134,000
Area: 116,324 square miles
Major Cities: Rome (capital), Milan, Naples, Turin

Nation: Spain
Population: 40,398,000
Area: 194,897 square miles
Major Cities: Madrid (capital), Barcelona, Valencia, Seville

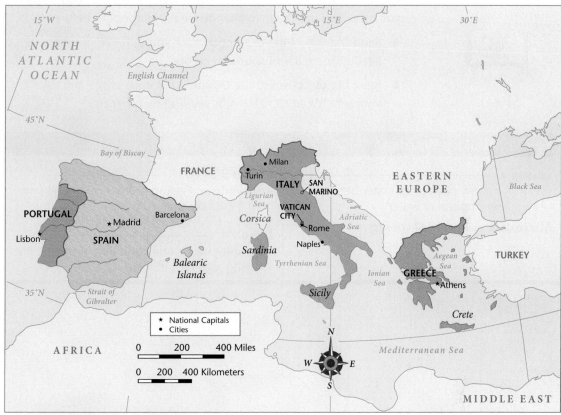

Map Skills

Southern Europe lies along the northern coast of the Mediterranean Sea. It is made up of the countries of Spain, Portugal, Italy, and Greece. The tiny countries of San Marino and Vatican City are also in southern Europe. Ancient Greece and Italy's ancient Rome are two of the oldest civilizations in the world. Some buildings from these civilizations still stand today. Like western Europe, many tourists visit southern Europe for its beauty and history.

Study the map and answer the following questions:

1. What sea lies to the east of Italy?

2. What is the capital of Greece? Italy? Spain? Portugal?

3. Between what degrees of latitude and longitude is most of southern Europe located?

4. Geographers often call southern Europe and northern Africa the Mediterranean Region. Why does this name fit?

5. Why is the Mediterranean Sea important to the countries of southern Europe?

Reading Strategy:
Predicting

When you predict something, you tell in advance what something may be. When you read something, you use what you already know and what you see to tell what you think you will read. After you read, you may have to change what you thought beforehand.

◆ Read the title of the chapter and ask yourself, "What do I already know about southern Europe?"

◆ Read the objectives at the beginning of each lesson and ask yourself, "What can I learn by reading this chapter?"

Key Vocabulary Words

Lesson 1 ————————————————

Strait A narrow passage of water between two larger bodies of water

Microstate A very small country

Lesson 3 ————————————————

Regionalism Feeling more loyal to one part of a country than to the whole country

Lesson 4 ————————————————

Unemployment The condition of people not being able to find jobs

---

Strait
A narrow passage of water between two larger bodies of water

Microstate
A very small country

The Italian peninsula is shaped like a boot.

Reading Strategy:
Predicting

Before you read this paragraph, what do you think the political regions are in southern Europe?

Where Is Southern Europe Located?

Most of southern Europe is located between 35 degrees and 45 degrees north of the equator. The area is sometimes called Mediterranean Europe because the countries of southern Europe are located on the Mediterranean Sea.

What Are Southern Europe's Physical Regions?

Three peninsulas make up southern Europe: the Iberian Peninsula, the Italian peninsula, and the Balkan Peninsula. These peninsulas are the three physical regions.

Spain and Portugal make up the Iberian Peninsula. Like all peninsulas, water surrounds it on three sides. The Bay of Biscay lies to the northwest. The Mediterranean Sea borders the east and south. The Atlantic Ocean touches the western coast of the peninsula. The **Strait** of Gibraltar links the Atlantic Ocean with the Mediterranean Sea. A strait is a narrow passage of water between two larger bodies of water. The Strait of Gibraltar is between Spain and northern Africa.

The Italian peninsula is surrounded by four seas, each a part of the Mediterranean Sea. The Adriatic Sea lies to the east. The Ionian Sea separates Italy from Greece in the southeast. The Tyrrhenian Sea lies off Italy's western coast, north of Sicily. The Ligurian Sea borders the northwestern coast.

The Balkan Peninsula is also bordered by seas. The Ionian Sea touches the western coast of Greece. The Aegean Sea is between Greece and Turkey and is part of the Mediterranean Sea. The Aegean Sea stretches from northeastern Greece to Crete, which is Greece's largest and southernmost island. Greece is the most southern part of the Balkan Peninsula.

What Political Regions Exist?

The four major nations of southern Europe are Spain, Portugal, Italy, and Greece. The tiny **microstate** of San Marino is also part of this region.

Spain is the largest of the countries. More than half of the country is a dry plateau that geographers call the *Meseta* or tableland. The *Meseta* receives little rainfall. Summers are hot. The region has little vegetation and is hard to farm. Most people in Spain live on coastal lowlands on the edge of the *Meseta*. The *Costa Brava,* or Rough Coast, lies in the north of Spain. To the south is the *Costa del Sol,* which means Coast of the Sun. Its year-round sunshine draws thousands of tourists.

Portugal's land looks a lot like Spain's. Much of it is a dry highland. Geographers call southern Portugal the Algarve. Northern Portugal receives more rain than the Algarve. Northern Portugal also has fertile soil and good farmland.

Mountains cover more than three-fourths of Italy and Greece. Most people in Italy live in mountain valleys or coastal plains. The western plains of Italy's Tyrrhenian coast are good for farming. In the south, the plains used to be swampy and marshy. However, farmers drained the swamps and marshes to create new farmland. Since most Greeks live on the coast, Greek farmers also drained swampy areas to create farmland.

Geography in Your Life

The Influence of Greek and Roman Architecture

Architecture is the art of designing and building places where humans live and work, worship, and do business. The ancient Greeks and Romans developed many styles of architecture and many ways to enclose space. Greek architects gave civilization three different styles with very different looking columns. They used them to build their temples for worship. Using the classical stone architecture of the Greeks, Romans put up buildings across Europe. Romans perfected the use of the arch, dome, and vault, which allowed them to cover large open spaces.

Today, architects still use columns, arches, domes, and vaults in buildings. They use them to build banks, colleges, government buildings, subways, and churches. If you visit Washington DC, you can see the great dome on the Capitol. The Romans gave us the idea for that. Look upward as you walk between its tall columns. We got the idea for those columns from the Greeks.

How Did Geography Shape History?

Because of the rugged land in which they lived, the people of southern Europe have always used the sea. These countries share a long history of sailing. The ancient Greeks were among the first people to trade with others by sailing the Mediterranean. During the 1300s and 1400s, Italian ships sailed on this sea. Merchants brought silks and spices overland from India and China to the eastern end of the Mediterranean Sea. Then Italian ships carried them to Italy and sold them in cities like Venice, Pisa, and Genoa.

Reading Strategy:
Predicting

What have you read so far that would let you predict how the geography of the area has influenced its history?

Soon Spain and Portugal began looking for their own trade routes. They wanted to have silks and spices to sell. During the 1400s, Portugal began to search for a sea route to India and China. Portuguese sailors sailed south down the Atlantic Ocean toward the tip of Africa. They were the first explorers to go around the tip of Africa to get to India.

Spanish sailors also tried to reach Asia by sea. However, they sailed west instead of south as the Portuguese had done. Christopher Columbus, an Italian sea captain, sailed from Spain. He tried to reach India and its spices by crossing the Atlantic Ocean. Instead, he reached the Americas.

Lesson 1 Review On a sheet of paper, write the word in parenthesis that makes each statement true.

1. Another name for southern Europe is (Atlantic, Mediterranean) Europe.

2. A (strait, bay) is a narrow passage of water between two larger bodies of water.

3. The (Ionian, North) Sea separates Italy from Greece.

4. (Plains, Mountains) cover more than three-fourths of Italy and Greece.

5. Explorers from Spain and Portugal tried to find new trade routes to (India, Italy) and China.

What do you think ?

How might history be different if most of southern Europe had fertile farmland instead of mountains?

Objectives

◆ To learn the
main physical
features and main
bodies of water in
southern Europe
◆ To describe
the climate of
southern Europe

What Are the Main Physical Features?

Southern Europe has many mountain ranges. The Pyrenees Mountains separate Spain from France and western Europe. Some of these mountain peaks are over 11,000 feet high. The Cantabrian Mountains are in northern Spain. While not as high as the Pyrenees, the Cantabrian range is almost as long.

The Dolomites, or Italian Alps, are a mountain range that borders northern Italy, Switzerland, and Austria. Just south of the Po River valley, the Apennine Mountains form the backbone of Italy. They stretch from northern to southern Italy. The biggest mountain range in Greece is the Pindus Mountains.

Southern Europe

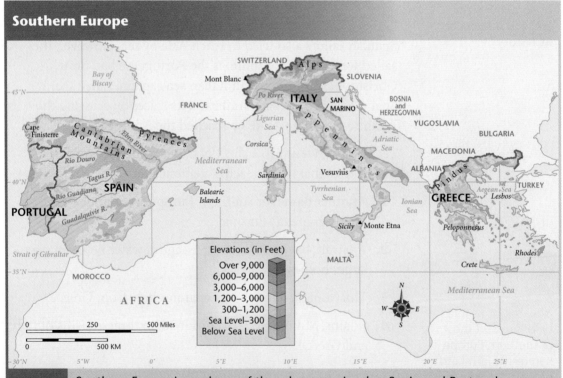

Map Study   Southern Europe is made up of three large peninsulas. Spain and Portugal are on the Iberian Peninsula. Italy and Greece are also peninsulas. What mountain ranges can be found in Spain? Which strait provides an opening for the Mediterranean Sea? What sea separates Greece from Turkey?

Southern Europe also has many islands. Greece includes an archipelago of over one thousand islands. In fact, islands make up about 20 percent of Greece. Its biggest islands are Crete and Rhodes in the eastern Mediterranean. The two largest islands in the Mediterranean are Sicily and Sardinia. They both belong to Italy. North of Sardinia is Corsica, which is part of France. Spain also has some important islands off its coast. The Balearic Islands are in the Mediterranean. The Canary Islands are 800 miles southwest of Spain in the Atlantic Ocean. They are only 70 miles from the northwestern coast of Africa.

What Are the Main Bodies of Water?

As you have learned, many seas touch the coasts of southern Europe. However, this area also has many rivers. Most of them are shallow and short. Portugal's most important river is the Rio Douro. Two important Spanish rivers flow out of the mountains. The Ebro and the Guadalquivir supply water for irrigation and hydroelectric power. Some of Spain's rivers dry up when rain does not fall.

The Po is the only navigable Italian river. The Po River valley has some of the best farmland in Europe. Other rivers in Italy are the Arno, the Tiber, the Dora, and the Taro. As in Spain, many of Italy's smaller rivers dry up in the hot summer months.

Reading Strategy:
Predicting

Based on what you have read, what do you predict the next page will be about?

Portofino, Italy, is a small town that tourists visit. Many people there fish for a living.

Greek rivers run short, winding from the highlands to the sea. None of them are navigable—large ships cannot sail on any of them. The Achelous is Greece's longest river. It is only 137 miles from beginning to end.

The most famous lakes of southern Europe are in Italy. Glaciers in the Alps formed them thousands of years ago. They include Lake Como, Lake Maggiore, and Lake Garda.

What Is the Climate Like?

Geographers usually describe the climate of southern Europe as Mediterranean. Summers are hot and dry; winters are short and mild. Rain usually falls in the winter. In fact, southern Europe has only two seasons: the dry season and the rainy season. However, some climate differences do occur in southern Europe. For example, more rain falls on its northern part than on its southern part. But, as a person travels south, temperatures remain about the same.

The height of the land also affects the climate. Mountain areas like the Alps receive more than 30 feet of snow a year. More rain and snow fall in the mountains, and temperatures are lower than on the coastal plains.

The best climate in southern Europe is probably on its islands. There, temperatures are almost the same throughout the entire year. Many tourists come to southern Europe every year because of the good climate.

Lesson 2 Review On a sheet of paper, write answers to each question. Use complete sentences.

1. What is the main physical feature of southern Europe?

2. What are the two biggest islands in the Mediterranean Sea?

3. What are two important rivers in Spain?

4. What is the climate of southern Europe?

5. Where do the temperatures remain almost the same the entire year?

Objectives

◆ To describe the main cultures of southern Europe

◆ To identify the religions of southern Europe

◆ To describe regionalism and why it is a problem

Reading Strategy:
Predicting

Based on what you have read in this chapter, what do you think may have shaped the cultures in southern Europe?

What Cultures Exist in Southern Europe?

Each country in southern Europe has its own culture. Spain, Portugal, and Italy are a mix of many people. Their cultures reflect the different people who once ruled the land. For example, Spain has several cultures, each one different from the other. Northern Spaniards descended from Celtic people. Southern Spain was strongly influenced by 700 years of Arab rule. Ancient Iberian tribes influenced the people of eastern Spain and Portugal. The Iberians were the first people in Portugal. Later the Celts and Romans arrived there. Still later, the Moors, Arab invaders from north Africa, overran Portugal and ruled the people there.

Most Italians have descended from the ancient Etruscans and Romans. During its long history, however, many different people have settled in Italy. Greeks sailed to the south of Italy and set up colonies. Later, Germanic and Norman people invaded Italy, defeated the people living there, and stayed.

The people of Greece call their country *Hellas;* they call themselves *Hellenes.* About 98 percent of the people of Greece have a Greek background. But people from other areas have also influenced Greece. Slavic people from the Balkans live in the northern part of the country. About 2 percent of the people living in Greece are Turkish. This is because the Turks ruled Greece for many years.

What Do Their Cultures Have in Common?

Southern European cultures share much in common. The people in Portugal, Spain, Italy, and Greece believe that the family is more important than anything else. They have extended families made up of parents, children, grandparents, aunts, uncles, and cousins.

Religion, history, and tradition play a big part in the lives of the people of southern Europe. Traditions are ideas, beliefs, and customs that people pass down to their descendants. Meals are an important part of daily life because they are a time for families to get together. Southern Europeans like good food—people all over the world like the foods of southern Europe.

What Religions Do They Practice?

Most people in Spain, Portugal, and Italy are Roman Catholics. Religious holidays are an important part of their culture. One of the biggest events in their year is Holy Week. This is the week that ends with the celebration of Easter.

More than 95 percent of Greeks belong to the Greek Orthodox Church. Most southern Europeans are Christians. Small groups of Jews and Muslims live in southern Europe.

The world center for Roman Catholics is Vatican City. It exists within the city of Rome, Italy. The pope, who is the head of the Roman Catholic Church, lives there. He runs Vatican City, which is an independent microstate.

Saint Peter's Square is a place for people to gather in Vatican City. Vatican City is within the city of Rome, Italy.

Regionalism

Feeling more loyal to one part of a country than to the whole country

Reading Strategy:
Predicting

Look at the subheads on this page. Predict what you think you will learn in this lesson.

What Languages Do These Europeans Speak?

All southern European languages, except Greek, are Romance languages that grew out of Latin. The people of Portugal speak Portuguese. Most people in Spain speak Spanish. The language of Italy is Italian. However, many people in Spain and Italy also speak a local dialect. Sometimes, people who speak one dialect do not understand people who speak another dialect. In Italy's border areas, many people speak German or French.

Where Do the People of This Region Live?

Before the 1940s, most southern Europeans lived in rural areas. After World War II, people left their farms and went to the cities to work in factories. Today, both Spain and Italy are very urban. Of the southern European countries, Italy has the most people. About 97 percent of Italians live in cities. In Spain, more than 90 percent live in cities. Portugal and Greece are more rural, but there too, more than half of the people live in cities.

Southern Europe has many big cities. Madrid and Barcelona are the two largest cities in Spain. About 2 million people live in each city. Italy's largest cities are Rome, Milan, Naples, and Turin. The capital of Portugal, Lisbon, has over 2 million people. More than one out of every three Greeks live in Athens.

What Problems Do the People Face?

One problem facing Spain and Italy is **regionalism**. That is, people feel more loyal to their part of the country than to the whole country. One example of this is the Basque people. They live in northern Spain. They speak their own language and have their own culture. Some Basques want to separate themselves from Spain. Regionalism is not as strong in Italy as in Spain.

Another problem is the large number of immigrants coming to the region. In the past, many people left southern Europe to live in other countries. Today, many people are moving to the region. Immigrants are coming from eastern Europe and from Asia. The long coast lines have made it easy for people to enter the countries from nearby Africa. The immigrants bring their own cultures, languages, and religions. But, they all need to find jobs and a place to live.

Celebrations

The Olympic Games

Ancient Greece was the site of the first Olympic Games in 776 B.C. The ancient Greek cities were usually at war with each other, but they agreed to stop fighting long enough to hold these games. Athletes, poets, musicians, and spectators gathered at a sacred place called Olympia. The first time they gathered, there was only one event—a short race. After that, Greeks held Olympic Games every four years and added more events. Athens, Greece, hosted the first modern games in 1896. Summer and winter games are now held two years apart in different cities in the world. The games celebrate strength and skill and let people compete without violence.

Critical Thinking In what ways are the modern Olympics like the ancient games?

Lesson 3 Review On a sheet of paper, write the letter of the answer that correctly completes each sentence.

1. Southern Spain was influenced by _____ rule.

    A French   **B** Arab   **C** Roman   **D** Germanic

2. Most southern Europeans are _____.

    A Greek Orthodox   **C** Muslim
    B Jewish   **D** Christians

3. The world center for Roman Catholics is Vatican City, which is located in _____.

    A Rome   **B** Lisbon   **C** Madrid   **D** Athens

4. The most urbanized country of southern Europe is _____.

    A Italy   **B** Portugal   **C** Spain   **D** Greece

5. Some Basque people want to separate themselves from _____.

    A Vatican City   **B** Portugal   **C** Spain   **D** Greece

What do you think

Which Italian foods do you like most and why?

Unemployment

The condition of people not being able to find jobs

What Is Southern Europe's Economy Like?

The economies of southern Europe differ. Spain, Italy, Greece, and Portugal are all members of the European Union. However, Italy is one of the richest countries in Europe; Greece is one of the poorest. Until World War II, all four countries had economies based on farming. Agriculture is still important in Greece and Portugal. Italy began to industrialize in the 1940s; Spain began in the 1960s–70s. Their economies grew quickly.

Unemployment is a problem in all the countries of southern Europe. Many young people in these countries cannot find jobs. A large number of immigrants from other countries adds to the unemployment problem.

What Are Southern Europe's Natural Resources?

None of the southern European countries are rich in natural resources. Italy produces some geothermal and hydroelectric power, but must import oil. Italy mines only mercury, sulfur, and marble in large amounts. It is the world's biggest producer of marble. People use Italian marble to build fine buildings.

Economy of Southern Europe

Country	People in the Workforce	Unemployment Rate	Exports (in billions)	Imports (in billions)	Key Industries
Spain	22 million	8%	$222	$324	textiles, clothing, automobiles, food, beverages
Portugal	6 million	8%	$47	$68	textiles, footwear, wood, pulp, paper
Italy	24 million	7%	$450	$445	tourism, machines, textiles, iron, steel
Greece	5 million	9%	$24	$59	tourism, food, tobacco processing

Chart Study This chart contains information about the economies of Spain, Portugal, Italy, and Greece. What is Spain's workforce? What is the unemployment rate in Italy? How much does Portugal export? How much does Greece import?

Biography

Galileo Galilei: 1564–1642

Many scientists call Galileo the founder of modern experimental science. This Italian astronomer and physicist made discoveries in mathematics and with a telescope. The law of freely falling bodies came from Galileo. Through experiments, he concluded that all objects fall at the same speed, no matter how big or heavy they are.

Galileo was the first scientist to use a large telescope to see the planets. He discovered new facts about the solar system. He confirmed the theory that Earth and the other planets revolve around the sun. Up to that time, people thought the sun revolved around Earth.

Spain uses its fast-moving mountain streams to produce hydroelectric power. Like Italy, Spain must import oil for its energy needs. It does mine some iron, coal, and zinc. Some mineral resources have been found in Portugal.

The most important mineral found in Greece is bauxite, which is used to produce aluminum. Oil has been discovered near some Greek islands. However, Turkey and Greece disagree as to who owns the rights for this oil.

What Are Some Major Industries?

Reading Strategy: Predicting

Based on what you have learned about southern Europe, can you predict what some of their industries are?

Agriculture is still an important part of the economy of Portugal, Spain, and Greece. Portugal is the world's leading producer of cork, which comes from cork oak trees. Spain and Greece export grain, olives, vegetables, and grapes. Fishing industries are important in Portugal and Greece. Shipping is also important to the Greek economy.

Thousands of people in southern Europe leave the countryside each year and move to factory jobs in the big cities. Other European Union countries have started manufacturing businesses in Spain. They have done this because Spanish people work for less money than German or French people.

An important Italian industry is textiles. Workers produce silk, cotton, and wool. People around the world buy Italian clothes and shoes. Italy also has a large chemical industry. Italian-made motorcycles and cars are sold everywhere.

Tourism is important to the region. Tourists come to see the ruins of ancient buildings and other historical sites. They also enjoy the swimming, fishing, sailing, and the weather.

What Environmental Challenges Exist?

The most serious environmental problem is water. In Spain and Greece, the problem is too little water. In Italy, the problem is too much water. The government has spent millions of dollars to try to stop flooding. No other place like Venice exists on Earth. The Italian city was built on supports in the Adriatic Sea over a thousand years ago, and it has been sinking ever since.

Water pollution is also a problem for southern Europe. Some factories let deadly chemicals flow into the rivers. Chemicals that farmers use run off the land and pollute the rivers.

Another environmental problem is soil erosion. Farmers have worked the land and raised goats for many years. Goats can live on land that is too rocky or too poor for farming. Goats eat plants down to the roots. Then the soil washes or blows away.

Lesson 4 Review On a sheet of paper, use the words from the Word Bank to complete each sentence correctly.

Word Bank
Greece
Italy
Portugal
Spain
Venice

1. _____ is one of the poorest countries in Europe.

2. _____ and Greece export grain, olives, and grapes.

3. People use marble from _____ to build fine buildings.

4. _____ is the world's leading producer of cork.

5. _____, which is built on supports in the Adriatic Sea, is different from any other city on Earth.

What do you think ?

Which country in this chapter do you think will have the strongest economy in the future? Explain your answer.

Siesta or Not?

My name is Angelo. I am 16 years old, and I live in Santiago, Spain. Each weekday, I attend school until 3:00 in the afternoon. Afterwards, if I don't have any sports, I go home. My home is empty when I arrive, just like it is for many American teens. I wait for my parents before eating dinner. Usually, that isn't until 9:30 or so.

Why so late? It has to do with the tradition of the siesta for Spanish workers. A siesta is a two- to three-hour lunch break combined with a short nap. Some people go home to eat their lunch and then sleep a bit. Others might rest in the back room of their business. My father often snoozes on a park bench outside. He says he feels ready to face the rest of the day afterwards.

Some business owners require a siesta lunch break for their employees. Many shops shut down from about 1 until 4 P.M. This means people like my father have to work longer into the evening. He does not leave for home until 8:00 or 8:30 at night. Those late hours push our family dinner into the late evening.

In January of 2006, our government did away with long lunch breaks for federal workers. The reasons were both social and economic. The government wanted our country to be on the same work schedule as other European countries. The government also decided the siesta schedule was bad for families. Working parents could not spend much time with their families. Many children spent long hours in day care. Others, like me, spent long hours alone after school.

The government has limited federal employee lunch breaks to 45 minutes. Most of their workers go home by 6:00. The hope is that private businesses will soon make the same change. But it's too early to tell whether anyone can change the long-time tradition of the siesta.

My mother works for the government, so now she gets home by 6:30 each evening. But my father still has to work until 8:30. My mother insists that we wait for him to get home so our family can eat dinner together. And so we do. But the good thing is that I get to spend more time with my mother now in the early evenings.

Wrap-Up

1. What is a siesta?

2. Why did the Spanish government eliminate long lunches for federal employees?

Chapter 10 S U M M A R Y

- Portugal, Spain, Italy, and Greece make up southern Europe. They are north of the Mediterranean Sea and south of western central Europe.

- Three peninsulas make up southern Europe: the Iberian, the Italian, and the Balkan. These countries are surrounded by the Bay of Biscay; the Atlantic Ocean; the Strait of Gibraltar; and the Mediterranean, Adriatic, Ionian, Tyrrhenian, Ligurian, and Aegean Seas.

- More than half of Spain is a dry plateau. Much of Portugal is a dry highland. Mountains cover more than three-fourths of Italy and Greece.

- Most rivers in southern Europe are shallow and short.

- The climate of southern Europe is Mediterranean. The mountainous areas have their own climate.

- Each southern European country has its own language and culture. Portugal, Spain, and Italy are a mix of people from other places. Southern Europeans believe that the family is most important.

- All southern European languages except Greek are Romance languages.

- Most people in Portugal, Spain, and Italy are Roman Catholics. More than 95 percent of Greeks belong to the Greek Orthodox Church.

- Most Spaniards and Italians live in urban areas. More than half the Greeks and Portuguese live in cities.

- The four countries of southern Europe have different economies. They all belong to the European Union. Italy is one of the richest European countries; Greece is one of the poorest.

- None of the southern European countries are rich in natural resources. Italy is the world's biggest producer of marble. Bauxite is Greece's most important mineral.

- Many southern Europeans are farmers. Portugal exports cork; Spain and Greece export grain and fruit.

- Both Spain and Italy are industrialized. One of Italy's industries is textiles. One of Spain's biggest industries is cars. Tourism is a large industry for southern Europe.

- Southern Europe faces the environment problems of either too little water or flooding. Water pollution and soil erosion are also problems.

Chapter 10 REVIEW

Word Bank

Adriatic 2
Gibraltar 4
Iberian 1
mountains 3
regionalism 5

On a sheet of paper, use the words from the Word Bank to complete each sentence correctly.

1. Spain and Portugal make up the _____ Peninsula.

2. The _____ Sea lies east of Italy.

3. Most of southern Europe is covered with _____.

4. The Strait of _____ links the Atlantic Ocean with the Mediterranean Sea.

5. When people feel more loyal to one part of a country than to the whole country, it is called _____.

On a sheet of paper, write the letter of the answer that correctly completes each sentence.

6. _____ is not a Romance language.

   A Portuguese   **C** Spanish
   B Italian   **D** Greek

7. The most serious environmental problem in southern Europe is _____.

   A air pollution   **C** soil erosion
   B deforestation   **D** too much or too little water

8. The climate of much of southern Europe is _____.

   A Mediterranean   **C** subtropical
   B continental   **D** arctic

9. Most people in Spain, Portugal, and Italy are _____.

   A Jewish   **C** Muslims
   B Roman Catholic   **D** Greek Orthodox

10. _____ is the world's largest producer of marble.

    A Spain   **C** Italy
    B Portugal   **D** Greece

On a sheet of paper, write the answer to each question. Use complete sentences.

11. How do the economies of the countries of southern Europe differ from one another?

12. In what way were the countries of Portugal, Spain, and Italy a mix of many cultures?

13. What makes southern Europe so popular with tourists?

Critical Thinking On a sheet of paper, write your response to each question. Use complete sentences.

14. Should the United States give countries like Greece and Italy money to save important ancient buildings? Explain your answer.

15. Some countries that do not have oil or natural gas energy resources build nuclear power plants. Is this a good idea? Explain your answer.

Applying the Five Themes of Geography

Movement

In the 1800s and 1900s, many people left Italy and Greece and moved to the United States. Why do you think they did this?

Test-Taking Tip

Do not wait until the night before a test to study. Plan your study time so that you can get a good night's sleep the night before a test. Study in short sessions rather than one long session. In the week before the test, spend time each evening reviewing your notes.

The History of Pizza

Pizza may be the favorite food of most American teenagers. Every day, people in the United States eat lots of pizza. Where did this favorite food come from? No one knows for sure.

Some historians think that the ancient Roman soldiers first made pizza. The word itself comes from the Latin word *picea*. *Picea* describes the blackening of the crust by the fire underneath. The first pizza was simply a piece of round bread with oil and spices on top. No cheese and no tomatoes topped it.

How did tomatoes become a topping for pizza? Columbus brought back tomato plants from the Americas. He discovered that the native people in the Americas grew a red, juicy fruit that tasted delicious. He carried tomato plants back to Europe. Europeans had never seen tomatoes. At first, some of them thought that this new fruit was poisonous. After a while, people came to like tomatoes, so they added them to their pizza.

In 1889, a famous pizza maker created a pizza for the queen of Italy. He wanted the pizza to show the red, green, and white of the new flag of Italy. He used tomatoes for the red. For the green, he used the herb basil. The white came from mozzarella cheese. Now pizza is sold all around the world.

Pizzas were cheap and filling, so even poor people could have them. This made pizza a popular food.

When Italian immigrants came to the United States, they brought their pizza recipe with them. In 1905, one of these Italian immigrants opened the first store that sold pizza in the United States. Today, Americans eat over 3 billion pizzas every year.

Wrap-Up

1. The word pizza comes from the Latin word *picea.* What does this Latin word mean?

2. Who brought tomato plants back from the Americas?

3. Why were there no tomatoes on the first pizzas?

4. Why did pizza end up having red, green, and white ingredients?

5. When did the first store selling pizzas open in the United States?

- The two big islands of Great Britain and Ireland and many small islands make up the British Isles. Iceland, Norway, Sweden, Denmark, and Finland are in northern Europe. France, the Netherlands, Belgium, Luxembourg, Austria, Germany, and Switzerland are in western central Europe. Portugal, Spain, Italy, and Greece are in southern Europe.

- Glaciers once covered much of Europe. When these melted, their water formed the North Sea, the English Channel, and the many lakes and fjords of northern Europe.

- The climate of the British Isles and western and northern Europe is marine West Coast because of the North Atlantic Drift. The mountainous areas have their own climate. Southern Europe has a Mediterranean climate.

- Almost all European countries have their own culture and language. English is the official language of the British Isles. Many languages of western and northern Europe are Germanic. French, Portuguese, Spanish, and Italian are Romance languages.

- Most Europeans are Christians. However, immigrants bring every major religion to Europe.

- Both western central Europe and Great Britain have a high population density. Northern Europe has a low population density. Most people in Europe live in cities.

- The British Isles and western central Europe have successful free-market economies. Northern Europe mixes a free-market economy with socialism. The countries of southern Europe have different economies.

- Other than coal, the British Isles and western central Europe have few natural resources. Northern Europe is rich in natural resources—oil, natural gas, iron, copper, lead, zinc, forests, and water. Southern Europe has few resources, except for marble in Italy and bauxite in Greece.

- Manufacturing is important in all of Europe. Many people farm in western and southern Europe. However, most people work in service industries. Trade and tourism are important.

- All industrialized countries face the problems of air and water pollution. Southern Europe faces the problems of too little water, flooding, or soil erosion.

Unit 5

Eastern Europe and Russia

In the last unit, you learned about northern, western, and southern Europe. Now you will learn about eastern Europe, the Balkans, Russia, and the republics of the former Soviet Union. The nations of this huge region have much in common. Most of their cultures and languages have common roots. Their histories are also linked. Perhaps most importantly, much of this region was once under Communist rule. Beginning in the late 1980s, Communism came to an end in this region. You will find out how this has affected these countries throughout the two chapters of Unit 5.

You will also learn about the varied geography of these lands. You will learn that Russia's influence over this area has been strong. It is an old country with some beautiful buildings. This is a photograph of Saint Basil's Cathedral in Moscow, Russia. It was built in the 1500s. The structures on the top are called onion domes, because they look like onions.

Russia remains a powerful nation and a strong influence in this region.

11

Eastern Europe

Eastern Europe is an area in which great change is taking place. For many years, the former Soviet Union controlled the many small countries in this area. It prevented them from trading with the rest of Europe and kept the region poor and underdeveloped. With the fall of Communism and the Soviet Union, the countries of eastern Europe demanded change. The countries held free elections, and the region is now trying to raise its standard of living to the level of the rest of Europe.

Goals for Learning

◆ To describe where eastern Europe is located

◆ To identify the most important physical features and climate of eastern Europe

◆ To describe the diverse cultures and explain where most people live

◆ To describe the economy and environmental challenges of the eastern European countries

Geo-Stats Key Nations of Eastern Europe

Nation: Ukraine
Population: 46,711,000
Area: 233,206 square miles
Major Cities: Kiev (capital), Kharkov

Nation: Poland
Population: 38,537,000
Area: 120,725 square miles
Major Cities: Warsaw (capital), Katowice

Nation: Hungary
Population: 9,981,000
Area: 35,919 square miles
Capital: Budapest

Nation: Romania
Population: 22,303,000
Area: 91,699 square miles
Capital: Bucharest

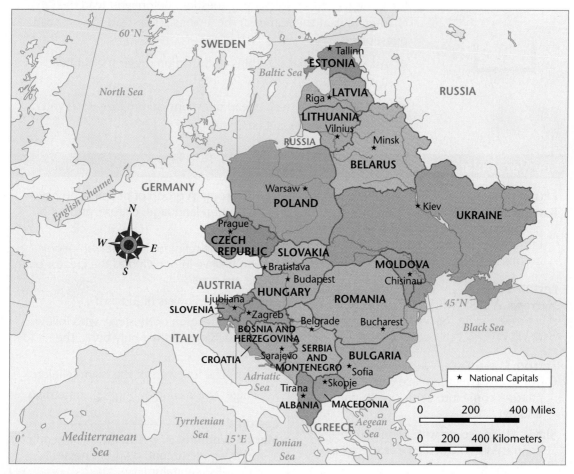

Map with labels: SWEDEN, Baltic Sea, North Sea, English Channel, GERMANY, RUSSIA, ESTONIA (Tallinn ★), LATVIA (Riga ★), LITHUANIA (Vilnius ★), Minsk ★, BELARUS, Warsaw ★, POLAND, Kiev ★, UKRAINE, Prague ★, CZECH REPUBLIC, SLOVAKIA, Bratislava ★, MOLDOVA, Chisinau ★, Budapest ★, AUSTRIA, Ljubljana ★, HUNGARY, ROMANIA, SLOVENIA, Zagreb ★, ITALY, BOSNIA AND HERZEGOVINA, Belgrade ★, Bucharest ★, Black Sea, Sarajevo ★, SERBIA AND MONTENEGRO, BULGARIA, Sofia ★, CROATIA, Adriatic Sea, Tirana ★, Skopje ★, ALBANIA, MACEDONIA, GREECE, Aegean Sea, Tyrrhenian Sea, Mediterranean Sea, Ionian Sea, 60°N, 45°N, 0°, 15°E

★ National Capitals

0   200   400 Miles

0   200   400 Kilometers

Map Skills

Eastern Europe is west of Russia and the Black Sea, north of the Mediterranean and Adriatic Seas, and east of western Europe and the Baltic Sea.

Study the map and answer the following questions:

1. Which countries border the Baltic Sea?

2. Which country is the farthest north?

3. Which country borders eastern Europe on the northeast?

4. What is the capital of Poland? Ukraine? Hungary?

5. Which southern European country is across the Adriatic Sea from eastern Europe?

Reading Strategy:
Text Structure

This text has chapters that are divided into lessons. The subheads are questions that you should be able to answer after you read the paragraphs that follow the question. Before you read this chapter, look at the names of the lessons. Then read the subhead questions.

◆ Ask yourself what you think each section under the subhead will be about.

◆ After reading these subhead questions, summarize what you think the chapter will be about.

Key Vocabulary Words

Lesson 1
Balkanization The breaking up of a geographical area or a group of people into smaller political groups; these smaller groups often fight with one another

Lesson 2
Narrows A place where a river becomes narrow; a strait that connects two bodies of water

Lesson 3
Cultural crossroad A place where different cultures come into contact with one another

Slavic Having to do with people from central Asia who settled in eastern Europe

Ethnic group A group of people who have a common language, culture, and set of values

Judaism The religion of the Jewish people who believe in one God as the creator of the universe

Jewish The followers of Judaism

Islam The religion of Muslims, who follow the teachings of their holy book, the Koran

Muslim The followers of the Islam religion

Shortage Not having enough of something

Lesson 4
Market economy A system in which people, not the government, own businesses—also called capitalism

Where Is Eastern Europe?

Eastern Europe is located in the middle latitudes. Most of the region lies between 40 degrees and 60 degrees north latitude. Western Europe borders the region to the west; Russia borders it on the east. Most of the countries of eastern Europe are landlocked. The combined population of all the countries in eastern Europe is about 180 million. Ukraine and Poland are the largest countries and have the most people. Eastern Europe also includes the smaller countries of Belarus, the Czech Republic, Slovakia, Moldova, and Hungary. It also includes the Balkan countries and the Baltic countries.

The Balkan countries are located on the Balkan Peninsula. The peninsula lies between the Adriatic Sea and the Black Sea. In the 1990s, Yugoslavia broke up into the independent states of Bosnia and Herzegovina, Croatia, Macedonia, and Slovenia. All that is left of Yugoslavia is the country of Serbia and Montenegro. Other countries on the peninsula include Albania, Bulgaria, and Romania. Greece lies to their south, but is part of southern Europe.

The three Baltic countries are all located on the east coast of the Baltic Sea. Estonia, Latvia, and Lithuania gained their independence soon after the Soviet Union broke apart in 1991.

This famous Mostar Bridge in Bosnia and Herzegovina was destroyed during a war in 1993. It was rebuilt, and it reopened in 2004.

Reading Strategy:
Text Structure

As you read this paragraph, look for the words *second, third,* and *fourth.* These words will help you identify the four regions.

Balkanization

The breaking up of a geographical area or a group of people into smaller political groups; these smaller groups often fight with one another

What Are the Four Physical Regions?

Eastern Europe has four physical regions. The North European Plain lies across the northern part of eastern Europe. This plain stretches across eastern Europe to the Ural Mountains in Russia. The land has gently rolling hills until they meet the high, Carpathian Mountains on the Poland-Slovakian border. Most of Ukraine, Belarus, Poland, and the Baltic countries are in this region.

Mountains and rugged hills of the Carpathian range form the second region. Slovakia and parts of the Czech Republic and Romania are in this region.

The third region, which is another plain, lies between the Carpathian Mountains and the Balkan Peninsula. Much of Hungary, Croatia, and the Danube River Valley of Romania are on this flat plain. The mountainous part of the Balkan Peninsula makes up the fourth region.

How Did Geography Shape History?

Geography has led to problems for the countries of eastern Europe. Poland is one large, flat area with no natural boundaries. Because of this, its more powerful neighbors have invaded Poland many times. Throughout its history, Poland's borders have changed often.

The Balkans are a very mountainous region. For over 400 years, Turkey controlled the Balkans. The mountains made governing these countries hard. It also made travel difficult. People who lived in this region were also cut off from their neighbors, so different cultures developed. Because of this, people began to mistrust those who were different from them. This is one of the reasons for fighting in the Balkans.

The winners of World War I broke up the old Turkish Empire. Afterward, a new word was added to the English language: **balkanization.** To balkanize is to break a geographical area or a group of people into smaller political groups. These smaller groups often fight with one another. The breakup of Yugoslavia into many countries is an example of balkanization.

Geography in Your Life

Radiation

Radioactivity is the energy in atoms. Marie Curie, a Polish-born French chemist, lived from 1867–1934. She and her husband, Pierre, studied radioactivity. X-rays are one use of radioactivity.

The Curies wanted everyone to benefit from their studies. During World War I, Marie helped fit ambulances with x-ray equipment to help find bullets in wounded soldiers. Her work was important to the study of nuclear physics and cancer therapy. Radioactivity is used to treat cancer, to date ancient objects, and is the source of nuclear energy. Too much radiation can be dangerous. People have to use caution when using equipment or materials that produce radiation.

Lesson 1 Review On a sheet of paper, write the word in parenthesis that makes each statement true.

1. Russia lies to the (west, east) of eastern Europe.

2. The (North, South) European Plain stretches across eastern Europe.

3. The (Carpathians, Alps) mountain range is in eastern Europe.

4. For over 400 years, (France, Turkey) controlled the Balkan countries.

5. To (balkanize, regionalize) is to break up a group of people or a geographical area into smaller political groups that are often fighting.

What do you think ?

Germany invaded Poland in World Wars I and II. How might the history of Poland be different if it had high mountains on the German-Polish border?

Objectives

- To describe the main physical features of eastern Europe
- To identify eastern Europe's major bodies of water
- To describe the climate in eastern Europe

Reading Strategy:
Text Structure

Read the subhead question. After you read the paragraphs, see if you can answer the question about physical features.

What Are the Physical Features of This Area?

Eastern Europe's main feature is its huge area of plains. In fact, Poland gets its name from the Slavic word *polonie* meaning plain. The plains region produces most of the grains that the people of eastern Europe use. Like in the Americas, windblown soil called loess helped create rich soil for farming. Farmers grow wheat, rye, corn, potatoes, sugar beets, cabbages, and tobacco on these rich plains.

Mountains are a second feature of eastern Europe. The Carpathian Mountains stretch across eastern Europe like a wide, curved line. Their highest peaks are in Romania. In the Czech Republic, Poland, and Slovakia, these mountains are not as high, and forests cover them.

The Rhodope Mountains are the highest mountains in the Balkan Peninsula. They join the Balkans near the Bulgarian capital of Sofia. The Balkan Mountains, however, give the Balkan Peninsula its name. In fact, *Balkan* is a Turkish word that means mountain. These mountains stretch from Serbia and Montenegro, through Bulgaria, to the Black Sea. The Dinaric Alps run down the Balkans along the Adriatic Coast. This region also has many small mountain ranges.

What Are the Major Bodies of Water?

Like other areas of Europe, glaciers helped to shape eastern Europe. Northern Poland has over 9,000 lakes. The largest lake in eastern Europe is Lake Balaton in Hungary.

The glaciers also created many rivers. The most important rivers of this region are the Dnepr and Danube. The Danube is 1,777 miles long and passes through or touches ten countries in Europe. It starts high in the Alps of Germany and Austria and flows eastward until it reaches the Black Sea. The Danube has many tributaries. The Dnepr or Dnieper River starts in Russia, flows through Belarus, and then through Ukraine into the Black Sea. It is an important source of hydroelectric power.

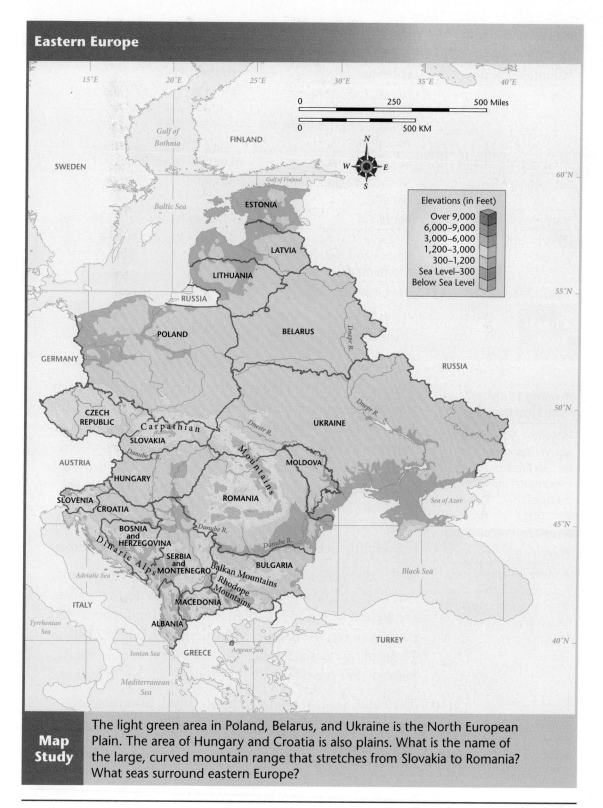

Eastern Europe

Elevations (in Feet)

- Over 9,000
- 6,000–9,000
- 3,000–6,000
- 1,200–3,000
- 300–1,200
- Sea Level–300
- Below Sea Level

Map Study
The light green area in Poland, Belarus, and Ukraine is the North European Plain. The area of Hungary and Croatia is also plains. What is the name of the large, curved mountain range that stretches from Slovakia to Romania? What seas surround eastern Europe?

Mountain Ranges in Eastern Europe and the Balkans

Mountain Range	Location	Highest Peak
Alps	France, Italy, Slovenia, Croatia, Bosnia and Herzegovina, Montenegro, Yugoslavia	Mont Blanc 15,771 feet
Rhodope Mountains	Bulgaria, Greece	Mount Musala 9,596 feet
Carpathian Mountains	Slovakia, Poland, Romania, Ukraine	Mount Gerlach 8,711 feet
Transylvanian Alps	Romania	Mount Moldoveanu 8,346 feet
Dinaric Alps	Slovenia, Croatia, Bosnia and Herzegovina, Montenegro	Bobotov Kuk 8,274 feet
Balkan Mountains	Bulgaria, Yugoslavia	Botev Peak 7,746 feet

Chart Study Eastern Europe and the Balkans have many mountains. This chart provides some information about the larger mountain ranges. Which mountain range is the tallest?

Reading Strategy:
Text Structure

How does the chart above help you understand the mountains in eastern Europe?

Narrows

A place where a river becomes narrow; a strait that connects two bodies of water

The Danube links all the countries of eastern Europe. Each year, people move millions of tons of goods on the river. It is deep enough to allow large ships to travel on it. However, the Danube has a **narrows** that geographers call the Iron Gate. Until workers dug a canal there, larger ships could not travel farther than that point. A narrows is a place where a river becomes narrow or where a strait connects two bodies of water. At the Iron Gate, the Danube flows through a small gap between the steep mountains between Romania and Serbia.

Rivers always flow from high land to low land. This means that all of Poland's rivers flow from south to north because the highest land is in the south. Rivers are important to each country in eastern Europe. Many of the rivers of the Balkan Peninsula are not navigable. However, they are important because they provide water for drinking and for irrigation.

The Baltic Sea is very important to Latvia, Estonia, and Lithuania. The Baltic ports of Riga and Tallinn are busy and important for trade.

What Is the Climate Like?

Eastern Europe has several climates. The western part of this region is affected by the North Atlantic Drift. It shares the same marine West Coast climate enjoyed by most of western Europe. The eastern part has a more humid continental climate. This is because it is farther away from the ocean. In these eastern lands north of the Danube River, winters are cold and snowy. Many rivers freeze during the winter. Summers may be hot with sudden thunderstorms.

Lands south of the Danube have a humid subtropical climate. Areas along the Adriatic coast have a Mediterranean climate. This mild weather draws tourists to the area.

Lesson 2 Review On a sheet of paper, write the letter of the answer that correctly completes each sentence.

1. The large area of plains in eastern Europe is an important _____ area.

   A industrial   **B** farming   **C** urban   **D** fishing

2. The _____ Mountains stretch across eastern Europe like a wide curved line.

   A Balkan   **B** Sudety   **C** Rhodope   **D** Carpathian

3. _____ formed Poland's many lakes.

   A Flooding   **B** Dikes   **C** Rain   **D** Glaciers

4. The _____ are the most important rivers of eastern Europe.

   A Danube and Dnepr   **C** Rhine and Rhône
   B Vistula and Dinaric   **D** Elbe and Carpathian

5. The western part of eastern Europe has a _____ climate.

   A marine West Coast   **C** Mediterranean
   B humid continental   **D** tropical

What do you think ?

What part of eastern Europe would you like to visit? Why?

Objectives

◆ To describe the cultures of this region

◆ To identify the languages and religions of the people

◆ To describe where the people live and the problems they face

Cultural crossroads

A place where different cultures come into contact with one another

Slavic

Having to do with people from central Asia who settled in eastern Europe

Ethnic group

A group of people who have a common language, culture, and set of values

Reading Strategy:
Text Structure

Look at the red subhead questions to identify what this page covers.

What Cultures Exist in This Region?

The people of eastern Europe and the Balkans have many cultures. In the past, this area was an important **cultural crossroads.** That is, it was a place where different cultures came into contact with one another. People from other places often invaded the area. Each set of invaders left behind some part of its culture.

The Germanic tribes and the Romans invaded from the west. People from central Asia called **Slavic** people invaded from the east. These Slavic tribes lived in some areas of eastern Europe thousands of years ago. They had different cultures and spoke different languages. Some settled in what is now Poland. Others became what today are called Czechs and Slovaks. Bulgarians, Serbs, and Russians are also Slavic people. Magyars from Asia invaded and settled modern Hungary. Turkey greatly influenced the Balkan countries. They left their mark in religion, architecture, and the customs of some of the people.

What Languages Do the People Speak?

Because of their history, eastern Europe and the Balkans have many different **ethnic groups.** An ethnic group is people who have a common language, culture, and set of values. These ethnic groups have lived in the same area for a long time. However, they often fought each other. Instead of looking at what they have in common, they look at their differences.

One key difference is language. Most of the languages spoken, such as Polish, Czech, Slovakian, Serbo-Croatian, and Bulgarian, are Slavic languages. Even though these languages are related to one another, they are quite different. The Estonian language is related to Finnish. In the western part of eastern Europe, most people use the Roman or Latin alphabet that is used in England and the United States. In the eastern part, including Ukraine and Belarus, they use an alphabet like the Russians use, called the Cyrillic alphabet.

What Religions Do the People Practice?

Another key difference among the people of this region is religion. Most people are Christians. The Roman Catholic Church greatly influenced the western part of this area. About two-thirds of the Hungarians are Roman Catholics. About 90 percent of the Polish people are Catholics. The Eastern Orthodox Church greatly influenced the eastern part of the region.

At one time, many people in Poland practiced **Judaism.** Judaism is an old religion of the **Jewish** people. They were the first to believe in one God as the creator of the universe. However, during World War II, Germany's Nazi Party rounded up most of these Jews. Then they put them in death camps called concentration camps. Historians call this the Holocaust. The Nazis killed as many as six million Jews in the Holocaust. Many of them came from eastern Europe.

Turkish rule brought a religion called **Islam** to the Balkans. Islam is a religion that follows the teachings of a holy book called the Koran. **Muslims** are the followers of Islam. When the Turks left the Balkans, small pockets of people who followed the Muslim religion stayed behind. Many people in Albania are Muslims. In the 1990s, ethnic and religious fighting broke out in this area. Many people were killed. Many more lost their homes and were forced to move.

Many people in eastern Europe live on farms like this one in Poland.

Where Do the People Live?

Eastern Europe is not as industrialized as the rest of Europe. Many people in this area still farm. For example, in Poland, Romania, and most of the Baltic countries, many people live on farms. As many as one out of every four people there make a living by farming. Fewer people farm in the other countries of eastern Europe. Still, more people farm than in the rest of Europe.

Shortage

Not having enough
of something

The biggest cities of eastern Europe are their capitals: Warsaw, Poland; Prague, Czech Republic; Sofia, Bulgaria; Bucharest, Romania; and Budapest, Hungary. Each of these cities has a population of more than a million people. Kharkov, Dnepropetrovsk, and Kiev, the capital of Ukraine, also have populations over a million. The capital cities are the business, governmental, and transportation centers of their countries. They are also centers for education and industry.

Reading Strategy:
Text Structure

Look for the words
first, second, and
biggest in these
paragraphs to
understand the
problems they face.

What Problems Do the People Face?

The eastern European people face three big problems. The first is a low standard of living. Employers do not pay workers very much. Many of the things workers need and want cost a lot of money, too. Many homes do not have heating that runs through the whole house. The electricity does not always work. People in a poor country like Bulgaria earn only about $200 a month. They must spend most of this for food, so they have little left for consumer goods. That means they cannot buy the things they want and need for themselves and their homes.

The countries with the highest standard of living are Poland, the Czech Republic, Hungary, and the Baltic countries. Workers in these countries are better off than workers in other eastern European and Balkan countries. However, they still earn much less than workers in western, southern, and northern Europe.

A second problem is **shortages,** or not having enough of something. Many of the countries have shortages in housing, food, and consumer goods. Many do not have modern machines.

Perhaps the biggest problem in the Balkans is ethnic fighting. In 1991, the country of Yugoslavia broke apart because of ethnic and religious differences. A civil war followed, killing many people. The wars destroyed railroads, roads, and buildings. Unless these people can overcome their differences, their economy will not improve.

Assumption Day

Polish Catholics honor Assumption Day each August. It is one of Poland's most important religious holidays. On this holiday, thousands of people make their way to the sacred town of Czestochowa. A famous painting hangs in Jasna Gora, a monastery in Czestochowa. This painting is over 500 years old. It shows the baby Jesus in the arms of Mary, his mother. Their faces are blackened by age, because the painting is so old. For this reason, it is called the Black Madonna.

During the Soviet era, many Polish Catholics considered their religion to be a statement against Communism, which had outlawed religion. The festival of the Black Madonna became a political statement. People sang protest songs as well as hymns.

Critical Thinking Why did Polish Catholics consider the festival a political protest during the Soviet era?

Word Bank

capitals

cultural crossroads

ethnic

Islam

Slavic

Lesson 3 Review On a sheet of paper, use the words from the Word Bank to complete each sentence correctly.

1. A place where different cultures meet is a _____.

2. An _____ group shares many common things.

3. Most eastern Europeans speak a _____ language.

4. Turkish rule brought _____ to the Balkans.

5. The largest cities of eastern Europe are their _____.

What do you think

What do you think was the effect on the people of eastern Europe of being controlled by Communism and the Soviet Union for many years?

Chernobyl

In 1983, Chernobyl, Ukraine, finished building a nuclear power plant. Its purpose was to provide electricity to the region. Three years later, an explosion in the plant killed 32 people and allowed radioactive material to escape.

That was only the beginning of the disaster. Winds blew the radioactive material from Chernobyl to northern Europe. In parts of Ukraine and Belarus, radioactive pollution fell on farmland and ruined it. Cows ate plants harmed by this radiation, which spoiled their milk, so people who drank it became ill. Radiation polluted the rivers and the fish.

Nearly 200,000 people had to leave the area around Chernobyl. Some communities, like the one in this photo, are still deserted. The people fled so quickly that they left their belongings behind. Some people who did not get away quickly enough are still sick today.

Ukraine is still struggling to recover from the disaster. This land may not be safe to use for thousands of years. Dealing with this hazard will continue to cost Ukrainians money.

Wrap-Up

1. What happened in Chernobyl in 1986?

2. Why was the explosion of Chernobyl so disastrous?

Make a Difference

Conserving energy can mean fewer power plants are necessary. Check your home to see which lights, computers, and appliances are on. Where can you save energy?

Objectives

◆ To describe the economy of eastern Europe and the Balkans

◆ To identify the natural resources of the region

◆ To describe the environmental challenges facing the region

Market economy

A system in which people, not the government, own businesses—also called capitalism

Reading Strategy: **Text Structure**

Make a two-column chart to use as you read this lesson. As you read, list each problem in the first column and a possible solution to the problem in the second column.

What Is the Economy of This Region Like?

For many years, eastern Europe had an economy based on Communism. In this economic system, the government owned most of the property and produced most of the goods. The government decided what goods the workers made and how and where they made them. It told farmers what crops they should grow.

In the early 1990s, the countries of eastern Europe and the Balkans refused to accept Communism any longer. They began to change their economies to a **market economy.** This is also called capitalism. In this system, individuals and private businesses make business decisions. More of the economy is in the hands of the people. This economic change has been more successful in Poland, the Czech Republic, Hungary, and the Baltic countries than in the rest of the countries. This is probably because these countries are more developed than the other countries in this area. The change is not easy. Some businesses had to close because they could not compete. This caused high unemployment and political problems for the governments. The countries of the region have made a lot of progress, but many problems remain.

Who Are the Major Trade Partners?

The economies of these countries have close ties with Russia. Until about 1990, most of their trade was with Russia and each other. Then Russia's economic problems caused problems for the economies of eastern Europe. Russia is still an important trade partner. Most of eastern Europe depends on Russia for minerals and energy resources. Many of the countries are looking toward improving their trade and political ties with western Europe. Poland, Hungary, Slovenia, the Czech Republic, and the Baltic countries now trade more with countries in western Europe. Many of these countries belong to the European Union.

What Natural Resources Are in the Area?

The region is not rich in mineral resources. Poland, Bulgaria, and the Adriatic Sea area have large coal deposits. Most of the coal is soft, brown coal called lignite. Other mineral resources common to the area are zinc, lead, tin, copper, and bauxite. The Czech Republic has some iron ore.

There are also some unusual minerals in the area. The mountains on the border of Germany and the Czech Republic have deposits of pitchblende. This ore contains radium. Albania has an unusual mineral called chromium.

The oil and natural gas deposits in Romania have been used up. The countries of this region import most of the energy they need.

What Are the Key Industries?

When Communists controlled eastern Europe, industries made cement, steel, ships, machinery, and trucks. The government controlled the economy. Often, what the workers produced was more for the good of the Soviet Union than for the local people. When the people threw out the Communists, the industries had a hard time keeping up with the global market. They could not sell their goods around the world at a price people would pay. Other countries in the West sold the same goods for less.

Most of the countries of this area are developing countries. People in developing countries are often poor. Many of them farm. Yet, manufacturing and service jobs are increasing. Poland manufactures machinery, iron and steel products, and chemicals. The Czech Republic's main industries are machine building, iron and steel production, chemicals, electronics, glass, and brewing. Over 60 percent of the people in the Baltic countries work in service industries.

The most industrialized countries of this area are Poland, the Czech Republic, Hungary, and Slovenia. They have tried to compete better by importing new machines and technology from the West. Foreign companies have poured money into the new industries of these four countries. Most of these companies are from western Europe, the United States, and Japan. The other countries have much less industry.

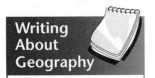

Writing About Geography

Eastern Europe and the Balkans have experienced great change in recent years. Their political and economic systems changed as they broke away from the Soviet Union. Write about how this might have affected the people living in these countries. Think about both the bad and good things that might have happened.

What Environmental Problems Do They Face?

Many countries in eastern Europe produced more and more goods while trying to industrialize. They paid little attention to the environment. Now they face air pollution and acid rain. Because lignite was the cheapest energy source, the people burned a lot of it. Lignite contains sulfur. When people burn it, the smoke mixes with rain or snow and becomes acid rain. Acid rain is a dangerous form of air pollution. It kills many trees and even eats away at the stone fronts of buildings. It also causes many people to get sick.

Water pollution is a second environmental problem for eastern Europe and the Balkans. Their industries have dumped chemical waste materials into the rivers and lakes. In February 2000, miners in Romania spilled a poison into the Lapus River. The polluted water flowed into the Tisza and Danube Rivers. Tons of dead fish floated to the surface. Many deer, ducks, and other animals drank the poisoned water and died. The spill affected not only Romania, but also other countries in the region. The effects will last many years.

Reading Strategy:
Text Structure

Review the lesson to see if you can answer each red subhead question.

Lesson 4 Review On a sheet of paper, write the answer to each question. Use complete sentences.

1. Who made economic decisions when the economy in eastern Europe was based on Communism?

2. What is a market economy?

3. Which countries do eastern European countries trade with?

4. Which kind of coal is common in this region?

5. What causes acid rain?

What do you think ?

Why do you think people are willing to work harder in a capitalist economy than under Communism?

Plenty of Mushrooms

My name is Lidia. I am 15 years old. I live in Sieraków, Poland, close to the German border. I am in my classroom looking out at the rain. I should be thinking about math, but I can't stop thinking about mushrooms!

Here in Poland, mushroom hunting is very common. Since much of Poland is covered in forest, mushrooms are plentiful. I have heard that in some countries, mushroom hunters keep their favorite spot a secret. They are afraid that others will take all the mushrooms. Polish people have no need for such secrets. Mushrooms are everywhere.

As my teacher talks numbers, my mouth waters. I like the *potrawka z kurczaka polska* (Polish chicken with mushrooms) my mother makes. I also enjoy my father's mushroom specialty. He makes stuffed mushrooms with shallots, garlic, parsley, breadcrumbs, and a salty sheep's milk cheese.

I have my own quick and easy way of preparing mushrooms. First, I clean away all the dirt. Then I cut the stems off and slice up the cap. With a bit of butter and salt in a frying pan, I sauté them until tender. Mmmmm! I like the bolete mushrooms best. Many of our recipes call for that type.

I look over at my best friend Anna in the desk next to me. She isn't looking at me, so I clear my throat. Anna looks at me curiously. I tilt my head toward the window. Ahhh! She nods with a small smile. We like to go hunting together. Some days, many kids from our class will head into the woods behind our school. Other days, just one or two of us go. I go whenever I can.

My father taught me which kinds are safe to eat. Some mushrooms are poisonous.

I always have a brown paper bag tucked in my pack to store the mushrooms I pick.

Autumn is the best time for mushroom hunting. Anna and I will bring home as many as we can. Our families keep mushrooms by drying or canning them. But I confess, sometimes I eat up every one I bring home!

Wrap-Up

1. What are some ways Polish people prepare mushrooms?

2. When is the best time of year for mushroom hunting?

- Eastern Europe is a region of two large countries and many small ones. Ukraine and Poland are the largest countries both in size and population. Eastern Europe is located in the middle latitudes. It is bordered by western Europe to the west and Russia on the east. The Balkan Peninsula sits between the Adriatic and Black Seas on the east and south. The Baltic countries are located on the east coast of the Baltic Sea.

- Eastern Europe is divided into four physical regions: the North European Plain; an area of the Carpathian Mountains and rugged hills; another plain between the Balkan Peninsula and the Carpathian Mountains; and the Balkan Peninsula.

- Because much of eastern Europe has no natural boundaries, many people have invaded it. The Turks ruled the Balkans for many years. The many invaders left their religions, architecture, and the customs of the people. The differences have sometimes led to war.

- The two main physical features of this area are huge plains and many mountains. Glaciers created many rivers throughout the area. The most important of these are the Danube and Dnepr or Dnieper.

- The western part of eastern Europe has a marine West Coast climate. The eastern part has a humid continental climate.

Land south of the Danube has a humid subtropical climate. Areas along the Adriatic Coast have a Mediterranean climate.

- The cultures of eastern Europe and the Balkans differ because this is a cultural crossroad. Germanic tribes, Romans, and Slavs invaded it and settled there. Turkey has greatly influenced the Balkan culture. Most people in this area speak a Slavic language, but these languages differ from one another.

- Most of the people are Christians. However, some Muslims live in the Balkans. This has led to ethnic and religious fighting.

- Eastern Europe and the Balkans are not as industrialized as the rest of Europe. Many people farm. The biggest cities are the capitals.

- For many years, these countries had Communist economies and close ties to Russia. Now, many countries have become capitalistic with close ties to western Europe. Many of the countries of eastern Europe have joined the European Union.

- This area's largest natural resource is lignite. The countries face the environmental problems of acid rain and water pollution. They face the social problems of a low standard of living, shortages, and ethnic fighting.

Chapter 11 REVIEW

Word Bank

acid rain 5
balkanize 1
cultural crossroads 3
free market 4
narrows 2

On a sheet of paper, use the words from the Word Bank to complete each sentence correctly.

1. To break a geographical area or a group of people into smaller political groups is to _____.

2. A _____ is a place where a river flows through a small gap between large mountains.

3. A _____ is a place where different cultures meet.

4. An economic system in which people, not the government, own businesses is called a _____.

5. A dangerous form of air pollution is _____.

On a sheet of paper, write the letter of the answer that correctly completes each sentence.

6. Eastern Europe and the Balkan countries are located in the _____ latitudes.

   A northern   **B** middle   **C** southern   **D** low

7. One of the main physical features of eastern Europe is its large area of _____.

   A rain forests **B** plains   **C** deserts   **D** beaches

8. A large number of _____ resulted from the glaciers that once covered eastern Europe.

   A lakes   **B** fjords   **C** seaways   **D** valleys

9. _____ greatly influenced the religion, architecture, and customs of the Balkans.

   A Poland   **B** Greece   **C** Germany   **D** Turkey

10. _____ are followers of Islam.

   A Buddhists   **B** Jews   **C** Muslims   **D** Christians

On a sheet of paper, write the answer to each question. Use complete sentences.

11. What are the four main regions of eastern Europe?

12. What are the four main climates found in this region?

13. What are two environmental challenges that the people of eastern Europe and the Balkans face?

Critical Thinking On a sheet of paper, write your response to each question. Use complete sentences.

14. Why are Poland, the Czech Republic, and Hungary more industrialized than the other countries of eastern Europe?

15. Do you think that some of the problems in eastern Europe and the Balkans can be traced back to their years of Communist control? Explain your answer.

Applying the Five Themes of Geography

Movement

How do the many cultures of eastern Europe and the Balkans reflect the theme of movement?

Test-Taking Tip

Read test directions twice. Sometimes they will give you a hint. For example, the directions may remind you to look for the "best" answer.

Russia

In 1991, a historic thing happened. The Soviet Union, a huge country created in 1917, suddenly broke apart. The Soviet Union had been made up of many republics or states, including Russia. Many of the republics of the old Soviet Union became independent. Despite the breakup, Russia is the largest country in the world.

Goals for Learning

◆ To describe where Russia is located

◆ To identify its most important physical features and climates

◆ To describe its diverse cultures and explain where most people in Russia live

◆ To describe the economy and the environmental challenges Russia faces

Geo-Stats   Russia

Nation: Russia
Population: 142,894,000
Area: 6,592,692 square miles
Length of Coastline: 23,340 miles
Length of Roads: 459,000 miles; Railroads 54,157 miles
Major Cities: Moscow (capital), St. Petersburg, Nizhniy Novgorod, Novosibirsk

Major Religions: Russian Orthodox and Islam
Major Languages: Russian, many other minority languages
Number of Cellular Phones: 120 million

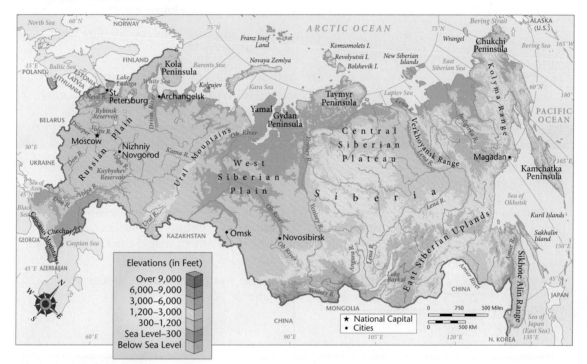

Map Skills

Russia is a huge country that stretches about 6.6 million square miles. Part of it lies in Europe and part of it in Asia. Traditionally, the Ural Mountains separate the European part from the Asian part. It is the largest country in the world. The territory of Siberia makes up about three-fourths of Russia. Since the fall of the Soviet Union, the official name of Russia has been the Russian Federation. It is made up of 89 internal regions, provinces, and territories. There is a small area of Russia surrounded by Poland, Lithuania, and Latvia.

Study the map and answer the following questions:

1. What is the capital of Russia?

2. What are three peninsulas in Russia?

3. What Scandinavian country is on Russia's northwestern border?

4. What ocean is north of Russia?

5. Why do you think most people live west of the Ural Mountains?

Reading Strategy:
Visualizing

When you visualize what you are reading, you are creating pictures in your mind. You can visualize things that you don't know about by using things that you do know about.

◆ The photographs in this chapter will help you visualize what Russia is like.

◆ Think about things that you already know. They might add to the information you get from the photographs in this chapter.

Key Vocabulary Words

Lesson 1
Czar A ruler or king

Lesson 2
Taiga A swampy, evergreen forest bordering on the arctic tundra

Polar climate A climate with long, cold winters and short, warm summers

Lesson 3
Atheist A person who does not believe in God

Pogrom An organized killing of groups of people, especially Jewish people

Lesson 4
Command economy An economy in which the government makes the key economic decisions

Nuclear waste The waste produced by atomic power plants

Only about 50 miles of water—the Bering Strait—separates the northeastern tip of Russia from Alaska.

Where Is Russia Located?

Russia is the world's biggest country. It stretches 6,000 miles from the Baltic Sea in Europe in the west to the Bering Sea in Asia in the east. The distance from Russia's most northern point to its most southern point is over 2,000 miles. It is about twice the size of the United States. It is so large that it has 11 time zones. The continental United States has only four. When it is 8:00 in the morning in the western part of Russia, it is 6:00 in the evening on its east coast.

The Baltic countries of Estonia and Latvia, as well as the countries of Belarus and the Ukraine, form Russia's western boundary. Russia's most important seaport, St. Petersburg, lies on its eastern border on the Baltic Sea. On the eastern coast of Russia is the Bering Sea, which separates Russia from Alaska. The Arctic Ocean lies north of Russia. China, Mongolia, and Kazakhstan are on its southern border.

What Are Russia's Physical Regions?

This huge area has three main physical regions. The first region is the Russian plain. It extends from the Northern European Plain that covers much of Europe. Three-fourths of the people live in this region. The three largest cities of Russia are located in this region. They are Moscow, St. Petersburg, and Nizhniy Novgorod. This region has the richest soil, a black soil called *chernozem*. It also has the most industry and the most navigable rivers.

The Ural Mountains form the second region. This low mountain range runs about 1,500 miles southward from the Arctic Ocean. Few of the mountains are higher than 4,000 feet. The Urals contain huge deposits of minerals. The Urals are the boundary between Europe and Asia. However, today geographers often call the landmass of both Europe and Asia together Eurasia.

Czar

A ruler or king

Siberia is the third and largest region. It is nearly one and a half times the size of the United States. There are three different subregions in Siberia. The vast West Siberian Plain lies east of the Ural Mountains. This flat lowland has many rivers, which often flood. As the plain extends eastward, it meets the Central Siberian Plateau. It is rich in undeveloped natural resources. Still farther east are the high mountains and forests of the East Siberian Uplands.

How Has Geography Influenced History?

Geography has often influenced Russian history. In the 1200s, the Mongols, or Tatars, from central Asia invaded the Russian plains. Genghis Khan led this army. For over 200 years, all of Russia was part of the Mongol empire that stretched from eastern Europe to China. Most Russians opposed foreign rule and this opposition united them.

To escape the invaders, many Russians headed north. In 1240, Alexander, a Russian prince, defeated the Swedes at the Neva River. In 1294, Alexander's youngest son, Daniel, became the ruler of Muscovy, or Moscow. Moscow became powerful and in 1480 overthrew the Mongols. One Russian prince, Ivan III, or Ivan the Great, was Russia's first national leader. Ivan IV, or Ivan the Terrible, was crowned Russia's first **czar**, which means ruler or king.

The Ural Mountains divide Russia. The western, or European, part of Russia has big cities and factories. Throughout the ages, it held almost all the political power. The eastern part of Russia is larger, but has fewer people. It has many natural resources.

Most of Russia's rivers flow north. During the winter, the water freezes, and the ports cannot be used. In the past, Russia has gone to war to capture ports that it could use year-round.

In the last 200 years, climate and size have kept Russia from being conquered. In 1812, Napoleon tried to capture Russia. He failed because the Russian soldiers kept retreating eastward, deeper and deeper into Russia. Finally, Napoleon ordered his troops home to France. Thousands of French soldiers died from hunger and from the cold.

The Kremlin is in Moscow, Russia. It is the center of Russian government. It overlooks the Moskva river.

From 1941 to 1942, German troops invaded Russia. Like Napoleon's troops, the German forces faced the cold Russian winter. The Russian army and the harsh winter cold caused the invasion to fail. The defeat was a turning point of World War II. Russia, along with the United States and their allies, won the war.

Lesson 1 Review On a sheet of paper, write answers to these questions. Use complete sentences.

1. How does Russia compare in size to the United States?

2. What is the largest physical region of Russia?

3. Which region is rich in natural resources that the Russians have only begun to develop?

4. How has Russia's climate affected its history?

5. How did geography and weather help defeat both Napoleon's army in 1812 and Germany's army from 1941 to 1942 when they tried to invade Russia?

What do you think ?

How would Siberia benefit from building more railroads?

Objectives

◆ To describe Russia's main physical features

◆ To identify its major rivers and lakes

◆ To describe Russia's climates

Taiga

A swampy, evergreen forest bordering on the arctic tundra

Reading Strategy:
Visualizing

Can you imagine what tundra looks like after reading this section? How about the taiga?

In 1905, the Trans-Siberian Railroad was completed. It runs 5,778 miles, from European Russia to the eastern coast.

What Are the Main Physical Features?

Plains are the most common physical feature of this region. The most productive land is in the Russian Plain in Europe. Most of the country's crops are grown here. Farmers grow potatoes, wheat, sugar beets, sunflowers, corn, barley, and other crops.

You have already learned about the tundra and the permafrost of Canada. Russia has these, too. Tundra covers much of the northern part of Russia. The tundra is a flat, treeless plain. The soil is thin and poor; the weather is cold. It receives little precipitation, usually less than 15 inches a year. Mosses and low shrubs are the only plant life. Geographers call its soil permafrost because a layer of soil is always frozen.

On the east side of the Ural Mountains is the Western Siberian Plain. This is an area of plains covered with swampy fields. These plains are frozen much of the year. South of the plain is the **taiga**. It is the world's largest forest. The Siberian taiga has so many trees that it is called a "green ocean." The taiga contains pine, fir, larch, and other evergreen trees. Trees take a long time to grow in the poor soil of the taiga. Summers in this region are short and cool. Winters are long and very cold. Like the tundra, the taiga has few people. The southern part of the plain has wild grasses and few trees.

Traveling eastward through Russia, the land gradually becomes higher. The Central Siberian Plateau lies between the Yenisey and Lena Rivers. High mountains rise in the eastern part of Russia. Mountains stretch all the way from the Pacific coast to north of Mongolia. They are about as high as the Rocky Mountains in the United States. The Kamchatka Peninsula in eastern Siberia has over 100 volcanoes. About 20 of them are active volcanoes.

What Are the Major Rivers and Lakes?

Russia has many large bodies of water. The Caspian Sea is part of Russia's southern border. Several rivers flow into the Caspian Sea. The huge Volga River, the largest in this region, is one of them. It begins around Moscow and flows over 2,000 miles. No rivers flow out of the Caspian Sea, the largest inland sea in the world. Other important rivers of western Russia are the Dnepr or Dnieper, Don, Dvina, Ural, and Kama. Canals link some of these rivers.

Siberia has four huge rivers that flow to the Arctic Ocean: the Angara, Lena, Ob, and Yenisey. They are so wide that you cannot see across them. The rivers are frozen much of the year.

All of Russia's rivers are important. They serve as highways because Russia still has few good roads and railroads. Russians have dammed many rivers to produce hydroelectric power.

Lake Baykal is the most famous lake in Russia. It is nearly one mile deep, and it holds as much water as all the Great Lakes combined. Its water is so pure that people bottle and sell it. Lake Baykal contains 80 percent of Russia's freshwater supply. Many rivers flow into Lake Baykal, but only the Angara flows out.

What Climates Does Russia Have?

Russia covers such a large area that it has many different climates. The far northern part of Russia is above the Arctic Circle. This tundra area has a polar climate. A **polar climate** has long, cold winters and short, warm summers. Little rain falls there.

Just south of this belt of polar climate is a large area of subarctic climate. This is like the polar climate except that it receives a little more rain and snow. The subarctic climate supports the huge forests of the taiga.

Most of European Russia has the humid continental climate. It has warm summers and cold winters. Rain falls throughout the year. It receives about 25 inches of snow and rain each year. This is about the same as in the Midwest in the United States.

This aerial photograph of Lake Baykal was taken from a helicopter. Lake Baykal is located in Siberia.

Reading Strategy:
Visualizing

Can you picture how a person who lives where it is so cold would dress to go outside on a cold day?

Russia's great size affects its climate. Most of the country is far from oceans. Water, whether a large lake or the ocean, has the effect of keeping weather from becoming too hot or too cold. Siberia, the huge region in the northeastern part of Russia, is so far from an ocean that its climate is very cold. The winter temperature may be as cold as 90°F below zero. Summer temperatures only reach 50°F.

Lesson 2 Review On a sheet of paper, use the words from the Word Bank to complete each sentence correctly.

Word Bank

Baykal

continental

plains

taiga

Volga

1. The most common physical feature of Russia is the _____.

2. The _____ is the largest forest in the world.

3. The _____ is a huge river in Russia.

4. Lake _____, Russia's most famous lake, contains 80 percent of Russia's freshwater supply.

5. Most people in Russia live in a humid _____ climate.

What do you think

Does climate have a big effect on where the people of Russia live? Explain your answer.

Objectives

- To describe the cultures of Russia
- To identify the languages and religions of Russia
- To describe some of Russia's political problems

Atheist

A person who does not believe in God

What Cultures Exist in Russia?

Like the United States, Russia is multicultural. Many ethnic groups, each with a different culture, live in Russia. The Russians are the largest ethnic group. Most of the people of Russia are Slavic people. They are related to the Slavs who settled eastern Europe and the Balkan countries.

Slavic Russia absorbed dozens of non-Slavic ethnic groups as it expanded south and east. More than 70 ethnic groups live in Russia. Among them are Tatars, Chechens, Bashkirs, Chuvashes, and Udmurts. In Soviet times, they had some rights to govern themselves, although the Soviet Union kept them under close watch. They kept their languages and religions.

What Languages Do the People Speak?

The most widely spoken language is Russian. Russia has about 150 million people. Over 80 percent speak Russian as their first and only language. However, each ethnic group has its own language. Many speak a Slavic language. Most speakers of a minority language also speak Russian. The Russian and other Slavic languages generally use the Cyrillic alphabet. The most popular of the minority languages is Tartar, spoken by about 3 percent of the people. The Bashkirs and the Udmurts live in the Ural Mountains and along the Volga River. They speak languages related to Hungarian and Finnish.

What Religions Do the People Practice?

The main religion in Russia is a branch of Christianity called the Russian Orthodox Church. Under the czars, the Russian Orthodox Church was the official church in Russia. After the Revolution of 1917, the Communists tried to make Russia an **atheist** country. They told the people they could not believe in God. The leaders banned religious holidays. They closed churches and other places of worship. However, many Russian people continued to worship at home. In 1991, Communist rule ended. Then people began to worship openly again.

Even though the Communists did not allow people to practice their religion, there are many beautiful churches in Russia.

Pogrom

An organized killing of groups of people, especially Jewish people

Russia's second largest religion is Islam. Russia today has seven regions that are mostly Muslim. Experts say that if current trends continue, more than half of Russia's population will be Muslim by 2050. As in many Western countries with growing Muslim populations, tensions are rising. Ethnic Russians worry that their country is losing its Russian Orthodox identity.

At one time, Judaism was a major religion in Russia. Around 1900, over 5 million Jews lived in Russia. However, they were treated poorly. After the Russian czar Alexander II was killed in 1881, there was a wave of **pogroms**. Pogroms are organized massacres of an ethnic group, especially Jews. Many Jews were forced to flee Russia and settle in other countries. Even in recent times, Jews have not felt welcome in Russia.

In the 1970s and 1980s, the Communist government allowed thousands of Jews to leave Russia. Many now live in the United States and Israel.

Do you think a city in Russia looks like a city in the United States? Why or why not?

What Are the Major Cities of This Region?

Moscow, the capital of Russia, is one of Russia's oldest cities. It played a big role in uniting the country. The city grew up around the Kremlin, an old fort. Even today, the Kremlin is the political center of Russia. Moscow has over 9 million people. It is the largest city in Europe. It is a large industrial and cultural center. In fact, some people call it the city of museums. The city is also famous for its ballet and opera.

In 1703, Peter the Great, a famous Russian leader, founded St. Petersburg. This beautiful city is Russia's biggest seaport on the Baltic Sea. St. Petersburg is Russia's second largest industrial and cultural center. Today, more than 5 million people live in St. Petersburg.

Biography

Vladimir Putin: 1952–

In March 2000, the people of Russia elected Vladimir Putin to be their new president. For many years, he worked as a spy for the KGB. This Soviet agency gathered information on the countries that were enemies of the Soviet Union. As the Soviet Union was collapsing in 1990, Putin left the KGB and entered politics. In 1999, Boris Yeltsin, the first president of Russia, made Putin prime minister of Russia. As president, Putin says he will strengthen Russia's security forces. This worries some Russians because they think he may turn away from Russia's new democracy.

St. Petersburg

It has been called Russia's crown jewel. St. Petersburg is a beautiful city of graceful palaces and grand cathedrals. The city is a cultural center for Russia. It is still home to Russia's world-famous ballet dancers and an inspiration to Russian writers.

The Russian czar, Peter the Great, ordered workers to begin constructing the city in 1703. It was to be his "window on Europe." It was an expensive order. Almost 100,000 people died of cold and hunger during its construction.

In 1712, the city became the capital of Russia. It remained the capital for 200 years. This photo is of Petrodvorets, which means Peter's Palace. It was built in the 1700s, but nearly destroyed by Nazis during World War II. After the war, it was restored.

The name of the city has changed throughout Russian history. Peter the Great named St. Petersburg for his patron saint. During World War I, the name was changed to Petrograd. When Soviet leader Vladimir Lenin died in 1924, the name changed to Leningrad. In 1991, even before Russia became its own country again, the city became St. Petersburg once more.

What Problems Do the People Face?

The people of Russia face many problems. The most important problem is whether the region, with its many minorities, can stay together. Many minorities live in areas where they are the majority. In the past, Moscow controlled everything. Today, the people want greater control over their own resources. They like their own cultures and their own language.

Some people think that Russia will split into several independent states in the future. Already, the world is seeing that some parts of Russia, like its republic of Chechnya, want to break away. The people of Chechnya have been fighting the Russian army for several years. They want to form an independent country. Russian soldiers have forced Chechnya to remain a part of Russia.

Reading Strategy:
Visualizing

Can you visualize the problem in Chechnya being similar to the problems in the United States before the Civil War?

Another problem is the breakdown of government. The Russian government seems unable to provide services for its citizens. Some people refuse to pay taxes.

Lesson 3 Review On a sheet of paper, write the word in parenthesis that makes each statement true.

1. The largest ethnic group in Russia is the (Tatars, Russians).

2. The most widely spoken language is (Russian, Slavic).

3. The main religion of most people in Russia is (Judaism, Russian Orthodox).

4. (St. Petersburg, Moscow) is Russia's biggest seaport on the Baltic Sea.

5. The (Kremlin, Kiev) is the political center of Russia.

What do you think ?

How would the breakup of Russia into several more independent republics affect the United States? Explain your answer.

Objectives

◆ To learn about Russia's economy

◆ To know some of Russia's natural resources

◆ To learn about Russia's industries

◆ To describe Russia's environmental problems

Command economy

An economy in which the government makes the key economic decisions

Reading Strategy: **Visualizing**

Does reading the words *first, second,* and *third* help you visualize what you are reading about Russia's problems?

What Is the Economy of Russia Like?

The economy of this region has undergone great change. After Communism failed, the republics changed from a **command economy** to a market economy. In a command economy, the government makes the key economic decisions. In a market economy, a business is privately owned. The people who own a business make decisions about it.

Making these changes was not easy. The first problem is that people who ran the factories and farms had little experience with privately-owned businesses. They made many mistakes. The second problem is that many of the big, government-owned businesses were old and not efficient. That is, the machinery in them was old, so the workers wasted time and energy producing goods. Because of this, the factories could not compete with businesses in other countries. Many workers lost their jobs. Some blamed their lack of jobs on new economic changes. A third problem is that foreign governments and companies were at first unwilling to invest money in Russia. Without money from overseas, the managers and workers had a hard time improving the economy.

Since 2000, Russia's economy has shown steady growth. Much of the growth is the result of high prices for Russia's oil and other natural resources. Foreign investment has grown and many Russians are hopeful about the future. Personal income has risen, and there is less poverty. The Russian government has been able to reduce its foreign debt. It continues to encourage reform and many Russians are starting businesses of their own. Nevertheless, serious problems remain. Economic growth is slowing while inflation remains high. Oil, natural gas, and other natural resources account for more than 80 percent of exports. World prices for such goods tend to go up and down. Russia's manufacturing base must be replaced or modernized. Other problems include a weak banking system and high-ranking people who are dishonest.

What Are Russia's Natural Resources?

Russia is rich in natural resources. This provides some hope for the future. Russia is the only industrialized country in the world that is almost self-sufficient in the natural resources it needs. The United States, China, Japan, and Europe must import oil; Russia does not. It has the world's largest supply of natural gas. However, the price of oil changes around the world. This greatly affects Russia.

Russia has iron ore, manganese, chromium, nickel, platinum, titanium, copper, tin, lead, tungsten, diamonds, phosphates, and gold. These natural resources provide Russia with money to buy the things it cannot produce itself. There are also rich deposits of minerals in Siberia. The problem is that many of the new discoveries are in places that are difficult to mine.

Reading Strategy:
Visualizing

Can you visualize the huge forests in Siberia? Remember that Siberia is about one-and-a-half times the size of the United States.

Russia has three other valuable natural resources—forests, furs, and fish. The forests of Siberia contain about one-fifth of the world's timber, so lumbering is a big industry. Russia is home to many animals, so the fur industry is important. Russia has a large fishing industry. Russians catch enough fish to sell to other countries, too.

What Are Some Major Industries?

In Russia, about 10 percent of people farm, about 30 percent work in factories, and the remaining 60 percent work in service industries.

Farmers use about 7 percent of Russia's land for farming. The most productive farmland is the Russian Plain. The climate in the other parts of Russia is too cold for growing many crops. In a command economy, the government owns the land. It is still not easy for Russian farmers to buy land for themselves. Many farmers do not have the necessary skills, machinery, or money to be successful. Wheat, barley, and corn are grown in Russia. Russia is the world's biggest grower of sunflower seeds, which are used to make cooking oil. The farmers also grow sugar beets and soybeans.

Why Are Industries in Trouble?

The manufacturing industries have troubles, too. Some heavy industries, like chemicals, steel, and automobiles, are not producing as much as they did under Communist rule. The Communists wanted to make the Soviet Union an industrial power. Because of this, the workers mostly produced goods for the military and for heavy industry.

They produced few consumer goods that people used in their homes. The goods they produced were not of high quality because the factories had no competition. The people had no choice but to buy what was available. Today, many industries that used to make military goods now make consumer goods.

Where Are the Main Industrial Areas?

Russia's major industrial areas are in the west. Manufacturing plants in Moscow produce cars and trucks, chemicals, and textiles. St. Petersburg's harbor is open all year around. It is close to the countries of the European Union, which provides a market for St. Petersburg's goods. St. Petersburg's industries include textiles, machinery, and ship building. The Volga River Valley's chief products are cars, chemicals, and food products. The river itself provides hydroelectric power and cheap transportation.

What Environmental Challenges Exist?

Russia faces both air and water pollution. The soft coal they use to make electricity puts harmful gases in the air. Many factories cannot keep these gases from escaping into the air. Cars and trucks give off harmful gases because cars do not have pollution control systems. People living near industrial areas have health problems. For example, the people who live in Siberian cities have a high rate of lung cancer and other lung diseases. Poor air quality causes these diseases.

Heavy industry can create a lot of harmful waste. The Soviet leaders used to dump these waste products into the rivers and lakes. Now, harmful chemicals have been washed into the water supply. Even Lake Baykal, which is a big source of water for Russia, shows signs of pollution.

An even bigger problem is **nuclear waste** and nuclear accidents. Atomic power plants produce nuclear waste. This waste used to be put into containers and dumped into the Arctic Ocean. Many people fear that the containers will leak. If this happens, many plants, animals, and people in Russia will die.

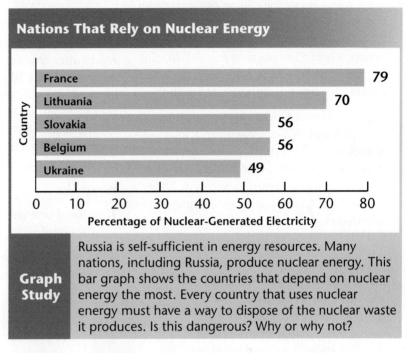

Nations That Rely on Nuclear Energy

Country	Percentage of Nuclear-Generated Electricity
France	79
Lithuania	70
Slovakia	56
Belgium	56
Ukraine	49

Graph Study Russia is self-sufficient in energy resources. Many nations, including Russia, produce nuclear energy. This bar graph shows the countries that depend on nuclear energy the most. Every country that uses nuclear energy must have a way to dispose of the nuclear waste it produces. Is this dangerous? Why or why not?

Word Bank

command ₁
fish ₃
natural ₂
service ₄
west ₅

Lesson 4 Review On a sheet of paper, use the words from the Word Bank to complete each sentence correctly.

1. Russia is having trouble changing from a _____ economy to a market economy.

2. Russia is rich in _____ resources.

3. Russians catch enough _____ that they can sell them to other countries.

4. Most Russians work in _____ industries.

5. Russia's major industrial areas are in the ____.

What do you think ?

Why did the leaders of the Soviet Union seem to care so little about the environment?

Living Without Parents

My name is Lev. I live in an orphanage in Yaroslavl, Russia. I came here two years ago, when I was 13. That year, my father went to prison. My mother became too sick to care for me. The orphanage is for children whose parents are dead or cannot care for them.

Right now there are 29 kids between the ages of 8 and 18 here. We go to a local school in our district. It's easy to tell the difference between other kids and us. Our clothes are usually worn, never new. Other kids tease us about our dirty hair and our mended clothes.

Those of us at my orphanage are lucky, though. We have painting and music classes. We often get fresh fruits and vegetables with our meals. We get two showers a week. And we earn a little money for the chores we do. I know boys from another orphanage who also attend my school. They get one shower a week, and no money, classes, or fresh fruit.

Our director told me she works hard to get money from people around the world. Sometimes people who donate money come here to help. They usually stay for a few weeks at a time. It is hard to say good-bye when they leave. One American man is now my pen pal. He might come back in a few years. I will be here unless my mother gets well enough to take me home. I can stay until I'm 18.

You have to be kind of tough to live in the orphanage, because most of the kids are tough. The hardships they've known have made them hard in return.

A lot of kids run away from the orphanage. Usually they do this within the first few weeks after arriving. But I don't want to live on my own. My director told me that the problem of homeless kids in Russia is very bad. I'm glad to have a place to sleep. My mattress is lumpy, and I wish I could have another blanket. And I never get any privacy. Still, I am grateful to have a bed.

Wrap-Up

1. What is one way Lev's orphanage is funded?

2. Why might some children run away from orphanages?

Chapter 12 S U M M A R Y

- Russia is the largest country in the world. The three main physical regions are the Russian plain, the Ural Mountains, and Siberia.

- Plains are Russia's main physical feature. The north has tundra and the taiga, the world's largest forest.

- Russia's largest river is the Volga. All rivers in this area are important because of the shortage of good roads and railroads. Lake Baykal contains 80 percent of Russia's freshwater supply.

- The far northern part of Russia has a polar climate. South of the polar climate is a subarctic climate. But the climate of most of European Russia is humid continental.

- This region is multicultural. The Russians are the largest ethnic group. Russian is the most widely spoken language, but each ethnic group has its own language. Many of these are Slavic languages.

- Most Russians are Russian Orthodox. However, many people are Muslims or atheists.

- Russia has changed from a command economy to a market economy. This change has been difficult. The major cities, both of which are industrial centers, are Moscow and St. Petersburg. Most major industries are in the western part of Russia.

- Russia is rich in natural resources. Russia possesses rich reserves of iron ore, manganese, chromium, nickel, platinum, titanium, copper, tin, lead, tungsten, diamonds, phosphates, and gold. Among Russia's other natural resources are forests, furs, and fish.

- Out of every 100 workers in Russia, 10 work on farms, 30 work in factories, and the rest work in service industries.

- Russia faces the environmental problems of pollution and the disposal of atomic waste. Social problems include independence movements, ethnic and religious conflict, and the breakdown of government.

Word Bank

Chechnya 5

Russian 4

Slavic 3

taiga 2

tundra 1

On a sheet of paper, use the words from the Word Bank to complete each sentence correctly.

1. The _____ is a flat, treeless plain that covers much of the northern part of Russia.

2. The _____ is a large forest region covered with pine, fir, larch, and other evergreen trees.

3. Most Russians are related to the _____ people who settled in eastern Europe and the Balkan countries.

4. Most Russians speak the _____ language.

5. The people of _____ have been fighting for several years against Russia to try to form an independent country.

On a sheet of paper, write the letter of the answer that correctly completes each sentence.

6. The largest country in the world is _____.

   A the United States   **C** Russia
   B Canada   **D** China

7. Two important cities located in European Russia are _____.

   A Moscow and St. Petersburg
   B Chernobyl and Siberia
   C Stockholm and Budapest
   D Omsk and Kiev

8. The most common physical feature of Russia is its _____.

   A mountains   **C** high plateaus
   B plains   **D** seas

9. The two main religions are Christianity and _____.

   A Judaism   **C** Buddhism
   B Hinduism   **D** Islam

10. The export of _____ provides Russia with money to buy things it cannot produce for itself.

A oil and natural gas   **C** food products
B consumer goods   **D** automobiles

On a sheet of paper, write the answer to each question. Use complete sentences.

11. What are the three main climates of Russia?

12. Why is this area of the world multicultural?

13. What environmental challenges does Russia face?

Critical Thinking On a sheet of paper, write your response to each question. Use complete sentences.

14. What would you do to solve the problem of ethnic conflict if you were Russia's president?

15. What would you do to make the new economy of Russia more successful?

Applying the Five Themes of Geography

Region

Imagine you are taking a trip across Russia from St. Petersburg in the west to the Sea of Okhotsk in the east. Describe what landforms you might see and the different climates you might experience.

Test-Taking Tip

If you do not know the answer to a test question, put a star beside it and go on. Then when you are finished, go back to any starred questions and try to answer them.

The Fabergé Easter Eggs

Before 1917, Easter was a special holiday for the Russian people. On Easter day, they gave gifts to the people they loved. Among these gifts were decorated Easter eggs. These eggs were a symbol of new life.

At that time, powerful rulers called czars controlled Russia. These czars lived in beautiful palaces filled with wonderful treasures. For a czar, the question was what Easter gift to give to a queen who had everything. An ordinary hen's egg would not do.

Each czar had a person who made jewelry for the czar's family. In 1884, Czar Alexander III asked Carl Fabergé, his jewelry maker, to create a special jeweled Easter egg for the queen. He wanted the egg to be beautiful and to contain a surprise inside.

Fabergé was a creative artist. He was also a master goldsmith and a mechanical genius. The first egg he made for the czar had an enameled gold shell. Inside the egg sat a tiny hen with eyes made of rubies. The czar was so pleased that he asked Fabergé to make a special egg for every year after that.

For more than 30 years, Fabergé made these Easter eggs for the czar's family. Each egg was different. In all, Fabergé made 49 special Easter eggs. Today at least 44 eggs still exist.

Fabergé made other beautiful jewelry. Still, people think that his Easter eggs are his greatest work. This is because of their unique design and the beautiful way he made them. Once you have seen a Fabergé Easter egg, no Easter egg will ever look the same again.

Wrap-Up

1. Who were the czars?

2. Who was Carl Fabergé?

3. What kind of Easter egg did Fabergé create for the czar's wife?

4. How many Fabergé Easter eggs still exist?

5. Why do some people think that the Fabergé Easter eggs are Fabergé's greatest work?

- Eastern Europe contains many countries, several of which are on the Balkan Peninsula. East of these countries lies Russia, the largest country in the world.

- The North European Plain extends from western Europe across eastern Europe into Russia. Eastern Europe also has mountains and rugged hills; another large plain; and the Balkan Peninsula. The three main physical regions of the land beyond eastern Europe are the North European Plain, the Ural Mountains, and Siberia.

- Plains and mountains are the main physical features of eastern Europe. Plains are the main feature of Russia. Northern Russia has tundra and the taiga.

- These regions have many climates. These range from the polar and subarctic in northern Russia, to humid continental climate, to humid subtropical south of the Danube River in eastern Europe. Some southerly parts have a Mediterranean climate.

- Both regions are multicultural with many ethnic groups. Most people speak a Slavic language. These languages differ from one another. Russian is the most widely spoken language in Russia.

- Most people in this part of the world are Christians. However, many Muslims live in the Balkans and in parts of Russia.

- Eastern Europe and the Balkans are not as industrialized as the rest of Europe, partly because they used to have a Communist government. Most industry in Russia is in the west. The countries of this region are trying to change from a command economy to a market economy.

- Eastern Europe's largest natural resource is lignite. Russia and the independent republics are rich in natural resources, such as oil, natural gas, forests, furs, and fish.

- Both regions face air and water pollution. Eastern Europe has a problem with acid rain. Russia has a problem with the disposal of atomic waste. They both face the social problems of ethnic and religious fighting.

Africa

Africa is a large continent south of the Mediterranean Sea, east of the Atlantic Ocean, and west of the Indian Ocean. It is a land of many nations, cultures, and huge open spaces. Africa is also home to the longest river in the world, the Nile, and the largest desert in the world, the Sahara.

This photograph was taken in Kenya in western Africa. Africa has many animal parks. People from all over the world travel to see African wildlife.

North Africa

North Africa is a cultural and historic crossroad. For thousands of years, people and ideas from Europe, Africa, and Asia came together here. North Africa stretches from the Atlantic and Mediterranean coasts in the north to the Sahara Desert in the south. The main physical feature of north Africa is the Sahara Desert.

Goals for Learning

◆ To describe where north Africa is located

◆ To learn north Africa's physical features and climate

◆ To identify the cultures of north Africa and explain where and how most north Africans live

◆ To understand north Africa's economy and the environmental challenges its people face

Geo-Stats   Key Nations of North Africa

Nation: Algeria
Population: 33,500,000
Area: 919,591 square miles
Capital: Algiers
Religion: Islam

Nation: Egypt
Population: 78,887,000
Area: 386,660 square miles
Cities: Cairo (capital), Alexandria
Religion: Islam

Nation: Morocco
Population: 31,700,000
Area: 172,413 square miles
Cities: Rabat (capital), Casablanca
Religion: Islam

Nation: Tunisia
Population: 10,175,000
Area: 63,170 square miles
Capital: Tunis
Religion: Islam

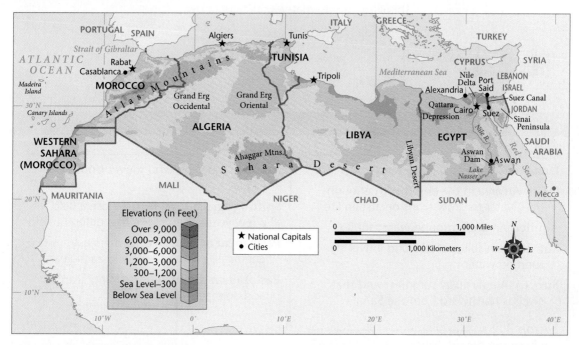

Map Skills

There are five countries in north Africa. North Africa is south of southern Europe and west of the Middle East. Western Sahara is controlled by Morocco.

Study the map and answer the following questions:

1. What are the five north African countries?

2. What seas do the nations of north Africa touch?

3. What body of water separates Egypt from Saudi Arabia?

4. What mountain ranges does the map show?

5. What large desert is in the south of the region?

Reading Strategy:
Inferencing

Inferencing means combining what you know with what you read. It builds what you know better than if you just read without thinking about what you already know.

◆ Think beyond the text.

◆ Predict what you will read next.

◆ Explain the cause and effect.

Key Vocabulary Words

Lesson 2

Dune Hill made of shifting sand

Oasis An area in the desert with enough freshwater to grow crops or sustain life

Aquifer An underground water source

Silt The rich soil carried along a river by running water

Sirocco A hot, dusty summer wind that sweeps northward from the Sahara

Lesson 3

Underemployment When a person trained for one job must accept another job that often pays less and requires fewer skills

Lesson 4

Nomad A person who moves from place to place

Shifting agriculture Farmers use a field for a few years, then move to a different field

Permanent agriculture Farmers use chemicals on the same field each year

Pastoralism Combining farming crops and animals

Where Is North Africa?

North Africa lies between the Mediterranean Sea to the north and the Sahara Desert to the south. The five countries of north Africa are Morocco, Algeria, Tunisia, Libya, and Egypt. Morocco, Algeria, and Tunisia are called the Maghreb nations. In Arabic, this means "land farthest west." The Red Sea divides north Africa from the Middle East. The Sinai Peninsula is separated from the main part of Egypt by the Suez Canal.

What Subregions Exist?

Geographers divide north Africa into three subregions. The first one is a narrow coastal plain in Morocco and Algeria. It includes the most fertile farmland.

The Nile River basin is a second subregion. People settled along the Nile because it was easy to farm there. Once a year, the Nile flooded, spreading rich, new soil. Today it continues to provide water for irrigation. Without the Nile, Egypt would only be a desert. Because of this, people call Egypt the "gift of the Nile."

The last subregion is the desert. The Sahara Desert is the world's largest desert. It covers 3.5 million square miles. Almost all of Europe could fit inside it. It covers 80 percent of Algeria and Libya.

The Great Pyramids of Giza are only a few miles from the skyscrapers of Cairo, in Egypt.

Reading Strategy:
Inferencing

What do you already know about the geography of this region?

How Did Geography Shape History?

The earliest civilizations grew up along river valleys. The Egyptian civilization, which grew along the Nile River, has lasted for more than 3,000 years. The Nile became an excellent highway for trade. The river flows north to the Mediterranean Sea. The river linked the Mediterranean Sea to the heart of Africa and united the areas of upper and lower Egypt.

Egypt prospered because of its natural boundaries. For most of its 4,100 miles, the river cuts through desert. Just before the Nile reaches the Mediterranean Sea, it forms a large, triangular-shaped delta of fertile farmland. The large delta was a rich farming area that grew more food than the people needed. This freed some people to become craftsmen, traders, religious leaders, and scientists. The Egyptians learned how to make paper. They were skilled builders. They invented a system of counting and used geometry to measure land.

Word Bank

delta 5
Egypt 3
Maghreb 1
Mediterranean 4
Sahara 2

Lesson 1 Review On a sheet of paper, use the words from the Word Bank to complete each sentence correctly.

1. Geographers sometimes call Morocco, Tunisia, and Algeria the _____ nations.
2. The largest desert in north Africa is the _____.
3. Many people call _____ the "gift of the Nile."
4. The Nile River empties into the _____ Sea.
5. The triangular-shaped area of fertile farmland at the mouth of the Nile is called a _____.

What do you think ?

Why did the first great civilizations develop in river valleys?

Objectives

◆ To describe the main physical features of north Africa

◆ To identify the major bodies of water

◆ To describe the climate of north Africa

Dune

Hill made of shifting sand

What Are the Main Physical Features?

The main physical feature of north Africa is the large area of desert. Many people think that sand covers deserts. It is true that much of Libya is covered with loose sand. Wind blows the sand into hills called **dunes.** However, only about one-fourth of the Sahara has sand dunes. Most of it is rocky plateaus and thin soil.

The large belt of desert lies between 15 degrees and 30 degrees north latitude. Most large deserts of the world are also located in this latitude. The air patterns create these subtropical deserts. Hot, wet air near the equator rises and cools. It drops its precipitation as heavy, tropical rains. The resulting cooler, drier air moves away from the equator. As the air reaches the subtropics, it drops down and warms. As a result, few clouds and little rain form.

This is an Arab village in Morocco. The houses are built on the slope of the mountains.

The Atlas Mountains stretch across Morocco, Algeria, and Tunisia. The Atlas are important because they are between the Mediterranean Sea and the Sahara Desert. In winter, they catch the rain-bearing winds. Because of this, most people live north of the mountains. Enough rain falls there to support farming.

An area in the desert with enough freshwater to grow crops or sustain life

Aquifer

An underground water source

Silt

The rich soil carried by river water

Reading Strategy:
Inferencing

After reading this section, what can you infer about the importance of water in north Africa?

What Are the Major Bodies of Water?

Life depends on water. Large parts of north Africa are almost empty because there is so little water. An **oasis** is a desert area with enough freshwater to grow crops or sustain life. Underground water sources called **aquifers** supply the water. In some places, a natural spring brings the water to the surface. In other places, people dig wells. Some of these wells are hundreds of years old.

In most places, the Nile River creates a narrow green belt through the desert. This belt is between two and five miles wide. Where it meets the sea, the river forms a delta about 100 miles long and 125 miles wide. Today, the Nile River valley and this delta support more than 75 million Egyptians.

Many of the water features were made by humans. In 1970, the Egyptian government built the Aswan Dam about 425 miles upstream from Cairo. The government wanted to control the flooding that took place every year. The dam created Lake Nasser. It is one of the largest human-made lakes in the world.

Lake Nasser provides irrigation water. The dam also produces hydroelectric power. However, the river no longer floods and leaves **silt**. Silt is the rich soil carried by the running water in a river. Farmers now have to use expensive fertilizers to make their crops grow.

Humans also made the Suez Canal, which opened in 1869. It allows large ocean-going ships to sail from the Mediterranean Sea, through the Red Sea, to the Indian Ocean. Because of this, ships do not have to take the long trip around the southern tip of Africa.

These boats are on the Nile River in Aswan, Egypt.

What Is the Climate Like?

This region has several climates. Most of it has a desert climate with hot days, cool nights, and little rainfall. In the summer, **siroccos** sweep northward from the Sahara. These hot, dusty winds sometimes cross the Mediterranean Sea and travel as far as southern Europe. Their fine dust covers everything.

The coastal areas around the Mediterranean Sea have a Mediterranean climate. Summers are hot; winters are mild with lots of rain. Spring is pleasant and cool.

Lesson 2 Review On a sheet of paper, write the letter of the answer that correctly completes each sentence.

1. _____ create the subtropical deserts located between 15 degrees and 30 degrees north latitude.

   A Air patterns   **C** Mountains
   B Oceans   **D** Rivers

2. Most of the Sahara Desert is covered with _____.

   A fine sand   **C** sand dunes
   B rocky plateaus   **D** oases

3. The Nile River no longer floods because of the _____.

   A Suez Canal   **C** Great Rift Valley
   B Aswan Dam   **D** Red Sea

4. The most important river of this region is the _____.

   A Mississippi   **C** Amazon
   B Volga   **D** Nile

5. A _____ is a hot, dusty summer wind that sweeps north from the Sahara.

   A steppe   **C** sirocco
   B oasis   **D** aquifer

What do you think ?

Do you think it was a mistake for Egypt to build the Aswan Dam? Explain your answer.

Objectives

◆ To identify the cultures of north Africa

◆ To explain where most people live

◆ To describe the main religion and languages of north Africa

Reading Strategy:
Inferencing

What does knowing the Five Pillars of Faith add to what you know about Islam?

These Muslims removed their shoes before going into the mosque to pray.

What Cultures Are In North Africa?

The major cultural group in north Africa is Arabs. The term "Arab" does not refer to a specific ethnic or racial group. Often, anyone who speaks Arabic is considered an Arab. Many north Africans are descended from Berbers. Berbers are light-skinned people who probably came from Europe or Asia. Most speak Arabic. Most of the people who live in Morocco, Algeria, and Tunisia are Berbers, but call themselves Arabs. However, in some places the people have kept their Berber culture.

What Religions Exist?

Over 90 percent of the people of north Africa follow the religion of Islam. This religion began in the 600s in what is now Saudi Arabia. An Arab named Muhammad believed that he should teach the word of God, who Muslims call Allah. Seven years after Muhammad died, Islam was brought to the Maghreb countries. An Arab army of 4,000 soldiers invaded north Africa. The Arabs brought Islam to the Berbers.

Muslims follow Muhammad's teachings as given in the Koran, often spelled Qur'an. This holy book is as important to Muslims as the Bible is to Christians and Jews.

The Five Pillars of Faith in the Koran list a Muslim's duties. First, they must state that God is Allah, and Muhammad is his prophet. Second, Muslims must pray five times a day at certain times. Third, they must give alms or money to the poor. Fourth, Muslims must not eat or drink from sunrise to sunset during the holy month of Ramadan, which is the ninth month of the Muslim calendar. Fifth, they must make the Hajj, a trip to Mecca in Saudi Arabia at least once, if they can afford it. Mecca is a holy city in the Islam religion.

This marketplace in Morocco sells goods that are made in north Africa.

Reading Strategy:
Inferencing

What can you infer about living in a family of eight children with little money?

What Languages Do the People Speak?

The most common language of north Africa is Arabic. The Koran is written in Arabic, which was among the earliest languages to have a written form. When European countries took over large areas of Africa in the 1800s, France ruled much of north Africa. Today, many people there still read and write using French. Some read newspapers printed in French, and many people use French for business. Since English has become the language of world business, many people in the business community also speak English.

What Are the Population Trends?

This region has one of the highest birthrates in the world. Islamic countries expect everyone to marry and have many children. Some families have as many as eight children. Most of the population is less than 15 years old. The population of Algeria, Tunisia, and Morocco has doubled in the last 40 years. It may double again in 30 years.

About 40 percent of north Africa's people still live in rural areas. However, many people are moving from rural areas to towns and cities. Some move because they cannot make a living farming. Some cities have doubled their size in 15 years. But some people are moving back to their villages after living in the city for a while. The reason is the high cost of land and high unemployment in the cities.

Cairo, Egypt, is the largest city in all of Africa. It has over 15 million people. Alexandria, Egypt's second-largest city, has over 3 million people. Algiers, the capital of Algeria, has over 3 million people and Rabat, the capital of Morocco, has over one million people.

First Home of Humans?

Many scientists believe that present-day humans came from Africa. The earliest known members of the human family may have appeared in Africa about 4 million years ago. The human family probably had many branches. Only one, Homo sapiens, still exists today. Scientists believe that Homo sapiens evolved, or changed over time, at least 100,000 years ago. Many years ago, an archaeologist found a jawbone near Lake Turkana in Africa. This jawbone belonged to a distant relative of humans. It may be over 4 million years old. The archaeologists below are sifting through the sand and rock to see what they may find.

Scientists use biological studies to show the links between people all over the world. Their studies suggest that human life began in Africa. From there, people migrated to the Middle East and then to Europe. Members of the human family also migrated to east Asia from Africa.

Scientists believe that language has made modern humans different from those who lived long ago. The development of language allowed humans to work together to obtain food and water. With language, they could exchange and share ideas. Most importantly, they could pass down what they had learned from one generation to the next.

Underemployment
When a person trained for one job must accept another job that often pays less and requires fewer skills

What Problems Do the People Face?

Like many developing countries, the greatest problem facing the countries of north Africa is poverty. North Africans are better off than many other Africans, but poverty is still widespread.

Many north Africans have health problems. Malaria is a disease spread by mosquitoes. Typhoid fever is a disease spread in dirty drinking water. Both diseases are common in villages and rural areas. While the number of people with HIV/AIDS in north Africa is small, it is growing. Another problem is the lack of good housing. The governments would also like to improve education, especially for women. Less than half of women in these countries can read and write.

Unemployment is a problem in this region. Many people who come to the cities cannot find jobs. The region also has **underemployment.** This is when a person who is trained for one job must accept another job that often pays less and requires fewer skills.

Lesson 3 Review On a sheet of paper, write the answer to each question. Use complete sentences.

1. Who are the Berbers?
2. What religion do most north Africans follow?
3. What is the holy book of Islam?
4. What language do most people of north Africa speak?
5. What is the largest city in north Africa?

What do you think ?

Do you think it would be better to live in rural north Africa or in one of the big cities? Explain.

Nomad

A person who moves from place to place

Shifting agriculture

Farmers use a field for a few years, then move to a different field

Permanent agriculture

Farmers use chemicals on the same field each year

Pastoralism

Combining farming crops and animals

Reading Strategy:
Inferencing

What can you infer about farming in north Africa? What words helped you make your inference?

What Is North Africa's Economy Like?

In this region, many people earn a living much as their ancestors did hundreds of years ago. Some are **nomads** who move from place to place, though the number of nomads is decreasing. Many tend herds of camels, sheep, or goats.

Even though the region has many deserts, nearly half of the people are farmers. Many are subsistence farmers. They rely on animal power and human labor instead of machines.

There are three major forms of traditional African farming. In **shifting agriculture**, farmers grow crops in a field for a few years and then move to a different field for a few years.

In **permanent agriculture**, farmers use the same land every year. Over time the land becomes less productive. Farmers then have to use expensive fertilizers.

The third type of farming is **pastoralism**. This form of farming combines growing crops with keeping herds of cattle and goats.

Along the Mediterranean coast, farmers grow enough crops to sell—barley, wheat, oranges, grapes, and olives. In the Nile River delta, farmers grow rice, cotton, sugar, barley, and wheat.

The growing population and environmental challenges facing north Africa have made farming more difficult. Long periods of drought and other natural as well as manmade disasters have caused many people to go hungry.

What Natural Resources Are Important?

Algeria and Libya have huge oil deposits. This oil is the most important part of their economies, supplying more than half of the national budget and almost all of their export earnings. Algeria is the third-largest natural gas exporter in the world. This region also has other mineral resources. Morocco is one of the world's largest producers of phosphates, used to make fertilizers. Morocco and Tunisia also have deposits of iron ore, manganese, lead, and zinc.

Reading Strategy:
Inferencing

What can you infer about the future of the environment in north Africa based on what you already know?

What Environmental Problems Exist?

North Africa faces many environmental problems. Pollution is a growing problem. The main reason for the pollution is the growing number of people. When people move to cities, the amount of pollution grows. As more industry develops, the region's countries begin to experience the same pollution common in developed countries. None of the countries have strong laws to protect the environment.

A second problem is the loss of farmland. Much farmland is lost as cities grow. The building of the Aswan Dam helped Egypt in many ways. However, it also created environmental problems. Before the dam was built, the Nile flushed out things that polluted the water. Now, the Nile flows more slowly, and is becoming more polluted. The Nile also used to wash harmful water snails out to sea. Now snails are working their way upstream. They spread a disease that affects workers in irrigated lands. Irrigation has also become a problem. It builds up salt in the soil. If this continues, the land will be useless for farming.

Lesson 4 Review On a sheet of paper, write the word in parenthesis that makes each statement true.

1. Nearly half of the people in this region are (nomads, farmers).

2. A form of farming that combines growing crops with keeping herds of cattle and goats is called (pastoralism, permanent farming).

3. (Algeria, Morocco) produces a large amount of phosphates.

4. (Libya, Egypt) has huge oil deposits.

5. The (Sahara, Aswan) Dam has caused problems.

What do you think ?

If you were in charge of setting national goals for the countries of north Africa, what would be your top three? Explain.

The Veils of Algeria

My name is Yamina. I am almost 18. I live with my family in Algiers, the capital of Algeria. Each day, I veil myself in a *haik.* This is a loose-fitting garment that covers my head and body. It is white and made of rayon. I also wear an *a'djar,* a kind of veil that covers the lower part of my face. My *a'djar* is made of finely embroidered silk.

I know many Americans do not understand why some women veil themselves. Veiling is an Islamic custom. Its purpose is to keep the honor of a woman and her family. The veil prevents men not related to a woman from seeing her.

Lately I've been seeing girls and women around the city not wearing veils. My father is angry that Algerian women try to look like American and European women.

Last year I did a school report on veiling. I learned that women in different parts of Algeria practice different styles of veiling. Here in Algiers, most wear the white *haik.* Some women choose silk instead of rayon.

In the central region of Algeria, women cover themselves even more. Most wrap themselves entirely in a large piece of white wool. It covers the face as well, leaving only one eye visible. This is also true for women in the desert region of the Sahara.

Women in the city of Constantine wear a veil called a *melia.* This is close-fitting and is made of a light-weight black fabric. It reaches all the way to a woman's feet. She wears a black *a'djar* to cover the lower half of her face.

In the city of Oran, women veil themselves in Moroccan style. They wear a long, loose-fitting robe called a *djellaba.* It has long sleeves and is usually dark in color. The *djellaba* has an attached hood, and women veil the lower half of their faces as well.

In some regions, veiling is far less strict. And the *Tuareg* women do not wear veils at all. Sometimes I wonder what it would be like to not veil myself. But I never do more than wonder. My father would never allow it.

Wrap-Up

1. What is the typical veil style in the city of Algiers?

2. How do women's veils in Constantine differ from those in Algiers?

- North Africa has five countries: Morocco, Algeria, Tunisia, Libya, and Egypt. This region has three subregions: the narrow coastal plain in Morocco and Algeria, the Nile River basin, and the desert. The Sahara Desert is the world's largest desert. It covers 3.5 million square miles.

- The Egyptian civilization, which grew along the Nile River, has lasted for more than 3,000 years. The Egyptian civilization developed because the large Nile delta was a rich farming area that grew a surplus of food. Humans made the Aswan Dam and the Suez Canal.

- The most important physical feature of north Africa is the large area of desert. Most of the Sahara Desert is covered with thin, rocky soil.

- Much of north Africa has a desert climate. The coastal areas around the Mediterranean have a Mediterranean climate.

- Arabs are the major cultural group in north Africa. Often, anyone who speaks Arabic is considered an Arab. Most of the people in Morocco, Algeria, and Tunisia are Berbers, but identify themselves as Arab.

- This region has one of the highest birthrates in the world.

- Over 90 percent of the people of north Africa follow the religion of Islam. Most people of north Africa speak Arabic.

- There are three major forms of traditional African farming: shifting farming, permanent farming, and pastoralism.

- Algeria and Libya have huge oil deposits. Morocco is one of the world's largest producers of phosphates.

- Pollution is a growing problem. The main reason for the pollution is the growing number of people. The loss of farmland as cities grow is a big problem.

- The Aswan Dam has helped Egypt, but it has also produced some environmental problems that threaten the land and its people.

Chapter 13 R E V I E W

Word Bank

Arabs ⁴

Egypt ³

Islam ⁵

Mediterranean ¹

Red ²

On a sheet of paper, use the words from the Word Bank to complete each sentence correctly.

1. The _____ Sea is north of northern Africa.

2. The _____ Sea divides north Africa from the Middle East.

3. _____ is often called the "gift of the Nile."

4. _____ are the major cultural group in north Africa.

5. Over 90 percent of the people of north Africa follow the religion of _____.

On a sheet of paper, write the letter of the answer that correctly completes each sentence.

6. The three Maghreb countries in north Africa that are located farthest west are Algeria, Tunisia, and _____.

   A Turkey   **C** Morocco
   B Egypt   **D** Iran

7. _____ cover most of the Sahara.

   A Rocky plateaus and thin soil
   B Savanna-like grasses
   C Sand dunes
   D Palm trees and oases

8. Shifting farming is when farmers _____.

   A rely on animal power and human labor
   B change fields every few years
   C use fertilizers in the same field
   D grow crops and farm animals

9. The third-largest exporter of natural gas in the world is _____.

   A Saudi Arabia   **C** Libya
   B Egypt   **D** Algeria

10. North Africa's biggest natural resource is _____.

    A silver   **C** gold

    B diamonds   **D** oil

On a sheet of paper, write the answer to each question. Use complete sentences.

11. What kind of climate does most of north Africa have?

12. What is the most important river of this region?

13. What two environmental problems does this region face?

Critical Thinking On a sheet of paper, write your response to each question. Use complete sentences.

14. A big problem in north Africa is the high birthrate. What do you think the countries of this region should do to limit population growth?

15. If you were a leader in north Africa, would you favor more food crops or more commercial farming?

Applying the Five Themes of Geography

Interaction

How does the Aswan Dam show both the good and the bad that can happen when people interact with their environment?

Test-Taking Tip

After you have taken a test, go back and reread the questions and your answers. Make sure that you have spelled the words correctly. Check to see that you have used proper grammar and punctuation in your sentences.

14

West and Central Africa

Some countries in west and central Africa are large and have many people. Others are small with few people. Rain forests cover some areas; deserts cover others. From the 1500s to the 1800s, west Africa supplied millions of slaves for the Caribbean, South America, and the United States. In the 1800s, the European powers divided Africa among themselves. Today, this area is one of the poorest in the world.

Goals for Learning

◆ To describe the location and regions of west and central Africa

◆ To identify the area's most important physical features and describe its climate

◆ To describe the cultures and people of the region

◆ To describe the region's natural resources, economy, and the environmental challenges it faces

---

Geo-Stats   Key Nations of West and Central Africa

Nation: Ghana
Population: 22,410,000
Area: 92,100 square miles
Capital: Accra

Nation: Niger
Population: 12,525,000
Area: 489,191 square miles
Capital: Niamey

Nation: Democratic Republic of the Congo
Population: 62,661,000
Area: 905,567 square miles
Capital: Kinshasa

Nation: Nigeria
Population: 131,860,000
Area: 356,669 square miles
Major Cities: Abuja (capital), Lagos, Ibadan

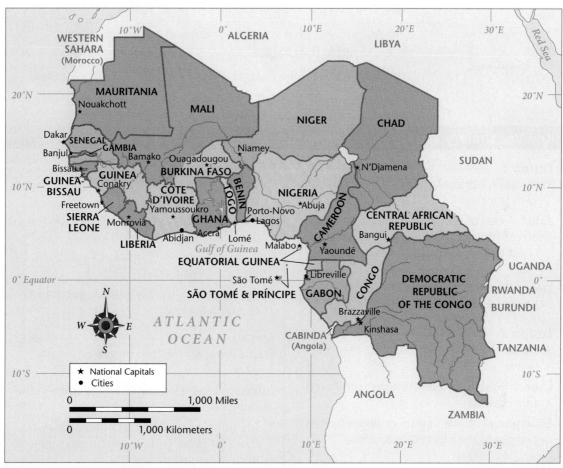

★ National Capitals
• Cities

0   1,000 Miles

0   1,000 Kilometers

Map Skills

Africa is the second largest continent in the world. It also has the second highest population. The Sahara Desert lies to the north of west and central Africa. The Gulf of Guinea in the Atlantic Ocean touches the western and southern shores of west and central Africa. Cape Verde is an island country in the Atlantic Ocean west of Senegal and Mauritania.

Study the map and answer the following questions:

1. What country on the map is actually made up of small islands?

2. Which gulf do many of the countries touch?

3. Which country in the region is farthest south?

4. Where are the capital cities of the countries along the Gulf of Guinea located?

5. Which countries does the equator run through?

Reading Strategy:
Metacognition

We call thinking about thinking metacognition. You can use metacognition to become a better reader.

◆ Look over the chapter before you begin reading.

◆ Ask yourself what you already know about the countries covered in the chapter.

◆ After you read the chapter, write a summary. Then compare it to the summary at the end of the chapter.

Key Vocabulary Words

Lesson 1
Savanna A flat, grassy plain in the Tropics with few trees

Sahel A belt of semiarid land that stretches across Africa from Senegal on the west coast to the highlands of Ethiopia in the east

Desertification The change from land that produces crops to desert land

Lesson 2
Sandbar A ridge of sand built up by ocean waves

Lagoon A shallow body of water separated from the sea

Escarpment A line of cliffs or slopes from a plateau to the plains or sea below

Lesson 3
Missionary A member of a church who travels to spread religious beliefs

Animist A person who believes that things in nature contain a spirit and who worships ancestors

Ancestor worship Worshiping members of one's family who lived long ago

Life expectancy The number of years an average person usually lives

Coup A sudden, usually violent, overthrow of a government

Lesson 4
Staple crop A food that people eat most often

Intercropping Planting different crops in the same field

Trade imbalance When a country is paying more for imports than what it receives from its exports

Objectives

◆ To identify the location of west and central Africa

◆ To describe their four physical regions

Where Are West and Central Africa Located?

West and central Africa make up a huge region. It covers an area larger than the size of the United States. The countries of Chad, the Democratic Republic of the Congo, and Niger alone are over half the size of the United States. Most of this region is in the low latitudes, near the equator. It includes 24 countries: Benin, Burkina Faso, Cameroon, Cape Verde, Central African Republic, Chad, Congo, Côte d'Ivoire (Ivory Coast), Democratic Republic of the Congo, Equatorial Guinea, Gabon, Gambia, Ghana, Guinea, Guinea-Bissau, Liberia, Mali, Mauritania, Niger, Nigeria, São Tomé and Príncipe, Senegal, Sierra Leone, and Togo. All of these countries, except for Cape Verde, are located on the west central part of the African mainland. Cape Verde is an island nation. The Atlantic Ocean and the Gulf of Guinea border many of these countries. However, some of them are landlocked, or surrounded by land.

What Physical Regions Exist?

West and central Africa have four physical regions. The first is the delta of the Niger River. Actually, this river has two deltas: the inland delta in Mali and the coastal delta in Nigeria. The inland delta is one of Africa's largest wetland areas. Mangroves, tropical trees that grow in swampy, coastal ground, cover much of the coastal delta.

The second region is the wide coastal plain. At one time, tropical rain forests completely covered this area. West Africans use the wood from these forests for fuel. In rural areas, wood is often the only energy source available. This area also exports lots of timber from these forests. For these reasons, many rain forests have been cut down.

Reading Strategy:
Metacognition
___

After you read this section, see if you can list the four physical regions.

Geography in Your Life

Insects in Africa

If you have ever had a mosquito bite or a bee sting, you know that some insects can be harmful. Some African insects, the tsetse fly and the black fly, are even deadly. They live in African grasses. The tsetse, shown here, sucks blood from humans and animals and can give them sleeping sickness. This disease damages the heart, changes a person's personality, causes head pain, and makes talking and walking difficult. Finally, the person goes into a long coma, or sleep, and dies.

Swarms of African black flies, each only 1/8 inch long, can cover a farm animal's body and bite it to death. This fly also bites humans and leaves behind small roundworms. The worms then blind the humans. The only way to control tsetse and black flies is to burn the grasses in which they live.

Savanna

A flat, grassy plain in the Tropics with few trees

Sahel

A belt of semiarid land that stretches across Africa from Senegal on the west coast to the highlands of Ethiopia in the east

Desertification

The process of land that produces crops changing into desert land

Reading Strategy:
Metacognition

Can you visualize the Sahel as a shore of the Sahara Desert?

The third region is the **savanna**. It is a flat, grassy plain in the Tropics. With few trees and rich soil, a savanna is good for farming. However, the tsetse fly and the black fly live there. The tsetse kills cattle and causes sleeping sickness in people. The black fly can blind people. It is most common along rivers, so people tend to avoid these areas, even though that land is best for farming.

The fourth region is the **Sahel.** This Arabic word means "shore." In this case, the "shore" is that of the Sahara Desert. The Sahel is a belt of semi-arid or dry land. It stretches across Africa from Senegal on the west coast through Mali, Niger, and Chad. Rainfall in this region varies each year. In the 1950s and 1960s, enough rain fell to raise crops. However, in the 1970s, almost no rain fell. Because of lack of rain, a way of life ended. Many nomads raised cattle, sheep, and goats, but the drought killed their animals. It also destroyed crops. Then farmers had no seed to start again when the rains returned in the 1980s. Many nomads and farmers migrated to cities. The desert gradually took over the deserted farmland. Geographers call this **desertification.** This change—when land that produces crops turns into desert land—is a major problem in Africa.

What Does Central Africa Look Like?

Much of central Africa is covered by tropical rain forests. The rain forests support many different types of plants. They are home to many birds and animals found no place else on Earth. The forests are in danger. People are cutting down the trees to earn money. Sometimes, they clear the land for farming. The soil is not rich and soon wears out. Over half of Africa's original rain forest is gone. In the southern part of central Africa, the rain forest gives way to savanna grasslands. The northern part of the region is desert.

Lesson 1 Review On a sheet of paper, write the word in parenthesis that makes each statement true.

1. (Cape Verde, Gambia) is an African island nation.

2. (Deserts, Mangroves) cover the coastal delta of Nigeria.

3. The (Sahel, delta) is experiencing desertification.

4. The (delta, savanna) is the home of the tsetse fly.

5. Much of central Africa is covered by (desert, rain forest).

What do you think ❓

What could stop desertification and the destruction of the African rain forest?

These workers are taking wood from a central African rain forest.

Sandbar

A ridge of sand built
up by ocean waves

Lagoon

A shallow body of
water separated from
the sea

Escarpment

A line of cliffs or
slopes from a plateau
to the plains or sea
below

What Are the Main Physical Features?

West Africa has a long coastline, but few harbors. The harbors have many **sandbars,** or ridges of sand built up by ocean waves. They also have **lagoons,** or shallow bodies of water separated from the sea. The only natural deepwater harbor is in Freetown, Sierra Leone. The two other important ports are Lagos in Nigeria and Abidjan in Côte d'Ivoire. Ships reach the Lagos harbor through a lagoon that must be regularly dredged, or dug out. To open up the Abidjan harbor, people dug a canal through a large sandbar. In recent years, many west African countries have tried to develop their coastal ports.

Many of Africa's geographic features can be explained by events that took place millions of years ago. While other large land masses broke apart and drifted away in what is called continental drift, Africa moved little. So, much of the land along Africa's coast drops sharply toward the sea in formations called **escarpments.** An escarpment is a line of cliffs or slopes from a plateau to the plains or sea below. This also explains why Africa has a rather smooth coastline. Compared to other continents, Africa has few harbors, bays, and peninsulas.

Africa's mountains are not as tall as those in South America and Asia. The highest mountains in west Africa are in Sierra Leone. The first Europeans who saw these mountains thought they looked like a sleeping lion, so they called them *Serra Lyoa.* This Portuguese term means "lion mountains" and became the name for the country. There are also mountain peaks on the border of Nigeria and Cameroon, north of the Sahel, and east of the Congo Basin.

There is a narrow coastal plain along the west coast of Africa. Moving inland from the plains and escarpments, the plains gradually change to a series of river systems, valleys, and basins, or lowlands. Higher land surrounds these basins. However, west and central Africa has few upland areas.

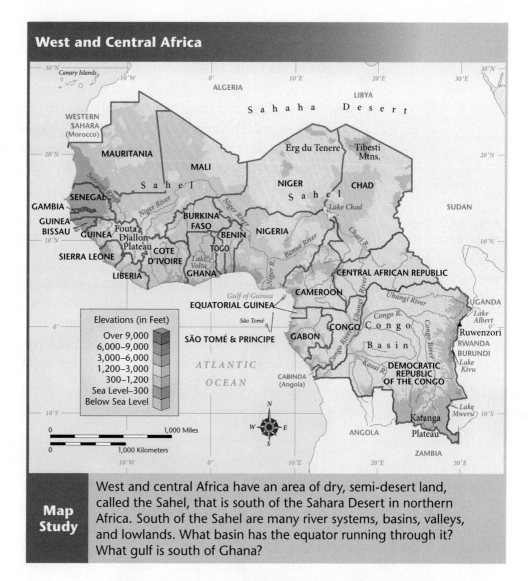

West and Central Africa

West and Central Africa

30°N · Canary Islands · 10°W · 0° · 10°E · 20°E · 30°E · 30°N

ALGERIA

LIBYA

S a h a h a   D e s e r t

WESTERN
SAHARA
(Morocco)

20°N · MAURITANIA · MALI · Erg du Tenere · Tibesti Mtns. · 20°N

S a h e l

NIGER · CHAD

S a h e l

Senegal River

SENEGAL

GAMBIA · Lake Chad · SUDAN

GUINEA
BISSAU · GUINEA · Fouta Djallon Plateau · BURKINA FASO · Niger River · Chari R.

Niger River

BENIN · NIGERIA · 10°N

SIERRA LEONE · COTE D'IVOIRE · TOGO · Benue River

LIBERIA · Lake Volta · GHANA · Niger R. · CENTRAL AFRICAN REPUBLIC

Gulf of Guinea · CAMEROON · UGANDA

EQUATORIAL GUINEA · Ubangi River · Lake Albert

0° · São Tomé · Congo R. · Ruwenzori

Elevations (in Feet)

Over 9,000
6,000–9,000
3,000–6,000
1,200–3,000
300–1,200
Sea Level–300
Below Sea Level

SÃO TOMÉ & PRINCIPE · GABON · CONGO · Congo · RWANDA

Basin · BURUNDI

ATLANTIC · Lake Kivu

OCEAN · Kasai R. · DEMOCRATIC REPUBLIC OF THE CONGO

CABINDA (Angola)

10°S · Lake Mweru · 10°S

Katanga

0 · 1,000 Miles · N · Plateau

W · E · ANGOLA

0 · 1,000 Kilometers · S · ZAMBIA

10°W · 0° · 10°E · 20°E · 30°E

Map Study

West and central Africa have an area of dry, semi-desert land, called the Sahel, that is south of the Sahara Desert in northern Africa. South of the Sahel are many river systems, basins, valleys, and lowlands. What basin has the equator running through it? What gulf is south of Ghana?

What Are the Major Rivers and Lakes?

The Congo River is the fifth longest river in the world and the second longest river in Africa. This 3,000-mile river begins in the Congo Basin of central Africa. Its depth and width depend on the location and time of year. It can be anywhere from one-half mile to ten miles wide. The Congo is an important "highway" to the middle of Africa. It is also an important source of food for people who live near it. It has several large tributaries, including the Ubangi and Kasai Rivers.

The Niger is the most important river in west Africa. Its 2,597 miles make it the third longest river in Africa. The Niger begins in the Fouta Djallon Plateau of Guinea in the west. It flows northward through Mali, then flows through the country of Niger and into Nigeria. Finally, it empties into the Gulf of Guinea. The Benue River is the Niger's biggest tributary. Other important rivers in west Africa are the Senegal, Volta, and Gambia. They provide hydroelectric power and water for irrigation.

Reading Strategy:
Metacognition

Remember to look at the physical map as you read about the physical features.

West and central Africa have many other rivers, but many of them are not navigable. Boats cannot navigate even the Congo in places because of the many waterfalls.

Lakes tend to form in the large basins. Many of these lakes are shallow and salty. Lake Chad is the largest lake in the area. It is about the same size as Lake Erie in the United States. Lake Chad is between Nigeria, Chad, and Niger. Lake Volta, a smaller lake, was created in 1965 when the Volta River was dammed.

The Congo River is an important "highway" to the middle of Africa.

What Is the Climate Like in This Region?

Most of west and central Africa has a tropical or a subtropical climate. Temperatures are high throughout the year. As a general rule, the climate is wettest on the coast. It becomes drier inland. Some of the upland areas, however, have more rain and lower temperatures than the surrounding lowlands.

Near the equator lies the belt of tropical rain forest climate. The closer an area is to the equator, the more rain it receives. Just north is a region with tropical savanna climate. The two climates differ in the amount of rainfall. The tropical rain forest climate has rain throughout the year. The tropical savanna climate has a dry season and a wet season. Along the coast, the rainy season lasts from May to October. Each year, as much as 200 inches of rain fall on the rain forest areas of Sierra Leone. The rainy season inland is shorter. The city of Timbuktu in Mali receives only about 8 inches per year.

Further north, the climate becomes much drier. The Sahel region has a dry steppe climate. Sometimes, there is enough rain to grow crops. In other years, people starve because there is too little rain to grow food or to feed their animals.

Word Bank

Chad 4
Congo 3
escarpment 2
lagoon 1
subtropical 5

Lesson 2 Review On a sheet of paper, use the words from the Word Bank to complete each sentence correctly.

1. A body of water separated from the sea is a _____.

2. A line of cliffs from a plateau to the plains or sea is an _____.

3. The _____ River is the fifth longest river in the world.

4. Lake _____ is the largest lake in central Africa.

5. Most of west and central Africa has a tropical or _____ climate.

What do you think ?

How might the lack of harbors affect the economy of west Africa?

Objectives

◆ To describe the cultures of west and central Africa

◆ To identify the languages spoken in the region

◆ To explain where most people in the region live

◆ To describe the major problems the region faces

What Are the Cultures of This Region?

Many people think that all Africans are alike. In fact, west and central Africa have a great deal of diversity. The countries in this region have many ethnic groups. Nigeria alone has more than 200 ethnic groups. The ethnic groups can be divided into two types of farmers who make their living in different ways.

Cultivators make up the first group. Cultivators are farmers who grow crops. They sell the crops to support themselves and their families. The largest ethnic groups of cultivators are the Mandinka in Senegal and Gambia, the Yoruba in Nigeria, the Mende in Sierra Leone, and the Ashanti in Ghana.

Pastoralists make up a second large group. Pastoralists look after animals. Sometimes they are nomads, moving from place to place. They travel long distances to search for water and grassy fields where their animals can eat and drink. The Fulani live in the savanna region. The Tuareg live further north in the Sahel region.

Reading Strategy:
Metacognition

Can you predict what languages are spoken in this part of Africa?

What Languages Do These Africans Speak?

More languages are spoken in central Africa than almost anywhere in the world. Each ethnic group has a language of its own. Over 200 languages are spoken in the Democratic Republic of the Congo alone. Many Africans speak one of the hundreds of Niger-Congo languages. People speaking different Niger-Congo languages can sometimes understand each other. Because of the great number of languages, many countries use a single western language as an official language. Many of the countries were colonies of European countries. Europeans controlled this area for a long time. Because of this, French, English, and Portuguese are among the official languages. Many people, especially in the Sahel and savanna regions, speak Arabic.

What Are the Major Religions?

West and central Africa is a region with many religions. Each African ethnic group has its own religion. European and American **missionaries** came to Africa's western coast. The missionaries spread their Christian beliefs, so some people there became Christians. Muslim traders crossed the Indian Ocean and introduced Islam to Africa. Muslim Arabs came to the dry northern area, so many people there became Muslims and practice Islam.

People in many rural communities keep their native beliefs. Many are **animists**. Animists believe that things in nature like trees, rivers, and the sky contain a spirit. They also practice **ancestor worship**. That is, they worship members of their family who lived long ago. An African chief once described his people as a "vast family, of which many are dead, few are living, and many more are not yet born."

Missionary

A member of a church who travels to spread religious beliefs

Animist

A person who believes that things in nature contain a spirit and who worships ancestors

Ancestor worship

Worshiping members of one's family who lived long ago

Celebrations

Festival of the Yams

Yams are a vegetable similar to sweet potatoes. They are an important food in west Africa. The beginning of August is the end of the rainy season. That is when the Yam Festival is held, and it lasts for several days. It is especially popular in Ghana and Nigeria.

First, villagers pray to the spirits of nature and their ancestors. They give thanks for the harvest. Then, the village chief, dressed in fine robes, tells stories. Afterward, all of the villagers bathe in the river, which represents a fresh start. Finally, everyone enjoys dancing, music, and eating.

Critical Thinking The Festival of the Yams celebrates a crop harvest. What holidays in your culture celebrate harvests?

Reading Strategy:
Metacognition

Note the main idea
and important details
about the paragraphs
on this page. Then
summarize what
you've read to make
sure you understand
this region of Africa.

Where Do Most People Live?

Most west Africans, especially those in the savanna region, live
in rural villages. Most are subsistence farmers who eat most of
what they grow and have little to sell. These farmers build their
homes with sun-baked mud bricks. They group their homes
into family units. The Islam religion allows men to have as
many as four wives. Muslim families are sometimes very large,
as women give birth to many children. In some villages, all the
people are members of the same family. Many people in the
Sahel keep cattle, sheep, or goats.

Of course, many people live in cities, too. Lagos in Nigeria has
about 9 million people. It is the largest city in the region. With
its high-rise buildings, Lagos looks like any large city in Europe
or North America.

Many farmers have moved to the cities. They live in the
shantytowns that surround these cities. In these slums, poor
people find shelter in cardboard boxes and other unfit places.
Dirt roads run through these shantytowns. The city does not
remove the garbage or provide sewers, water, or transportation.
Often the people drink unclean water.

What Are the Population Trends?

Population growth in west Africa is among the highest in the
world for two reasons. First, the countries have a high birthrate.
Families need many children to work in the fields or to herd
the animals. Second, the death rate is falling. In the past, many
children died as babies. Now, modern medicine has changed
that, and not as many babies die.

Many countries have a growth rate that is between 2 and
4 percent. A growth rate of 2.9 percent will double a population
in 23 years. Children under the age of 15 make up about half
of the population of many of these countries. Governments
need money to pay for education, medical care, and other
important services.

This town in Nigeria shows that poverty is a big problem.

What Problems Do These Countries Face?

Poverty is the region's biggest problem. Many of the world's poorest countries are in this region. Another problem is **life expectancy**, or the number of years an average person usually lives. Life expectancy is lower in west and central Africa than anywhere in the world. In Chad, it is only 47 years. Compare this to almost 78 years in the United States.

West Africa has other problems that result from poverty. Farmers cannot keep up with the growing number of people. This has caused widespread hunger. Most countries in the region depend on food aid and other aid from countries like the United States.

Coup

A sudden, usually violent, overthrow of a government

Reading Strategy:
Metacognition

Can you now summarize the problems in west Africa?

Shortages of everything from water to food have caused widespread fighting. Fighting has also broken out over who will control the region's vast mineral wealth. Many of west and central Africa's problems go back to when European countries took over Africa. Europeans drew the borders, but they did not think about human geography. They sometimes divided an ethnic group among several countries. They also put people who had been enemies into the same country. This has led to ethnic and religious wars. Thousands of people die every year.

The governments of most of these countries have kept the people from solving these problems. Many countries have a history of one-person rule. This often leads to dishonesty. The leader and those in high positions often become rich while most of the people stay poor. Many countries have had five or more **coups** since becoming independent in the 1950s and 1960s. A coup is a sudden overthrow of the government that is usually violent. In some countries, an army official has taken over the government.

Lesson 3 Review On a sheet of paper, write the answer to each question. Use complete sentences.

1. What is the difference between a cultivator and a pastoralist?

2. Why are European languages the official languages of some African nations?

3. What major religions do west and central Africans practice?

4. What is the largest city in Nigeria?

5. What did the Europeans do that has led to ethnic and religious wars?

What do you think ?

Should the United States and the United Nations send soldiers to Africa to stop the killing of innocent people in the ethnic wars there? Explain your answer.

Famine in Africa

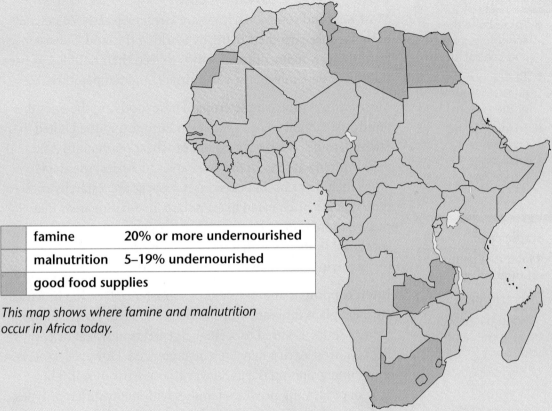

	famine	20% or more undernourished
	malnutrition	5–19% undernourished
	good food supplies	

This map shows where famine and malnutrition occur in Africa today.

Every year, about 30 million people die around the world from famine or malnutrition. Many of these people die in Africa. Famine is an extreme shortage of food. Malnutrition means not getting enough of the right kinds of food to stay healthy. Undernourished is another word for malnutrition.

Famine has many causes. Some causes, such as floods or not enough rain, are natural. Humans can also cause famine. War and overpopulation are two causes that humans create.

Wrap-Up

1. What are some causes of famine?

2. Do you think people in other parts of the world suffer from malnutrition?

Make a Difference

Write a letter to your local newspaper explaining the African famine situation. Include the names and addresses of two organizations to which people can send money.

Objectives

◆ To describe the economies of west and central Africa

◆ To describe the natural resources of the region

◆ To identify the environmental challenges the region faces

Staple crop

A food that people eat most often

Intercropping

Planting different crops in the same field

What Is the Economy Like?

Most west and central Africans are farmers. Nearly 70 percent of the people earn their living by working the land. Subsistence farmers grow many different crops to feed their families. What they grow depends on the soil, rainfall, and temperature.

Most farmers grow **staple crops**. These foods are the ones the family usually eats. For example, in Europe and the United States, families often eat a potato or wheat product. In Asia, people often eat rice. In the drier areas of Africa, the staple crops include yams and cassavas. Cassavas are a starchy root crop that are often eaten like a potato. In African areas that receive more rain, subsistence farmers grow corn, millet, and sorghum. In the areas that receive the most rain, farmers grow tropical fruits like mangoes, bananas, and papayas.

Intercropping is another kind of subsistence farming in Africa. Farmers plant different crops in the same field. People in the United States are used to seeing large fields of wheat or corn, so fields in west Africa may look disorganized. However, experts think intercropping is a good way to use African soil. This system of farming provides families with many different types of foods. The larger plants shade the smaller plants that might not do well in the hot sun. Also, the thick crop cover protects the soil from erosion during heavy storms.

Some farmers in the savanna and forest areas practice shifting agriculture. They move from place to place every few years. To clear a plot of land, they cut and burn the trees and grasses. At first, the ash from the fire makes the soil better for growing crops. However, in a year or two, the heavy rains wash away all the valuable minerals in the soil. The farmers then move to another place and start all over again.

Gradually, farming the same land each year is replacing shifting agriculture. This is because these countries have less land to farm and more and more people to feed.

West Africa produces cash crops such as cacao, coffee, peanuts, and cotton. Today, Africa is the main cacao supplier, with 75 percent of the world's cacao crop. Côte d'Ivoire is a large producer of cacao. Farmers in Nigeria and Senegal grow peanuts. Farmers raise cotton in Mali, Nigeria, and Côte d'Ivoire. Senegal exports a lot of shellfish and fish.

What Are Their Natural Resources?

This region is rich in natural resources. Nigeria, the Democratic Republic of the Congo, Cameroon, Côte d'Ivoire, Gabon, and Equatorial Guinea are all big oil producers. Africa provides about 14 percent of United States oil imports. This is almost as much as the United States imports from the Middle East. Nigeria has large deposits of oil, tin, and coal. It has about half of the world's supply of columbite, a metal that hardens stainless steel. Guinea is the world's second largest producer of bauxite. Niger is the second largest producer of uranium. The Democratic Republic of the Congo is rich in diamonds, copper, and cobalt. Sierra Leone has diamonds. Ghana produces more manganese, used to produce steel, than any other country.

At one time, west Africa was an important producer of gold. In fact, people once called Ghana the "Gold Coast." Workers in Ghana and Mali still mine gold, but production has dropped.

A miner drives a small train through a tunnel in a gold mine in Ghana. Many miners work underground.

How Does Trade Affect the Region's Economy?

Many west and central African countries trade mainly with the European countries that at one time ruled them. For example, Senegal still trades with France. Ghana and Nigeria still trade with Great Britain. The worldwide demand for oil has resulted in increased trade with the United States and China. The main exports of the region are oil, minerals, and farm products like cacao, coffee, palm oil, and cotton.

Exports bring in some money to these African countries, but they import more products than they export. This has led to a **trade imbalance.** This makes them owe money to countries they import from. To make up the difference, these African countries must borrow money. Now they need to figure out how to pay the debt they owe to other countries.

Dakar in Senegal is an important port city.

Recall what you
have read about
environmental
problems in other
countries to see if
these problems are
similar or different.

What Are Some Environmental Problems?

The region's growing population has been hard on the environment. The main environmental problems are water shortages, pollution, deforestation, soil erosion, and desertification. These problems affect one another. For example, the loss of forests can cause soil erosion. Trees hold soil in place, but rain can wash away treeless soil. Wind also blows it away. This turns an area into desert.

In urban areas, the biggest environmental problems are a result of overcrowding. Housing is often poorly built. In the large shantytowns, people do not have proper places to live.

Lesson 4 Review On a sheet of paper, write the letter of the answer that correctly completes each sentence.

Writing About Geography

Imagine that you are a political leader in Africa. Look back over this chapter. Then list one problem African nations face. Write an action plan for how you would solve this problem. Give details for how you will make the plan work.

What do you think

What might the trading partners of west Africa do to help these African countries solve their problem of high foreign debt?

1. Most people of west and central Africa make their living from _____.

   A natural resources   **C** fishing
   B mining   **D** farming

2. _____ are the foods that people most often eat.

   A Meats   **C** Junk food
   B Staple crops **D** Carbohydrates

3. _____ is the planting of different crops in the same field.

   A Intercropping   **C** Commercial farming
   B Shifting agriculture **D** Organic farming

4. The west African country of _____ has large deposits of oil, tin, coal, and columbite.

   A Mali   **C** Ghana
   B Nigeria **D** Niger

5. In urban areas, the biggest environmental problems are a result of _____.

   A logging **C** overcrowding
   B exports **D** imports

A Typical Day in Tibati

My name is Sylvie. I am 14 years old. I live in Tibati in Cameroon's Adamawa Province. My family is larger than most American families. That's because my father has four wives, each with her own children.

Families here live in mud hut compounds. My father has his own hut. Each wife also has her own hut where she lives with her children. There are huts for the goats and cattle, for grain storage, and for cooking.

Three of my half brothers live in our hut, not with their mother. My father divorced their mother. In our country, the father keeps the children after a divorce.

The first thing I do each day is go to the local well. I make several trips, carrying the jugs on my head. It's best to go early. Depending on the rains, the well is sometimes empty by the end of the day.

We use the water for cooking, washing, and praying. We pray to Allah five times each day. Not all Muslims wash before praying, but we do.

Some days I go to school. There are about 75 children in my class. My teacher is very busy! I love school, even though my French is not good. I speak Fulfulde, so there is a lot I do not understand yet. Still, I am happy to be there.

My mother keeps me home when she needs me. I care for my younger brothers and sisters in the compound. Often I have to help raise the vegetables we grow. We sell them in the market to make extra money.

My mother does not care when I miss school. She thinks it's foolish since my future is as a wife and mother. In two or three years, she and my father will arrange my marriage. Whoever asks to marry me will offer my parents gifts of wine, wood, money, or salt. My parents will decide whether the man can provide for me and our future children. I will be expected to have children, cook, and look after the hut. But, until I become a wife, I will keep studying, because I like to learn new things.

Wrap-Up

1. Why do Sylvie's brothers live with her and not their own mother?

2. What does Sylvie's future hold?

Chapter 14 SUMMARY

- Africa is the second largest continent. The 24 countries of west and central Africa cover an area larger than the size of the United States.

- West and central Africa have four physical regions: the Niger River delta, the wide coastal plain, the savanna, and the Sahel. Most of west Africa is plains and basins with a few uplands. It has a long coastline, but few harbors.

- The region's most important rivers are the Congo and the Niger. Rivers provide hydroelectric power and water for irrigation. The largest lake is Lake Chad.

- West and central Africa has several climates. Near the equator is a belt of tropical rain forest climate. Just north is a region with tropical savanna climate. The Sahel region has a steppe climate.

- Hundreds of ethnic groups live in these countries. They form two cultural groups: cultivators who farm and pastoralists who raise animals.

- In the past, European countries controlled west Africa. Because of this, French, English, and Portuguese are official languages. However, each ethnic group has its own language. Many people also speak Arabic.

- Many coastal west Africans are Christian. Northern people are Muslims. Many people are animists who believe that spirits live in nature.

- Most west and central Africans live in rural villages on the savanna and are subsistence farmers. Other farmers raise cash crops, such as cacao, coffee, peanuts, and cotton. Because of drought, many farmers have moved to overcrowded cities.

- Population growth is among the highest in the world. The governments in this African region have little money to provide education, medical care, clean water, sewage, and other services.

- West and central Africa have a low life expectancy, ethnic and religious wars, and poor political leadership. Poverty is the biggest problem. Many people die from hunger or malnutrition.

- West and central Africa are rich in natural resources including oil. Other minerals found in the region are bauxite, uranium, copper, cobalt, manganese, gold, and diamonds.

- West and central African countries trade mainly with Europe. The worldwide demand for oil has resulted in increased trade with the United States and China. Many countries import more than they export so they are in debt.

- West and central Africa's main environmental problems are water shortages, pollution, deforestation, soil erosion, and desertification.

Chapter 14 REVIEW

Word Bank

animists 4
farming 5
pastoralists 3
Sahel 1
staple 2

On a sheet of paper, use the words from the Word Bank to complete each sentence correctly.

1. The region of west and central Africa that is experiencing desertification is the _____.

2. Foods that people eat most often are called _____ crops.

3. Farmers called _____ make their living by looking after animals.

4. People called _____ believe that things in nature contain a spirit.

5. Most people of west and central Africa make their living _____.

On a sheet of paper, write the letter of the answer that correctly completes each sentence.

6. West Africa has a long coastline but few _____.

   A harbors   **C** basins
   B forests   **D** lakes

7. The _____ is the most important river in west Africa.

   A Nile   **C** Volta
   B Niger   **D** Congo

8. _____ are areas of poor shelters that surround the big cities of west and central Africa.

   A Barrios   **C** Shantytowns
   B Intercrops   **D** Suburbs

9. Cassavas and yams are _____ crops, because most west Africans eat them.

   A cash   **C** share
   B pastoral   **D** staple

10. West and central Africa's growing _____ has been hard on the environment.

    A rain forests   **C** population
    B intercropping   **D** life expectancy

On a sheet of paper, write the answer to each question. Use complete sentences.

11. What is the climate of west Africa like?

12. What are the two different ways that farmers make a living in Africa?

13. What are some environmental problems of west and central Africa?

Critical Thinking On a sheet of paper, write your response to each question. Use complete sentences.

14. In the past, slave ships carried millions of slaves away from west Africa to the United States. Should the United States pay the west African countries money to make up for what they lost? Explain your answer.

15. Should west and central African countries encourage more farmers to grow cash crops? Why or why not?

Applying the Five Themes of Geography

Interaction

How has poor management of the environment added to Africa's problems?

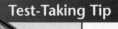

Test-Taking Tip

Read test questions carefully to identify those questions that require more than one answer. Read your answers to make sure that you answered all the questions.

15

East and Southern Africa

East Africa is a highland region with a cool climate and rich soil. Southern Africa is a vast plateau surrounded by a narrow coastal plain. For nearly 300 years, European countries ruled most of southern Africa. South Africa's small white population controlled the much larger black population until 1994. It was only then that the black majority was able to take control of the government.

Goals for Learning

◆ To describe the countries of east and southern Africa

◆ To identify the most important physical features and climate of this region

◆ To describe the diverse cultures of southern and eastern Africa and how the people live

◆ To describe their economies and the environmental challenges they face

Geo-Stats Key Nations of East and Southern Africa

Nation: Ethiopia
Population: 74,778,000
Area: 424,934 square miles
Capital: Addis Ababa

Nation: Kenya
Population: 34,708,000
Area: 228,861 square miles
Major Cities: Nairobi (capital), Mombasa

Nation: South Africa
Population: 44,188,000
Area: 471,445 square miles
Major Cities: Pretoria, Cape Town (capitals), Johannesburg

Nation: Mozambique
Population: 19,687,000
Area: 308,642 square miles
Capital: Maputo

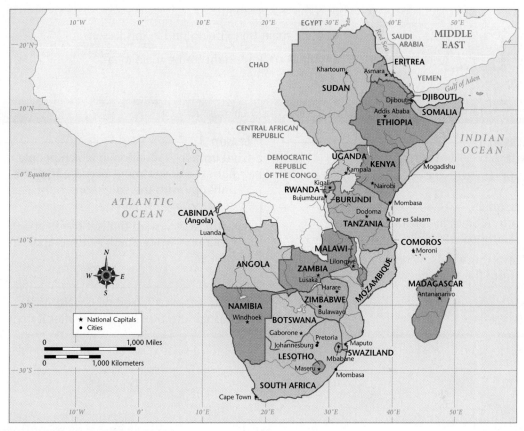

Map Skills

East Africa is known as the "horn of Africa" because it is shaped like the horn of a rhinoceros. The horn includes the countries of Somalia, Ethiopia, and Djibouti. The countries south of the equator are considered southern Africa. Some countries in this area include South Africa, Zimbabwe, and Mozambique. Southern Africa also includes the island nations of Madagascar, Comoros, Mauritius, and Seychelles.

Study the map and answer the following questions:

1. What country lies farthest east on the African continent?

2. What country is a large island east of Mozambique?

3. What big geographic problem do you think Lesotho faces?

4. What is Africa's southern most city?

5. What might make east Africa's location so important?

Reading Strategy:
Summarizing

Readers who summarize ask questions as they are reading. While reading this chapter, ask yourself these questions:

◆ What is this lesson about?

◆ What is the main thing being said in this lesson?

◆ What details are important to the main idea?

Key Vocabulary Words

Lesson 1

Rift A break in Earth's crust

Veld A grassy plain in southern Africa

Lesson 2

Fault A break in Earth's crust where earthquakes usually happen

Prevailing winds Winds that usually blow from the same direction

Lesson 3

Civil unrest A situation in which people fight the government because they are unhappy with the conditions in their country

Apartheid A system that set blacks and other non-white South Africans apart from whites

Lesson 4

Runoff Material mixed with water that washes into rivers and lakes after it rains

Objectives

◆ To describe the location of east and southern Africa

◆ To describe how the geography of the region affected its history

◆ To identify the physical regions of east and southern Africa

Where Are East and Southern Africa?

East Africa borders the Red Sea and the Gulf of Aden on the north and the Indian Ocean on the east. Central Africa lies to the west. East Africa includes Sudan, Eritrea, Ethiopia, Djibouti, Somalia, Uganda, Kenya, Rwanda, Burundi, and Tanzania. Southern Africa stretches from about 10 degrees to about 35 degrees south latitude, at the southern end of the African continent. Angola, Cabinda, Zambia, Malawi, and Mozambique are in southern Africa. The most southern countries are South Africa, Lesotho, and Swaziland. Sandwiched between are Namibia, Botswana, and Zimbabwe.

Southern Africa also includes the four island nations of Madagascar, the Seychelles, the Comoros, and Mauritius. They are located in the Indian Ocean, which borders the eastern shore of southern Africa. The Atlantic Ocean borders Angola, Namibia, and South Africa's western side. Lesotho, Swaziland, Botswana, Zimbabwe, Zambia, Malawi, Burundi, Rwanda, Uganda, and Ethiopia are the southern and eastern African countries that are landlocked.

Reading Strategy:
Summarizing

After reading this section, you should be able to tell how geography shaped the region's history.

How Did Geography Shape History?

In the 1400s, Europeans began to look for a sea route to Asia. They did this because the country that controlled the trade route to Asia would become rich and powerful. It would be cheaper to transport goods by sea than on land. As explorers sailed down the west coast of Africa, the Portuguese found its southern tip. They called it the Cape of Good Hope. In 1652, the Dutch built a small settlement on Africa's tip. They called it Cape Town. Later, German, French, and British settlers joined the Dutch. Southern Africa offered them rich farmland and a mild climate. The settlement grew. Soon the European holdings also grew. The white settlers fought with the native blacks.

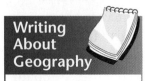

In 1886, gold-bearing rocks were found on a farm in South Africa. News of this spread quickly. Soon thousands of people rushed there, searching for gold. A small town grew up near the gold site. It became Johannesburg, South Africa. Today, it is the economic center of South Africa.

East Africa was at first of little interest to the European powers. Italy entered the scramble for Africa late. It took over two territories on the horn of Africa, Eritrea and Somalia. Italy thought that by conquering Ethiopia it could form a bridge between its two territories. Today, east Africa's location is important for military reasons. The countries on the horn of Africa guard the way into the Red Sea. Oil-producing countries in the Middle East sell much of the world's oil. For this reason, the United States, which buys some of the oil, wants to keep this area free of conflict.

What Regions Exist?

East Africa is a highland region of plains and plateaus. On the east of the Ethiopian Highlands is a large **rift** valley. A rift is a break in Earth's crust. The Great Rift Valley is on the eastern edge of some of Africa's tallest mountains. It also contains some of the deepest lakes in the world. The Great Rift Valley runs through Ethiopia, Kenya, and Tanzania. The valley is large and wide.

Southern Africa has four main physical regions. In the southern part, the plateaus and the Drakensberg Mountains make up a highland region.

A second region is the **veld.** This grassy plain stretches across central South Africa to western Lesotho and Zimbabwe. The veld is like the steppes of Russia, the pampas of Argentina, and the American prairie. The only difference is the type of grass that grows on the land. All these grasslands have rich soil for growing grain.

The Namib Desert covers much of Namibia.

The third region is a desert region. A large desert stretches across the western part of southern Africa. The Namib covers western Namibia. The Kalahari is the largest desert in southern Africa. It covers two-thirds of Botswana and stretches into Namibia and South Africa.

The fourth region is the low-lying plain of the northern part of southern Africa. This region receives the most rainfall, and is covered by forests. Woodlands cover the northern parts of Zambia, Malawi, and Mozambique. A low coastal plain is located to the east. In southern Mozambique, this coastal plain broadens. Heavy rains sometimes cause its many rivers to flood.

Lesson 1 Review On a sheet of paper, write the word in parenthesis that makes each statement true.

1. (Cape Town, Johannesburg) is the economic center of South Africa.

2. East Africa is an area of (highlands, lowlands).

3. The (veld, desert) is like the American prairie.

4. The Kalahari is a (lake, desert) in southern Africa.

5. Two thirds of Botswana is covered by the (Sahara, Kalahari) desert.

Reading Strategy:
Summarizing

Can you now list the four regions in east and southern Africa?

What do you think

Think about what you have learned about Africa. Why did Europeans prefer to settle in southern or east Africa rather than in west Africa?

What Are the Main Physical Features?

The Great Rift Valley is the main physical feature of east Africa. The rift has been forming for 30 million years. It is the result of several tectonic plates shifting. The valley is over 4,000 miles long. It is a geological **fault.** A fault is a break in Earth's crust, or outer layer. Solid rock on one side of the fault may move up, down, or sideways from the rock on the other side. Sometimes, the movement is slow and no one notices it. At other times, the movement is quick and causes earthquakes. Along the fault line are many beautiful mountains, valleys, and lakes.

The shape of southern Africa's land is like an upside-down plate. Much of the land is a large plateau. Along the coast, the plateau drops sharply to a coastal plain. Escarpments form the edges of the plateau. One escarpment is the Drakensberg Mountains in eastern South Africa.

The Kalahari Desert is also part of the plateau area. Most people think of deserts as having few plants. However, grass and shrubs cover the Kalahari. The area only gets about 16 inches of rain per year. Underground water near the surface supports the plants. The Namib Desert runs along the entire west coast of Namibia. This desert is much drier than the Kalahari. Because of this, huge sand dunes with few plants cover most of the Namib.

Some of the Drakensberg Mountains in South Africa have flat tops. They are an example of an escarpment.

Major Deserts of the World

Desert	Location	Area in Square Miles
Sahara	North Africa	3,500,000
Gobi	Mongolia/Northeastern China	500,000
Patagonian	Argentina	260,000
Rub' al-Khali	Southern Arabian Peninsula	250,000
Chihuahuan	Mexico/Southwestern United States	140,000
Taklamakan	Northern China	140,000
Great Sandy	Northwestern Australia	130,000
Great Victoria	Southwestern Australia	130,000
Kalahari	Southwestern Africa	100,000
Kyzyl Kum	Uzbekistan	100,000

Chart Study The world has many large deserts. Two of the ten largest are in Africa. The largest is the Sahara in north Africa. The Kalahari in southern Africa is the ninth largest. How large is the Sahara? What deserts are located in Asia?

Reading Strategy:
Summarizing

Look at the chart above. Which large deserts are in Africa?

What Are the Major Rivers and Lakes?

Lake Victoria is Africa's largest lake. It is located in east Africa on the border of Tanzania, Kenya, and Uganda. Lake Tanganyika is located in the Great Rift Valley. It separates Tanzania from its central African neighbor, the Democratic Republic of the Congo. It is the largest rift lake in Africa. Lake Malawi is a freshwater lake along the border between Malawi and Mozambique. The lakes east of the Great Rift Valley are shallow. They are located in areas with high average temperatures. This causes the water to evaporate. That is, the water turns into water vapor. When the water evaporates, it leaves behind salt and other minerals. The water is too salty for most animals.

East Africa has many rivers. The Nile is a major river that flows into Egypt. The rivers have a variety of wildlife including giraffes, cheetahs, lions, leopards, hyenas, buffalo, hippos, and crocodiles.

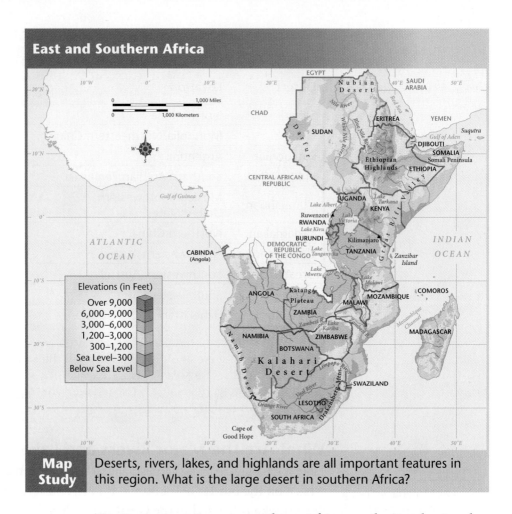

East and Southern Africa

Elevations (in Feet)
- Over 9,000
- 6,000–9,000
- 3,000–6,000
- 1,200–3,000
- 300–1,200
- Sea Level–300
- Below Sea Level

Map Study Deserts, rivers, lakes, and highlands are all important features in this region. What is the large desert in southern Africa?

Two important rivers in southern Africa are the Zambezi and the Orange. The Zambezi is southern Africa's longest river. It flows between Zambia and Zimbabwe. Victoria Falls, on the Zambezi, is more than one mile across and drops 354 feet. The Zambezi River flows into Mozambique and then into the Indian Ocean. The Orange River begins in the highlands of Lesotho, flows through South Africa, and empties into the Atlantic Ocean. Many rivers in the western part of southern Africa are dry during much of the year.

Southern Africa's largest lakes were formed by damming the Zambezi River. Lake Kariba is on the Zambia-Zimbabwe border. Lake Cahora Bassa is in Mozambique. Lake Malawi is between Malawi, Tanzania, and Mozambique. It drains into the Zambezi River.

The dams provide hydroelectric power. Fish have been added to the lake to improve the diet of people in Mozambique. Southern Africa also has salt lakes, which are dry for much of the year.

What Is the Climate of This Region Like?

East Africa has many different climates. The coastal strip and the low valley areas are warm all year. Djibouti, Somalia, and Eritrea are mostly desert. Their northernmost parts have temperatures close to 100°F for much of the year. The Ethiopian Highlands enjoy cooler and wetter weather than the savanna areas that surround them.

East Africa is suffering from a long drought. Life depends on the rains. Many people of Kenya and Ethiopia are starving partly from the lack of rain.

Southern Africa has four climate types. The southernmost tip has a Mediterranean climate with mild winters. The most rain falls during the winter months of May to August.

Prevailing winds affect the Drakensberg Mountain slopes in southern Africa. These winds usually blow from the same direction. Air always flows from places of high air pressure to places where the air pressure is lower. This is the way heat is spread around the globe. Areas with warm temperatures like the Tropics have low air pressure. Areas with cooler temperatures like the Polar regions have high air pressure.

The prevailing winds affect the ocean currents. The ocean currents carry warm water toward the poles and cold water toward the equator. This circular flow of water and air is very important to maintaining life on Earth.

Ocean currents affect southern Africa greatly. The western shore of Namibia is very dry, even along the coast. This is because the prevailing winds flow away from the land. Maritime climates like those of the eastern coast of South Africa are the result of the prevailing winds blowing from the Indian Ocean toward the land. This moist air rises as it hits the windward slopes of the Drakensberg Mountains. As the air rises, it cools, and then it rains.

Victoria Falls on the Zambezi River are more than one mile across. They drop 354 feet.

Reading Strategy:
Summarizing

Why do some areas of southern Africa receive rain, while some areas are a desert?

Much of the inner part of southern Africa is far from the ocean. The prevailing winds drop most of their precipitation as they rise over the mountains. The result is a dry steppe or desert climate. Winters are dry, with clear skies and high temperatures. The little bit of rain comes mostly in the summer.

The eastern coastal area of southern Africa has a humid subtropical climate. Summers are hot and humid; winters are mild. Rain falls throughout the year, but mostly in the summer months.

Word Bank

Drakensberg 1

Victoria 2

Namib 3

prevailing 5

Zambezi 4

Lesson 2 Review On a sheet of paper, use the words from the Word Bank to complete each sentence correctly.

1. One escarpment is the _____ Mountains in eastern South Africa.

2. The largest lake in Africa is Lake _____.

3. Large sand dunes cover the _____ desert.

4. Dams on the _____ River provide hydroelectric power.

5. Winds that usually blow from the same direction are called _____ winds.

What do you think ?

Why might a person want to travel to east or southern Africa?

Objectives
◆ To describe the cultures of east and southern Africa
◆ To describe the religions of the region
◆ To identify some of the social problems the region faces

What Cultures Exist in This Region?

East Africa is home to many different ethnic groups. In Kenya alone, there are over 70 different groups. Each group has its own culture and language. The countries in the coastal areas have a different culture than those farther inland. The coastal areas of east Africa had contacts with India, Egypt, west Asia, and even with China long before other parts of Africa did. As time passed, Arabs and people from India settled in east Africa. During the colonial period, many people from Europe settled in east Africa.

This region's people can be divided into two groups: the Bantu and the Nilotic people. The Bantu mostly farm. In the beginning, many of them lived in west Africa. Three large subgroups of the Bantu are the Kikuyu in Kenya, the Sukuma in Tanzania, and the Baganda in Uganda.

The Nilotic people are mostly animal herders. They include the Lango in Uganda and the Luo in Kenya. One of the largest groups of Nilotic people is the Masai. They live in southern Kenya and northern Tanzania. Another large group is the Somalis. They are the largest ethnic group in Somalia, but some Somalis also live in Ethiopia, Kenya, and Djibouti. The Hutu and the Tutsi are the two major ethnic groups in Rwanda and Burundi. They were at war for many years. Over half a million people died in these wars.

For many years, only a few people lived in southern Africa. Most of them had come from somewhere else. This long history of people migrating to southern Africa has created diversity. Today, the main population groups include African peoples, Europeans, Asians, and a growing number of people of mixed race.

These farmers in Ethiopia grow papayas to sell.

Outsiders usually divide the people of southern Africa simply into black people and white people. However, both are made up of many different ethnic groups. For example, about 75 percent of the people of South Africa are blacks. However, this group includes many different ethnic groups. A small number of people trace their roots back to the earliest settlers, the San or "Bushmen." One large ethnic group is the Nguni. They include the Zulu, Swazi, Ndebele, Pondo, Temba, and Xhosa people. Two other large groups are the Sotho and the Tswana.

The white people in South Africa also differ. Most of them are descendents of Dutch, German, French, and British colonists. The ancestors of the largest group, the Afrikaners, came from the Netherlands. They make up about 13 percent of the population. People of mixed race and people of Indian ancestry make up the rest.

Why Do People Still Migrate in This Region?

As in many other areas we have studied, people in east and southern Africa migrate from rural villages to towns and cities to find more safety and better jobs. Many men from neighboring countries come to South Africa to work in mines, on farms, and in factories. War also causes people to leave their homeland. During a long civil war in Somalia, over 300,000 people left the country. Many of them sought safety in refugee camps in several neighboring countries. People have also left the Darfur region of Sudan. Millions of people have died in conflicts in Sudan, and more people have fled or died from starvation there.

Reading Strategy:
Summarizing

Can you explain two reasons people migrate in Africa?

What Religions Do People Practice?

In the 1800s, the European colonists introduced Christianity to many parts of Africa. Because of this, many people in Mozambique are Roman Catholic. In South Africa and Namibia, many people are Protestant.

Muslim traders who crossed the Indian Ocean brought the religion of Islam to east Africa. Islam is strongest in parts of Ethiopia, Somalia, and Tanzania. Many people in the northern coastal areas of Mozambique also practice Islam. A large group of South Africans migrated there from India. They practice Hinduism, a religion they brought from India.

Over 2,000 years ago, a small group of Jewish people settled in Ethiopia. They are called "Falashas" or "Black Jews." They lived and practiced their religion in peace for hundreds of years. Because of recent ethnic violence, many of the Falashas have been forced to migrate to Israel.

Of course, many people in southern Africa practice their traditional African religions like animism. Africans sometimes add parts of European religions to their own beliefs.

What Languages Do They Speak?

There are almost as many languages and dialects as there are ethnic groups in this region. Visitors to the big cities may hear European languages like English and French. Many people speak several languages. The Cushite language is spoken in parts of east Africa. The language spoken by most east Africans is Swahili. Swahili developed as a language of trade. It combined words from Arabic with African words. Swahili is the official language of Kenya and Tanzania.

People in southern Africa also speak many languages. Many black Africans speak one of the Niger, or Bantu, languages. Another language family, spoken by the San people, is Khoisan. This language uses different clicking sounds made by the tongue and the roof of the mouth.

Reading Strategy:
Summarizing

Can you summarize what is true about the languages in Africa?

The official languages of many countries in southern Africa go back to the colonial period. People from Mozambique and Angola speak Portuguese. Some people in Namibia still speak German. English is widely spoken in South Africa and Zimbabwe. The most commonly spoken language among whites is Afrikaans. This language is a mixture of Dutch and African languages. People in South Africa, Namibia, and Zimbabwe speak Afrikaans.

Between one quarter to one half of the population of these countries lives on less than $2 a day.

What Are the Population Trends?

The population of east and southern Africa is growing fast. There are many young people. Ethiopia may double its population in 25 years. Uganda's population may double in 50 years. Many of the people of this region are below the age of 18. As they grow up and have children, the growth rate will probably increase.

What Problems Do the People Face?

There is widespread poverty. In the past, most countries in this region raised enough food to feed all their people. Then, as the population grew, many countries began to spend lots of money to import food. Countries then had little money left to provide services to the people. To improve daily life, the government must find a way to slow population growth.

Civil unrest is another problem. It occurs when people fight the government because they are unhappy with the conditions in their country. In east Africa there is ethnic conflict in many countries. There was a long civil war in Somalia. Fighting in Rwanda and Sudan killed thousands of people and drove many more from their homes. The fighting disrupts everything. Herders cannot take care of their animals. Farmers have a hard time tending their crops. Armed gangs take what little food is grown.

In 1948, the whites in South Africa introduced **apartheid,** which means *apartness.* This system set blacks and other nonwhite South Africans apart from whites. Apartheid laws defined whom blacks could marry and where they could travel, what they could eat, or if they could go to school. Only white people could vote. Whites decided where nonwhites could live. Apartheid ended in 1992. Two years later, the people elected a black president, Nelson Mandela. But black political groups and whites still fight. Crime has increased. There is little law and order.

Africans do not always have farm machinery to help them. These Zimbabwe women are planting corn in a field.

Another problem in southern Africa is that whites controlled much of the land for many years. Whites numbered less than 1 percent of the people in Zimbabwe, but they owned 70 percent of the land. The Zimbabwe leaders tried land reform. This was a program to buy land from the whites and to give it to poor blacks. However, the government had no money to buy the land. So it looked the other way when blacks decided to take the land by force. This resulted in many white farmers leaving. But most blacks had no training in large-scale farming. They did not manage the land well and farm production dropped. Zimbabwe no longer produces enough food for the people who live there.

In South Africa, blacks make up 75 percent of the population, but they live on less than 15 percent of the land. The African National Congress came to power in South Africa in 1994. Land reform was one of their main promises. But only 3 percent of farmland that whites owned is now owned by blacks.

Perhaps Africa's biggest problem is AIDS. Africa has 70 percent of the world's population infected with HIV/AIDS. There are over 5 million people living with HIV in South Africa. Almost 1,000 AIDS deaths occur every day. In Botswana, Lesotho, Swaziland, and Zimbabwe, more than 30 percent of the adult population is HIV-positive.

The AIDS epidemic has a big effect on the economy. The deaths of farmers has cut food production. The number of orphans and old people that need care has grown. Some children cannot attend school because they have to take care of sick family members.

Biography

Nelson Mandela: 1918–

Nelson Mandela, the son of a Tembu chief, was the first black president of South Africa. When apartheid began in 1948, Mandela practiced peaceful protest. Mandela believed in nonviolence. He became a leader of the African National Congress. When Mandela protested the killing of some unarmed black Africans at Sharpeville in 1960, the government arrested him.

He spent the next 28 years in prison. During that time, he became a symbol for his people. In 1990, the white government freed Mandela. He continued to work to end apartheid. This happened in 1992, followed by free elections in April 1994. Mandela was elected president and developed a new democratic constitution. He served as president until 1999. In 1993, he received the Nobel Peace Prize, the highest peace honor in the world.

Lesson 3 Review On a sheet of paper, write the answer to each question. Use complete sentences.

1. How did trade influence the culture of east Africa?

2. Why do people migrate?

3. What religions besides Christianity do the people of east and southern Africa practice?

4. What is the Swahili language and where is it spoken?

5. What was apartheid?

What do you think ?

Whites own much of the land in southern Africa. Would you change this situation? Explain your answer.

Objectives

◆ To describe the economies of east and southern Africa

◆ To identify the natural resources of this region

◆ To learn some of the environmental problems the region faces

What Is the Economy Like?

Farming is the main activity in east and southern Africa. Most of the people are farmers. Many of them are subsistence farmers. Some families have animals to help with the work, but most people do their farm work by hand. They grow millet, sorghum, barley, wheat, corn, cassava, and matoke, a banana-like fruit. They raise cattle, sheep, and goats. The land is not as productive as it was in the past. There are also long periods with little rain. This has made it difficult to raise enough food to feed all the people. Many countries rely on food imports.

Crops are different in each country. The main crop in Botswana is sorghum, a type of grain. In Mozambique, it is cassava, which is like a sweet potato. In Lesotho and Zimbabwe, the main crop is corn. Kenya and Uganda produce coffee and tea.

Some people in southern Africa earn their living by farming on large plantations. Workers use machinery to plow, plant, and harvest. The plantation owners make money by exporting much of what the workers grow. The plantation crops are also different in each country. In Mozambique, farmers grow cotton. South Africa produces fruit and wine. Swaziland exports sugarcane. In Zimbabwe, cotton and tobacco are important exports. Botswana and Namibia are too dry for farming, so people raise cattle. In fact, twice as many cattle as people live in Botswana. The cows supply families with milk and meat.

Reading Strategy:
Summarizing

Now summarize the economy of east and southern Africa.

Many people must work two jobs to make enough money to live. For example, in Botswana, 85 percent of the people are farmers. However, farming earns them less than 35 percent of their income. Their farmland is poor and the weather is dry. One or more family members, usually men, must work in the cities or in the mines to support their families.

What Are Some Important Industries?

South Africa and Zimbabwe have large manufacturing industries. In fact, about one-fourth of South Africans have jobs in manufacturing. The biggest manufacturing industries are automobiles, metalworking, machinery, textiles, iron, and steel. South Africa produces many of the cars and buses that people in other parts of Africa use. Zimbabwe produces iron, steel, cement, food, textiles, and consumer goods.

What Natural Resources Exist?

People mine more gold in South Africa than in any other country in the world.

Many people in this region work as miners. Their working conditions are difficult and dangerous. However, the miners earn more than they could in their rural villages. Iron, copper, and gold have been mined for hundreds of years. South Africa is the largest exporter of gold, platinum, and chromium in the world. It also exports diamonds and uranium. It has large coal deposits.

Not all mining is done under ground. This is a gold mine in southern Africa.

Geography in Your Life

Tourism

Would you like working with people in a fun industry? You might be interested in a job in tourism. In Africa and other parts of the world, people work in service jobs in tourism. They work in hotels, restaurants, transportation industries, or recreation industries. Anything related to travel is part of the tourism business.

Ecotourism has created a new type of tourist job. Ecotourism workers say, "Take nothing but photographs and leave behind nothing but footprints." These workers help people enjoy nature without destroying it. Kenya was one of the first countries to ask workers to be part of ecotourism. It collected fees from tourists going into the national parks to look at wild animals. Kenya used this money to take care of the park and the animals. Kenya has shown that ecotourism brings more money to the native people than farming does. Workers in this new service industry want to keep parks, rain forests, wildlife, and beautiful land alive and well. Their job is to encourage people to respect nature.

Zimbabwe has huge deposits of chromium as well as coal, asbestos, copper, nickel, gold, platinum, and iron ore. Most of Botswana's exports are diamonds, copper, and nickel. Zambia depends on its large copper and cobalt deposits for about half of its income. Angola has large oil deposits. It exports much of its oil to the United States and China. Angola also produces diamonds.

Reading Strategy:
Summarizing

Summarize why the landscape in Africa is different from the landscape in the United States.

The landscape and wildlife of east and southern Africa are important natural resources. Tourists come to this area to see the wildlife: lions, elephants, giraffes, wildebeest, zebras, gazelles, buffalo, hippopotami, topi, warthogs, leopards, and hyenas. Many of these animals live on the grassy savannas of the Serengeti National Park in Tanzania. Tourists travel from all over the world to visit the natural beauty of Africa.

What Environmental Problems Exist?

This region shares many of the same environmental problems as the rest of Africa. The biggest problem is that there are too many people. There is too little good farmland. Few of the countries can produce enough food to feed all their people. Southern Africa has another big problem. How can it balance the needs of poor people with the needs of wildlife? The high population growth rate in many countries puts pressure on the environment. For example, thousands of poor villagers need wood for firewood, so they chop down trees. In rural areas, the animals are an important source of meat.

Tourism is both good and bad for southern Africa. Often, people from other countries own the hotels and restaurants. Because of this, the money tourists bring into a country soon leaves the country. Also, some of these owners build hotels and other tourist spots without taking care of the environment. Large numbers of tourists threaten the animals the tourists come to see. The cars, buses, and vans the tourists use add to air pollution.

Cape Town, South Africa, is located on the southern end of the African continent.

Material mixed with water that washes into rivers and lakes after it rains

Mining can be harmful, too. Hills of yellow waste materials from gold mines surround Johannesburg. **Runoff** from the mines pollutes rivers. Runoff is material mixed with water that washes into rivers and lakes after it rains. The coal-burning power stations also produce air pollution.

Lesson 4 Review On a sheet of paper, write the letter of the answer that correctly completes each sentence.

1. Most of the people in east and southern Africa work in _____.

   A gold mining   **C** manufacturing
   B agriculture   **D** diamond mining

2. Different countries raise different _____.

   A crops   **C** cattle
   B plantations   **D** cassava

3. _____ is the largest producer of gold in the world.

   A Namibia   **C** Mozambique
   B South Africa   **D** Botswana

4. _____ has large oil deposits and exports oil to the United States and China.

   A Zimbabwe   **C** Angola
   B Zambia   **D** South Africa

5. East and southern Africa's biggest problem is _____.

   A too many people and not enough good farmland
   B hotel owners from other countries
   C too much wildlife
   D too much tourism

What do you think ?

What is the best way for other countries to help the starving people in Africa?

The Lost Boys of Sudan

In 2001, the United States government brought 3,600 boys from Sudan to America. The boys had survived against all odds in their civil-war torn country. Starting over was possible, but healing would be hard.

In the late 1980s, around 26,000 Sudanese boys ran from the soldiers coming to their villages. Soldiers killed their parents and older brothers and took their sisters as slaves. The boys fled for their lives into the wilderness. They found thousands of other boys doing the same.

The large band walked endlessly in the African heat, hoping to find safety. Older boys took care of younger boys. But many boys died. They were chased by soldiers and wild animals. Disease and lack of food and water took many lives. Drowning was also common.

After about two months, they arrived in Ethiopia. There, they spent about three years in various refugee camps. Then gunfire chased them away again. The boys walked for nearly another year, through Sudan to Kenya.

Only about 10,000 of the original boys arrived at Kakuma Refugee Camp in 1992. Most were between the ages of 8 and 18. Those who are still at the camp suffer from hunger, disease, and lack of water. They receive small amounts of food and water each day.

The 3,600 Lost Boys who came to America now live in about 38 U.S. cities. Some have had a hard time living in America. If they

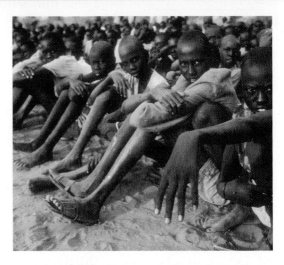

were under 18, they got to finish high school. They could attend junior college for free. But those over 18 weren't able to go to school. They had to find jobs. Without education and the right skills, their jobs have been low paying.

Other Lost Boys stories are happier. Some were adopted by American families. Some work during the day and attend classes at night. Many save just enough of their wages to pay the rent, and they send the rest to relatives. One boy has done remarkably well. He was accepted at Stanford, a well-known university in California.

Almost all of the Lost Boys—some now men—have nightmares about their past. But their courage and strength provide hope to anyone who knows their story.

Wrap-Up

1. About how many boys fled Sudan in the late 1980s?

2. How do the lives of boys still at the camp and boys in America differ?

- East Africa is a highland region of plains and Ethiopian Highlands. Southern Africa has four main regions: the southern highlands, the veld, the western deserts, and the northern low-lying plain covered with forests.

- The main physical feature of east Africa is the Great Rift Valley. Much of southern Africa is a large plateau with mountains. The most important deserts of southern Africa are the Kalahari and the Namib.

- Lake Victoria is Africa's largest lake. Lake Tanganyika is located in the Great Rift Valley. The main rivers are the Nile, Zambezi, and the Orange.

- The coastal strip and the low valley areas of east Africa are warm all year. Djibouti, Somalia, and Eritrea are mostly desert. The Ethiopian Highlands enjoy cooler and wetter weather than the savanna areas that surround them. The southernmost tip of Africa has a Mediterranean climate. The slopes of the Drakensberg Mountains have a maritime climate. Much of the inner part of southern Africa has a steppe climate.

- This region's people can be divided into two groups: the Bantu and the Nilotic people. The Bantu mostly farm. The Nilotic people are mostly animal herders. Many ethnic groups live in southern Africa. Many ethnic groups have migrated to southern Africa.

- Christianity, Islam, Hinduism, and animism are the major religions.

- The language spoken by most east Africans is Swahili. The people of southern Africa speak different languages, such as Bantu, Portuguese, German, or English. The most common language among whites is Afrikaans.

- High population growth, widespread poverty, civil unrest, and an AIDS epidemic are among the many problems in this region. Most east and southern Africans are subsistence farmers or they raise cattle. Most countries in the region do not raise enough food to feed all of their people.

- East and southern Africa are rich in minerals. Angola is a major oil producer. South Africa is the most industrial of the countries of southern Africa. Tourism is an important source of money for the region. The main environmental problem is that it has too many people and too little farmland.

Chapter 15 REVIEW

Word Bank

apartheid 5
fault 1
Kalahari 2
Swahili 4
Zambezi 3

On a sheet of paper, use the words from the Word Bank to complete each sentence correctly.

1. A _____ is a break in Earth's crust where rock may move.

2. The largest desert in southern Africa is the _____.

3. The longest river in southern Africa is the _____ River.

4. Many people in east Africa speak _____, which began as a language of trade.

5. The policy of _____ in South Africa kept blacks apart from whites.

On a sheet of paper, write the letter of the answer that correctly completes each sentence.

6. The east African countries of Djibouti, Ethiopia, and Somalia make up the _____.

   A poorest countries   **C** horn of Africa
   B Sahel   **D** largest rain forest

7. The _____ is the grassy plain of central southern Africa.

   A steppe   **C** pampas
   B veld   **D** prairie

8. The main physical feature of east Africa is the _____.

   A Orange River   **C** Drakensberg Mountains
   B Great Rift Valley   **D** Red Sea

9. In the 1800s, European colonists introduced _____ to parts of Africa.

   A Islam   **C** Christianity
   B Judaism   **D** Hinduism

10. The richest and most industrialized country of southern Africa is _____.

    A Botswana   **C** Mozambique
    B Zimbabwe   **D** South Africa

On a sheet of paper, write the answer to each question. Use complete sentences.

11. Where is east Africa located?

12. How has HIV/AIDS affected southern Africa?

13. What are two environmental problems that the countries of east and southern Africa face?

Critical Thinking On a sheet of paper, write your response to each question. Use complete sentences.

14. Why do you think a small white minority in South Africa adopted a policy of apartheid?

15. Should the United States and other rich countries do more to help the struggling countries of this region? Explain your answer.

Applying the Five Themes of Geography

Movement

How does the history of southern Africa reflect the theme of movement?

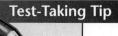

Test-Taking Tip

After you have completed a test, reread each question and answer. Ask yourself, "Have I answered the question that was asked? Have I answered all parts of the question?"

Diamonds: Southern Africa's Best Friend

Southern Africa has the world's largest supply of diamonds. In 1867, a 15-year-old boy discovered the first diamond in this area. Erasmus Jacobs found it on his father's farm on the south branch of the Orange River in South Africa.

The discovery set off a diamond rush. Many British fortune-seekers came to southern Africa. They bought land and made a claim to the diamonds. Soon, two of these English immigrants bought out all the claims. Cecil Rhodes brought together the holdings of the two men. In 1889, he founded the De Beers Company. Today, his company sells most of the diamonds in the world.

High temperatures and pressure deep within the earth form diamonds. The action of volcanoes brings these diamonds to the surface. Diamonds lie in volcanic pipes called kimberlite.

Skilled workers cut and polish the diamonds to bring out their color and sparkle. The best diamonds become gems used in diamond rings and other jewelry.

The poorer diamonds are not as pretty, but they are still important. Industries use them to grind, smooth, or polish other materials.

Seven countries control 80 percent of the world's diamond production. Four of these countries are in southern Africa. They are Botswana, Zaire, Angola, and South Africa. However, today people can make diamonds rather than mine them. These industrial diamonds are competing for sales with gem diamonds that come from mines.

Wrap-Up

1. When and where were the first diamonds discovered in southern Africa?

2. Who was Cecil Rhodes and what was his connection to the diamond industry?

3. What is kimberlite?

4. What is the difference between gem diamonds and industrial diamonds?

5. What four southern African countries produce the most diamonds?

- Africa is the second largest continent. It is south of Europe. The Red Sea divides it from the Middle East.

- Africa has many regions with deltas, coastal plains, deserts, basins, mountains, plateaus, and valleys.

- Some physical features are the Niger River and Nile River deltas; the Sahara, Kalahari, and Namib deserts; the Drakensberg Mountains; and the Great Rift Valley.

- Africa has many climates that include subtropical, steppe, Mediterranean, and desert.

- Several hundred ethnic groups live in west Africa. Many ethnic groups and descendants of European settlers live in southern Africa. Most people in central and east Africa can be divided into two groups: the Bantu and the Nilotic. More than half of the people of north Africa are Arabs.

- These ethnic groups speak many different languages, such as Bantu, Cushite, Swahili, Arabic, and a number of European languages.

- Among the religions people practice are Christianity, Islam, and Judaism. Many African people practice their own native religions. Some people practice Hinduism.

- Most people in Africa are farmers. Many are subsistence farmers. Others raise cash crops.

- Central and east Africa have fewer minerals than the rest of Africa. North Africa has oil deposits. Tourism is an important source of money. Tourists come to southern Africa to see the wildlife.

- Population growth is high in this region. Fighting among different ethnic groups throughout Africa is a problem.

Unit
7

The Middle East and Central Asia

The Middle East and central Asia are southeast of Europe and northeast of Africa. The Middle East is sometimes called southwest Asia because it is the southwest part of the Asian continent. It has much in common with parts of north Africa and with central Asia. This unit will show you how the Middle East and central Asia are two regions that are of growing importance in the modern world.

This photo is of a street in the old part of Damascus, Syria. It shows goods that are made in the Middle Eastern area of the world.

16

The Middle East

People have lived in this region for thousands of years. Historians say that civilization began in the Fertile Crescent, between the Tigris and Euphrates Rivers. The Middle East is still an important crossroads. Many people and ideas came together here. The region is the birthplace of three great world religions. The area has plenty of oil, but little water. There has been much fighting over religion, oil, and water in this important part of the world.

Goals for Learning

◆ To describe where the Middle East is located

◆ To identify its most important physical features and climate

◆ To identify the cultures of the Middle East and to explain how most people live

◆ To describe the economy and the environmental challenges the Middle East faces

Geo-Stats   Key Nations of the Middle East

Nation: Iran
Population:
6,8,688,000
Area: 636,296 square miles
Cities: Tehran (capital), Esfahan, Mashhad

Nation: Israel
Population:
6,352,000
Area: 8,019 square miles
Cities: Jerusalem (capital), Tel Aviv

Nation: Iraq
Population:
26,783,000
Area: 169,235 square miles
Cities: Baghdad (capital), Arbil, Basra, Mosul

Nation: Saudi Arabia
Population:
27,020,000
Area: 830,000 square miles
Cities: Riyadh (capital), Jeddah, Mecca

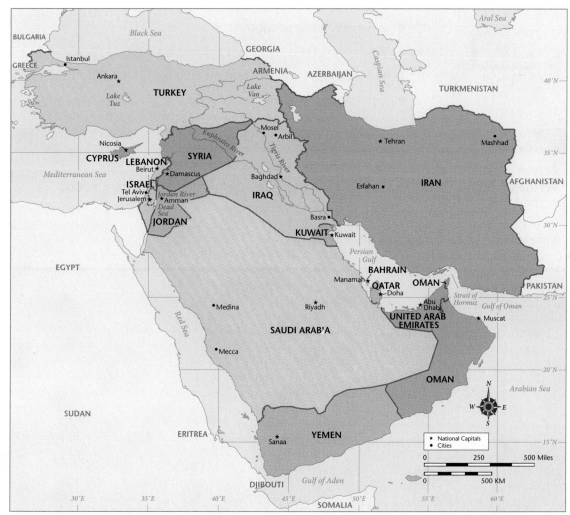

Map Skills

The Middle East is part of Asia. The Middle Eastern nations begin with Turkey, which is between the Black and Mediterranean Seas. From there, the Middle East extends southeast to the Arabian Sea.

Study the map and answer the following questions:

1. What are the largest countries in the Middle East?

2. What countries have borders on the Persian Gulf?

3. What is the capital of Iraq? Yemen? Jordan?

4. What sea is north of Iran?

5. What six countries does Iraq border? How might this explain Iraq's importance to the region?

Reading Strategy:
Questioning

Questioning as you read will help you become a more active reader. It will help you understand and remember more of what you read. As you read, ask yourself:

◆ What do I know about this subject?

◆ What in my life is like what I am reading?

◆ How can I remember important facts as I am reading?

◆ Can I summarize what I just read?

Key Vocabulary Words

Lesson 1

Fertile Crescent The rich farmland between the Tigris and Euphrates Rivers in Iraq and along the Jordan River in Israel and Jordan

Levant The coastal farming region of Syria, Lebanon, and Israel

Lesson 3

Monotheism A belief in only one God

Objectives

◆ To know where the Middle East is located

◆ To identify the four subregions of the Middle East

◆ To describe how geography shaped the history of the region

Fertile Crescent

The rich farmland between the Tigris and Euphrates Rivers in Iraq and along the Jordan River in Israel and Jordan

Levant

The coastal farming region of Syria, Lebanon, and Israel

Where Is the Middle East Located?

The Middle East is part of Asia. Geographers often link the Middle East with north Africa because of their religious and cultural ties. The Middle Eastern countries are Turkey, Syria, Lebanon, Israel, Saudi Arabia, Jordan, Iran, Iraq, Kuwait, United Arab Emirates, Bahrain, Qatar, Oman, and Yemen. Geographers often group Cyprus with the Middle East. Cyprus is an island nation in the Mediterranean Sea.

What Are the Subregions?

The Middle East has four subregions. The first is the area of rich farmland between the Tigris and Euphrates Rivers in Iraq and along the Jordan River in Israel and Jordan. This subregion is shaped like a crescent, or quarter moon, so it is called the **Fertile Crescent**. Thousands of years ago, this area was home to many early civilizations.

Another area of rich farmland is the **Levant.** It is the coastal farming region of Syria, Lebanon, and Israel. It borders the Mediterranean Sea. Arabs living there sometimes refer to it as *Mashriq,* meaning the country where the sun rises.

The third subregion is the Plateau of Anatolia. It is sometimes called Asia Minor. It includes most of Turkey and the mountains of Iran and Afghanistan. The plateau is over 3,000 feet high. There are rugged mountain ranges both to the north and south of it. It is located along a huge fault line and has many earthquakes.

The final subregion is the Rub' al-Khali. It is the huge desert located on the Arabian Peninsula. This desert has so few people that geographers sometimes call it the "empty quarter." Rub' al-Khali is the largest sand desert in the world and has the tallest sand dunes.

The Fertile Crescent is an area of rich farmland.

Why do you think the location of the Middle East could have helped shape its history?

How Did Geography Help Shape History?

The Middle East has been an important crossroads for thousands of years. Turkey lies between Europe and Asia. Many of the coastal areas of the Middle East along the Mediterranean Sea were colonized by ancient Greeks. The Phoenicians lived in what is now Lebanon. They traded cloth, glass, wood, and beautiful metal objects with people in other lands. They sailed to England to search for tin and copper. They traveled to parts of Africa for ivory. They founded colonies in France, Spain, and present-day Tunisia. The Phoenicians and other traders sold goods for their neighbors in north Africa, Arabia, and the Fertile Crescent.

Iran used to be called Persia. The people who live there are called Persians.

Over thousands of years, many different people have fought over this area because of its location. As a result, it has many diverse cultures. In ancient times, the Greeks and Persians fought for control of the region. In modern times, wars have broken out among the countries of the Middle East. Sometimes, countries outside the region like the United States and Russia have become involved.

This is a view of Istanbul, Turkey. In the foreground is the Mosque of Süleyman I the Magnificent. Mosques are places where Muslims worship.

Biography

Princess Basma Bint Ali: 1970–

Princess Basma is a member of the royal family of Jordan and is a major in the Jordanian army. In the 1990s, she became the first Jordanian woman to qualify as a navy diver. However, she is famous worldwide because she works to protect the undersea world in the Gulf of Aqaba. It is part of Jordan's coastline along the Red Sea. No other place matches the Red Sea for coral life, so many scuba divers come there. Princess Basma is president of the Jordan Royal Ecological Diving Society. She works to conserve this beautiful part of the world. She is also active in the politics of Jordan.

Word Bank

Fertile Crescent 1
Levant 2
Phoenicians 4
Rub' al-Khali 3
wars 5

Lesson 1 Review On a sheet of paper, use the words from the Word Bank to complete each sentence correctly.

1. The subregion of rich farmland that is shaped like a quarter moon is the _____.

2. The _____ is the coastal farming region of Syria, Lebanon, and Israel.

3. The huge empty desert on the Arabian Peninsula is called the _____.

4. The _____ traded goods from north Africa, Arabia, and the Fertile Crescent.

5. Because of its location, many _____ have been fought in this region.

What do you think ?

Why would the Middle East be important to European and Asian traders?

Objectives

◆ To describe the main physical features of the Middle East

◆ To identify the main bodies of water

◆ To describe the climates of the region

Reading Strategy:
Questioning

Ask yourself, "Can I name the main physical features of the Middle East?"

What Are the Middle East's Physical Features?

The main physical feature of the Middle East is the Arabian Peninsula. It is a large triangle-shaped piece of land separated from Africa by the Red Sea and from the rest of Asia by the Persian Gulf. Like most of north Africa, much of the Arabian Peninsula is desert. The Rub' al-Khali Desert is the world's largest sea of sand. It covers more than 250,000 square miles. It makes up most of Saudi Arabia, as well as parts of Oman, Yemen, and the United Arab Emirates. It is one of the hottest and driest places on Earth. Most people consider this desert a vast wasteland.

A second feature of this region is its highlands and high plateaus. Saudi Arabia's Hejaz Mountains rise along the Red Sea. Mountains border the high plateaus of Turkey and Iran. In northern Turkey are the Pontic Mountains. The tallest and most rugged mountains in the Middle East are the Taurus Mountains in southern Turkey. Mount Ararat, in eastern Turkey near the Iranian border, is almost 17,000 feet high. Iran has the Elburz Mountains in the north and the Zagros to the west.

Three large tectonic plates come together in Turkey and Iran. When the plates collided with each other long ago, the edge of one plate slid up over another and formed mountains. This created all the mountains in the region. Today, the plates still shift, causing deadly earthquakes.

What Are the Major Bodies of Water?

Fresh water is an important resource because there is so little of it in the Middle East. This is one reason why the area's rivers are so important. The Tigris and the Euphrates are two of the most important rivers in this region. The Euphrates River is the longest river in the Middle East. It begins in the Turkish mountains and flows through Turkey, Syria, and Iraq. In Iraq, it joins the Tigris before emptying into the Persian Gulf. The Tigris also begins in the mountains of Turkey. It has many tributaries. In ancient times, these rivers flooded every spring.

Middle East

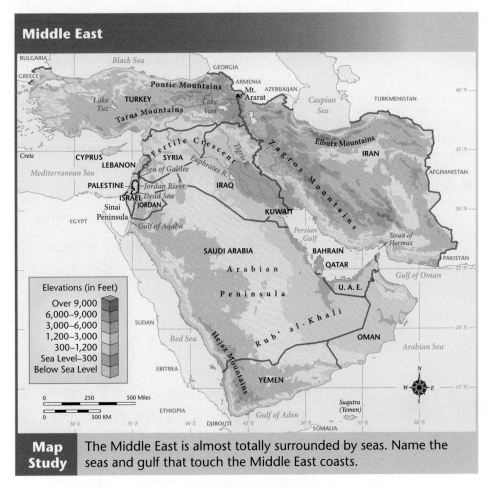

Map Study The Middle East is almost totally surrounded by seas. Name the seas and gulf that touch the Middle East coasts.

The floods carried much-needed water and silt—fertile soil and small rocky pieces. The floods left this silt behind in the river valleys. It helped form deltas and fertile farmland.

Reading Strategy:
Questioning

Does looking at the map help you visualize what you are reading about?

The Jordan River is a small but important river. It starts in the mountains of Lebanon and flows south. It forms the boundary between Jordan and Israel. It ends at the Dead Sea, which is a landlocked salt lake. The Dead Sea is so salty that very few plants or fish can live in it. People do not use the water for drinking or irrigation. But they do consider it healthy to bathe in. People have been coming to the lake for thousands of years to bathe in its waters and to soak in its black, mineral mud.

The Sea of Galilee is a small lake in Israel. It provides Israel with half its fresh water. The area around the lake has many beaches and is home to many types of birds.

What Is the Climate Like?

The Middle East has several climates. Much of it has a desert climate: hot days, cold nights, and little rainfall. The northern highlands of Turkey and Iran have a steppe climate. They are much wetter than the rest of the region except for the coast.

The coastal areas around the Mediterranean Sea have a Mediterranean climate. Summers are hot; winters are mild with lots of rain. Spring is pleasant and cool.

Reading Strategy:
Questioning
___

What is a steppe climate? If you cannot remember, look in the Glossary for a definition.

Lesson 2 Review On a sheet of paper, write the letter of the answer that correctly completes each sentence.

1. The world's largest sea of sand is the _____ desert.

A Sahara **C** Rub' al-Khali

B Sonora **D** Gobi

2. The highest mountains in the Middle East are the _____ Mountains in southern Turkey.

A Taurus **C** Hejaz

B Elburz **D** Zagros

3. The mountains and high plateaus of this region were formed by colliding _____.

A volcanoes **C** tectonic plates

B earthquakes **D** floods

4. The longest river in the Middle East is the _____.

A Tigris **C** Jordan

B Euphrates **D** Danube

5. The _____ provides Israel with over half of its fresh water.

A Tigris River **C** Dead Sea

B Nile River **D** Sea of Galilee

What do you think ?

Why might nations in conflict in the Middle East want to control highland areas?

Reading Strategy:
Questioning

Before reading the Geography in Your Life, ask yourself, "Did any ancient Arabs make a difference in what I do in math class?"

What Cultures Exist In This Region?

Arabs are the biggest cultural group in the Middle East. More than half of the people are Arabs. They share three things: they speak the same language, 90 percent are Muslims, and they are proud of their culture.

At one time, the Arab world was the center of learning in the world. Arabs made important contributions in science, mathematics, literature, art, and medicine. Hundreds of years ago, an Arab doctor wrote a set of 25 books about medicine. There were many Arab scholars who were experts in subjects such as science, geography, and math.

Arab scientists were the first to study light. They learned that curving a lens causes things to appear larger. They were the first to figure out that the world was round. They correctly guessed that it was about 25,000 miles around.

Poetry is important to Arab culture. Arabs are also famous for creating beautiful designs for rugs, leather goods, and swords. Muslims decorate their mosques, or places of worship, with beautiful designs and letters.

Geography in Your Life

The Ancient Islamic Influence on Math

After A.D. 750, the Islamic Empire produced many famous scholars in mathematics. They invented algebra. In this type of mathematics, letters and symbols represent unknown numbers. One Arab mathematician worked on trigonometry.

Arab scholars also expanded on what they learned from other people. They kept alive the important mathematical works of the Greeks. From India, they borrowed the nine numbers that we still use today. We call these "Arabic numbers" even though they came from India. From the Hindus, the Arab mathematicians borrowed the decimal system. They based this new system on the number 10. It includes the idea of 0. This system has served us well for hundreds of years. Before that time, many people used the Babylonian system. It was based on the number 60.

Although most people in the Middle East are Arabs, it is also home to many non-Arabs. The Turkish people originally came from Central Asia. They conquered and ruled a large area. At one time, their empire included much of the Middle East and north Africa. This empire lasted more than 600 years.

Iran was once called Persia. Its history goes back more than 2,500 years. Greeks, Arabs, Mongols, and Turks invaded this land. The culture reflects all of these invaders, yet it remains different. Even today, Iranians still memorize parts of an epic (long) poem about ancient heroes. The Persian poet Firdawsi wrote the poem a thousand years ago.

About 6 million people of the Middle East are Israelis, most of whom are Jews. They live in the country of Israel. Many migrated there after 1948 when modern-day Israel was founded. These immigrants came from Europe, the Middle East, north Africa, Asia, Russia, and the Americas.

The Kurds are a large ethnic group with no country of their own. About 25 million Kurds live in Turkey, Iraq, and Syria. They have kept their own culture even though other groups have controlled them for centuries. The Kurds call the whole area where they live Kurdistan. Many Kurds have fought for years to try to make this area an independent country.

What Religions Exist?

The Middle East is the birthplace of three major religions. The oldest of these is Judaism. This religion is over 3,000 years old. Abraham, a Hebrew leader long ago, encouraged his people to believe in only one god. This idea is called **monotheism.** The ancient Jews lived near present-day Lebanon and Israel.

The Hebrews settled in a land called Palestine. Later, they migrated to Egypt, where they became slaves. Moses, their greatest prophet, led the Hebrews out of Egypt and out of slavery. The journey out of Egypt was called the Exodus. It is a key event in Jewish history. During the Exodus, God gave Moses the Ten Commandments. These commandments are basic to Judaism, as well as to Christianity and Islam.

When the Hebrews returned to Palestine, they formed the Kingdom of Israel. This kingdom existed off and on from 1025 B.C. to A.D. 70 when the Romans ended it. The Jews were then scattered all around the world.

Reading Strategy:
Questioning

Why do you think the Middle East was the birthplace of three important religions?

Most people in the Middle East practice Islam, another religion that comes from the region. There are two main branches of Islam: Sunnism and Shiism. The split began right after their leader, Muhammad, died in the 600s. Muslims disagreed about who would be the new leader. One group believed that the new leader should be elected by the whole Muslim community. They supported Abu Bakr. The members of this group became the Sunnis. Most Arabs in the Middle East are Sunnis.

The other group believed that Muhammad had chosen his own son-in-law, Ali, as his successor. They believed that Muhammad had passed special religious powers to Ali. Ali's followers came to be known as Shiites. The only countries where Shiites outnumber Sunnis are Iran and Iraq.

Celebrations

Passover

Many Jewish holidays celebrate events in history. Passover is one such holiday. It is in memory of the Exodus, the Hebrews' escape from ancient Egypt. Passover celebrates the idea of freedom.

On the first night (and sometimes the second) of Passover, Jewish people serve a ritual meal called a Seder. At the beginning of the Seder, the story of Passover is told. The centerpiece of the Seder is a beautiful plate that contains special foods. These foods remind the Jews of the journey to freedom.

The joyful feast includes many songs and prayers. Some Jewish people celebrate seven days of Passover, and some celebrate eight.

Critical Thinking Why do you think the overall spirit of Passover is joyful rather than serious?

The third religion to come out of the Middle East was Christianity. Christianity began as a branch of Judaism and both religions share some common beliefs. Christianity is based on the teachings of Jesus Christ who lived in Palestine about 2,000 years ago. His followers believe that Jesus is the son of God. Today, Christianity is the world's largest religion with over 2 billion followers around the world.

What Languages Do the People Speak?

Most people of the Middle East speak Arabic. This language is closely tied to Islam. Most Muslims want to read the Koran, or Qur'an, the holy book of Islam. It is written in Arabic. Written Arabic is the same for all Arabic speakers across the region. The spoken language, however, differs from country to country. In countries that are far from one another, the differences in the spoken language can be great.

All large minority groups speak their own language. The Turks speak Turkish. The Kurds speak Kurdish. The Iranians speak Farsi, an Indo-European language related to English. The people of Israel speak a modern version of Hebrew.

Reading Strategy:
Questioning

Does this map help you visualize where most Muslims live today?

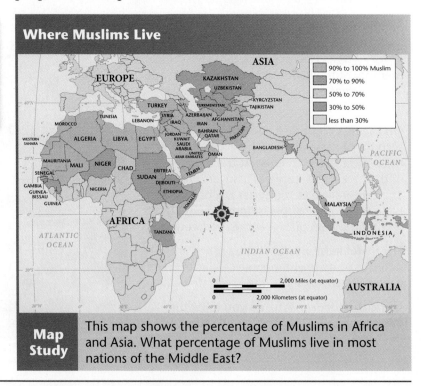

Where Muslims Live

90% to 100% Muslim
70% to 90%
50% to 70%
30% to 50%
less than 30%

Map Study
This map shows the percentage of Muslims in Africa and Asia. What percentage of Muslims live in most nations of the Middle East?

Persian New Year

One of the biggest holidays in Iran is Noruz, which means the New Day. It is celebrated in March. This holiday began long before Islam came to Iran. Celebrating Noruz sometimes involves building a fire, which people jump over. As they jump, they believe that all the bad luck they have collected during the past year burns away. Then, they can start fresh.

This practice is probably left over from Zoroastrianism, which was an ancient Persian religion. This ancient religion taught that two great forces rule the world—one good, one evil. Good is associated with fire and light, and evil with darkness. Good and evil are locked in a never-ending struggle. Some people in Iran still practice this religion.

Critical Thinking Why is spring an appropriate season to celebrate this holiday?

Where Do Most Middle Eastern People Live?

About one third of the people in the Middle East still live in rural areas. The original people of the Arabian Peninsula are Bedouins. The Bedouins are Arabic speakers who travel with their herds of goats and camels from place to place. As in many other places, people in the Middle East are moving from rural areas to towns and cities. Many of the countries have grown rich with money from oil. With the money, the governments have built large, modern cities.

Cities are growing quickly. Some are doubling in size in just 15 years. Over 9 million people live in Istanbul, Turkey. It is the largest city in this region. There are 22 cities with over 1 million people and five with over 3 million. Other large cities are Tehran, Iran; Baghdad, Iraq; Riyadh, Saudi Arabia; and Ankara, Turkey. The population in the entire region is increasing quickly.

Writing About Geography

Look for an article about fighting in the Middle East. Read the article and highlight the main ideas. Finally, write an editorial, an article giving your opinion, on the main idea of the newspaper or magazine article.

What Problems Do the People Face?

People of different cultures and religions sometimes disagree. This may cause war. Israel and its Arab neighbors have fought six wars since 1948, the year Israel became a nation. Israel's Arab neighbors do not think the Israelis have a right to live on the land. Israel has won all the wars. But, some of the defeated Arab countries still refuse to recognize Israel as a nation.

The Palestinians are Arabs who were forced out or chose to leave Israel in 1948. Now they are demanding a homeland. Some Palestinians formed the Palestinian Liberation Organization (PLO). Some PLO members believe they need to use force to gain a homeland. The United States has tried to get Israel and its neighbors to settle their differences. Israel has signed agreements with Egypt and Jordan. However, Israel has not reached an agreement with the Palestinians or with Syria.

Iran and Iraq also have disagreements. In late 1980, Iraqi forces invaded Iran and fought an eight-year war. Iraq then took over Kuwait and its rich oil fields. The United Nations told Iraq to leave Kuwait. Iraq refused. This led to the Persian Gulf War in 1991. Forces from many countries defeated the Iraqis.

In Libya, Syria, and Saudi Arabia, the leaders have almost total control over their countries. Iran is controlled by religious leaders. Iraq was ruled by Saddam Hussein from 1979–2003. Hussein was a Sunni Muslim. In December, 2002, the United States and its allies attacked Iraq to overthrow Hussein. After Hussein lost power, fighting broke out between the Sunnis and the Shiites. Thousands of Iraqi people, many U.S. and other soldiers, and others have been killed in the conflict.

Lesson 3 Review On a sheet of paper, write the answer to each question. Use complete sentences.

1. What did Arabs contribute to math and science?

2. What three religions developed in the Middle East?

3. What language do most people in the Middle East speak?

4. What is happening to the population in the Middle East?

5. What has caused many wars in this region?

What do you think

Why do you think fighting has broken out between the Sunnis and the Shiites in Iraq?

Objectives

- To describe the economies of the Middle East
- To describe the natural resources of the region
- To identify some of the environmental problems the region faces

What Natural Resources Are Important?

The most valuable natural resource in the Middle East is oil. Until oil was discovered there, little attention was given to the region. Oil is the key to the economies of almost all Middle Eastern countries. Saudi Arabia has one-fourth of the known deposits of oil in the world. The United Arab Emirates, Qatar, Bahrain, Kuwait, Iraq, and Iran also have large oil fields.

People all over the world use oil for fuel, and many everyday things are made from it. Oil is used in the making of plastics, paint, clothing, and detergent. Because of this, the Middle East has a lot of economic power. In 1960, the world's main oil producing countries formed the Organization of Petroleum Exporting Countries (OPEC). This group tries to control the supply of oil by setting production limits. The sale of oil pays for the building of roads, housing, and schools. With oil money, the governments of these countries can develop other parts of their economy, such as manufacturing and tourism.

World Oil Reserves by Country

Country	Oil Reserves (Billion Barrels)
Saudi Arabia	264
Canada	179
Iran	133
Iraq	115
Kuwait	102
United Arab Emirates	98
Venezuela	80
Russia	60
Libya	39
Nigeria	36
United States	21

Chart Study This chart shows the countries that have the largest oil reserves. Which country has the largest reserves? Which of these countries are in the Middle East?

What Are the Economies Like?

The money from the sale of oil has changed the economies of the Middle East. Before oil was discovered in 1938, Saudi Arabia was largely home to animal herders and nomads. Today, Saudi Arabia has a well-educated population, many of whom live in the capital city of Riyadh. The oil-rich states on the Persian Gulf are trying to branch out to other industries so they are not so dependent on oil. Nevertheless, oil is the chief export and provides most of the wealth for these countries.

Countries like Syria, Jordan, and Israel have not shared in the oil wealth. Syria and Jordan have much poverty and unemployment. Israel depends on imported oil, but it has become an important industrial, urban country. Nearly a third of its people work in industry. It manufactures airplanes, communications equipment, computer equipment, and fiber optics. Its leading exports are cut diamonds and high technology equipment. Agriculture is also important. Israel grows almost all the food it needs and exports many crops such as tomatoes, fruit, potatoes, and cotton.

Because of all the conflict in the Middle East, the economy has suffered. In Israel, many businesses have closed and many people are out of work. Lebanon's economy suffered because of its conflict with Israel. Tourism, an important source of income in Israel, is down because people are afraid to travel there. Despite the war in Iraq, the economies of the oil-producing countries are doing well.

This oil rig is in the Persian Gulf. You can tell how big it is by looking at the huge ship in the foreground.

What Environmental Problems Exist?

Many of the countries in the Middle East share the same environmental problems. The biggest problem is the shortage of water. There are few rivers and lakes and underground water resources are being used up. Some countries have used their oil wealth to build plants to remove salt from water. These plants turn seawater into fresh drinking water.

Desertification is another big problem—when farmland changes into desert. Also, too much irrigation can cause salts to build up in the soil. It is hard to grow crops when this happens. The removal of plants and the poor management of farmland can cause soil erosion. Long periods of little rain can also cause soil erosion.

Reading Strategy:
Questioning

Where does the water you drink come from?

Lesson 4 Review On a sheet of paper, write the letter of the answer that correctly completes each sentence.

1. The most valuable natural resource in the Middle East is _____.

   A oil　　　**B** sand　　　**C** detergents　　　**D** salt

2. _____ has one-fourth of the known deposits of oil in the world.

   A United Arab Emirates　　　**C** Israel
   B Kuwait　　　**D** Saudi Arabia

3. _____ tries to control the world's oil supply.

   A Palestine Liberation Organization (PLO)
   B Organization of Petroleum Exporting Countries (OPEC)
   C United Arab Emirates (UAE)
   D Rubʿ al-Khali

4. _____ has much poverty and unemployment.

   A United Arab Emirates　　　**C** Syria
   B Kuwait　　　**D** Turkey

5. The environmental problem of farmland turning into desert is called _____.

   A drought　　　**C** desertification
   B soil erosion　　　**D** shortage

What do you think ?

Should OPEC have the power to set production limits on oil? Explain your answer.

Sleeping in the Sukkah

My name is Adan. I am 17 years old, and I live in Dimona, Israel. Because we are Jewish, we celebrate Sukkot. This joyous holiday begins the fifth day after Yom Kippur, in the fall. Sukkot is a harvest festival. Sukkot also honors the journey of our ancestors from Egypt to the Promised Land. They wandered for 40 years in the desert, living in temporary shelters.

That's why, each year, we build a little hut called a sukkah. One of our religious commandments is this: You will dwell in booths for seven days; all natives of Israel shall dwell in booths. So, for seven days, our lives revolve around the sukkah.

We obey the commandment to "dwell" by eating all of our meals in the sukkah. Many Israeli Jews also entertain in their sukkahs. Usually we sleep in it, too. I like sleeping in the sukkah, in our backyard garden.

The first two days of Sukkot are like other Jewish holidays. We don't go to work or school. Most people stay home with their families and go to synagogue, which is our house of worship. Of course, we spend all of our time at home in the sukkah we have built. After the first two days, we go back to normal routines but always eat and relax in our sukkah. The last day of the seven is called Hoshana Rabbah. It is a day with many special customs.

The sukkah can be built in a garden, on a balcony, or on a roof. It is great fun to build, almost like building a fort. A sukkah has 2½, 3, or 4 walls. They can be made of anything. The roof, however, must be made from something that grew from the ground and was cut off. We use palms, willow branches, or bamboo.

Most people try to make the sukkah as beautiful as possible. My family likes to hang fruit and vegetables from the ceiling. My little sisters make drawings for the walls. My mother likes to use her best tablecloth, rugs, and dishes in our sukkah.

Sukkot is a joyous time. I look forward to it every year.

Wrap-Up

1. What does Sukkot celebrate?
2. Where do Israeli Jews spend most of their time during Sukkot?

Chapter 16 S U M M A R Y

- The Middle East is part of Asia. Turkey, Syria, Lebanon, Israel, Saudi Arabia, Jordan, Iran, Iraq, Kuwait, the United Arab Emirates, Bahrain, Qatar, Oman, Yemen, and the island nation of Cyprus make up the Middle East.

- The Middle East has four subregions: the Fertile Crescent, the Levant, the Plateau of Anatolia, and the Rub' al-Khali Desert.

- The most important physical feature of the Middle East is the Arabian Peninsula. A second feature is its rugged highlands and high plateaus. The most important rivers of the Middle East are the Tigris, Euphrates, and Jordan Rivers.

- Much of the Middle East has a desert climate. The northern highlands of Turkey and Iran have a steppe climate. The coastal areas around the Mediterranean have a Mediterranean climate.

- Most of the people in the Middle East are Arabs who speak Arabic and practice Islam. Other groups include the Turks, Persians, Kurds, and Jews. Minority groups may speak their own languages.

- The Middle East is the birthplace of three important religions: Judaism, Christianity, and Islam. There are two major branches of Islam: Sunnism and Shiism.

- Most people in the Middle East speak Arabic. However, the minority groups speak their own language.

- People in the Middle East are moving from rural to urban areas. Oil is the key to the economies of almost all Middle Eastern countries. The biggest environmental problem is the shortage of water. There are few rivers and lakes and underground water resources are being used up.

Chapter 16 REVIEW

Word Bank
Arabs 4
Islam 5
Fertile Crescent 2
Judaism 3
Rub' al-Khali 1

On a sheet of paper, use the words from the Word Bank to complete each sentence correctly.

1. The large desert on the Arabian Peninsula is the _____.

2. The area of rich farmland between the Tigris and Euphrates Rivers is the _____.

3. _____ was the first religion to believe in only one God.

4. _____ are the largest cultural group in the Middle East.

5. Most people of the Middle East practice the _____ religion.

On a sheet of paper, write the letter of the answer that correctly completes each sentence.

6. The first leader of Islam was _____.

   A Muhammad   **C** Abu Bakr
   B Ali   **D** Shiite

7. The Rub' al-Khali is covered mostly with _____.

   A rocky plateaus and infertile plains
   B savanna-like grasses
   C sand dunes
   D palm trees and oases

8. One-fourth of the world's oil deposits are in _____.

   A Saudi Arabia   **C** Libya
   B Iran   **D** Kuwait

9. Most people in the Middle East speak _____.

   A English   **C** Jewish
   B Arabic   **D** Kurdish

10. The biggest environmental problem in the Middle East is a shortage of _____.

   A natural gas   **C** water
   B farmland   **D** oil

On a sheet of paper, write the answer to each question. Use complete sentences.

11. What are the two branches of Islam?

12. What kind of climate does most of the Middle East have?

13. What are the three main rivers of this region?

Critical Thinking On a sheet of paper, write your response to each question. Use complete sentences.

14. A big problem in the Middle East is the fighting between different religious groups. How would you try to stop the groups from fighting?

15. How could the oil wealth of the Middle East be used to improve the lives of the people who live there?

Applying the Five Themes of Geography

Interaction
What effect has human activity had on the environment of the Middle East?

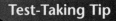

Test-Taking Tip

Restate test directions in your own words. Tell yourself what you are expected to do.

17

Central Asia and the Caucasus States

In the 1990s, over 20 new countries appeared on the map. These included 15 new countries that were created when the old Soviet Union broke up. Many of the new countries are in central Asia and the Caucasus region. In this chapter, we will be studying Georgia, Armenia, Azerbaijan, Turkmenistan, Uzbekistan, Tajikistan, Kyrgyzstan, and Kazakhstan.

Goals for Learning

◆ To describe where central Asia and the Caucasus States are located

◆ To identify the most important physical features and climate of the region

◆ To describe the cultures of central Asia and the Caucasus States and where the people live

◆ To describe the economy and the environmental challenges the region faces

---

Geo-Stats — Key Nations of Central Asia and the Caucasus States

Nation: Kazakhstan
Population:
   15,233,000
Area: 1,049,155 square miles
Major Cities: Astana (capital), Almaty

Nation: Georgia
Population:
   4,661,000
Area: 26,911 square miles
Capital: Tbilisi

Nation: Uzbekistan
Population:
   27,307,000
Area: 172,700 square miles
Capital: Tashkent

Nation: Azerbaijan
Population:
   7, 900, 000
Area: 33,400 square miles
Capital: Baku

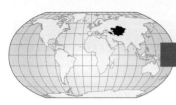

Map Skills

Georgia, Azerbaijan, and Armenia are west of the Caspian Sea. They are called the Caucasus States. Turkmenistan and Kazakhstan are east of the Caspian Sea. Russia is north of Kazakhstan. China is east of Kyrgyzstan, Tajikistan, and Kazakhstan.

Study the map and answer the following questions:

1. What sea is surrounded by Kazakhstan and Uzbekistan?

2. What sea is between Azerbaijan and Turkmenistan?

3. What is the capital of Azerbaijan? Georgia?

4. What region is south of the Caucasus States?

5. What three countries in this region are the farthest east?

Reading Strategy:
Predicting

When you preview a chapter, you can think about what you already know about that chapter. It will also prepare you to look for new information—so you can predict what will come next. As you make predictions about this chapter:

◆ Read all the subheads in all the lessons.

◆ Look at the photos in the chapter.

◆ Use what you know to predict what you will read.

Key Vocabulary Words

Lesson 2 ————————————

Reservoir A place where water is collected and stored, usually created by damming a river

Lesson 3 ————————————

Radical Using extreme measures or force to get a result

Enclave A part of a country that is separated from the main part

Yurt A tent with a wooden frame covered with rolls of wool

Objectives

◆ To know where
central Asia and
the Caucasus
region is located

◆ To identify the
major subregions

◆ To describe how
geography shaped
the region's
history

Where Are Central Asia and Caucasus States?

Central Asia and the Caucasus States take up an area as large as all of western Europe. The area stretches from the Black Sea on the west to China on the east. Russia lies to the north and the Middle East to the south. The Caucasus Mountains form the border between Russia and the Caucasus States. The Caucasus States include the three countries of Armenia, Azerbaijan, and Georgia. The area is sometimes called Transcaucasia. Central Asia includes five countries: Kazakhstan, Kyrgyzstan, Tajikistan, Turkmenistan, and Uzbekistan.

What Subregions Exist?

There are three geographical subregions. One is the large area of steppes that is a continuation of the West Siberian plain. The steppe region is very dry and not suited for farming. It is a large, open area with few people. There are still many nomads who live in tents and wander with their animals from place to place. The western part of the steppe is a low, flat basin. In the east is a hilly plateau.

The second subregion is the Turan Plain. This area is located between the Caspian Sea and the mountains of central Asia. The Turan Plain is in southwestern Kazakhstan and northwestern Uzbekistan. Much of it is a desert with only 4 to 8 inches of rain a year. Very few people live there.

The third subregion is desert. The Kyzyl Kum Desert is one of the largest deserts in the world. It is located in north central Uzbekistan and extends into Kazakhstan. The Ustyurt Plateau is between the Caspian and Aral Seas.

Reading Strategy:
Predicting

You have just read about the location of this region. What can you predict about how geography has influenced the history of this area?

How Did Geography Shape History?

Many people think of central Asia as a huge, empty wasteland. Nevertheless, it has played a very important role in world history because of its location. It is located between Europe and much of Asia. So, it is a kind of bridge between the two continents.

How Computers Help the Study of Geography

Like most people today, geographers use computers. Computers help geographers do things faster, cheaper, and more accurately and detailed than by hand. Geographers use computers called Geographic Information Systems (GIS). They are used to collect and store information about Earth and its people. This information is then used to answer questions or to solve problems. Geographers can see patterns in society or how the land has changed over time. They can also create models to predict what may happen to the land or people in the future.

Geographers are not the only people who use computers to study geography. Meteorologists, for example, use computers to study the weather. Many businesses, schools, and government groups also use them. For example, someone in the restaurant business could use a GIS to find out the best place to build a restaurant. A computer could find the cheapest place to build a new restaurant that has the most people nearby to become its customers. This saves time and prevents poor business decisions.

At one time, the people of Europe and the people of Asia knew very little about each other. Eventually, they began to trade along an overland trade route known as the Silk Road. Many traders made the long, difficult trip to China. Religions such as Islam and Buddhism moved east along the Silk Road. Chinese inventions such as gunpowder and the printing press moved west. The Silk Road was probably at its busiest from 1200 to 1400.

Lesson 1 Review On a sheet of paper, use the words from the Word Bank to complete each sentence correctly.

Word Bank

Caucasus 1
Kyzyl Kum 4
Russia 2
Silk Road 5
Turan 3

1. The three countries of Armenia, Azerbaijan, and Georgia are sometimes called the _____ States.

2. The Caucasus Mountains form the border between _____ and the Caucasus States.

3. The _____ Plain is located between the Caspian Sea and the mountains of central Asia.

4. The _____ is one of the world's largest deserts.

5. The trade route between Europe and China was called the _____.

What do you think

How does trade bring people of different countries closer together?

Objectives

◆ To describe the main physical features

◆ To list the major bodies of water

◆ To describe the climates of the region

What Are the Main Physical Features?

The most important physical features of the region are mountains and deserts. The Caucasus region is an area of mountains and valleys between the Black Sea and the Caspian Sea. The high Caucasus Mountains separate the area from Russia. The highest peak is Mount Elbrus. It is 18,510 feet high.

Central Asia is mostly plains and low plateaus surrounded by high mountains. Many of the countries are landlocked. Kyrgyzstan is very mountainous. The Tian Shan Mountains form part of the border between Kyrgyzstan and China. Tajikistan is 90 percent mountains. The Trans Alai range is in the north and the Pamirs are in the southeast.

Central Asia and the Caucasus States

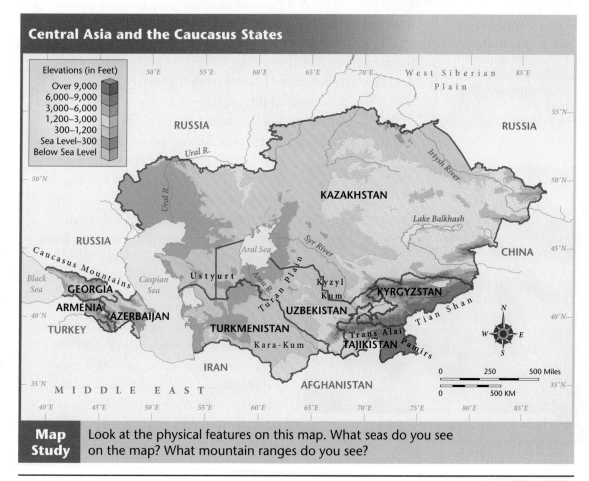

Elevations (in Feet)

Over 9,000
6,000–9,000
3,000–6,000
1,200–3,000
300–1,200
Sea Level–300
Below Sea Level

Map Study Look at the physical features on this map. What seas do you see on the map? What mountain ranges do you see?

The Pamir Mountains are some of the highest mountains in the world. Its three highest mountains are over 23,000 feet high. Travel is limited to only a few mountain passes. The Pamir Mountains have many glaciers. One of its largest glaciers is Fedchenko Glacier, which is about 45 miles long.

The large area of desert is the second main physical feature of most of this large region. Much of Turkmenistan is covered by the Kara-Kum Desert. The country is 80 percent desert. Uzbekistan's flat-to-rolling plains are covered with sandy desert and dunes. The Kyzyl Kum Desert covers most of western Uzbekistan. Central and southern Kazakhstan is also mostly desert. Communication and transportation are very difficult in this harsh environment. Few people live in these deserts.

What Are the Major Bodies of Water?

Large parts of central Asia are almost empty because there is so little water. Two great rivers flow through central Asia, the Syr and the Amu. Both flow from the Tian Shan Mountains. From the mountains, the rivers enter the steppe and empty into the Aral Sea. Life depends on water from these rivers. When the Soviet Union controlled this area, so much water was taken out of the rivers that little water reached the Aral Sea. Both rivers have many dams and **reservoirs.** Reservoirs are places where water is collected and stored. The water is used for irrigation. The water flowing over the dam generates hydroelectric power. Sometimes, the shortage of water causes conflict. This prevents the countries from working on projects that would help all of them.

There is more water in the Caucasus region. Many rivers flow down from the mountains to the lowlands of Azerbaijan. The Kura is the longest river. It begins in Georgia and flows southeast. Its main tributary is the Araks River. The Araks forms most of Armenia's border with Turkey and Iran, and flows into Azerbaijan.

This farm in Kyrgyzstan is near the Tien Shan Mountains.

Lake Balkhash is a large lake in southwestern Kazakhstan. It is shrinking because of all the water taken out of the rivers that feed it. The western half of the lake is fresh water, but the eastern half is salt water. There are thousands of small lakes in the Caucasus region.

What Is the Climate Like?

Most of the Caucasus region has a highland climate. The eastern part of the Caucasus region is drier than the western part. There is a big range in temperature because the high mountains block the warm winds from the Mediterranean and Black Seas. Winters are very cold with a lot of snow. The coastal area of Georgia has a mild humid subtropical climate.

Central Asia is such a large area that it has several climates. The north has a steppe climate with hot summers and cold winters. The areas south of the steppe have a desert climate. The mountain areas of central Asia have a highland climate.

Lesson 2 Review On a sheet of paper, write the letter of the answer that correctly completes each sentence.

1. The two most important physical features of central Asia and the Caucasus States are _____.

   A rivers and lakes   **C** plains and plateaus
   B mountains and deserts   **D** peninsulas and water

2. The country in central Asia with the most mountains is _____.

   A Armenia   **B** Kazakhstan   **C** Tajikistan   **D** Uzbekistan

3. The _____ Mountains are some of the highest mountains in the world.

   A Pamir   **B** Rocky   **C** Tian Shan   **D** Caucasus

4. The two great rivers flowing through central Asia are the _____ Rivers.

   A Syr and Amu   **C** Debet and Akstafa
   B Indus and Brahmaputra   **D** Rhine and Danube

5. Much of the Caucasus region has a _____ climate.

   A highland   **B** Mediterranean   **C** steppe   **D** desert

Reading Strategy:
Predicting

Use what you know about mountains and deserts to predict what the climates may be.

What do you think ❓

Can a country have economic growth and still protect the environment?

Objectives

◆ To describe the cultures of the Caucasus States and central Asia

◆ To identify the major religions

◆ To learn the languages that are spoken there

◆ To describe the main problems the people of the region face

What Cultures Exist in This Region?

Many cultures exist in the Caucasus region. The mountains made it difficult for people to travel and communicate so different cultures and languages developed in the valleys. The region has been invaded by foreigners many times. Armenia, the smallest country of the region, has been invaded by Romans, Persians, Turks, Mongols, and Russians. Each group of foreigners influenced the cultures. Most Armenians today are ethnic Armenians. Like many of the people of the region, they are very independent and proud of their ethnic background.

Some of the countries have many ethnic groups. Some groups want to break away and be independent. Fighting between different ethnic groups is common in this region.

The countries of central Asia also are home to many ethnic groups. In the past, each ethnic group lived in one area. They could live as they wanted without much contact with other groups. When the Soviet Union took control of central Asia, they divided it up into separate countries. Each country had one main ethnic group. Uzbekistan's people were mostly ethnic Uzbeks. Tajikistan's people were mostly Tajiks. However, each country had large numbers of other ethnic groups. For example, many ethnic Russians and Tatars live in Uzbekistan. Kazakhstan has many ethnic Russians. Nearly one-fourth of the people of Tajikistan are Uzbeks.

The people of the steppe region of central Asia are either Turkic or Mongol. The two groups are ethnically related. Their languages are also related. The Turkic people are related to the people who founded what is today called Turkey. The Mongol people came from the steppe region. In the 1200s, their empire stretched across Asia and central Europe.

Tajikistan stands out from the other countries of central Asia. The Tajik people are neither Turkic nor Mongol, but are related to the people of Iran. They are descended from Persians who ruled the area about 2,500 years ago.

What Religions Exist?

Even though there are many ethnic groups in central Asia, many of the people share the same religion, Islam. Islam was brought to the region by Muslim armies in the 700s and 800s. During the Soviet era, the governments discouraged religion throughout the region. No money was given to mosques, which are Islamic places of worship. All students had to study Communism. Factories did not give workers time for the daily prayers required of Muslims.

Now that the central Asian republics are independent, people are freer to practice their religion. Mosques have been reopened, partly with the aid of other Muslim countries like Saudi Arabia and Pakistan. However, Communists and dictators still hold power in some places. They see Islam as a threat to their control. An estimated 6,500 people are in jail in Uzbekistan because of their religious or political beliefs. One worry is that some central Asian Muslims are becoming **radical** or extreme. Radical Muslims believe that force is needed to set up religious governments. Most Muslims do not believe in violence.

Radical

Using extreme measures or force to get a result

Reading Strategy:
Predicting

What religions do you think the people of this region may practice?

Mosques were closed while the Communists were in power. Now mosques like this one in Samarkand, Uzbekistan, are open for Muslim worshippers.

Many people of the Caucasus States are also Muslims. Islam arrived in Azerbaijan with Arab invaders in the 600s. Today, almost 90 percent of the Azerbaijan population is Muslim. However, many people of the Caucasus region are Christian. Armenia is proud to be the first country to adopt Christianity as an official religion. Christianity was introduced into Georgia in the 300s. Georgia became the second country in the world to make Christianity its state religion. After Islam, Christianity is the second official religion of Azerbaijan.

Enclave

A part of a country that is separated from the main part

Yurt

A tent with a wooden frame covered with rolls of wool

алфавит

This is what the word alphabet *looks like using Cyrillic letters.*

What Languages Do the People Speak?

Ancient Arab geographers called the Caucasus "the mountains of tongues." Hundreds of languages are spoken. Many people speak a Slavic language. Russian, one of the Slavic languages, is spoken by many people. Armenian is spoken mainly in Armenia but also in parts of neighboring Azerbaijan, Georgia, and Turkey. Most of the people of Georgia speak Georgian.

Most central Asian people speak Turkic languages. Turkic refers to a large family of languages including Turkish, Kazakh, Kyrgyz, Uzbek, Azeri, and others. When the Soviet Union controlled central Asia, Russian was the official language. The people of the region were forced to use the Cyrillic alphabet and speak Russian. After independence, many countries rejected both. Today, most countries use the same alphabet used in most of the world. The new alphabet is now used in schools and on television. The old Turkic languages are spoken again.

What Problems Do the People Face?

Since the fall of the Soviet Union, there has been much fighting in this region. The reasons for the conflicts are religious, ethnic, and political differences. The people of this region also have different ideas about the type of government they want. Fighting has broken out between some of the countries. Azerbaijan has a conflict with Armenia over the Azerbaijani Nagorno-Karabakh **enclave.** An enclave is a part of a country that is separated from the main part. Nagorno-Karabakh is surrounded by Azerbaijan, but most of the people living there are ethnic Armenians. Since fighting began, over a half million people have left the area, becoming refugees. Georgia has been fighting a civil war. Two of its territories, Abkhaz and South Ossetia, have broken away. They are supported by Russia and are not controlled by the government of Georgia.

When so much in the region is changing, it is hard to preserve traditions. But this region is not well developed, and some people still live as they always have. Some people are nomads who move often and own very few things. They live in tents called **yurts.** The word yurt is originally from the Turkic word meaning "home." A yurt is a tent with a wooden frame covered with rolls of wool.

These two women are weaving cloth on a portable loom. They are outside of their yurt.

Kazakhstan has found new wealth in oil and natural gas. This had led to the rapid growth of its cities. Many people have moved from rural areas to cities to find jobs. This had led to problems such as overcrowding and greater pollution. Astana, Kazakhstan's capital, grew into a modern city in just 10 years.

Lesson 3 Review On a sheet of paper, write the answer to each question. Use complete sentences.

1. Why are there so many different cultures in the Caucasus region?

2. What do the Turkic and Mongol people of the steppe region of central Asia have in common?

3. What happened to religion during the Communist rule?

4. What countries in the region are mostly Christian?

5. What is the reason for much of the fighting in this region?

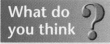

What do you think

What differences do you think cause so much of the conflict in this region?

Objectives

◆ To describe the economy of the region

◆ To know the importance of the area's natural resources

◆ To learn the environmental problems the region faces

What Is the Economy of This Region Like?

When the region was under Soviet control, its economy was closely tied to the Soviet Union. When the Soviet Union broke apart, the economies of the region suffered. The trade links between it and the Soviet Union fell apart. The countries had a difficult time adjusting to the change. They were used to having the state run industries and farming. Now, many businesses are privately owned. The people have little experience running companies. One result is that much less is produced. But the region is recovering, and people hope their future will be better.

Russia is still a major trade partner. But like so many other things in this region, this is also changing. The Caucasus States have new trade partners. Armenia's trade partners include Germany, Iran, and Belgium. Azerbaijan does more trade with Italy than with Russia.

In contrast, the chief trade partner of most of the countries of central Asia is still Russia. However, this too is changing. Trade with China, Japan, the European Union, and the United States is increasing.

What Natural Resources Exist?

Reading Strategy:
Predicting

What do you know about the region that may help you predict what natural resources it may have?

Many countries in central Asia have large deposits of natural resources such as oil and natural gas. Kazakhstan is rich in fossil fuels like coal, oil, and natural gas and in other minerals and metals. Turkmenistan has large undeveloped deposits of gas and oil resources. Tajikistan, the poorest of the countries of central Asia, has no oil. It has some mineral resources. Among the Caucasus countries, only Azerbaijan is rich in oil. Oil is its main export.

Western companies and China have invested huge amounts of money to develop the oil fields of the area. Western companies have built a $4 billion pipeline from Baku, Azerbaijan, to Turkey's Mediterranean port of Ceyhan. China has invested huge amounts of money in Kazakhstan's oil and gas.

Pipelines carry oil or other petroleum products. China has built pipelines in Azerbaijan and Kazakhstan.

China has built a 620-mile pipeline in Kazakhstan. Trade ties between the two countries have increased greatly. Kazakhstan supplies China with oil, and China supplies Kazakhstan with low-cost goods.

As in most other countries, farming is also important. Kazakhstan's many farmers grow grains and raise livestock. Uzbekistan is a dry, landlocked country. Crops can be grown on only 11 percent of the land. Because of irrigation, Uzbekistan is the fifth largest producer of cotton in the world. Turkmenistan and Tajikistan are also large producers of cotton.

The Caucasus region depends heavily on farming. Armenia has moved away from the big Soviet collective farms to small private farms. Most of the farmers are very poor. They cannot afford to buy modern equipment. Most of Georgia's people farm. They grow grapes, citrus fruits, hazelnuts, and tea.

What Industries Exist?

Much of the industry of this region is related to its natural resources. Mining and processing oil are key industries. Some of the countries are developing industries that make construction equipment, tractors, and other farm machinery. Many of the factories built in the Soviet era are old and can no longer be used.

Saving the Aral Sea

The Aral Sea lies between Kazakhstan and Uzbekistan. It is fed by two rivers, the Syr and the Amu. In the 1950s, the Soviets built the Karakum Canal. It took water from both the Syr and Amu rivers. They used the water to irrigate cotton fields.

With less water coming in, the Aral Sea began to shrink. As it shrank, it grew more salty. Freshwater fish living in the sea began to die. Ships were stranded on the salty deserts that were once seashores. Salt blew over the lands nearby and damaged the soil. The soil could no longer be used as farmland.

In 1960, the Aral Sea was the world's fourth largest sea. Today, the Aral Sea is about half the size it was in 1960. The city of Muynak, which used to be an important fishing community, is now miles from the sea. Their fish-canning industry has literally dried up.

The five nations of this area signed an agreement in 1992 to use the water more wisely. The countries did not keep their word, however. Little progress has been made in keeping the Aral Sea from shrinking.

Wrap-Up

1. What problems did the saltiness of the Aral Sea cause?

2. Why would a body of water get saltier?

Make a Difference

Contact your local water authority. Ask them to send information on how to save water. Make a list of their suggestions, and put a check next to the ways you save water now. Then, circle two more ways you can try to save water from now on.

What Environmental Problems Exist?

The Aral Sea is an environmental disaster. Taking water from both the Syr and the Amu rivers means less water reaches the Aral Sea.

Reading Strategy:
Predicting

Use what you have learned about the area that was under Communist rule to predict what some of their environmental problems are.

The Soviets were more interested in growing cotton than the environment. To improve production, the Soviets used harmful chemicals to kill pests and protect against plant diseases. Many chemical fertilizers were used in the cotton fields. This caused a lot of pollution. People who live in the area were being harmed. Unfortunately, the economy of some central Asian countries still depends heavily on cotton, so little has changed.

Another big problem is the effect of nuclear testing. In Soviet times, the test site for most nuclear weapons was an area in northeastern Kazakhstan. Nearly 500 nuclear devices were tested from the 1940s to the 1980s. The winds carried nuclear waste over a large area. The testing caused health risks for both people and animals. Illnesses like cancer were common. Even though the testing stopped in 1989, the effects continue.

Lesson 4 Review On a sheet of paper, write the word in parenthesis that makes each statement true.

1. A major trading partner of the Caucasus States and central Asia is still (Russia, the European Union).

2. Many countries in (central Asia, Caucasus region) have large deposits of oil and natural gas.

3. Among the Caucasus States, only (Azerbaijan, Armenia) is rich in oil.

4. (Uzbekistan, Kazakhstan) is the fifth largest producer of cotton in the world.

5. The (Aral Sea, oil industry) is an environmental disaster.

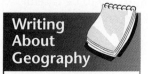

Writing About Geography

What would you do to solve the problem of the Aral Sea? Write a paragraph explaining how you would keep the farmers who need water happy while fixing the problem.

What do you think ?

Do the increased ties between central Asia and China pose a problem for the United States?

Kyrgyzstan Kidnappings

My name is Alina, and I am 18 years old. I live in a small Kyrgyzstan village near Osh. I am not yet married. But here, women are often surprised by their own weddings. It could happen at any time to me, as it did to my sister Aida.

One day last year, Aida went to the market but never came home. My parents didn't seem worried. The next day, three men came to our farm while my father was shearing sheep. At first, he seemed serious. But soon he was laughing with them, shaking their hands when they left.

Inside, my father told us Aida was marrying into a good family. He and my mother seemed calm. I was so surprised! Aida had not mentioned it to me. In two days, she came home with her husband, wearing a new scarf.

In private, Aida told me what had happened. She had been shopping for vegetables. Suddenly, a man grabbed her. He pushed her into a car full of strangers, all men. They drove her to a house, leaving her with a group of women.

The women tried to talk Aida into marrying one man from the car. They were his relatives. But my sister said no, she had never met him! The women said Aida's family and our village would not be happy if she did not follow this custom.

They promised Aida kind treatment and spoke well of her future husband. They explained how they'd been kidnapped, too. But now they were happily married.

Aida is stubborn. She thought at first that it would be fine if the village was unhappy with her. But she also knew the truth. It would be hard for her to support herself in the village without a husband. She would have to move to a bigger city, alone. Aida told me she would miss us too much. So, eventually, she let the groom's mother put the scarf on her head, making her marriage official.

What happened to Aida happens often in our country. Even though it is not legal, police usually do nothing about it. Some women do get to choose who they want to marry. But my friends and I try to be careful whenever we go out. Life can change quickly here.

Wrap-Up

1. Why did Aida agree to the marriage?

2. What made the marriage official?

Chapter 17 S U M M A R Y

- Central Asia and the Caucasus States take up as large an area as western Europe. The Caucasus countries are Armenia, Azerbaijan, and Georgia. The central Asian countries are Kazakhstan, Kyrgyzstan, Tajikistan, Turkmenistan, and Uzbekistan.

- The three physical subregions of central Asia and the Caucasus States are the steppe, the Turan Plain, and the desert.

- The Silk Road was a trade route taken that linked Europe and Asia. Trading posts along the route grew into cities.

- The Caucasus region is an area of mountains and valleys between the Black Sea and the Caspian Sea. The high Caucasus Mountains separate the area from Russia. Central Asia is mostly plains and low plateaus surrounded by high mountains. Many of the countries are landlocked.

- Much of central Asia is covered with desert. The Kyzul Kum Desert is one of the largest deserts in the world. Two great rivers flow through central Asia, the Syr River and the Amu River.

- Most of the Caucasus region has a highland climate. Central Asia has three climates: steppe, desert, and highland.

- There are many cultures in the Caucasus region. The region was invaded by foreigners many times. Each group of foreigners influenced the cultures. When the Soviet Union took control of central Asia, they divided it into separate countries. Each country had one main ethnic group.

- Many of the people of central Asia are Muslims. The people of the Caucasus region are mostly Muslim or Christian. The state religion of Armenia and Georgia is Christianity.

- Many countries in central Asia have large deposits of natural resources such as oil and natural gas. The Aral Sea is an environmental disaster. Another big problem in central Asia is nuclear waste from nuclear testing.

Word Bank

enclave

Kyzul Kum

reservoir

Silk Road

yurt

On a sheet of paper, use the words from the Word Bank to complete each sentence correctly.

1. A _____ is a place where water is collected and stored.

2. An _____ is a part of a country that is separated from the main part.

3. The trade route between Europe and China was called the _____.

4. A _____ is a tent with a wooden frame covered with rolls of wool.

5. One of the world's largest deserts is the _____ in central Asia.

On a sheet of paper, write the letter of the answer that correctly completes each sentence.

6. The most important physical features of central Asia and the Caucasus States are mountains and _____.

A deserts   **C** peninsulas

B plateaus   **D** coastal plains

7. The mountain areas of central Asia have a _____ climate.

A Mediterranean   **C** steppe

B desert   **D** highland

8. Some people of the Caucasus region have been able to keep their own culture because they live in _____.

A mountain valleys   **C** urban areas

B the desert   **D** cities

9. The people of Armenia are proud that they were the first to adopt _____ as an official religion.

A Judaism   **C** Christianity

B Islam   **D** Buddhism

10. Many countries in central Asia have large deposits of _____.

   A grains and livestock   **C** oil and natural gas
   B irrigation   **D** cotton

On a sheet of paper, write the answer to each question. Use complete sentences.

11. What is the biggest industry of central Asia?

12. Why is the Aral Sea an environmental disaster?

13. What does this region have in common with much of the Middle East?

Critical Thinking On a sheet of paper, write your response to each question. Use complete sentences.

14. What effect did control by the Soviet Union have on central Asia and the Caucasus States?

15. What is the relationship between geography and the homes people live in?

Applying the Five Themes of Geography

Movement

Give an example of the theme of movement as it applies to central Asia and the Caucasus States.

Test-Taking Tip

Restate the test directions in your own words. Tell yourself what you are expected to do.

The Silk Road

Silk is a light, strong cloth woven from threads made by silkworms. The Chinese people discovered how to make this cloth almost 5,000 years ago. They kept the process secret. People who wanted silk had to go to China. In ancient Rome, silk was valuable. Many traders made the long and difficult journey from Europe to China.

Over time, a regular route developed. It was called the Silk Road. It was not an actual road, but an overland trade route. It ran from the Mediterranean coast through Persia and central Asia into China. Trading posts along the route grew into lively cities.

Religions such as Islam and Buddhism moved east along the Silk Road. Inventions such as gunpowder and the printing press moved west. The Silk Road was probably at its busiest in the days of the Mongol empire. But, after the 1500s, sea travel became popular. Trade along the Silk Road died out.

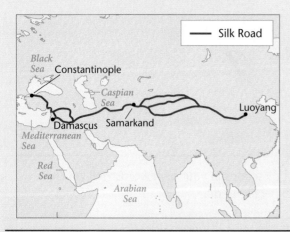

Wrap-Up

1. What is silk made of?

2. Where did people go to get silk?

3. What was the route of the Silk Road?

4. What religions moved along the Silk Road?

5. What made trade along the route die out?

- The Middle East and central Asia are southeast of Europe and northeast of Africa. The Middle East is sometimes called Southwest Asia.

- The Middle East has four subregions: the Fertile Crescent, the Levant, the Plateau of Anatolia, and the Rub' al-Khali Desert. Central Asia has the steppe, the Turan Plain, and the desert regions.

- The most important physical feature of the Middle East is the Arabian Peninsula. The Caucasus region is an area of the Caucasus Mountains and valleys. Much of central Asia is covered with desert.

- Much of the Middle East has a desert climate. Most of the Caucasus region has a highland climate. Central Asia has steppe, desert, and highland climates.

- Most of the people in the Middle East are Arabs who speak Arabic and practice Islam. Most of the people of the Caucasus States are Muslim or Christians. There are many cultures in the Caucasus region. There are many ethnic groups in central Asia. There are many languages spoken in central Asia.

- The Middle East is the birthplace of three important religions: Judaism, Christianity, and Islam. Most people in Israel are Jewish. Armenia and Georgia have Christianity as their state religion. Most of the people of the region are Muslim.

- Oil is the key to the economies of almost all Middle Eastern countries. It is also important to many countries in central Asia.

- The biggest environmental problem in the Middle East is the lack of water. In central Asia, the Aral Sea is an environmental disaster. Nuclear waste is also a big problem.

Unit 8

South Asia

India, Sri Lanka, Nepal, Bhutan, Bangladesh, Afghanistan, and Pakistan make up South Asia. India is its largest country and has more than a billion people. It has an ancient civilization and is the birthplace of two of the world's great religions, Buddhism and Hinduism. South Asia is a region of great economic, political, cultural, and geographical differences. The photo shows people using Himalayan yaks in Nepal.

India and Its Neighbors

India is the largest country in south Asia and has more than a billion people. Its neighbors—Bangladesh, Sri Lanka, Nepal, and Bhutan—are small in comparison. Many foreigners have come to this region over hundreds of years. Different groups settled and ruled. Each group brought with it a different set of ideas and customs.

Goals for Learning

◆ To describe the location of India and its neighbors

◆ To identify their most important physical features and climates

◆ To describe the diverse cultures and explain where and how most people live

◆ To describe the economy and the environmental challenges the region faces

Geo-Stats — India and Its Neighbors

Nation: India
Population:
   1,095,352,000
Area: 1,269,346 square miles
Major Cities: New Delhi (capital), Mumbai, Kolkata, Delhi

Nation: Bangladesh
Population:
   147,365,000
Area: 55,598 square miles
Major Cities: Dhaka (capital), Chittagong, Khulna

Nation: Sri Lanka
Population:
   20,222,000
Area: 25,332 square miles
Capital: Colombo

Nation: Nepal
Population:
   28,287,147
Area: 56,827
   square miles
Capital: Kathmandu

India and Its Neighbors

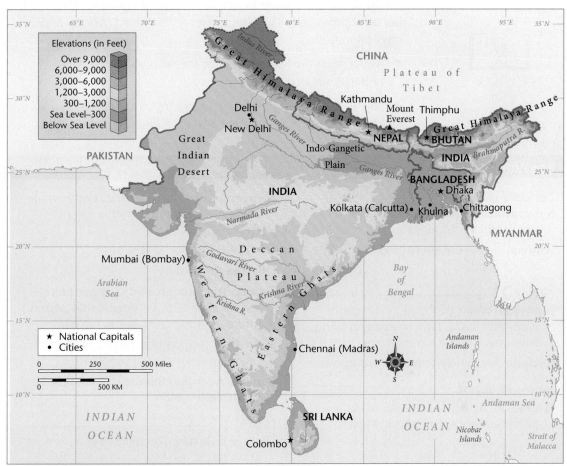

Map Skills

This map shows five countries—India and its neighbors of Bangladesh, Sri Lanka, Nepal, and Bhutan. The mountains in the northern part separate the region from China. The Himalayas contain some of the highest peaks in the world, including Mount Everest. The Ganges and Brahmaputra Rivers are important to this region.

Study the map and answer the following questions:

1. Which two mountain ranges are located on the western and eastern coasts of India?

2. Which countries border China?

3. Which island nation is located southeast of India?

4. Which bodies of water surround India?

5. How do you think the geography of this region affects the people?

Reading Strategy:
Text Structure

When you know how a textbook is organized, it helps you understand what you are learning. Each chapter in this book has a map before the lessons begin. Sometimes it is a political map, but sometimes, as in this chapter, it is a combined political and physical map.

◆ As you read the lessons, refer to the map to help you understand what you are reading.

◆ As you read about a physical feature, river, mountain, or plateau, locate it on the map from the description in the text.

Key Vocabulary Words

Lesson 1

Subcontinent A large landmass that is smaller than a continent

Alluvial Fertile soil left behind by a river after a flood

Lesson 2

Monsoon Winds that change direction according to the time of year and bring heavy rains in the summer

Cyclone A storm system with strong winds

Lesson 3

Hinduism A religion and way of life practiced by most people in India

Reincarnation The belief that every living creature is reborn as another living creature

Caste A Hindu social group

Dharma One's duty

Karma The force created by a person's actions that helps determine that person's future

Sikhism A religion that combines parts of the Islam religion with Hinduism

Jainism A religion that began as a protest to the caste system

Lesson 4

Cottage industry The making of a product at home

Subcontinent

A large landmass that is smaller than a continent

Where Is the Indian Subcontinent?

The peninsula of south Asia is sometimes called a **subcontinent**. It is a large landmass that is smaller than a continent. India, Sri Lanka, Bangladesh, Nepal, and Bhutan are in this region. It covers about 1.5 million square miles, which is about half the size of the United States. Most of the subcontinent is located in the low latitudes between the equator and the Tropic of Cancer.

Geographers think that millions of years ago the subcontinent was a huge island floating on a large tectonic plate. This plate drifted northward until it crashed into the Eurasian plate. The Indian plate pushed under the Eurasian plate to create the Himalayan Mountains. They are the highest mountains in the world. They separate the Indian Peninsula from China.

The Indian subcontinent is a peninsula surrounded by the Indian Ocean. The western part of this ocean is the Arabian Sea. The eastern part is the Bay of Bengal. The Indian subcontinent is between the Middle East and Africa to the west and Southeast Asia to the east.

Sri Lanka is a tear-shaped island located 22 miles off the coast of southeastern India. India's neighbor to the east is Bangladesh. Nepal and Bhutan are located in the Himalayas.

How Did Geography Shape History?

Much of the time, mountains protected the Indian peninsula from invaders. However, many armies have marched into the region. They reached India through mountain passes like the Khyber Pass.

The people who came through the mountain passes changed the history of the subcontinent. Each group brought new ideas. The newcomers sometimes had children with the people who had come before. The cultures of the region today reflect the many different groups that came through the passes.

Many Indians wash themselves and their clothes in the Ganges River.

What Regions Are on the Peninsula?

The region can be divided into four geographical regions. Mountains are the first region. The Himalayan Mountains stretch across the northern part of the Indian peninsula. Few people live on the steep slopes of these mountains.

The Indo-Gangetic Plain is a second region. Most of India's people live on this plain. It begins at the Indus River in Pakistan and stretches about 1,900 miles east. It includes the delta of the Ganges River. Flooding rivers leave behind **alluvial** soil. The flooding of the Ganges deposits rich alluvial soil on the floodplain.

The third region is the peninsula itself. Its largest part is the Deccan Plateau south of the Indo-Gangetic Plain. Much of India's mineral wealth is in the northeastern part of the peninsula.

The Thar, or Great Indian Desert, is the fourth region. This western desert covers about 77,000 square miles and separates India from Pakistan.

Lesson 1 Review On a sheet of paper, write the word in parenthesis that makes each statement true.

1. The Indian subcontinent is a huge (island, peninsula).

2. The body of water east of India is the (Bay of Bengal, Arabian Sea).

3. Nepal and Bhutan are located among the (Himalayas, Thar Desert).

4. Armies marched into India through the (Khyber Pass, Sri Lanka).

5. Most of India's people live on the (Indo-Gangetic Plain, Himalayan Mountains).

What do you think ?

In what ways do you think geography has helped or hurt the people of South Asia?

Objectives

◆ To describe the main physical features of India, Sri Lanka, Bangladesh, Nepal, and Bhutan

◆ To know their major rivers

◆ To describe the region's climates

Reading Strategy:
Text Structure

Refer to the map on page 423 as you read the pages in Lesson 2.

Mount Everest is Earth's tallest mountain.

What Are the Main Physical Features?

The Himalayan Mountains form the natural boundary between India and China. These mountains are one of the main physical features of the region. Eight of the world's 10 highest peaks are in Nepal, including Mount Everest, the world's tallest, and Kanchenjunga, the third tallest. Mount Everest is located near the border between Nepal and China. Himalaya means "home of the snows" in Nepali, the official language of Nepal. Glaciers and snow cover the mountains year round.

The Deccan Plateau is another important physical feature. Part of it is 600 million years old. The plateau covers most of the Indian subcontinent. Most of this flat land is about 3,200 feet high. The highlands of the Eastern and Western Ghats border the plateau. Some parts of the plateau have rich volcanic soil. However, much of it is dry. Enough rain falls in the northeast to support farming. The western and southern parts have little rain, so farming is difficult. The plateau drops sharply along the Arabian Sea. This narrow coast is ideal for growing spices such as pepper, ginger, and cardamom.

Most of Bangladesh is a large alluvial plain. The plain is really the floodplain and delta of large rivers that flow down from the Himalayas. Much of the land is just a few feet above sea level. This low-lying delta is one of the most densely populated places in the world. Each year, during the rainy season, much of the country is flooded. The rivers flood much of the floodplain and destroy the crops. Fields often lie under water.

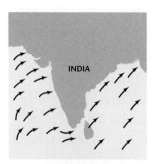

Summer monsoon winds

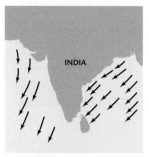

Winter monsoon winds

What Are the Major Rivers?

The Indian subcontinent has many rivers. The two most important rivers are the Ganges and the Brahmaputra. They are called Himalayan rivers because they begin in the mountains. They are fed by the melting snows and keep a high to medium rate of flow throughout the year. The Ganges River begins in the Himalayas and flows to the Indo-Gangetic Plain. The Ganges is called the *Ganga* in India. One third of India's people live on this plain. The Ganges joins the Brahmaputra River in the eastern part of the plain. The Brahmaputra has the greatest volume of water of all the rivers in India because of the heavy rains that fall in the lands it drains. The low floodplain and delta of the two rivers make up most of Bangladesh.

India has other important rivers. The Krishna River starts in the Western Ghats and flows east into the Bay of Bengal. The river is long but does not carry much water. The Godavari also begins in the Western Ghats and flows southwesterly for over 600 miles until it too empties into the Bay of Bengal. Its delta on the east coast is one of India's main rice-growing areas. The Narmada flows into the Arabian Sea.

What Is the Climate Like in This Region?

The Indian subcontinent has many climates. The **monsoon** winds influence the Indian climate. These winds change direction according to the time of year. Two monsoon winds blow over India. In summer, winds blow from the Arabian Sea and the Bay of Bengal and bring in heavy rains. In winter, little rain falls. In autumn, the monsoon changes to the northeast. This wind is weaker than the summer monsoon, but farmers in east India still depend on it. The northeast monsoon can form **cyclones** off the Bay of Bengal. Cyclones are storms with strong winds that spin in a circular motion. They damage low-lying coastal areas, and have killed people in India and Bangladesh.

Most of India, Sri Lanka, and Bangladesh have either tropical monsoon or tropical savanna climates. The high northern mountains block the cold from central Asia and keep most of India warm or hot year around. Temperatures are also hot because these areas are close to the equator.

This aerial view shows some of the geography of Sri Lanka.

The coastal areas of India that receive high seasonal rainfall have monsoon forests. Most of the Deccan Plateau has a tropical savanna climate. Its natural vegetation is grasses with a few trees.

Nepal and Bhutan have highland climates. The weather ranges from freezing cold in the higher areas in the Himalayas to subtropical in the lowlands. The middle parts of Nepal have a moderate climate. However, the summer temperatures can reach over 100°F.

Lesson 2 Review On a sheet of paper, use the words from the Word Bank to complete each sentence correctly.

Word Bank

Brahmaputra 3

Deccan 2

highland 5

Himalayas 1

monsoon 4

1. The _____ form a natural border between India and China.

2. The _____ Plateau is 600 million years old.

3. Two major Himalayan rivers are the Ganges and the _____.

4. A _____ is a wind that changes direction according to the time of year.

5. Nepal and Bhutan have a _____ climate.

What do you think ?

What do you think would happen if the monsoon winds fail to bring rain?

Objectives

◆ To describe
the cultures of
India, Sri Lanka,
Bangladesh,
Nepal, and Bhutan

◆ To name some
of the languages
spoken in this
region

◆ To describe
Hinduism and
the caste system
of India

Hinduism

A religion and way of
life practiced by most
people in India

What Cultures Are in This Region?

This region has many cultures with great diversity in religions,
languages, and education. The culture of the people who live
in villages differs from those who live in cities. People from the
east and south are usually shorter and have darker skin than
people in the north. People in different areas eat different foods
and dress in different ways. Technology, education, and contact
with other cultures are changing this region.

What Languages Do the People Speak?

Hindi is the national language of India. But only about one-
third of Indians, mainly in the north, speak Hindi. There are
many other languages spoken by the millions of people in India.
Each of the 25 states in India has an official language. From
1750–1947, India was a colony of Great Britain, so English is
the language of government and larger businesses. The many
languages cause communication problems.

Many people in Bangladesh also speak English, but most
people speak Bengali. Many people in the southern part of the
subcontinent speak Dravidian languages. Among these is Tamil.
It is one of the two languages spoken in Sri Lanka. The other
language is Sinhalese. Most of the people living in Nepal and
about a quarter of those living in Bhutan speak Nepali. Bhutan's
official language is Dzongkha. All together, there are more than
200 languages spoken on the subcontinent.

What Is Hinduism?

Many people in this region practice **Hinduism**. This religion
began about 5,000 years ago. Unlike some other religions,
Hinduism had no one founder. Most Indians and Nepalese are
Hindu. Hindus worship many gods. Hinduism has no single
holy book. It has many sacred texts; one is called the Vedas.

Reincarnation

The belief that every living creature is reborn as another living creature

Dharma

One's duty

Karma

The force created by a person's actions that helps determine that person's future

Caste

A Hindu social group

Sikhism

A religion that combines parts of the Islam religion with Hinduism

Jainism

A religion that began as a protest against the caste system

Reading Strategy:
Text Structure

After reading about dharma, karma, and castes, can you guess what the Hindu religion is based on?

Hindus believe that every living creature has a soul that is a part of a larger spirit. According to Hindus, when a person dies, the person's soul is reborn into another living form. This is called **reincarnation**. Many Hindus think of life as a play in which each person plays a part. This is their **dharma**, or duty. The way they perform their dharma creates a force, called **karma,** that helps determine their future. If they follow their dharma well and have good karma, they may break this cycle of reincarnation.

Hinduism is both a religion and a way of life. Hindus believe that hurting people and animals is wrong, so they do not eat meat. They also believe that a person is born into a **caste**, or social group. There are four main castes. The priests and teachers belong to the highest caste. Other castes include rulers and warriors; farmers, traders, and makers of crafts; and laborers. People who do not belong to a caste are called untouchables. They have the dirty, lowest jobs. The caste you are born into determines who you can marry, what foods you can eat, and what job you can have. People cannot change the caste they are born into. However, if they fulfill their dharma, they may return in a higher caste in the next life.

In modern India, the caste system is not as powerful as it once was. However, it remains strong in rural villages.

What Other Religions Do the People Practice?

Islam is also a common religion in this region. In India, 14 percent of the people are Muslims. The Taj Mahal, a tomb of a Muslim queen, is often called the world's most beautiful building. Almost all of the people of Bangladesh are Muslims.

A large number of Buddhists live in Bhutan and Sri Lanka. Millions of Sikhs live in northern India. **Sikhism** was founded in the 1500s. It combines the Muslim belief in one god with the Hindu belief in reincarnation. However, it has no caste system. Sikhism and **Jainism** began as protests against the caste system. Jains respect all life. They do not even kill insects. They do not farm because they might harm living things. Because of this, many Jains have successful businesses. About 30 million Christians also live in India. Most of them live in the south.

What Problems Do the People Face?

The biggest problem in India and its neighboring countries is poverty. People lack food, housing, health care, or educational services. The average income in India is only $530 per year.

Location and religion influence what people eat. People who live along the coasts eat lots of fish. In southern India, people eat a lot of rice. In the north, people usually eat bread with their meal. Hindus never eat meat. Muslims do not eat pork. Many people cannot afford to eat a healthy diet.

The caste system is another problem. The Indian government has tried to end this system and give people in the lower castes more opportunities. But some Hindus think that the caste is an important part of their religion.

Reading Strategy:
Text Structure

Notice how each new paragraph introduces a new problem.

Part of the poverty problem may be overpopulation, a problem in the whole region. Bangladesh has one of the highest population densities in the world. Its population is about two-thirds the size of the population of the United States. Yet, the people all live in an area about the size of Wisconsin.

 Biography

Mother Teresa: 1910–1997

Mother Teresa's family was Albanian. At the age of 12, she knew she wanted to be a Christian missionary. She became a nun and joined the Sisters of Loreto, a community of nuns with missions in India. In 1931, she was sent to India. She saw a lot of suffering and poverty. In 1948, she began working among the poorest of the poor. People began to call her "the saint of the gutters." She formed the Missionaries of Charity. She and other nuns cared for the dying, sick, old people, and children that had been given up in India's large cities. She also started missions in other parts of the world. In 1979, Mother Teresa won the Nobel Peace Prize for her work.

There are many effects of overpopulation. Many people are poor. There are not enough jobs. Dozens of people may share a house. People live in areas that are likely to flood. Often, they do not get enough to eat so many children starve. Many people suffer from poor health.

Another big problem is urbanization and migration. Most people still live in rural areas, but people are moving into urban areas to find work. Many end up living in shantytowns.

What Are the Religious Problems?

In 1947, India became independent of Great Britain. However, the British split India into two parts. One was India, a country with a Hindu majority. The other was Pakistan, a Muslim nation. Hindus rushed out of Pakistan into India. Millions of Muslims fled from India to Pakistan. Fighting occurred throughout the region. About 500,000 people were killed.

Kashmir is a state on the border between India and Pakistan. Most of the people of Kashmir are Muslims, but India claims that Kashmir is part of its country. The risk of war is high. Thousands of Indian and Pakistani troops stay in the area.

There are other examples of religious and civil unrest. Some Sikhs want a state of their own. In Sri Lanka, thousands of people have died in ethnic fighting. In Nepal, Communist rebels have been trying to take over the government. The political situation there is not very stable.

Lesson 3 Review On a sheet of paper, write the answer to each question. Use complete sentences.

1. Why are the many languages spoken in India a problem?
2. What is the caste system of the Hindu religion?
3. What is the biggest problem in this region?
4. What country has the highest population density in the world?
5. What is the cause of the fighting in Kashmir?

What do you think

Do you think the caste system keeps India from developing faster? Explain.

Objectives

◆ To describe the economies of India, Sri Lanka, Bangladesh, Nepal, and Bhutan

◆ To describe their natural resources and major industries

◆ To learn the environmental challenges facing the region

Reading Strategy:
Text Structure

Look back at the unit opener photo on page 420. How does it tie into this section about subsistence farmers?

What Is the Economy Like?

More than half of the people of India and its neighboring countries are farmers. The only exception is Sri Lanka. In Nepal and Bhutan, more than 90 percent of the people farm. Most are subsistence farmers. More than one-third do not own the land. They work someone else's land in exchange for a share of the crops. They use simple tools and little machinery. In some places, farmers still use wooden plows pulled by oxen.

More than half of the land in India and Bangladesh is farmland. Many farmers depend on monsoon rains to grow crops. In the Indo-Gangetic Plain, farmers grow rice, wheat, corn, potatoes, beans, spices, sugarcane, and fruit. In areas that receive much rain, the main crop is rice. Farmers on the Deccan Plateau need to irrigate their fields because too little rain falls. They grow cotton, wheat, peas, and beans. The main food crop of Bangladesh is rice, using about 75 percent of the farmland.

Commercial farming is also common. India's main exports are cotton, tea, rice, cashew nuts, and spices. It also produces sugarcane, coffee, and jute. Rope and bags are made from jute.

The other nations of the Indian subcontinent also export crops. Sri Lanka is the world's biggest exporter of tea. Bhutan exports cardamom—a spice used for baking and cooking.

What Natural Resources Exist?

This region is rich in natural resources. The fast-flowing rivers of Nepal and Bhutan create cheap hydroelectric power. India's Deccan Plateau has huge deposits of coal, iron ore, bauxite, and copper. India gets some of the oil it needs from its own wells. India also has limestone and manganese in large amounts.

Sri Lanka exports many gemstones like diamonds, emeralds, and rubies. Bangladesh has few natural resources other than natural gas. Bhutan and Nepal have mineral wealth, but very little has been mined.

What Are the Main Industries?

Though most Indians are farmers, India is rapidly developing its industrial base. India has iron ore and coal needed for a modern steel industry. However, many of India's steel mills are old and inefficient. India is a big producer of aircraft, ships, locomotives, heavy electrical machinery, construction equipment, chemicals, and communication equipment.

Since the 1980s, India's economy is one of the fastest growing economies in the world. Textiles is one of the largest industries in the country. It employs millions of people. Computers and cars are two newer industries. One of India's major exports is computer software. Many multinational corporations are investing in India. The country's rail system, roads, and communication system have improved. India is the world's fastest growing cell phone market.

Weaving rugs is a cottage industry in India.

A result has been a steady improvement in the standard of living. Even though a quarter of the people live on less than $1 a day, India's middle class is growing. Many people now have cars, televisions, computers, bicycles, and radios.

Even though they are small, **cottage industries** are an important part of the subcontinent's economy. Cottage industries are ones in which people make products in their homes. Family members pass along the skills needed to make needlework, tie-dye, papier-mâché, baskets, jewelry, and carpets. Whole families often work together to make carpets.

In the past, Bangladesh's most important export was jute. Now it is an important exporter of ready-made clothes, shrimp, fish, and leather goods. Its chief agricultural exports are rice, tea, fresh fruits, flowers, and vegetables. The country is trying to build up its industry, but it lacks resources.

Geography in Your Life

Micro-Credit

Muhammad Yunus, a Bangladeshi economist, came up with an idea called micro-credit. This idea would help poor people start businesses. His idea was to start a small bank, Grameen Bank, to grant small loans. With $300 of his own money, Yunus began lending small sums of money. Today, 97 percent of the bank's 7 million borrowers are women. Almost all the people have paid back their loans. This program has helped more than 80 percent of poor families in Bangladesh. For his idea, in 2006 Yunus was awarded one of the world's most important honors, the Nobel Peace Prize.

Reading Strategy:
Text Structure

Notice that the Geography in Your Life feature is about something that relates to the lesson. But it is not a direct part of the lesson.

What Environmental Problems Exist?

Air pollution is an environmental problem, especially in India. India's cities are growing and so is the traffic. Its industries are booming. The smoke from cars and trucks and untreated industrial smoke are the chief causes of air pollution. India has more than 20 cities with populations over 1 million. New Delhi, Bombay, and Chennai are among the world's most polluted cities. India's air pollution may cause 40,000 deaths per year.

Water pollution is also a problem. Only a few towns on the subcontinent have systems to remove human waste. Businesses often dump untreated animal waste and factory runoff into the nearest river. Human waste usually ends up in the river, too. Many rivers are polluted. Parts of the Ganges River are so badly polluted that bathing in and drinking its water has become dangerous. Water pollution is also a problem in Bangladesh. The water is polluted with chemicals.

Other environmental problems are deforestation and soil erosion. Forests have been cut down to build dams and to develop new mines. This leads to soil erosion. The governments and environmental groups want to save the remaining forests.

Many people in India make a living from commercial fishing. These men are loading their fishing nets into their boats on the western shore of India.

India, Nepal, and Bangladesh worry about flood control, preventing drought, and generating hydroelectric power. The three countries are working together to make the best use of their water resources.

Lesson 4 Review On a sheet of paper, write the letter of the answer that correctly completes each sentence.

1. Most people in this region are _____.

   A farmers   **C** miners
   B basket weavers   **D** fishers

2. Sri Lanka is the world's largest exporter of _____.

   A jute   **B** spices   **C** tea   **D** cardamom

3. Since the 1980s, _____ has had one of the fastest growing economies in the world.

   A Nepal   **B** Sri Lanka   **C** Bangladesh   **D** India

4. Making products in one's home is called a _____ industry.

   A growing   **B** computer   **C** cottage   **D** heavy

5. Cars, trucks, and untreated smoke create _____ pollution.

   A water   **B** air   **C** river   **D** soil

Writing About Geography

In this book, you have learned about many sources of energy. What do you think will be the main energy source in the future? Write your opinion. Include at least three details or facts to support your opinion.

What do you think ?

What does the growth of high-tech businesses tell you about the level of education in India?

Carrying a Load

My name is Santosh. I am 15 years old. My family grows corn on a farm outside Kathmandu, Nepal. But I don't help farm. I earn more money for my family working as a porter.

During the summer, I get up at 3:00 A.M. and walk one hour into Kathmandu. I arrive at the market with the first truckloads of vegetables. Vendors pay me to unload them.

Afterward, I walk to a bus park. Many people come to Nepal to climb mountains or trek foothills. I earn money loading and unloading their luggage. It isn't always easy to get work in the city. Many boys—and some girls—try for these jobs. We agree with the employers beforehand how much they will pay us. They always hire those who ask for the lowest pay.

During other seasons, I work in the hills. People hire porters at a market center where the highway ends. Mostly I carry construction items over the steep hills. These items include blocks and pipes and materials for building bridges. Sometimes I carry large sacks of grain, or crates of fruits and vegetables. Or, I carry luggage for tourists who come to trek the hills, or climb mountains.

I usually carry my loads in a large basket on my back. The basket is supported underneath by a strap that runs over the top of my head. I also carry a T-shaped stick used to support my load while I rest. My wages on these long trips depends on the weight of the load. I carry as much as I'm able so I can make more money.

I am gone for many days at a time, sometimes for weeks. My mother packs flour, rice, and dry vegetables for me to take. Not all young porters are so lucky. Some use all their wages to buy food for that trip. Some rely on mangos, oranges, and bananas along the journey.

Once, when I was 12, I fell into a river while working. I was not hurt, but I did lose my shoes in the water. I had to finish that journey barefoot. I consider that trip my worst. Now I am more careful.

Wrap-Up

1. What is challenging about working as a porter in the city?

2. What is challenging about working as a porter in the hills?

- India, Bangladesh, Nepal, Bhutan, and Sri Lanka make up much of south Asia. India has more than a billion people. The Indian peninsula is surrounded by the Indian Ocean.

- The subcontinent has four geographical regions: the Himalayas, the Indo-Gangetic Plain, Deccan Plateau, and the Thar or Great Indian Desert.

- The main physical feature is the Himalayas. Most of Bangladesh is a large alluvial plain. Sri Lanka is an island. The major rivers are the Ganges and Brahmaputra.

- The monsoon winds influence the many climates. Most of India, Sri Lanka, and Bangladesh have either a tropical monsoon climate or a tropical savanna climate. Nepal and Bhutan have a highland climate.

- English is the language of government and big business. However, India's national language is Hindi. India has more than a thousand other languages. All of these languages cause communication problems.

- India is the birthplace of Hinduism. Islam, Sikhism, and Jainism also have a large following. About 30 million Christians also live in India.

- The biggest social problems are poverty and population growth. Other problems are urbanization, migration, civil unrest, and religious conflict.

- More than half of the people in the region are farmers. Farmers depend on the monsoon rains. Most are subsistence farmers. But some sell and export their crops of cotton, tea, rice, cashew nuts, spices, sugarcane, and coffee. Sri Lanka is the world's biggest exporter of tea.

- India has big oil, coal, and iron ore deposits. The fast-flowing rivers of Nepal and Bhutan supply cheap hydroelectric power. Sri Lanka exports many gemstones like diamonds, emeralds, and rubies.

- India's economy is one of the fastest growing economies in the world. Textiles, cars, and computers are new industries. Cottage industries are an important part of the subcontinent's economy. Bangladesh exports clothes, shrimp, fish, leather goods, and agricultural products.

- The main environmental problems are air and water pollution, deforestation, and soil erosion.

Chapter 18 REVIEW

Word Bank

farmers

Ganges

monsoon

passes

peninsula

On a sheet of paper, use the words from the Word Bank to complete each sentence correctly.

1. The Indian subcontinent is a huge _____.

2. Mountain _____ have enabled invaders to reach India.

3. The _____ begins in the Himalayas and flows to the heartland of India.

4. The _____ winds change direction according to the time of year and bring rain to farmers.

5. Most of the people in India are _____.

On a sheet of paper, write the letter of the answer that correctly completes each sentence.

6. The island nation off the southeastern coast of India is _____.

A Nepal **C** Bhutan
B Bangladesh **D** Sri Lanka

7. Most of India's people live on the _____.

A Himalayas **C** Indo-Gangetic Plain
B island **D** Great Indian Desert

8. Most people who live in India and Nepal are _____.

A Buddhists **C** Muslim
B Hindus **D** Christian

9. The caste system is a feature of _____.

A Buddhism **C** Islam
B Sikhism **D** Hinduism

10. One of India's newest major exports is _____.

A oil **C** computer software
B cars **D** tea

On a sheet of paper, write the answer to each question. Use complete sentences.

11. Where is the Indian subcontinent located?

12. What is happening to India's economy?

13. What are the major environmental problems the region faces?

Critical Thinking On a sheet of paper, write your response to each question. Use complete sentences.

14. What do you think are the best ways to fight poverty in the world? Explain your answer.

15. Do you think religion plays too big of a role in life on the Indian subcontinent? Explain your answer.

Applying the Five Themes of Geography

Place
How is Bangladesh different from most other countries?

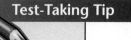

Test-Taking Tip

When answering a multiple-choice question, first identify the choices you know are wrong.

Chapter

19

Pakistan and Afghanistan

Afghanistan and Pakistan are two countries of south Asia. Like India, Pakistan is the birthplace of an ancient civilization. Thousands of years ago, villages grew into cities along the Indus River Valley. Afghanistan also has a very long history. North Afghanistan was one of the earliest places where people began to grow crops and raise animals. The two countries have much in common, but also have important differences.

Goals for Learning

◆ To describe Pakistan and Afghanistan

◆ To identify their most important physical features and climates

◆ To describe their diverse cultures and where and how most people live

◆ To describe their economies and the environmental challenges they face

Geo-Stats   Pakistan and Afghanistan

Nation: Pakistan
Population:
   165,804,000
Area: 307,374 square miles
Major Cities: Islamabad
   (capital), Karachi, Lahore,
   Faisalabad
Major Religion: Islam

Nation: Afghanistan
Population:
   31,056,000
Area: 251,825 square miles
Major Cities: Kabul (capital),
   Kandahar
Major Religion: Islam

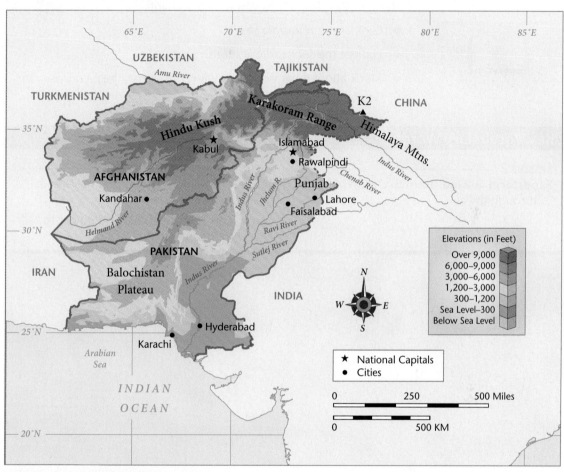

Map Skills

Pakistan and Afghanistan are neighboring countries in southern Asia. Mountains separate the two countries. Afghanistan is landlocked. Pakistan has a major port in Karachi. Both countries are united by a common religion, Islam.

Study the map and answer the following questions:

1. What mountain range is in eastern Afghanistan?

2. What country borders Pakistan on the east?

3. What country borders Afghanistan on the west?

4. What river flows through most of Pakistan?

5. How do you think geography affects these countries?

Reading Strategy:
Visualizing

Think about what you have heard about Pakistan and Afghanistan in the news. This will help you visualize the countries you will learn about in this chapter. As you read the chapter:

◆ Look at the photographs.

◆ Look at the subhead questions.

◆ Think about what you already know that may help you visualize what you learn from this chapter.

Key Vocabulary Words

Lesson 2	*Lesson 3*
Sandstorm A wind storm that blows sand through the air	**Taliban** A religious group that believes in a strict form of Islam
	Terrorism The use of fear and power to control people

- To know where Pakistan and Afghanistan are located
- To describe how the geography of the region shaped its history
- To identify the major subregions

Reading Strategy:
Visualizing

Look at the map at the beginning of the chapter. Visualize the dark brown areas as mountains.

Where Are Pakistan and Afghanistan Located?

Pakistan is located on the Indian subcontinent. The mountain ranges in the north separate Pakistan from China and Afghanistan. They include the Karakoram, the Hindu Kush, and part of the Himalayas. Some of these mountains are more than 20,000 feet high. They are among the highest in the world. The Arabian Sea borders southern Pakistan. Pakistan is about the size of Texas in the United States.

Afghanistan is north and west of Pakistan. Iran is west of Afghanistan. China and the central Asian republics of Turkmenistan, Uzbekistan, and Tajikistan border it on the north.

How Did Geography Shape History?

Historically, Afghanistan and Pakistan have always been an important crossroads. People traveling to and from China, central Asia, India, Europe, and the Middle East traveled through Afghanistan. In 330 B.C., Alexander the Great, a Greek warrior, invaded. In A.D. 642, Arabs invaded and introduced the religion of Islam. At different times, Afghanistan was ruled by the Persians and the Mongols. In the 1800s, Great Britain and Russia fought in Afghanistan. The invaders came through the few mountain passes. The most famous is the Khyber Pass. It connects northwest Pakistan with Kabul in Afghanistan. The Tochi Pass and the Gamal Pass also allow passage through the high mountains between the two countries.

Afghanistan has an important location. This is the reason why so many different groups have tried to control it. It is at a crossroads for the movement of oil and other natural resources. Afghanistan is likely to become even more important as the demand for oil and other natural resources increases. This demand is growing, especially in Asia.

The Indus River has an important part in world history. One of the first great civilizations developed in the Indus River Valley. The river begins in the Himalaya Mountains in India. When the snow melted, the river flooded. The water left silt behind. Because this rich soil is good for growing crops, people settled along the Indus River Valley. The ruins of two cities, Harappa and Mohenjo Daro, are still there.

What Are the Regions in These Countries?

Pakistan can be divided into three regions. In the north are mountains. The high mountainous region includes the Karakoram, the Hindu Kush, and part of the Himalayas. Southwestern Pakistan is a dry plateau. The lowlands along the Indus River make up the third and most important region. This region is where most Pakistanis live. It includes the cities of Karachi, Islamabad, Lahore, and Rawalpindi. The lowlands have rich farmland. The river water is used for irrigation. Most of Pakistan's food is grown in this region.

Afghanistan also has three regions. Two-thirds of the country is covered by the highlands that include the Hindu Kush Mountains that separate it from Pakistan. In the north is an area of dry plains. The southwestern lowlands are mostly desert. The best farmland is near the city of Kandahar in southeast Afghanistan.

Lesson 1 Review On a sheet of paper, write the word in parenthesis that makes each statement true.

1. (Pakistan, Afghanistan) is located on the Indian subcontinent.

2. The body of water that borders southern Pakistan is the (Bay of Bengal, Arabian Sea).

3. One of the first great civilizations developed in the (Indus, Hindu Kush) River Valley.

4. Most of Pakistan's people live in the (highlands, lowlands) region.

5. The best farmland in (Afghanistan, Pakistan) is near Kandahar.

Reading Strategy: Visualizing

Look at the map at the beginning of the chapter to see where these cities are located.

What do you think

Would you expect Afghanistan and Pakistan to have a close relationship? Explain.

Objectives

♦ To describe the main physical features of Afghanistan and Pakistan

♦ To identify the main rivers

♦ To describe the climate

Sandstorm

A wind storm that blows sand through the air

Reading Strategy:
Visualizing

Does this photo help you visualize a sandstorm?

What Are the Main Physical Features?

Mountains are the main physical feature of Pakistan and Afghanistan. The Himalayas, the Karakoram, and the Hindu Kush contain some of the world's highest peaks. K2 is the second highest mountain in the world. The mountains are still growing as several tectonic plates smash into each other. Earthquakes are very common. The mountains are snow covered and contain over 300 glaciers. Two of the most famous glaciers are Baltoro and Pasu. The glaciers are important. When they melt, they feed the Indus River and its tributaries.

The Balochistan Plateau covers much of Pakistan. The average height of the plateau is about 2,000 feet. The plateau is stony and dry. The rivers and streams contain water only after it rains. The area is well-known for its sudden **sandstorms**. A sandstorm has winds that blow sand through the air.

What Are the Major Rivers?

The Indus River flows through much of Pakistan. It is one of the world's longest rivers. It runs 1,800 miles from the Himalaya Mountains to the Arabian Sea. It is fed by the melting ice and snow of the mountains. It carries twice as much water as the Nile River does. It has five important tributaries: the Jhelum, Chenab, Ravi, Beas, and Sutlej rivers.

Sandstorms are common in this area. The sand in the air makes it hard to see and hard to breathe.

The rivers form a large floodplain that is the richest farm region of Pakistan. The Pakistani province of Punjab is in the northern part of this region. Punjab means "the five waters." The people call the area Punjab because the five important tributaries of the Indus flow through it.

Life in Pakistan depends on the waters of the Indus River. The waters of this river and its tributaries have supplied irrigation to the plains of Pakistan since ancient times. They supply most of Pakistan's drinking water. Most of Pakistan's people live in the province of Punjab.

Reading Strategy:
Visualizing

Do any rivers or streams in your area flow only when it rains?

Afghanistan shares the Amu River with several countries of central Asia. It is on Afghanistan's border with Tajikistan and Uzbekistan. Afghanistan has three other important rivers: the Helmand, the Harirud, and the Kabul. Most of Afghanistan's rivers are shallow and flow only when it rains. Afghanistan has built several dams to try to use the water for irrigation and hydroelectricity. The dams have not been cared for, and none of them are working well.

What Is the Climate Like?

The Indus River Valley of Pakistan and much of Afghanistan have a steppe climate. Extreme temperatures are common. The mountains are cold and snow covered in summer and winter. Even the world's best mountain climbers are limited to a few weeks in May and June because of the extreme cold. The areas close to the mountains are also cold. Temperatures on the plateau can be very hot. Summer temperatures are often over 100°F. In the summer months, a strong steady wind blows. The wind causes blinding sandstorms and drought. Winters are very cold and snowy with some blizzards.

The lowlands are hot. The climate of the coastal areas of Pakistan is moderated by sea breezes, but is usually warm. Both countries receive little rainfall. Most of the rain comes in late summer.

Geography in Your Life

The Richter Scale

Seismologists study earthquakes. A machine that records ground movements caused by earthquakes is a seismograph, shown below. Charles Richter, who was a seismologist, developed the Richter scale in 1935. The scale is a series of numbers that shows how strong an earthquake is. Each number on the scale represents a tenfold increase in the distance the ground moves. Imagine that an earthquake records 7 on the scale. That would mean that the ground moved 10 times more than it moved for a 6 on the scale.

While moving the ground, an earthquake releases energy. Each number on the Richter scale represents a release of about 30 times the amount of energy represented by the number below it. An earthquake that records as a 7 would release 30 times the energy of a 6.

Earthquakes that are 5 or less on the scale cause little damage. However, earthquakes about 7 or higher can kill people and cause great damage. For example, an earthquake of 6.9 on the Richter scale killed over 4,700 people in Afghanistan in 1998.

Word Bank
Amu
mountains
plateau
Punjab
steppe

Lesson 2 Review On a sheet of paper, use the words from the Word Bank to complete each sentence correctly.

1. The main physical feature of Pakistan and Afghanistan is _____.

2. A 2,000-foot-high _____ covers much of Pakistan.

3. Afghanistan shares the _____ River with several central Asian countries.

4. _____ is the area of Pakistan where most of its people live.

5. The Indus River Valley of Pakistan and much of Afghanistan have a _____ climate.

What do you think ?

What conditions make it difficult to fight a war in Afghanistan?

Lesson 3 — The People and Cultures

Objectives

- To describe the cultures of Pakistan and Afghanistan
- To identify the languages that are spoken there
- To describe their religion
- To describe the major social problems

What Are Pakistan and Afghanistan's Cultures?

Pakistan and Afghanistan have many ethnic groups. Each group has its own language and culture. Most people of Pakistan feel more loyalty to their ethnic group than to their country. Conflict between ethnic groups is common. Punjabis are the main ethnic group in both Pakistan and Afghanistan. Pashtuns are the main ethnic group in northwestern Pakistan. The Pashtuns are independent and loyal to their tribe.

In northern Afghanistan, a quarter of the people are Tajiks. They are the second largest ethnic group. The Hazara, a people of mixed Mongol background, make up about 18 percent of Afghanistan's population. The cultures in both countries have many things in common with other Asian cultures. The languages and religion are similar to those in Iran.

What Languages Do the People Speak?

Each ethnic group speaks its own language. Many people speak more than one language. The national language of Pakistan is Urdu. People who live in the major cities speak Urdu. It is also taught in all of Pakistan's schools. However, the most common spoken language is Punjabi.

Afghanistan has two main languages—Pashto and Afghan Persian, or Dari. Pashto is spoken only by the Pashtuns. Dari is the first language of Tajiks and Hazara, but it is a widely spoken second language for others. In the north, Turkic languages are common. There are at least 30 other languages.

What Religion Do the People Practice?

The people in Pakistan and Afghanistan are Muslims. This gives everyday life a certain unity throughout the region. Most people in Pakistan and Afghanistan are Sunni Muslims. Both countries have Shiite minorities too. Islam is an important part of the lives of most people in both countries. They organize their day around the five times of prayer required of Muslims.

Muslim women and men live very separate lives. Children get a religious education from their families. Children may also go to regular schools. In Pakistan, few girls attend school.

In 1992, a Muslim group called the **Taliban** took control of Kabul, Afghanistan. The Taliban follow a strict form of Islam. They believe women cannot work outside the home. Girls cannot attend school. Boys have limited education. The Taliban does not allow television or computers. By 1998, the Taliban controlled almost all of Afghanistan. The United States attacked the Taliban in 1998 and 2001, and defeated some Taliban forces. The people now have more freedom. Girls can go to school. Still, the Taliban continues to influence Afghanistan.

What Problems Do the People Face?

Poverty is the biggest problem; many people are very poor. Population growth is also a problem. The growth rate in Pakistan means the population may double by 2030.

Reading Strategy:
Visualizing

Some people in these countries live on $1 per day. Can you visualize how poor the people in these countries are?

The Taliban continues to be a problem. The United States views the Taliban as a threat. It links the Taliban with **terrorism**. Terrorism is the use of fear and power to control people. The United States has had troops in Afghanistan for years. The border between Pakistan and Afghanistan is an area that is difficult to reach or control. Neither Pakistan nor Afghanistan has kept the Taliban under control.

Pakistan also has problems with its neighbors, especially India. The constant fighting in Afghanistan created refugees; many of them settled in Pakistan.

Lesson 3 Review On a sheet of paper, write the answer to each question. Use complete sentences.

1. Why might loyalty to an ethnic group instead of a country be a problem?

2. What is the national language of Pakistan?

3. What is the major religion in Pakistan and Afghanistan?

4. What is the Taliban?

5. What are the biggest problems in these countries?

What do you think ?

What do you think is the best way for the United States to fight terrorism?

The Arms Race

When the United States used atomic bombs against Japan in World War II, the world changed. Ever since, the world has faced the risk of a nuclear war. The competition among countries to develop nuclear bombs is called the Arms Race.

The Cold War was a period from about 1945 to the early 1990s. During this time, both the Soviets and the Americans built a supply of nuclear weapons to threaten each other. Even now, both Russia and the United States have many of these bombs. Other nations have built atomic bombs, too.

India exploded its first test nuclear bomb in 1998. Much of the rest of the world was alarmed. India, however, said that it had become a major power—a nuclear power. India said it needed to protect itself from enemies such as Pakistan. Months later, Pakistan exploded its own test atomic bomb. The United States invaded Iraq in 2003 saying that it thought Iraq had weapons that could kill many people. There are concerns about Iran's and North Korea's ability to produce such bombs, too.

One result of this arms race is a new effort to ban these bombs. These bombs can quickly cause many deaths. Years later, the material released by the bomb can still kill people who touched or breathed those materials.

Several treaties to control the spread of nuclear weapons have passed. However, some countries with atomic weapons have not signed treaties. Many people are afraid that even more countries will develop nuclear weapons.

Wrap-Up

1. Why did India feel it needed to have atomic bombs?

2. Why might the United States believe there is a need to keep a stock of nuclear weapons today?

Make a Difference

Find out what your representative in Congress thinks about banning nuclear weapons in the world. Then write a letter to the representative, agreeing or disagreeing with his or her position.

Objectives

◆ To learn about Pakistan's and Afghanistan's economies

◆ To describe their natural resources and industries

◆ To learn about the environmental problems these countries face

Reading Strategy:
Visualizing

Can you visualize nomads raising sheep?

What Is the Economy Like?

Many people in Pakistan and Afghanistan are farmers. In Pakistan, about half the population is involved in some form of agriculture. In Afghanistan, the percentage is even higher. Most farmers work small plots of land. They use water buffalo, oxen, donkeys, and other animals for heavy work such as plowing. In some parts of the region, goats and sheep are raised by nomads.

The farms that produce the most crops are in the Indus River Valley of Pakistan. Using irrigation, farmers there can grow enough cotton and rice to export.

In Afghanistan, the major crops are corn, rice, barley, wheat, vegetables, and nuts. Many Afghan farmers grow opium poppies to sell. They are easy to grow and are an important source of income for poor farmers. People make illegal drugs such as heroin and opium from the flowers of this plant. Afghanistan produces more than 90 percent of the world's opium.

Both Pakistan and Afghanistan are poor countries. Both receive large amounts of foreign aid from the United States and other countries. Afghanistan does not have good road and rail systems. The growing population means there is less land available for farming. At the same time, more people means that they need to grow more food. The shortage of water, the high cost of fertilizer, and the constant fighting make both countries dependent on food imported from developed countries.

This is a field of opium poppies. They grow well in Pakistan and Afghanistan.

What Are Their Natural Resources?

Pakistan has some natural resources. It has lots of natural gas and some oil. Pakistanis mine chromite, used to make metals. They also mine limestone and rock salt. Northeastern Pakistan has large forests. Much of the land there is used for forestry.

Afghanistan has not developed its resources. It has natural gas, iron ore, copper, and chromium. It also has some gemstones such as lapis, emeralds, and rubies.

What Are Their Industries?

Pakistan is more developed than Afghanistan. Pakistan has a growing industrial base. About one-fifth of the Pakistani people work in industries and offices in Pakistan's cities. However, cottage industries are common. People make baskets, pottery, carpets, furniture, metal ware, and leather goods in their homes. Pakistan also has a thriving repair business. Appliances and technical goods are hard to get and expensive. So people tend to keep everything that can be fixed.

Pakistan has a growing textile industry. Its factories produce clothes, bed linens, and cotton cloth. About 80 percent of the textile industry is cotton, but factories also produce other fibers. Its biggest export trade partner is the United States.

Other important industries include food processing, chemical manufacturing, and iron and steel industries. Food processing is considered Pakistan's largest industry.

Afghanistan has almost no industries.

Reading Strategy:
Visualizing

Visualize Islamabad covered by a thick cloud of smog.

What Environmental Problems Exist?

Air and water pollution are the biggest problems. In Pakistan, factories, cars, and trucks produce pollution. Its two largest cities, Karachi and Lahore, are badly polluted. Islamabad, the capital, is covered by a thick cloud of smog. The air quality is so poor that thousands of people are hospitalized each year for air-pollution-related illnesses. Many people have trouble breathing, and many children suffer from diseases related to the pollution.

The level of water pollution is also high. Karachi's Lyari River is stained black with sewage and toxic waste. The river's banks are lined with piles of burning garbage. The city's water and sewer systems are terrible. Karachi produces 8,000 tons of garbage each day, but only 40 percent is collected.

Pakistan is trying to grow enough food for its people. It is also trying to develop industries. Pakistan has not paid much attention to the environment.

Other environmental problems are deforestation and soil erosion. In both Pakistan and Afghanistan, people cut trees for firewood. So much of Pakistan's forests are being cut down that in 10 years, there may be no forest left.

Lesson 4 Review On a sheet of paper, write the letter of the answer that correctly completes each sentence.

1. The most productive farms in Pakistan are in the _____.

   A Indus Valley   **C** Hindu Kush
   B mountain regions   **D** Nile River Valley

2. Afghanistan produces most of the world's _____.

   A jute   **C** opium
   B spices   **D** cotton

3. About one-fifth of Pakistan's people work in _____.

   A mining   **C** industry
   B farming   **D** fishing

4. Pakistan's most plentiful resource is _____.

   A emeralds   **C** oil
   B cottage industries   **D** natural gas

5. Air and water quality are poor in Pakistan's port city, _____.

   A Islamabad   **C** Kabul
   B Karachi   **D** Lahore

What do you think ?

Pakistan has a large number of refugees from the fighting in Afghanistan. Do you think the developed countries of the world should provide more help to Pakistan?

Adjusting in Afghanistan

I am 14 years old, and my name is Sofia. I live in eastern Afghanistan near the city of Jalalabad. Many things have changed for me since 2001. In 2001, the United States drove out the government here called the Taliban. The Taliban is a Sunni Islamic group—a religious group. The Taliban denied women and girls many freedoms.

While the Taliban were in power, I could not be seen outside the home by men or boys. I could only perform indoor chores. Today, I work in the pasture. I collect cow dung. Then, I stick it to the walls of my home to dry. My family burns it as fuel for cooking fires.

Most families near my village are farmers. They grow wheat, rice, and vegetables. Women and girls here now do things they never used to do to help out. They tend crops. They carry water. Because women and girls want to wear proper Muslim dress, they still wear chadors, or veils, over their heads. But now many women and girls wear pants under their long dresses. The Taliban did not allow females to wear pants.

As I work, I see a caravan of camels passing by. The camels carry people, tents, and supplies. I know that these travelers are searching for better grazing pastures for their animals. I am glad to live in one place. Otherwise I would not be able to attend school. I am the first girl in my family to attend school.

Under the Taliban, it was illegal for girls to get an education. To attend school in my teacher's home, I must walk 30 minutes into the village. I see the damage from the last 20 years of war. The roads are filled with holes from land mines. Bombed-out buildings and homes are everywhere.

Even though it is legal for girls to go to school, I tell no one that I go. It could be dangerous for me, my classmates, and my teacher. Many Taliban supporters attack girls' schools. Many Afghanistan schools for girls have been attacked. I am always careful to go straight to the house of my teacher. Even though I am often afraid, I am grateful for the freedom to attend school.

Wrap-Up

1. What are some things girls now do in Afghanistan?

2. What are the signs of war Sofia sees on her walk?

- Pakistan is located on the Indian subcontinent. Afghanistan is north and west of Pakistan. Iran, China, Turkmenistan, Uzbekistan, India, and Tajikistan are their neighbors. Pakistan is on the Arabian Sea.

- Afghanistan and Pakistan have always been an important crossroads. People traveling to and from China, central Asia, India, Europe, and the Middle East traveled through Afghanistan. One of the first great civilizations in the world developed in the Indus River Valley.

- Pakistan can be divided into three regions. The north is mountainous. Southwestern Pakistan is a dry plateau. The lowlands along the Indus River make up the third and most important region. Afghanistan has three regions: the central highlands, an area of dry plains, and the mostly desert southwestern lowlands.

- Mountains are the main physical feature of Pakistan and Afghanistan. The Himalayas, the Karakoram, and the Hindu Kush contain some of the world's highest peaks. The Indus River is Pakistan's longest river. The Indus River Valley of Pakistan and much of Afghanistan have a steppe climate. Temperature extremes are common.

- Pakistan and Afghanistan have many ethnic groups. Each group has its own language and culture. Pashtuns are the main ethnic group in Pakistan and Afghanistan.

- The national language of Pakistan is Urdu. Afghanistan has two main languages, Pashto and Dari. The people of both Pakistan and Afghanistan are Muslims who practice Islam.

- In Pakistan, about half the population works in agriculture. In Afghanistan, even more people are farmers. The most productive farms are in the Indus Valley of Pakistan.

- Pakistan is not rich in natural resources. Its most plentiful resource is natural gas. Afghanistan's known resources have not been developed. It has natural gas, iron ore, copper, and chromium.

- Pakistan has a growing textile industry. Its factories produce clothes, bed linens, and cotton cloth. Food processing is considered Pakistan's largest industry.

- Pakistan's and Afghanistan's main environmental problems are air and water pollution, deforestation, and soil erosion.

Chapter 19 REVIEW

Word Bank
Hindu Kush 5
Indus 3
Islam 4
Khyber 2
Pashtun 1

On a sheet of paper, use the words from the Word Bank to complete each sentence correctly.

1. The main ethnic group of both Pakistan and Afghanistan is _____.

2. The _____ Pass is the most famous pass through the high mountains.

3. The _____ River begins in the Himalayas and flows through Pakistan.

4. The religion of _____ unites the people of Pakistan and Afghanistan.

5. The _____ is a mountain range in Afghanistan.

On a sheet of paper, write the letter of the answer that correctly completes each sentence.

6. The _____ River Valley is one of the first places civilization developed.

    A Ganges   C Indus
    B Brahmaputra   D Hindu Kush

7. Most of Pakistan's people live _____.

    A on a plateau   C in the river valley
    B on a peninsula   D in deserts

8. The most common spoken language in Pakistan is _____.

    A English   C Urdu
    B Punjabi   D Bengali

9. Much of Pakistan and Afghanistan have a _____ climate.

    A subtropical   C Mediterranean
    B steppe   D humid continental

10. Pakistan's biggest industry is _____.

    A forestry   C fishing
    B textiles   D food processing

On a sheet of paper, write the answer to each question. Use complete sentences.

11. In what ways does Islam determine what a girl can do in Afghanistan?

12. What is the Taliban?

13. What are the major environmental problems Pakistan faces?

Critical Thinking On a sheet of paper, write your response to each question. Use complete sentences.

14. Do you think it is more important to be loyal to an ethnic group than to a country? Explain your answer.

15. Do you think religion plays too big a role in the lives of the people of Pakistan and Afghanistan? Explain your answer.

Applying the Five Themes of Geography

Movement
Afghanistan has been a crossroads for centuries. How does its culture reflect the theme of movement?

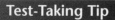

Test-Taking Tip

To choose the answer that correctly completes a sentence, read the sentence using each answer choice. Then choose the answer that makes the most sense when you read the entire sentence. Or, choose the answer that makes the sentence true.

Bollywood

Unless you are of Indian descent, you probably have never heard of Bollywood. Bollywood is the nickname for India's film industry. India has been making films for more than 100 years. Some years, India produces more than 600 films.

The filmmaking industry is centered in Mumbai (Bombay). The filmmakers create their films in 17 different Indian languages. The films and the actors who appear in them are popular. Rural communities sometimes build temples to actors who play the roles of gods in the films.

Few of the Indian films are original. Many are fairy tales based on religious stories. The films contain music and dance. The actors appear in brightly colored costumes. Beautiful green landscapes are often the setting. These films offer the poor people of India a brief escape from poverty.

Many of these films are popular with Indians who have migrated to other countries. Indian audiences in the United States, Great Britain, the Persian Gulf countries, and some countries in Africa enjoy these films. They remind them of the India they left behind. Some films make more money overseas than they do in India.

Wrap-Up

1. What is Bollywood?

2. Where is Bollywood?

3. Why are these films so popular in India?

4. Why are the films popular with Indians who now live overseas?

5. What are some places with large Indian communities?

- India, Bangladesh, Nepal, Bhutan, and Sri Lanka make up much of south Asia. The Indian peninsula is surrounded by the Indian Ocean. Pakistan is located on the Indian subcontinent. Afghanistan is north and west of Pakistan.

- The Himalayas are the main physical feature of south Asia. Mountains are the main physical feature of Pakistan and Afghanistan. The Indus River is Pakistan's longest river. The major rivers in south Asia are the Ganges and Brahmaputra.

- Most of India, Sri Lanka, and Bangladesh have either a tropical monsoon or a tropical savanna climate. Nepal and Bhutan have a highland climate. The Indus River Valley of Pakistan and much of Afghanistan have a steppe climate.

- India has over a billion people. India is the birthplace of Hinduism. Most Indians are Hindus. About 30 million Christians also live in India. Most people in Pakistan and Afghanistan are Muslims.

- English is the language of government and big business in south Asia. India's national language is Hindi. India has many other languages. Urdu is Pakistan's national language. Pashto and Dari are the main languages in Afghanistan.

- More than half the people are farmers who depend on rain or irrigation to grow crops. Cotton, tea, rice, cashew nuts, spices, sugarcane, and coffee are the most important cash crops.

- Pakistan has natural gas. Afghanistan's resources have not been developed. India has oil, coal, and iron ore deposits. India has a fast-growing economy. Textiles, cars, and computers are new industries. Pakistan's main industry is food processing. Afghanistan does not have much industry.

- Poverty is a problem in the area. The main environmental problems are air and water pollution, deforestation, and soil erosion.

Southeast and East Asia

Southeast Asia includes Indonesia, an archipelago of over 13,000 islands. It also includes other island nations such as the Philippines and Brunei. East Asia includes China, Japan, and North and South Korea. This is a photo of Mount Fuji in Japan. Mount Fuji is the highest mountain peak in Japan. It is a dormant volcano that last erupted in 1707.

Did you know that this region has far more people than any other region of the world? You will learn about this large region's geography, culture, and economies. You will learn about terrace farming and great, modern cities like Tokyo and Shanghai. You will also learn about the religions of Buddhism and Shinto.

20

Southeast Asia

Southeast Asia is home to over 500 million people. The countries of Southeast Asia differ from one another in many ways. They have different forms of government. Some are large; others are small. Some have many natural resources; others have few. Many have developing economies; others have some of the fastest growing economies in the world. Some people still live much as their ancestors did hundreds of years ago.

Goals for Learning

◆ To describe where Southeast Asia is located and how geography shaped its history

◆ To identify its most important physical features and its climate

◆ To describe its diverse cultures and explain how and where most Southeast Asians live

◆ To describe Southeast Asia's economy and environmental challenges

Geo-Stats   Key Nations of Southeast Asia

Nation: Indonesia
Population: 245,453,000
Area: 741,101 square miles
Major Cities: Jakarta (capital), Bandung, Surabaya

Nation: Malaysia
Population: 24,386,000
Area: 127,317 square miles
Capital: Kuala Lumpur

Nation: Thailand
Population: 64,632,000
Area: 198,457 square miles
Capital: Bangkok

Nation: Vietnam
Population: 84,403,000
Area: 127,242 square miles
Major Cities: Hanoi (capital), Ho Chi Minh City, Haiphong

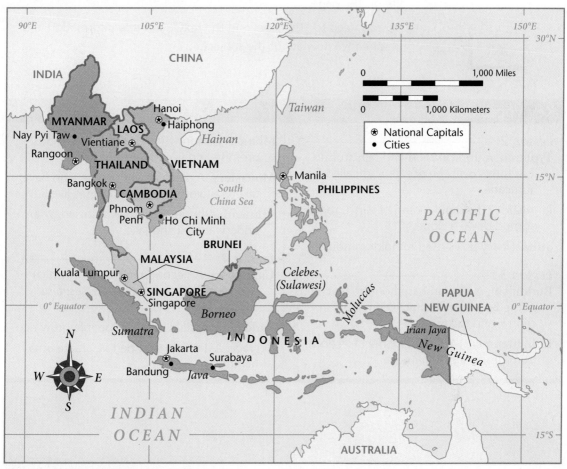

Map Skills

The large peninsula of Southeast Asia is east of India and south of China. Southeast Asia also includes many island nations in the Indian Ocean and the south Pacific Ocean. This map shows the main countries of this region.

Study the map and answer the following questions:

1. What body of water does Vietnam border?

2. In what direction would one have to travel to get from Vietnam to the Philippines?

3. What is the capital of Thailand? Cambodia?

4. Which large country borders Southeast Asia on the south?

5. Which of these countries is landlocked?

Reading Strategy:
Inferencing

Inferencing combines what you know with what you read. Sometimes you need to understand more than just the words that are on the page.

◆ You need to "think beyond the text," and add information you already know about the subject.

Key Vocabulary Words

Lesson 2

Typhoon A tropical wind and rain storm that forms over the ocean, also called a hurricane

Landslide The rapid sliding of earth, rocks, or mud down a slope

Stilts Heavy poles used to hold up houses

Lesson 3

Buddhism A religion based on the teachings of the Buddha and practiced mainly in central and eastern Asia

Enlightenment A state of perfect freedom from desire and suffering

Monk A person who has made a religious promise and lives in a monastery

Monastery A place where people who have taken religious vows or promises live

Tsunami A huge ocean wave caused by an underwater earthquake

Lesson 4

Capitalism An economic system in which people own their own businesses; also called a market economy

Paddy A wet field in which people grow rice

Terrace A flat field that people create on a hillside

Where Is Southeast Asia Located?

Southeast Asia is located in the Tropics. It extends from about 25 degrees north latitude to about 10 degrees south. It is made up of peninsulas and islands. Geographers call the largest peninsula the Indo-Chinese Peninsula. It extends southeast off of the mainland of Asia and borders both India and China. Vietnam, Laos, and Cambodia are located on this peninsula. Most of Myanmar and Thailand are also on the peninsula.

Stretching southward from this peninsula is the long, narrow Malay Peninsula. The rest of Thailand and Myanmar are located in the northern part of this peninsula. Malaysia is on the southern part. The small island country of Singapore is located off the southern tip of the Malay Peninsula.

The Philippine Islands are named after King Philip of Spain.

All of the other countries of Southeast Asia are islands in the Pacific Ocean. Thousands of islands stretch over 3,000 miles from east to west. They stretch almost to Australia. Some islands have no people living on them. All are near the equator. The other countries include Indonesia, the Philippines, and Brunei. Indonesia is the largest of these countries. The west half of the island of New Guinea, called Irian Jaya, is part of Indonesia. Indonesia's total land area is three times the size of Texas. The Philippines is another archipelago, made up of more than 7,000 islands.

How Did Geography Shape History?

Southeast Asia's location makes it an important region. It is located between the Indian and the Pacific Oceans. In the past, this was the main water route between China and India. Today, Southeast Asia is located on one of the world's most important shipping routes. Much of the world's trade passes through its busy seaports.

Reading Strategy:
Inferencing

What do you know
about spices? Think
about what you know
as you read about the
Spice Islands.

Europeans arrived in Southeast Asia in the 1500s. They first came as traders and missionaries. They discovered that Southeast Asia was rich in mineral and agricultural resources. The riches of the Spice Islands of eastern Indonesia attracted the Europeans. The Spice Islands are called the Moluccas. At that time, spices like pepper, cloves, and nutmeg were far more valuable than they are today. People had no refrigerators, so food spoiled quickly. Spices kept food from spoiling and made it taste better. These spices would not grow in Europe.

Soon all the countries of Southeast Asia except for Thailand became European colonies. Portugal, the Netherlands, Great Britain, Spain, and France controlled most of the countries. The United States controlled the Philippines from 1898 until 1946.

Geography also helps to explain the many diverse cultures of Southeast Asia. Because of its location, it attracted people from many different lands. The Malays came from China. Other groups followed. Each group brought its customs, cultures, and lifestyles. Traders from India introduced the religions of Hinduism and Buddhism. Muslim traders brought Islam to Malaysia and Indonesia. Europeans introduced Western ideas, including Christianity, while in control of the region.

Word Bank

Archipelago 4

Islam 5

Peninsula 2

spices 3

Tropics 1

Lesson 1 Review On a sheet of paper, use the words from the Word Bank to complete each sentence correctly.

1. Southeast Asia is located in the _____.

2. The mainland nations are located on the Indo-Chinese _____.

3. One of the reasons Europeans were first attracted to the region was the _____ that grew there.

4. The island nations of the region are all part of the Malay _____.

5. Muslim traders brought _____ to Malaysia and Indonesia.

What do you think

The people of Indonesia and the Philippines are spread over many islands. How might this affect the unity of these countries?

Objectives

◆ To describe the main physical features of Southeast Asia

◆ To identify the main bodies of water

◆ To describe the climate

◆ To learn how people adapted to their environment

Reading Strategy:
Inferencing

What do you already know about volcanoes? What do you think living along the Ring of Fire must be like?

What Are Southeast Asia's Physical Features?

The physical features of "mainland" and "island" Southeast Asia are different. The mainland countries of Cambodia, Laos, Vietnam, Myanmar, and Thailand have high mountains in the north. These mountains separate them from the countries of India and China. Several mountain ranges extend southward through the Indo-Chinese Peninsula. They stretch all the way to the sea and make east-west travel and communication hard. Thick, tropical rainforests cover many mountains.

Much of Southeast Asia is located along the "Ring of Fire." This arch of active volcanoes circles the Pacific Ocean. There are earthquakes along these faults, too. It stretches from New Zealand, along the eastern edge of Asia, north to Alaska, and south along the coast of North and South America.

Indonesia and the Philippines have more than 200 active volcanoes. In 1883, the largest volcanic eruption ever recorded occurred on the Indonesian island of Krakatau. It killed more than 36,000 people.

What Are Southeast Asia's Bodies of Water?

Between the mountain ranges of the Indo-Chinese Peninsula are valleys with several rivers. The Irrawaddy and the Salween rivers run south through Myanmar. The Chao Phraya is in Thailand. The Mekong River winds its way through Thailand, Laos, Cambodia, and Vietnam. Each year, these rivers flood, leaving silt behind. It forms fertile, flat, fan-shaped deltas. Farmers grow rice on them.

Many parts of Southeast Asia have few railroads or good roads. Because of this, some people and goods also travel up and down the rivers. In dry areas, farmers irrigate with river water. Southeast Asia has only a few dams. Most of the people of mainland Southeast Asia live in cities in river valleys, and on deltas. Cities on rivers include Rangoon in Myanmar, Bangkok in Thailand, and Ho Chi Minh City and Hanoi in Vietnam.

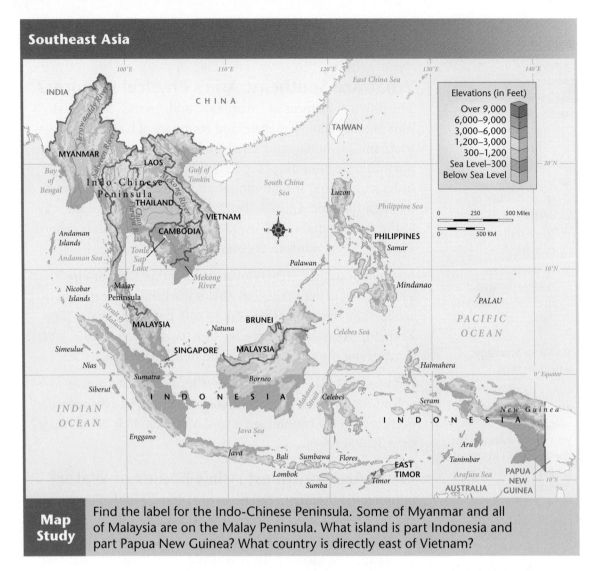

Southeast Asia

Map Study Find the label for the Indo-Chinese Peninsula. Some of Myanmar and all of Malaysia are on the Malay Peninsula. What island is part Indonesia and part Papua New Guinea? What country is directly east of Vietnam?

Mainland Southeast Asia has only one large lake. Tonle Sap, or Great Lake, is located in the lowland of Cambodia. The ocean is also important to Southeast Asia. All of the countries, except for landlocked Laos, have long coastlines. Many people fish for a living. The ocean provides fish for eating and tropical fish for pets. People around the world collect tropical fish.

What Is the Climate Like?

Most of Southeast Asia is close to the equator, so much of the region has a tropical climate. It is hot and humid throughout the year. Only highland areas have cooler weather.

Typhoon

A tropical wind and rain storm that forms over the ocean; also called a hurricane

Landslide

The rapid sliding of earth, rocks, or mud down a slope

Rainfall, not temperature, divides the seasons. A lot of rain falls on some places; other places receive much less. The northern and southern areas have a dry season that may last six months. Places near the equator have no dry season. Monsoons also affect the climate. The rainy season on the Indo-Chinese Peninsula usually lasts from May to September. It rains almost every day.

Island nations like Indonesia, Brunei, and the southern part of the Philippines have a tropical rain forest climate. Rain falls almost daily. It is always hot and humid. This rainforest is the second largest on Earth; only the Amazon's is larger. **Typhoons** destroy homes and crops and kill hundreds of people. A typhoon is a wind and rain storm that forms over the ocean. Sometimes these typhoons cause floods and **landslides.** A landslide occurs when a mass of dirt, rocks, or mud falls quickly down a slope.

If the islands were flat, the temperature and rainfall would be similar on each island. However, some islands have mountains. The windward sides of these mountains receive more rain. Temperatures are cooler in mountain areas. Snow covers some mountain peaks all year.

 Biography

Aung San Suu Kyi: 1945–

Since 1988, Aung San Suu Kyi has led the fight for democracy in Myanmar. Until 1989, Myanmar was called Burma. Leadership is a family trait. Her father, Aung San, is called the father of independent Burma.

In 1988, Burmans protested against military rule. As a result, troops arrested thousands. Many people were killed. Aung San spoke out for human rights. She helped the National League for Democracy win 80 percent of the seats in the legislature. The rulers ignored the results and kept her under house arrest for six years. In 1991, she won the Nobel Peace Prize. But the generals still limit her freedom to speak and travel.

This house is built on stilts. When the water rises, the house does not flood.

How Does the Climate Affect the People?

The tropical climate of Southeast Asia affects daily life. For example, people don't need shelter from cold. Houses in rural areas are usually small, simple, and open to the breeze. Bamboo grows quickly in this climate. People use bamboo and grasses as building materials. Most rural homes have dirt floors.

The rivers tend to flood during the summer monsoons. In the lowlands, people live in houses built on **stilts.** These heavy poles keep the houses high above the ground. Floods do not usually wash away houses on stilts. Stilts also provide protection from wild animals. The space below the house also shelters a family's work animals, usually water buffalo.

Lesson 2 Review On a sheet of paper, write the word in parenthesis that makes each statement true.

1. (Islands, Mountains) are the main physical feature of mainland Southeast Asia.

2. Thousands of volcanic (islands, rainforests) are in Southeast Asia.

3. The most important (rivers, islands) of Southeast Asia are the Irrawaddy, the Chao Phraya, and the Mekong.

4. The only Southeast Asian country without a coastline is (Laos, Vietnam).

5. (Temperature, Rainfall) divides the seasons.

Objectives

- ◆ To describe the cultures of Southeast Asia
- ◆ To know the languages they speak and the religions they practice
- ◆ To learn where most Southeast Asians live and the problems they face

Reading Strategy:
Inferencing

What do you think it would be like to live on an island with 125 million people?

English, French, and Spanish are also related languages. However, many people can only understand one.

What Are the Cultures in Southeast Asia?

Almost all of the countries of Southeast Asia have many different ethnic groups. For example, the Burmans are the largest group in Myanmar, but the country also has several other groups. Members of these ethnic groups have fought against the government since the country gained its independence in 1948.

In Malaysia, the population is almost equally divided between the Malays and the Malaysian Chinese. The Thais are Thailand's largest group, but large groups of Malay, Miao or Hmong, Vietnamese, and Laotian peoples also live in Thailand.

The largest ethnic group in Indonesia is the Javanese. About 125 million people live on the island of Java. This is one of the most densely populated places in the world. Almost all the people of the Philippines are Filipino except for a small group of Chinese and other foreigners.

As in Africa, colonial powers drew the borders of many Southeast Asian countries. These borders separated people with strong cultural links to one another.

What Languages Do Southeast Asians Speak?

Southeast Asia's diverse peoples speak many different languages. The main languages of island Southeast Asia are of Malay origin. However, people speaking different languages cannot easily understand each other.

There are over 500 dialects or languages spoken in Indonesia. There are nine native languages spoken in the different parts of the Philippines, and two are official languages—Filipino and English. Most Cambodians speak Khmer. The people of Myanmar speak Burmese. Thai is the main language of Thailand. Vietnamese is the main language of Vietnam.

Buddhism

A religion based on the teachings of the Buddha and practiced mainly in central and eastern Asia

Enlightenment

A state of perfect freedom from desire and suffering

Monk

A person who has made a religious promise and lives in a monastery

Monastery

A place where people who have taken religious vows or promises live

What Religions Do Southeast Asians Practice?

Indian traders brought Hinduism to Southeast Asia. Today, it is the main religion only on the Indonesian islands of Bali and Lombok. About 90 percent of the people of Indonesia follow Islam, which is also the main religion of Brunei and Malaysia. Large groups of Muslims also live in the southern Philippines.

Most people in Myanmar, Thailand, Laos, Cambodia, and Vietnam are Buddhists. Traders from India and Sri Lanka helped spread **Buddhism** to these countries. Buddhism is a religion based on the teachings of the Buddha, who lived in about 500 B.C. Buddhists do not worship gods.

Buddhists seek release from being reborn again and again. To do this, they seek **enlightenment,** a state of perfect freedom from desire and suffering. Buddhists believe in karma, or that the force of a person's actions helps determine the person's future. Karma is also a belief of Hinduism.

Most Buddhist men in Thailand and Myanmar become **monks** at some time in their lives. They make a religious promise, or vow, and live in a **monastery.** A monastery is a place where religious people live. Some men become monks for only a short time, some after they retire. Some spend their lives as monks.

Christianity is also found in Southeast Asia. Missionaries from Europe and the United States brought it there. They were most successful in spreading Christianity in the Philippines. Today, 90 percent of the Philippine people are Christian.

Where Do Most Southeast Asians Live?

Indonesia has the fourth largest population in the world. About 60 percent of Indonesians live on Java. This island covers only about 6 percent of Indonesia's land area. Java's 130 million people live in an area about the size of New York State. Irian Jaya, part of the island of New Guinea, is three times the size of Java. It has about 2 million people.

Most of Southeast Asia's people live in small rural villages and farm for a living. Often the villages are located along rivers, canals, or roads. Gardens and fields surround the village.

Coffee is sometimes nicknamed "java." That's because Java was once a major source of the world's coffee.

Most Buddhist men in Thailand and Myanmar become monks at some time in their lives.

The cities of Southeast Asia are growing rapidly. Each year, thousands of people migrate to the cities. There are two huge cities in Southeast Asia. Jakarta, the capital of Indonesia, has over 13 million people. Bangkok, the capital of Thailand, has close to 9 million. Manila is the largest city and capital of the Philippines. Vietnam has two large urban centers: Ho Chi Minh City and Hanoi. The country of Singapore is made up entirely of cities and suburbs. Rangoon or Yangôn is the largest city in Myanmar. Almost all the big cities are the center of government and business. They are also important seaports.

What Are the Population Trends?

The population of Southeast Asia is growing. Better health care, food, and living conditions have helped this happen. Fewer babies now become sick and die, and adults live longer. The birthrate is over 3 percent. This means that in less than 25 years, the population of Southeast Asia will double.

What Problems Do the People Face?

The biggest problem of Southeast Asia is poverty. Most of its countries are poor. Two out of three people farm for a living. But farms are often too small to support each farmer's family.

Disease is a problem in the tropics. Malaria is widespread, especially in rural areas. Mosquitoes spread this disease. Tuberculosis, a deadly lung disease, is a problem. Cholera and typhoid fever are diseases caused by drinking untreated water.

Ethnic and religious differences threaten to break up some countries. A strong military rule held Indonesia together until 1998. Then the dictator was forced to leave office. The country had no strong government to hold it together. People fought for independence. Fighting has also occurred in Irian Jaya and the Moluccas. In the Philippines, Muslims on the island of Mindanao have tried for greater independence. The Malays are the majority in Malasia, but China controls their economy.

Earthquakes, volcanoes, and **tsunamis** are common. A tsunami is a huge wave caused by an underwater earthquake. A tsunami in 2004 killed many thousands of people in Southeast Asia.

Celebrations

Tet Festival

Tet is the biggest holiday of the year in Vietnam. It celebrates the lunar new year. This is a time when the living honor their ancestors. They believe the spirits of their ancestors visit Earth during Tet.

Preparations for the festival begin weeks in advance. People return to their home villages if they can. People clean and decorate their ancestors' graves. They celebrate with parades and floats. On the last night of the old year, the family lights candles at a family altar and says prayers. At midnight, the spirits of the ancestors enter the house.

Critical Thinking What is the biggest holiday of the year where you live? How is it similar to and different from Tet?

Writing About Geography

Poverty is a problem throughout the world. List five things related to geography that can cause poverty. Then choose one, and write three ways to prevent this from being a cause.

What do you think

What would happen if Indonesia or the Philippines broke up into smaller countries?

Lesson 3 Review On a sheet of paper, write the letter of the answer that correctly completes each sentence.

1. Countries in Southeast Asia have many __D__ groups.

   A farming **B** family **C** mountain **D** ethnic

2. Most of the languages of island Southeast Asia belong to the __A__ language group.

   A Malay **B** Chinese **C** Vietnamese **D** English

3. Most people in Myanmar, Thailand, Laos, Cambodia, and Vietnam are __A__.

   A Buddhists **B** Christians **C** Hindus **D** Muslim

4. Most Southeast Asians live in _____ areas.

   A urban **B** rural **C** landslide **D** desert

5. The biggest problem facing Southeast Asians is _____.

   A health care   **C** poverty
   B a low birthrate   **D** independence

Capitalism

An economic system in which people own their own businesses; also called a market economy

Paddy

A wet field in which people grow rice

Terrace

A flat field that people create on a hillside

In Malaysia, people grow rice in flooded fields called paddies.

What Is Southeast Asia's Economy Like?

The economic geography of Southeast Asian countries varies. Vietnam and Laos have Communist economies. The military controls Myanmar's economy. The other countries of Southeast Asia practice **capitalism**. In this economic system, people own their own businesses and encourage foreign investment. The government does not run these businesses.

Most Southeast Asian countries except Singapore have poorly developed economies. The climate, the lack of roads, and the thick jungles have slowed development in Southeast Asia. Many people live as their ancestors did hundreds of years ago. Two out of three people farm, but they don't have good farmland. But, the weather is warm and it rains often. The river deltas and soil on the islands of Southeast Asia have good farmland.

Most of the farmers are subsistence farmers. Poor farmers often clear the land by cutting down the forest and burning it. Because this damages the soil, the farmers must move to a new field in a few years. The farmers of Southeast Asia grow cassavas, yams, beans, corn, peanuts, and some fruit.

Rice is the main cash crop in this region. Farmers use over half of their farmland to grow three crops of rice per year. Rice **paddies** cover much of the land. A paddy is a wet field in which people grow rice. There is little flat farmland, so people built **terraces**. A terrace is a flat area that people create on a hillside.

During the many years of colonial rule, Europeans introduced large plantation farming. Today, some big plantations still exist, but many have been divided into smaller plantations. Plantations still export rubber, coffee, sugarcane, oil palms, rice, spices, and coconuts.

Some countries are developing their economies rapidly. Singapore is Southeast Asia's richest country. It is on the important sea route linking Europe and the Middle East with east Asia. This has made Singapore one of the world's busiest seaports. Singapore is also an important manufacturing center. Shipbuilding, food processing, machinery making, and technology products are the leading industries. This island country is Southeast Asia's banking center and oil refiner.

Thailand, Malaysia, and Indonesia are also growing. Textiles and garments are Thailand's largest industries. In the 1990s, Thailand developed a fast-growing automobile industry. Thailand also is the world's second largest maker of motorcycles. Electronics are Thailand's biggest export. About 300,000 people work in factories producing computers and other electronic consumer products.

Indonesia's industry is also growing. Textiles and finished clothes are major exports. Batik, an Indonesian hand-printed cloth, is a major cottage industry. Indonesia also produces automobiles, electronics, and telephones.

Reading Strategy:
Inferencing

You have read that industry is growing rapidly in Southeast Asia. Based on what you know, how do you think this is changing the life of the people there?

Geography in Your Life

Rice

Rice is a staple in the diet of more than half of the people in the world. Asian farmers grow nearly 90 percent of it because rice needs to grow in a warm, wet climate. Thailand, Vietnam, and Indonesia are among the top producers of rice.

Farmers in Southeast Asia flood their fields before planting. This gives moisture to the plants and kills weeds and bugs. The farmers drain their rice fields about three weeks before the harvest. They do most work in the rice fields by hand. Some farmers use oxen or water buffaloes to pull their plows.

The people of Southeast Asia eat most of the rice they grow. Less than 5 percent of the rice crop in the world is traded. However, Thailand is one of the chief exporters of rice.

What Natural Resources Are Important?

Most Southeast Asian countries have natural resources, such as tropical forests. They export wood to Japan and Europe where people use it to make products such as furniture. The most valuable Southeast Asian woods are mahogany, ebony, and teak.

Southeast Asia also has mineral resources. Malaysia, Thailand, and Indonesia produce more than half of the world's tin. Indonesia, Malaysia, and Brunei are important exporters of oil and natural gas, especially to Japan. Indonesia and Malaysia export bauxite. The Philippines are a leading producer of chromium, nickel, copper, and gold.

What Environmental Problems Exist?

Deforestation is a problem in nearly every Southeast Asian country. Each year, rain forests are destroyed.

Air pollution, soil erosion, and water pollution are problems, too. Cars and factories pollute the air. Forest fires add to Indonesian air pollution. Jakarta's air is among the dirtiest in the world. The water around Indonesia is very polluted. Farming on steep slopes has caused soil erosion. The Chao Phraya River south of Bangkok is so polluted that nothing can grow or live in it.

Another problem for Southeast Asia is its fast-growing cities. There is not enough housing. Many people live in slums. Jakarta and Bangkok are among the fastest growing cities in the world. To provide drinking water, people have built many wells. They are pumping so much water out of the ground that Bangkok is sinking three inches a year. Many wells are polluted.

Lesson 4 Review On a sheet of paper, write the answer to each question. Use complete sentences.

1. How do most Southeast Asians earn their living?

2. What is the main cash crop of Southeast Asia?

3. What is Southeast Asia's richest country?

4. What countries buy much of Southeast Asia's wood?

5. What are two of the fastest growing cities?

Reading Strategy:
Inferencing

You've read about many countries that have serious air and water pollution. What can you infer about how that affects peoples' daily lives?

What do you think ❓

Would you like to live in Bangkok or Jakarta? Why or why not?

The Games They Play

My name is Carlos. I am 13 years old, and I live in the Philippines. Because it is so warm here, my friends and I spend a lot of time playing outside. There are many ways to have fun here.

We love to play basketball. If no one has a real basketball, we use any ball we can find. And if there isn't a hoop available, we make our own. Sometimes we use a reed basket hung on a pole. We make reed baskets from the tall grasses. Cardboard boxes hung on a tree also work just as well. We aren't fussy about the courts, either. Mostly we play on hardened dirt, not concrete.

One thing my friends and I like to do is make a *tirador*. This is a slingshot. Every kid I know has one. We shoot stones at trees to knock down ripe fruit. My farming friends use a *tirador* to keep birds out of the fields.

Many games we play have been played on our islands for years. *Luksong-tinik* is a game where we jump over a stick or someone's hands. In the game *sipa,* we kick a palm or paper ball. *Sungka* is a game of buried treasure. Shells or stones are put into holes, and then a friend tries to find them.

Spider fighting is my favorite way to pass the time, though. Most kids probably think so, too. We find spiders outside in the trees. After we catch them, we place two spiders on a stick. They wrestle each other. Sometimes one gets pushed off. Sometimes one ends up wrapping the other in its web.

Our parents don't want us betting on these fights, but sometimes we do anyway. I keep my champions in matchboxes in between fights. But even when one loses, I don't worry. In the Philippines, you can always find another spider.

Wrap-Up

1. What do children in the Philippines do with slingshots?

2. What is spider fighting?

- Southeast Asia is a large peninsula south of China and east of the Indian subcontinent. It includes many island countries in the Indian and South Pacific Oceans.

- Geography shaped Southeast Asia's history because it is located on the water route between China and India. In the 1500s, Europeans began to colonize the region because of the valuable spices grown there.

- The main physical feature of mainland Southeast Asia is mountains. Volcanic islands are the main island feature. Some volcanoes are active.

- The most important rivers in Southeast Asia are the Irrawaddy, the Chao Phraya, and the Mekong.

- Most of Southeast Asia is close to the equator, so it has tropical climates. Rainfall, not temperature, divides the seasons. Monsoons also affect the climate.

- Southeast Asia has many diverse cultures. The people speak many different languages. The main languages of island Southeast Asia are of Malay origin.

- Among the religions of Southeast Asia are Hinduism, Islam, Buddhism, and Christianity.

- Most of the people of mainland Southeast Asia live in small villages in river valleys and deltas. Cities are growing rapidly as people migrate to them.

- Two out of three people of Southeast Asia farm. Most are subsistence farmers. Over half of Southeast Asia's farmland is used to grow rice, which is a staple crop.

- Most Southeast Asian countries have poorly developed economies. The climate, lack of transportation, and thick jungles have slowed economic development in Southeast Asia. Southeast Asia is rich in natural and mineral resources and exports wood products from its many tropical rain forests.

- Southeast Asia's main environmental problems are deforestation, air pollution, and water pollution. Its rapidly growing cities cannot provide all the services that are needed. Southeast Asia's biggest social problem is poverty. It also has civil unrest and religious conflict.

Chapter 20 REVIEW

Word Bank

farming

Malay

seasons

teak

Tropics

On a sheet of paper, use the words from the Word Bank to complete each sentence correctly.

1. Southeast Asia is located in the _____.

2. In Southeast Asia, _____ are defined by when the most rain falls.

3. The main languages of the island nations of Southeast Asia are of _____ origin.

4. Two out of three Southeast Asians earn their living by _____.

5. Wood cut from the forests of Southeast Asia include mahogany, ebony, and _____.

On a sheet of paper, write the letter of the answer that correctly completes each sentence.

6. _____ frequently occur on the islands of Southeast Asia.

   A Blizzards   **C** Volcanic eruptions
   B Tornadoes   **D** Killer bees

7. To create more flat land for farming, Southeast Asian farmers have _____.

   A built hillside terraces
   B drained swamps
   C irrigated hilly areas
   D filled coastal bays with landfill

8. Much of Southeast Asia has a _____ climate.

   A continental   **C** highland
   B arctic   **D** tropical

9. The richest country in Southeast Asia is _____.

   A Indonesia   **C** Singapore
   B the Philippines   **D** Vietnam

10. Most Southeast Asian countries practice _____, which is an economy in which people own their own businesses.

   A Communism   **C** subsistence
   B capitalism   **D** cash crop

On a sheet of paper, write the answer to each question. Use complete sentences.

11. What makes Southeast Asia's location so important?

12. What religions do Southeast Asians practice?

13. What environmental problems does Southeast Asia face?

Critical Thinking On a sheet of paper, write your response to each question. Use complete sentences.

14. Imagine that a U.S. company hires you to give advice about expanding overseas. Would you recommend building in Southeast Asia? Explain your answer.

15. Indonesia's national motto is "Unity in Diversity." Do you think this would be a good motto for the United States, too? Explain your answer.

Applying the Five Themes of Geography

Which of the five themes of geography explains why the economy of Southeast Asia is growing? Explain your answer.

Test-Taking Tip

If you do not know the meaning of a word in a question, read the question to yourself, leaving out the word. Try to figure out the meaning of the word from its use in the sentence.

21

China and Its Neighbors

People have lived in China for thousands of years. In fact, farming began there more than 8,000 years ago. From the 1950s to the 1980s, the Communist government owned and controlled everything in this large country. Since then, many changes have taken place. China's economy is now one of the fastest growing economies in the world.

Goals for Learning

◆ To describe the locations and regions of China, Mongolia, and Taiwan

◆ To identify their most important physical features and climates

◆ To describe the people and cultures of China, Mongolia, and Taiwan

◆ To describe the economies and the environmental challenges of China and its neighbors

Geo-Stats   China and Its Neighbors

 Nation: China
Population:
   1,313,974,000
Area: 3,705,829 square miles
Major Cities: Beijing (capital), Shanghai, Tianjin, Chongqing, Shenyang, Guangzhou

Nation: Mongolia
Population:
   2,832,000
Area: 603,749 square miles
Capital: Ulaanbaatar

 Nation: Taiwan
Population:
   22,894,000
Area: 13,888 square miles
Major Cities: Taipei (capital), Kaohsiung

China and Its Neighbors

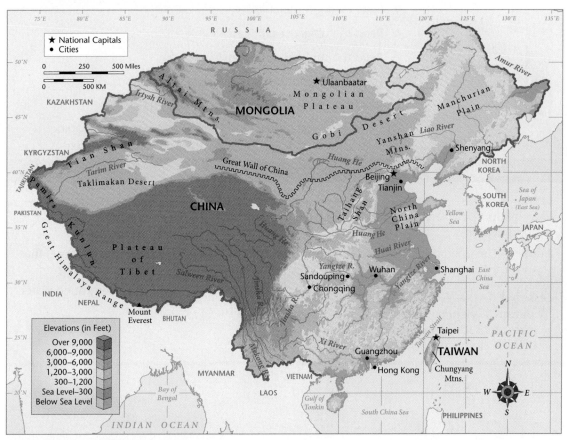

Map Skills

China is the fourth largest country in area in the world. China and Mongolia are located south of Russia and north of the Indian subcontinent and Southeast Asia. The Pacific Ocean and several seas touch China's shores to the east. The island of Taiwan is located in the East China Sea, which is east of China. China has a population of over 1.3 billion people. This means that one out of every five people in the world lives in China.

Study the map and answer the following questions:

1. What is China's capital city?

2. What large plateau is in southwestern China?

3. Which desert is located in northern China and southern Mongolia?

4. What nations are across the Yellow Sea from China?

5. Where do you think the first civilizations started in China? Explain your answer.

Reading Strategy:
Metacognition

Metacognition means "thinking about your thinking." It can help you become a better reader. As you begin a new chapter:

◆ Page through the chapter.

◆ Read the objectives for each lesson.

◆ Read the subhead questions.

◆ Look at the photographs and read the captions.

◆ Read the chapter summary.

This may help you understand the chapter as you are reading.

Key Vocabulary Words

Lesson 2 _____

Floodplain A level area of land built up by flood deposits

Adobe A sun-dried brick made from mud and straw

Lesson 3 _____

Ideogram A picture, symbol, or mark that stands for a thing or an idea in the Chinese language; a character

Lesson 4 _____

Reform A change in how people do something to make things better

Light industry The making of products that people use every day

Water table The level of underground water

Objectives

◆ To know where China, Mongolia, and Taiwan are located

◆ To describe how China's geography shaped its history

◆ To identify the different regions in China

Where Are China, Mongolia, and Taiwan?

China is located almost entirely in the middle latitudes, between the Tropic of Cancer and 50 degrees north latitude. This is about the same as the United States. Russia, Canada, and the United States are larger than China. Mongolia and China share borders with Russia to the north; Southeast Asia and Bhutan to the south; and India, Nepal, Pakistan, Kazakhstan, Kyrgyzstan, and Tajikistan to the west. The Koreas, the Yellow Sea, the East China Sea, and the South China Sea are located to the east of China. Taiwan is an island located about 100 miles from the southeast coast of China.

How Did Geography Shape China's History?

Geography has played a big role in China's history. Civilization first developed there in the valley of the Huang He or Yellow River. *Huang* means yellow in Chinese. The river got its name

from the fine silt it carries. The Huang He runs through plains of fertile loess soil deposited by the wind. The Huang He region had everything necessary for civilization to develop, especially rich farmland and a good water supply. People could also use the river for transportation.

China's natural borders include high mountains, huge deserts, and seas. These natural barriers isolated and protected China from foreign invaders. There is no natural barrier separating the rich farmland of northern China from the steppes and deserts of central Asia. To stop invaders, the Chinese built a huge wall that today is called the Great Wall. Its main part is over 2,000 miles long and about 25 feet high.

The Great Wall of China has many towers like the one in this photo. The wall is from 15 to 25 feet wide.

What Regions Exist in China?

China has four regions. The North China Plain is in eastern China. The Yanshan Mountains border the plain on the north. The Taihang Mountains are on the west. The plain has fertile yellow-brown loess soil for farming. It is densely populated. Beijing, the capital, and Tianjin, an industrial city and port, are on its northeast edge. The Huang He flows through the plain.

Reading Strategy:
Metacognition

Think about the definitions of *plain* and *plateau* as you read the next paragraphs.

China's second region is the Manchurian Plain. It is north of the North China Plain. The Manchurian Plain also has fertile soil. It has rich coal and iron deposits. This has made it China's industrial area. Most of Manchuria's people live in the southern part of the plain near the Liao River.

Highlands and high plateaus make up China's third region. Mountains cover one-third of China. The highest ones are in the west. They include the Himalayas, the Pamirs, the Kunlun, and the Tian Shan. The mountains surround the Plateau of Tibet, also called Qinghai-Tibet Plateau. It is the largest highland region in the world. It is known as "the roof of the world." Few people live in this part of China because of its harsh climate and geography. Eastern China has highland areas covered with forests.

Deserts and steppes make up China's fourth region. The Taklimakan Desert in northwestern China is one of the world's largest and driest deserts. The Gobi Desert shares China's border with Mongolia. Steppes are south and east of the deserts. Nomadic Mongols and Tibetans have raised sheep and goats there for many years. Lack of rainfall makes farming hard.

Word Bank

China
Great Wall
Huang He
Plateau of Tibet
Taklimakan

What do you think?

Do you think that all Chinese people live in the same type of houses and eat the same foods? Explain your answer.

Lesson 1 Review On a sheet of paper, use the words from the Word Bank to complete each sentence correctly.

1. _____ is the fourth largest country in the world.

2. The Chinese built the _____ to protect themselves.

3. The _____ is yellow because of its silt.

4. People call the _____ "the roof of the world."

5. The _____ is one of the driest deserts in the world.

Objectives

Objectives

- ◆ To describe the main physical features
- ◆ To identify China's main rivers
- ◆ To describe the climates of China and its neighbors

What Are the Main Physical Features?

Mountains are China's main physical feature. Nearly one-third of China is covered with mountains. Western China has some of the highest mountain ranges in the world. Two large tectonic plates smashed together to create these mountains. The two plates are still pushing against each other, so the mountains grow a few inches higher each year.

Plateaus are another important feature. They make up about one-fourth of China. The Plateau of Tibet is located in southwestern China. It is over 14,000 feet high.

Plains cover much of eastern China. About 95 percent of the Chinese people live on these fertile plains, yet they make up only about 12 percent of the land in China. Farmers have built terraces into the hillsides to create new farming areas. Terraces are common throughout Asia.

Sun Moon Lake in Taiwan is a popular place for tourists.

Taiwan's main physical feature is the mountains that run from north to south on the island. About half of Taiwan is covered by the Chungyang Range. The mountains are covered with tropical rainforest. The east coast of China, facing the Taiwan Strait, is a large coastal plain. The strait separates Taiwan from China.

Mongolia's physical features are very much like those of northern China. The main feature is the Mongolian Plateau, a region of high grasslands that covers about two-thirds of central Mongolia. The high mountains of the Altai Range along Mongolia's southwestern border separate it from China. The Gobi Desert is the most important physical feature of the southern third of Mongolia.

What Are China's Main Rivers?

China has over 1,500 large rivers. Most of them begin in the high western mountains. The Huang He is the longest northern river. People call it "China's Sorrow" because it has flooded so often. In 1931, the Huang He flooded and killed over 3.7 million people. Today, a system of dams and dikes controls most floods.

Rivers like the Huang He carry huge amounts of silt down from the mountains. Over millions of years, the silt deposits build up. Geographers call the flat land on both sides of a river a **floodplain.** The huge floodplain of the Huang He became the North China Plain.

The Yangtze is the longest river in Asia. It divides northern China from southern China. The Yangtze flows nearly 4,000 miles from the mountains to the East China Sea. It has 700 tributaries, some of which are themselves important rivers. The wide, fertile plain of the lower Yangtze is one of China's best agricultural areas.

Huai He is between the Huang He and Yangtze rivers. But, it does not flow all the way to the sea. This causes it to flood often. The Xi is another important Chinese river. The city of Guangzhou is located on the delta of the Xi River. The island of Hong Kong lies at its mouth.

What Is the Climate Like?

This region has many different climates. The mountainous areas of western China have highland climates. People call the Plateau of Tibet the "Land of Snows" because some snow remains on the ground in some places all year. The harsh climate is the main reason so few people live in the area.

Much of the Mongolian Plateau and west central China have steppe or desert climates. Sheep and ponies can graze on the short grasses of the steppes. China's steppes and deserts have great temperature extremes. Summers are hot; winters are cold. Dust storms and droughts are common. More animals live there than people.

The parts of northern China that are closer to the sea, such as the Manchurian Plain, have a humid continental climate with four seasons.

Most of southeastern China and northern Taiwan have a subtropical climate. The climate is affected by the seasonal monsoon winds. From May to September the winds bring heat and moisture from the Indian and the Pacific oceans. The areas closest to the sea receive the most rain. The summers are long, hot, and wet. Winters are short.

How Does the Geography Affect the People?

The people who live in the western mountain regions live in **adobe** houses. They are made of sun-dried bricks made from mud and straw. Adobe houses protect people from the harsh climate. Farmers grow mostly wheat. People eat noodles, bread, and lamb. People of the North China Plain live in mud-based houses. They eat wheat products and potatoes.

In southern China, the climate is milder. People call the valley between the Yangtze and the Xi rivers "China's Rice Bowl." Farmers grow about half of China's rice in this area. Houses are built on hills, leaving the flatter land for farming. People eat rice and more vegetables than the people in other parts of China because the climate is good for growing vegetables. People living near the sea eat fish at nearly every meal.

Adobe

A sun-dried brick made from mud and straw

Because of the geography of Mongolia, few people live there. Millions of animals graze on the grasslands that cover most of the country.

This nomad in Mongolia uses a long stick to guide the horses together. Grasslands cover most of Mongolia.

Writing About Geography

Think about where you live. How does where you live affect how you live? Does the climate affect your life? What foods do you eat? List five ways that the area in which you live affects your life.

China and Its Neighbors Chapter 21 **491**

The Building of the Three Gorges Dam

In 1994, China began building the Three Gorges Dam at Sandouping. It is the world's largest dam. It has an almost 400-mile-long reservoir, or lake, behind it. The dam will control flooding along the Yangtze River. It will also provide hydroelectricity that will reduce air pollution from burning coal. Finally, the dam will allow ships to travel about 1,400 miles up the Yangtze River.

When totally filled, the dam's reservoir will flood hundreds of thousands of acres of good farmland. This area includes nearly 2,000 villages, towns, and cities. Over one million people had to move from the area. Environmentalists say that the Chinese alligator, the finless porpoise, the river dolphin, and the white crane will become extinct because of the change in the river.

Some scientists fear that the reservoir's weight will cause an earthquake that will destroy the dam. Because of all this, many engineers believe that a series of smaller dams along the Yangtze would have been better. However, the dam wall was completed in 2006.

Lesson 2 Review On a sheet of paper, write the answer to each question. Use complete sentences.

1. What is the main physical feature of China?

2. What is the main physical feature of Mongolia?

3. What are four important rivers of China?

4. What part of China has a subtropical climate?

5. How does geography affect what Chinese people eat and how they live?

What do you think ?

Do you think the Three Gorges dam will do more good than harm? Explain.

Objectives

- To describe the cultures of the region
- To identify their religions
- To name the languages spoken
- To describe where most people in China, Mongolia, and Taiwan live

What Cultures Exist in These Countries?

China has over 50 different ethnic groups. Over 90 percent of Chinese people are Han Chinese. This cultural group began in the valley of the Huang He about 5,000 years ago.

Of the remaining 100 million Chinese people, the largest minority is the Zhuang. They live mostly in south-central China. Another large group is the Uygurs. They live in the mountainous, desert areas of western China. The largest ethnic group in Mongolia is the Mongols. Mongols also live in the northern part of China. There are also over 2 million Tibetans, living mostly on the Plateau of Tibet. In 1950, Chinese soldiers invaded Tibet, which was an independent country. Since that time, Tibet has been part of China. However, the Tibetans have kept their culture.

Most of Taiwan's people and culture are Chinese. Over 20 million people live on Taiwan. Most call themselves Taiwanese. Their families have lived in Taiwan for hundreds of years. When Communists took over China after World War II, several million Chinese fled to Taiwan. They are called "mainlanders." The Chinese government considers Taiwan a part of China. The majority of people on Taiwan consider their island to be an independent country. They have their own government.

Reading Strategy:
Metacognition

Do you already know something about the religions the Chinese practice? Have you heard of Confucius?

What Religions Are Practiced?

The Communists who rule China allow some religious freedom. Many Chinese people follow their ancient beliefs. Respect for one's parents and ancestors is part of their religion. The Chinese believe that prayers and sacrifices to these ancestors join the worlds of the living and the dead.

The teachings of Confucius have influenced Chinese beliefs. Confucius lived more than 2,500 years ago. He did not think of his teachings as a religion. He taught that each person has a place in society.

Ideogram

A picture, symbol, or mark that stands for a thing or an idea in the Chinese language; a character

Confucius also taught that the family and respect for elders are important. These ideas remain today. The Chinese also believe that people can improve themselves through effort and study.

The Chinese have had other influences. Buddhism was introduced from India over 2,000 years ago. Traders brought Islam from the Middle East to China. Christian missionaries tried to bring Christianity to China. But only a small percentage of people follow these religions in China.

Most people in Taiwan and Mongolia are Buddhists. There is a small Christian community in Taiwan.

What Languages Do the Chinese Speak?

Over 90 percent of the people in China speak Chinese. About one-fifth of the world's people speak Chinese. The written Chinese language does not have an alphabet with letters that stand for sounds. The Chinese make up sentences from thousands of characters, or **ideograms.** These pictures, symbols, or marks stand for things or ideas. Ideograms must be memorized. A 12-year-old knows about 3,000 characters. A highly educated adult might learn 10,000 characters. Chinese people everywhere can read these ideograms. This is not true of spoken Chinese, since there are dozens of dialects. About two-thirds of the Chinese people speak the Mandarin dialect. Most large minority groups in China speak their own languages. Most people on Taiwan also speak Chinese. However, the official language of Mongolia is Mongolian.

These are the Chinese ideograms for peace and for love. The written Chinese language has an ideogram for each word or idea. The Chinese people memorize the ideograms.

Languages of the World

Language	Speakers in Millions	Main Areas Where Spoken
Han Chinese (Mandarin)	over 1 billion	China, Taiwan, Singapore
English	508	United States, Great Britain, Canada, Zimbabwe, South Africa, Caribbean
Hindi	497	India
Spanish	392	South and Central America, Spain, Mexico
Russian	277	Russia, Belarus, Kazakhstan, Central Asia
Arabic	246	Middle East
Bengali	211	Bangladesh
Portuguese	191	Brazil, Angola, Mozambique, Portugal
Malay-Indonesian	159	Indonesia, Malaysia
French	129	France, Belgium, Rwanda, Cameroon, Haiti

Chart Study This chart lists the world's top ten languages and the number of speakers per language. What is the most commonly spoken language? How many people speak Spanish? English?

Reading Strategy:
Metacognition

What have you already read that might help you know about where most Chinese people live?

Where Do the People Live?

China has more people than any other country. About 90 percent of its people live on about 20 percent of the land. Most Chinese live in the eastern and southeastern regions. Few people live in western China. Two-thirds of Chinese are farmers; about a third of Chinese live in urban areas. China has almost 40 cities with more than a million people each.

Three Chinese cities have more than 10 million people each. Shanghai is China's largest city. More than 20 million people live in this port city and its suburbs. Beijing, China's second largest city with 15 million people, is its capital. Tianjin has over 10 million. Other large cities include Hong Kong, Shenyang, and Wuhan.

Taiwan and Mongolia are also urbanized. Nearly 75 percent of Taiwan's people live in urban areas. More than one-fourth of all Taiwan's people live in the capital city of Taipei. Even though Mongolia only has 2.5 million people living in an area as large as Europe, one-quarter of them live in the capital, Ulaanbaatar. More than half of Mongolia's people live either in the capital or in small towns.

What Is the Population Trend?

Population growth is a big problem in China. Between 1950 and 1990, China's population doubled. A growing population needs food, housing, schools, and medical care. China also has a growing number of older people. The government needs to meet all their care needs. This population growth affects the quality of life of every Chinese person.

The government passed a law in 1980 to control the population growth. The government decided it had to do this if it wanted to develop the country. This law is a "one child" rule for the people living in China's cities. If a couple has one child, the government gives the parents money. If a couple has more than one child, they have to pay the government money. People living in rural areas and ethnic minorities can have more children.

The "one child" rule has worked at slowing population growth. However, some families have chosen to have only boy babies. Many girls have been given up for adoption. Because of this, China faces a serious shortage of women in the years ahead.

What Other Problems Do the People Face?

The lack of city housing is a problem. Apartments are small and hard to get. Several families may share bathrooms or kitchens. In Shanghai, some families live in small apartments with no running water.

China has three cities with more than 10 million people each. Shanghai is China's largest city. More than 20 million people live in this city and its suburbs.

Some Chinese people wait seven or eight years to get an apartment.

China's cities are growing. China began to make changes to its economy in 1978. The growing number of factories in the cities needed thousands of unskilled workers. Over 3 million migrants have moved to Beijing. Most of them live in poor housing on the edge of the city. They have no running water and few schools. Many people can find only part-time work at low-paying jobs. But people living in cities earn more than three times what a farmer earns. So farmers are leaving for better paying jobs in the cities. Some people move back and forth from rural areas to the cities.

China's relationship with Taiwan is a political problem. In 1949, a long civil war ended in China. The Communists won the war. People who did not want to live under Communism fled to the nearby island of Taiwan. They established the Republic of China. The government of China considers Taiwan part of China. It does not accept Taiwan as an independent state. From time to time, China threatens to take over Taiwan by force.

Reading Strategy: Metacognition

From what you have read, do you understand why some people would flee to Taiwan from China?

Lesson 3 Review On a sheet of paper, write the word in parenthesis that makes each statement true.

1. Over 90 percent of the Chinese people are (Han Chinese, Zhuang).

2. The teachings of (Buddha, Confucius) have influenced Chinese beliefs.

3. Most Chinese live in the eastern and (southeastern, northern) regions.

4. To help slow down population growth, the Chinese government introduced the ("two child", "one child") rule.

5. People living in China's cities usually earn (more, less) than what a farmer earns.

What do you think ?

Is China's government right in forcing urban couples to limit themselves to having only one child? Explain your answer.

Objectives

- To describe the economies of the region
- To name the region's natural resources
- To describe the environmental problems the region faces

Reform

A change in how people do something to make things better

Reading Strategy: Metacognition

When you think about Taiwan's economy, think about things you have seen that are "Made in Taiwan."

What Is the Economy Like?

In 1949, Communists took over China. The government tried to control every part of Chinese life. It told the Chinese people what to grow, where to live, where to work, and what books to read. The leaders wanted to make China an industrial power without any help from other countries.

In 1979, Chinese leader Deng Xiaoping introduced a new plan for economic **reform**, or change. He let people once again own businesses and property. He invited foreign countries to invest in China. Since that time, China's economy has changed. Now China's economy is moving toward becoming a free-market economy. People, not government, decide what to buy and sell.

Today, Chinese farmers grow what they like and sell their crops at a price they set. Many people have opened businesses. Incomes are rising. Many people are able to buy things that they want, such as cars, televisions, radios, fans, watches, washing machines, and refrigerators.

China's economy is one of the fastest growing in the world. Its economy is among the world's largest. Many foreign companies are investing in China. They are taking advantage of the low cost of labor in China compared to most developed countries. They see China's huge population as a market for their products. One of China's biggest customers is the United States.

Taiwan's economy has also changed. Until the 1960s, Taiwan was a mostly agricultural country. Gradually, Taiwan began to industrialize. It became known as one of Asia's "Four Tigers," along with South Korea, Singapore, and Hong Kong. All have growing economies. Taiwan's per capita income increased 10 times from the 1950s to the 1990s. Today, Taiwan produces high-technology goods such as electronics.

What Are Their Natural Resources?

China was the first country to mine coal to use as an energy source. Today, China produces a third of the world's coal. Coal provides much of China's energy needs.

The open lands of northwest China have huge, undeveloped deposits of oil. Getting the oil out of the ground costs a lot of money. Bringing it to places where it can be processed is expensive, too. The Chinese government is allowing foreign oil companies to develop new oil fields in China's seas.

China has large deposits of bauxite, uranium, tungsten, and low-grade iron ore. Most of these resources are underdeveloped because they are located far from the centers of industry. China does not have a transportation system to get these resources to the cities. Waterpower is another underdeveloped resource. China's many fast-moving rivers could make it the world's largest producer of hydroelectric power.

Mongolia also has many undeveloped natural resources. It has many mineral resources including oil, coal, copper, and zinc. It is working with China and Russia to develop its resources.

What Economic Problems Does China Face?

China's energy needs are growing. It does not produce enough oil to meet the needs of its fast-growing industries. It needs oil for its growing number of cars. China is investing in the oil-rich areas of central Asia, Africa, and Kazakhstan. It buys oil from Sudan, Saudi Arabia, and other Middle Eastern countries.

It costs a great deal of money to develop industries, a modern transportation system, and new urban areas. China has borrowed billions of dollars and has a huge debt. This may hurt its economy.

Despite its mass transit, Beijing has traffic jams.

These people are harvesting rice in China. Rice is one of China's main crops.

What Are Some Important Chinese Industries?

Most Chinese people still farm for a living. Their farms are small. The staple crop north of the Yangtze River is wheat. Farmers also grow sorghum, corn, millet, and soybeans. South of the Yangtze, the climate is more subtropical. There, rice is the main crop. Other crops include tea, tobacco, silk, rubber, and fruits. Farmers grow vegetables, such as cabbage, onions, and beans, all over China. Because most farmers have little machinery, they do most of their work by hand.

Only about 20 percent of China's workers work in industry. However, more industrial jobs are being created. China's economy is moving from heavy industry to **light industry.** Light industry is the making of products that people use every day, such as clothing, appliances, and bicycles.

Most of China's industrial growth has taken place in the southeast. In the 1970s, the Chinese government created four areas called Special Economic Zones (SEZs). Industries in these zones pay lower taxes. This made it easier for foreign companies to invest in China. These four zones have been successful. Huge fields that once grew rice are now industrial areas with factories, apartments, schools, and traffic jams.

Today, China's economy produces many goods. It is the world's leading producer of silk. It also produces cotton. It is an important producer of iron and steel. Its large industries make machines, chemical fertilizers, cement, weapons, and cars.

What Environmental Problems Exist?

China's economic growth has come at a high price to the environment. The burning of coal for power has caused bad air pollution. Seven of the world's ten most polluted cities are in China. Beijing has some of the worst air quality in the world. Air pollution makes breathing hard. It causes many health problems. Diseases from air pollution are the leading cause of death in China. China is trying to change. It is introducing solar and wind power. In Beijing, all city buses now run on natural gas. Beijing has also expanded its subway and light rail systems to cut pollution from cars.

Water table

The level of underground water

Some Chinese cities are growing so fast that the government cannot provide all of the services the people need. Half the people do not have safe water to drink. Human and industrial waste flow into the sea without being treated.

Some farmers cut down trees on steep hills to provide more farmland for their families. This can cause soil erosion. China has lost farmland because of economic development. Homes, factories, and businesses now cover land that used to be farmed.

Another problem is finding enough water. As many as 300 Chinese cities may face water shortages. The **water table** is dropping. The water table is the level at which underground water is found. People have to drill deeper into the ground to find water. The problem is most serious in western China.

Mongolia also has serious environmental problems. It has very limited water resources. Deforestation, overgrazing, soil erosion, and desertification are big problems.

Lesson 4 Review On a sheet of paper, write the letter of the answer that correctly completes each sentence.

1. The Chinese economy is moving toward becoming a
   ___A___ economy.

   A free-market   **C** socialist
   B staple   **D** Communist

2. ___B___ provides a large percentage of China's energy needs.

   A Oil   **C** Hydroelectric power
   B Coal   **D** Atomic energy

3. China does not produce enough ___D___ to meet its needs.

   A cotton   **B** appliances   **C** rice   **D** oil

4. China is the world's leading producer of ___C___.

   A cars   **B** computers   **C** silk   **D** steel

5. As many as 300 Chinese cities face serious ___A___.

   A water shortages   **C** global warming
   B deforestation   **D** desertification

What do you think

What effects do you think China's booming economy has on the rest of the world?

What's in a Name?

My name is Chen Yi. I am 13 years old. I live in Nanjing, China. Names are different here than in America. What Americans call a last name is considered a family name in China. Our family name is Chen. And what Americans call a first name is considered a given name. My parents gave me the name of Yi. In China, we say our family name first, followed by our given name.

In China, many parents give their children a milk name, as we call it. It is a temporary name. My parents took nearly a month to choose my given name. During that time, they called me by my milk name—Chwun Yu. This translates into *spring rain,* because I was born on a rainy spring day. My friend Wu Hui's milk name meant *Small Tiger.* His mother dreamt of a tiger the night before he was born.

Most kids in China have a family nickname. It often is a shortened version of their full name. For example, if your name was Liu Xiaoping, your parents or siblings might call you Ah Ping. Girls' nicknames are often the last syllable, repeated. My parents call me Yiyi. In larger families, kids are called Second Son, Third Sister, and so on.

Chinese kids do not address any adults by their given name. At my best friend's house, I call her mother "Ayi." This is the proper term for addressing any woman one generation older than oneself. We call our teachers "Teacher."

How I address my aunts and uncles depends upon which side of the family they are from. For example, "Shushu" is the term for my father's brother. Of course, it is always acceptable to use an adult's full name. When I talk to my classmates, I use their given name, their whole name, or a nickname. They are all acceptable.

I know that in America, children are sometimes named after someone else. In China, it is rare to do that. Given names are chosen to reflect nature, periods in history, or a characteristic. Take my name, for example. Yi means cheerful.

Wrap-Up

1. What are some ways that Chinese families create nicknames for kids?

2. How are given names typically chosen in China?

Chapter 21 S U M M A R Y

- China is the fourth largest country in the world. High mountains, huge deserts, and seas isolated China for centuries. Mongolia is a large, landlocked country on China's northern border. Taiwan is an island about 100 miles from the southeast coast of China.

- China has four geographic regions: the North China Plain, the Manchurian Plain, highlands and plateaus, and deserts and steppes.

- Mountains are the most important physical feature of China and Taiwan. The most important physical feature of Mongolia is the Mongolian Plateau, a region of steppes that covers about two-thirds of central Mongolia.

- The most important Chinese rivers are the Huang He, the Yangtze, Huai He, and the Xi. All four rivers are important highways to the middle of China.

- Over 90 percent of Chinese people are Han Chinese. Mongols are the largest ethnic group in Mongolia. Most of Taiwan's people and culture are Chinese.

- Many Chinese people still follow their ancient beliefs. Confucius greatly influenced them. Most people in Taiwan and Mongolia practice Buddhism.

- Most people in China and Taiwan speak Mandarin Chinese. There are dozens of different dialects. There is only one written language. Most of the large minority groups speak their own dialects. Most people in Mongolia speak Mongolian.

- China has more people than any other country. About 90 percent of these people live on about 20 percent of the land. Most Chinese are farmers. About a third of all Chinese live in urban areas. China has almost 40 cities with more than a million people each. Many people in Mongolia are nomadic herders.

- China's economy is one of the fastest growing in the world. About 20 percent of the people work in industry. Many foreign companies invest in China.

- China and Mongolia have many natural resources. Many have not been developed because they are located far from the centers of industry.

- China's main problems are population growth, lack of city housing, air pollution, deforestation, soil erosion, water shortages, and its relationship with Taiwan.

Word Bank

farmland [1]

floodplain 3

ideograms 4

light 5

terraces 2

On a sheet of paper, use the words from the Word Bank to complete each sentence correctly.

1. To protect their rich _____, the Chinese built the Great Wall.

2. Chinese farmers create new areas to farm by building _____ in the hillsides.

3. A _____ is an area of level land that a flooding river creates over hundreds of years.

4. The written Chinese language uses thousands of _____, or symbols.

5. A _____ industry makes products that people use every day.

On a sheet of paper, write the letter of the answer that correctly completes each sentence.

6. China is located almost completely in the ___B___ latitudes.

    A low   **C** high

    B middle   **D** arctic

7. The main feature of Mongolia is its ___C___.

    A desert   **C** plateau

    B mountains   **D** forests

8. The ___C___ River is called "China's Sorrow" because it floods so often.

    A Yangtze   **C** Huang He

    B Xi   **D** Liao

9. The Plateau of ___A___, called "the roof of the world," is the largest highland region in the world.

    A Tibet   **C** Himalayan

    B Xi   **D** North China

10. The largest city in China is ___D___.

    A Beijing   **C** Wuhan

    B Hong Kong   **D** Shanghai

On a sheet of paper, write the answer to each question. Use complete sentences.

11. What is China's most important physical feature?

12. How have the teachings of Confucius influenced Chinese culture?

13. What are China's most serious environmental problems?

Critical Thinking On a sheet of paper, write your response to each question. Use complete sentences.

14. Why are businesses all over the world interested in investing in China?

15. Why have economic reforms worked in China?

Applying the Five Themes of Geography

Place and Movement

Why is there a housing shortage in most Chinese cities?

Test-Taking Tip

Before writing out a Critical Thinking answer on a test, read the question twice to make sure you understand what it is asking.

22

Japan

Japan is an island nation. About 80 percent of it is covered with mountains. It has few natural resources. But, Japan is very industrialized. The Japanese people enjoy one of the highest standards of living in the world. Japan is a modern country with huge cities. It has a highly developed transportation system. Even though its lifestyle is very much like that of Europeans and Americans, Japanese culture is unique.

Goals for Learning

◆ To describe where Japan is located

◆ To identify its most important features and climate

◆ To describe the culture of Japan and to explain how and where most Japanese live

◆ To describe Japan's economy and the environmental challenges it faces

Geo-Stats   Japan

Population: 126,745,000
Area: 145,875 square miles
Major Cities: Tokyo (capital), Yokohama, Osaka, Nagoya, Sapporo
Major Religions: Shinto, Buddhism, Christianity

Major Language: Japanese
Number of Daily Newspapers: 121
Number of Television Sets: 100 million
Number of telephones, including cellular: 155 million
Literacy rate: 99 percent

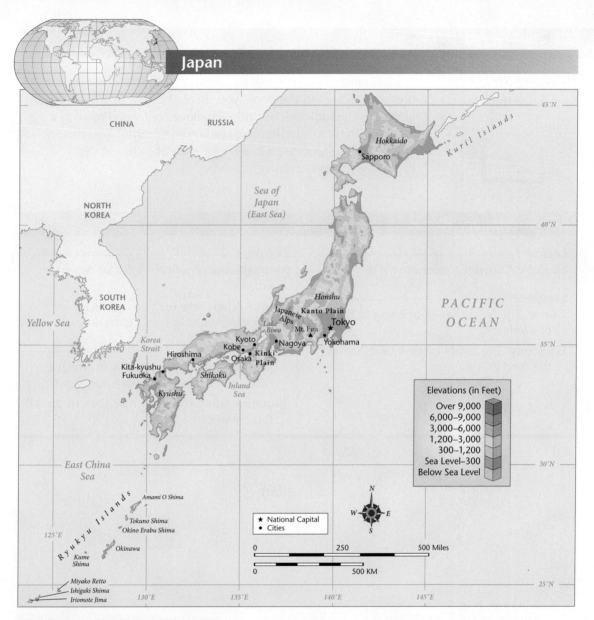

Japan

Map Skills

Japan has four large and many small islands. This country is off the eastern coast of Asia. Its closest neighbors are the Koreas, China, and Russia.

Study the map and answer the following questions:

1. Which four large islands make up Japan?

2. What is the capital of Japan?

3. What strait separates Japan from South Korea?

4. What Japanese islands are located southwest of the four main islands in the East China Sea?

5. Why might you expect Japan, the Koreas, and China to have close relations?

Reading Strategy: Summarizing

Readers who summarize can answer questions that occur as they are reading. In this book, you should be able to answer the questions the subheads ask after you have completed reading a section. After you have finished reading the chapter, you should also be able to provide an answer for each objective at the beginning of the lessons.

Key Vocabulary Words

Lesson 1 —————————————
Shogun A powerful Japanese military leader

Lesson 2 —————————————
Crater The bowl-shaped opening at the top of a volcano

Harmony The ability to work together and to blend in

Lesson 3 —————————————
Manual labor Physical work that requires little skill

Shinto A Japanese religion in which followers worship spirits in nature

Lesson 4 —————————————
Export economy An economy in which a country depends on exports for growth

Robotics Using robots or machines to do factory work

◆ To learn where Japan is located

◆ To describe how geography shaped Japan's history

Nearly 80 percent of Japan's people live on the island of Honshu.

Reading Strategy:
Summarizing

Ask yourself, "Where is Japan located?"

Where Is Japan Located?

Japan is a nation of islands. It stretches from about 25 to 45 degrees north latitude and from about 125 to 145 degrees east longitude. The Japanese archipelago is made up of nearly 4,000 islands. This string of islands curves around northeast Asia's mainland for about 1,500 miles. The Sea of Japan separates the Asian continent from the Japanese archipelago. The Korean Strait lies between the Koreas and Japan. The Japanese call Japan *Source of the Sun,* because at one time they thought that they were the first people to see the sun each day.

Four main islands make up 95 percent of Japan's land area. The northernmost island is Hokkaido. About 5 percent of Japan's people live there. South of Hokkaido is Honshu, Japan's largest island. Nearly 80 percent of Japan's 126 million people live there. The Pacific coastline of Honshu is one of the most densely populated areas in the world. Tokyo, Japan's capital city, is located on Honshu. South of Honshu is Shikoku, the smallest of the four large islands. Fewer people live on Shikoku than on the other three islands. Between Honshu and Shikoku is the Inland Sea. The southernmost of the four main islands is Kyushu, which is home to about 11 percent of Japan's people.

Many of Japan's smaller islands are part of the Ryukyu Islands. These islands are southwest of Japan's four larger islands.

Japan is a small country, especially when compared with its neighbors Russia and China. Together, the islands of Japan are about as large as the state of California in the United States.

This modern Japanese man is dressed how a shogun may have dressed hundreds of years ago.

How Did Geography Shape Japan's History?

Japan's nearest neighbors are Korea and China. Less than 150 miles of water separates Korea and Japan. About 450 miles of water separates Japan from China. In the past, sailing the seas was difficult, so these distances were great barriers. Water isolated Japan geographically.

Throughout much of its history, civil war divided Japan. For hundreds of years, powerful military leaders called **shoguns** fought each other for control of the land. In 1600, Tokugawa Ieyasu won an important battle. He united all of Japan. The Tokugawa family ruled Japan until 1867. They believed that dealing with foreigners was bad for their country. In 1635, the ruling family made all foreigners leave Japan. The rulers did not let Japanese people travel to other lands. Japan remained closed to outsiders for more than 200 years.

Shogun

A powerful Japanese military leader

Lesson 1 Review On a sheet of paper, write the word in parenthesis that makes each statement true.

1. Nearly (1,000, 4,000) islands make up the Japanese archipelago.

2. (Honshu, Hokkaido) is the largest Japanese island and the one on which nearly 80 percent of the Japanese people live.

3. The Korea Strait, a narrow passageway less than 150 miles wide, separates Japan from (China, Korea).

4. About (150, 450) miles of water separates Japan from China.

5. In 1600, (Tokugawa Ieyasu, Confucius) united all of Japan.

What do you think ?

What effects do you think the long period of isolation had on Japanese culture?

Objectives

◆ To learn the physical features of Japan

◆ To describe Japan's climates

◆ To tell how the environment affects the people

Reading Strategy:
Summarizing

Do you know what Japan's main physical feature is?

Only 11 percent of the land in Japan can be used for farming.

What Are the Physical Features of Japan?

Mountains cover nearly 80 percent of Japan. It is part of the "Ring of Fire." Japan is located in an area where three tectonic plates come together. Erupting volcanoes formed the Japanese islands millions of years ago. The tectonic plates continue to rub against each other. This causes earthquakes and tsunamis—huge ocean waves. Japan has about 1,000 earthquakes every year. Most are mild and cause little or no damage.

Some earthquakes cause a great deal of damage to Japan's urban areas. Damage also comes from tsunamis caused by underwater earthquakes. Sometimes fires start after earthquakes because of broken gas lines. In the last 100 years, Japan has had more than 20 destructive earthquakes. In 1995, a bad earthquake hit the city of Kobe. More than 5,500 people were killed. Because Japan experiences so many earthquakes, all its newer buildings are built to stay up during most earthquakes.

The Japanese Alps is Japan's longest and highest mountain range. It runs like a backbone down the length of Honshu. Mount Fuji is on the Pacific coast of Honshu. It is Japan's highest peak and most famous landmark. This volcano, which has not erupted since 1707, has an almost perfectly shaped cone.

Japan's other main landform is a narrow coastal plain. Almost all of the Japanese people live on it. The largest area of flat land is the Kanto Plain of east-central Honshu. It is an important center of population, farming, and industry. Tokyo, the capital of Japan, and Yokohama, an important seaport, are both located on the Kanto Plain. The Kinki Plain stretches across southern Honshu. The cities of Osaka, Kyoto, and Kobe are located on this coastal plain.

Crater

The bowl-shaped opening at the top of a volcano

Writing About Geography

Write a poem about harmony, as defined on the next page. In the poem, explain what you think harmony means and why it might be important to some people.

Reading Strategy: **Summarizing**

Can you compare Japan's climate to the climate where you live?

What Are the Main Bodies of Water?

The rivers of Japan are short, swift streams. In the past, they were important for travel. Today, trains and trucks have replaced the slow riverboats. However, the rivers are still important. The people use them to irrigate their crops and to create hydroelectric power.

Many of Japan's lakes are located in the mountains. Some lakes form when volcanic material dams a river. Others form when rain fills the bowl-shaped opening at the top of a volcano. This is called a **crater.** The largest of Japan's many lakes is Lake Biwa near Kyoto on Honshu. Millions of people depend on the lake waters for their freshwater needs.

The seas surrounding Japan and Korea provide fish and seaweed. The Japanese dry the seaweed. Then they use it to add flavor and protein to their food. A Japanese meal often includes fish and rice. Japan is one of the world's leading fishing nations.

What Is the Climate Like in Japan?

Japan has several climates like those on the East Coast of the United States. Northern Japan has the long, harsh winters of the humid continental climate. Icy winds blow from Siberia in Russia. As these winds cross the Sea of Japan, they pick up moisture. When the winds reach the Japanese Alps, they drop their moisture in the form of snow. The northwestern coastal regions of Honshu can receive five or six feet of snow per year.

Southern Japan includes the southern half of Honshu and the islands of Kyushu and Shikoku. This area has a subtropical climate. Winters are usually mild and sunny. The Japan Current is much like the North Atlantic Drift that warms western Europe. This warm water current helps keep temperatures mild along Japan's coastal plain.

The far north and south of Japan have very different climates. In March, for example, you can go sunbathing in the south and snow skiing in the north.

During late summer and fall, typhoons sometimes cause flooding in Japan. These tropical storms bring strong winds and heavy rains and sometimes damage homes and crops.

Harmony

The ability to work together and to blend in

These Japanese women are collecting shellfish on the beach.

Word Bank

continental 4

mountains 1

tsunami 3

typhoon 5

volcanoes 2

How Does the Environment Affect the People?

The mountains and the sea play important parts in Japanese culture. A love of nature is expressed in Japanese poetry and art. Respect for nature is a key feature of one of Japan's main religions. No part of Japan is more than 70 miles from the sea. The sea influences Japan's climate, is important for trade, and is a source of food.

Because of the mountains, most people live on the coasts. Living in a small, crowded space led the Japanese to develop a formal system of getting along with one another. Correct manners are very important to the Japanese. In America, people are encouraged to act and think for themselves. The Japanese people think of themselves as members of a group. The group can be the family, school, community, company, or country. The Japanese do what is best for the group. **Harmony,** or the ability to work together and to blend in, is important to the Japanese.

The crowded conditions have caused the Japanese to use space wisely. They store things on top of one another. They also fold things and roll them up to save space.

Lesson 2 Review On a sheet of paper, use the words from the Word Bank to complete each sentence correctly.

1. The main physical feature of Japan is _____.

2. The Japanese islands were formed by _____.

3. An earthquake can cause a _____, or huge ocean wave.

4. Northern Japan has a humid _____ climate.

5. A _____ is a tropical wind and rain storm that forms over the ocean.

What do you think ?

Why are none of Japan's main cities located in the mountains?

Objectives

◆ To explain Japan's cultures

◆ To learn what languages they speak

◆ To describe Japan's religions and the problems the people face

Manual labor

Physical work that requires little skill

Reading Strategy:
Summarizing

Can you state in a sentence or two what Japan's culture is like?

What Cultures Exist in This Region?

Japanese culture has much in common with China and the rest of east Asia. One written form of the Japanese language uses a writing system that came from China. Buddhism came to Japan from China through Korea. Early rulers of Japan stressed Chinese values of orderly society. People were taught to obey the people in power.

Japan has little cultural diversity. Most Japanese people see themselves as a single people, living in a united country. However, Japan does have three minority groups.

The Ainu are the original people of Japan. At one time, Ainu lived on all or most of the Japanese islands. Starting in the 700s, invaders forced the Ainu out of most of Japan, except Hokkaido. Today, there are only about 24,000 Japanese people with some Ainu ancestry. They have their own language and culture. Today, both are close to being extinct.

Koreans are the largest non-Japanese group living in Japan. Between 1910 and 1945, Japan ruled Korea. During that time, the Japanese forced many Koreans to work in Japanese factories. The majority of Koreans living in Japan have lived in Japan for a long time. They now speak only Japanese. However, they have not been totally accepted into Japanese society.

In recent years, foreign workers from China and the Philippines have come to Japan. Many entered illegally. They do **manual labor,** or physical work that requires little skill. Often, they do the work that Japanese do not want to do. Most foreign workers are poor. Also, some children of Japanese in South America have returned to Japan. Their parents went to South America during World War II.

What Languages Do the People Speak?

Nearly everyone living in Japan speaks Japanese. This language developed over thousands of years. What makes it hard for Westerners to learn is its different speech levels. Teenagers use one level of speech when talking to their teachers. They use another level with their friends. They may use a third level with their family.

Japanese writing goes from top to bottom instead of from left to right. A written page begins in the upper right corner. Japanese books begin at what Westerners would call the "back" and read through to the "front." Newspapers, however, go from top to bottom and left to right.

Geography in Your Life

The Arts in Japan

Japan has three traditional forms of plays. The *Noh* play presents history and legend with music, dance, and a chorus. This is a photo of a *Noh* play. Everything in the *Noh* play follows a traditional rule. *Banraku,* Japanese puppet theater, uses puppets that stand up to four feet high. A *kabuki* play uses colorful costumes and makeup. The actors' movements are made with more energy than normal.

After World War II, many artists turned away from Japan's traditional art forms. The government began to pick artists who had the courage to practice the old art forms. Japan calls these artists "Living National Treasures." These "living treasures" may dye the kimonos that women wear; weave bamboo baskets; perform with puppets. Others make swords; shape pottery; fold paper to make birds, flowers, and fish in the origami style; or act in *Noh* plays. Each artist keeps alive the treasured art forms of Japan's past.

What Religions Do the People Practice?

Shinto

A Japanese religion in which followers worship spirits in nature

The main religions in Japan are **Shinto** and Buddhism. Not many Japanese go to a place of worship or pray regularly. However, many Japanese follow both Buddhist and Shinto customs in their everyday life.

This painted bridge is a Shinto shrine. It is located on Hokkaido, Japan.

The word *Shinto* means way of the gods. This religion began thousands of years ago in Japan. The early Japanese believed that gods or spirits existed all around them in nature. Shinto gods take the form of things important to life. Mountains, trees, rocks, rivers, and the wind and rain are gods. By worshipping these spirits, the Japanese tried to live in harmony with nature. Nearly every Japanese town and city has a Shinto shrine. People visit the shrine to celebrate the New Year and to ask the gods for help in hard times.

Shinto is not a formal religion with firm rules. It has no founder and no sacred texts. It took shape gradually over the course of Japan's early history. Shinto is more like a way to live life.

Buddhism came to Japan in the 500s. Most Japanese Buddhists are Zen Buddhists. They believe that humans must clean their hearts and minds. Arranging flowers in a special way and participating in a tea ceremony help them purify themselves. Japanese Buddhists also want to get rid of personal desire. They believe that judo, archery, and fencing help them do this. Fencing is a sport using swords.

***Reading Strategy:* Summarizing**

What are the two religions practiced in Japan?

Buddhists believe in reincarnation. They believe that when people die, their souls are reborn into another living form. This happens until they reach enlightenment. Most Japanese pray to the Buddha as they get older. Most funerals are Buddhist, and Buddhist priests lead the funerals. They say prayers for the person who died. Most Japanese see no problem in believing in more than one religion.

What Problems Do the People Face?

One of Japan's biggest problems is its aging population. People are having fewer children, so the number of younger people is falling. However, the number of older people is rising. The Japanese have the longest life expectancy of any ethnic group. People born today in Japan may expect to live more than 81 years. The number of people in the workforce is getting smaller. There are fewer young people to fill the jobs. At the same time, more older people are retiring. By 2020, over one-fourth of Japanese will be over age 65.

Urbanization is a second problem for Japan. Much of Japan's population is crowded into a few cities along the coast. In 2005, 12 of Japan's cities had more than a million people. Some are so close to each other that they form a megalopolis. The Tokyo-Yokohama megalopolis is the largest in the world. More than 35 million people live in it. It is very densely populated. Osaka, Kyoto, and Kobe make up another large urban area.

Reading Strategy:
Summarizing

What are two of the problems in Japan?

Tokyo, Japan, stretches as far as a person can see.

Most Populated Cities in the World in 2005

Metropolitan Area	Country	Population
Tokyo area	Japan	35,197,000
Seoul area	Korea	22,770,000
Mexico City area	Mexico	19,411,000
New York City area	United States	18,747,000
São Paulo area	Brazil	18,333,000
Bombay (Mumbai) area	India	18,196,000
Delhi area	India	15,048,000
Shanghai area	China	14,503,000
Calcutta (Kolkata) area	India	14,277,000
Moscow area	Russia	13,400,000

Chart Study The world has many cities with large populations. This chart shows what the United Nations thinks are the ten most populated metropolitan areas in the world. Each is a megalopolis, not a single city. Which megalopolis on the list is in the United States? What is the population of the largest metropolitan area in Japan?

Lesson 3 Review On a sheet of paper, write the answer to each question. Use complete sentences.

1. What are the original people of Japan called?

2. What makes the Japanese language so difficult for Westerners to learn?

3. What are the two most widely practiced religions in Japan?

4. What do Buddhists believe happens when a person dies?

5. Why is the aging population a problem for Japan?

What do you think ?

Two atomic bombs were dropped on Japan near the end of World War II. How do you think this may have affected Japanese attitudes toward war and nuclear weapons?

Objectives

- ◆ To learn about Japan's economy
- ◆ To learn about its natural resources and industries
- ◆ To describe Japan's environmental problems

Export economy

An economy in which a country depends on exports for growth

Reading Strategy:
Summarizing

Now, summarize what the Japanese economy is like.

What Is the Economy Like?

Japan's economy is the second strongest in the world. Only the economy of the United States is larger. Japan's economy is an **export economy.** In this type of economy, a country depends on exports for growth. Trade with other countries is very important. One example is the automobile industry. Of all passenger cars sold in the United States, 40 percent have Japanese brands. North American factories assemble about two-thirds of Japanese brand vehicles sold in the United States.

Japan has huge investments in other countries. Labor and other costs are high in Japan. Japanese companies have built factories in countries where costs are lower, such as China, Taiwan, Vietnam, and Malaysia. Japan has huge investments in the United States. More than 56,000 Americans work in Japanese-owned automobile plants.

Today, less than 2 percent of Japanese people farm. Most farms are small. Japanese farmers grow enough rice to feed all of Japan's people. Farmers use machines, chemicals, and other labor-saving devices.

Japan has one of the world's largest fishing fleets. It catches about 15 percent of all the fish people eat in the world. Fish farming is an important part of the Japanese fishing industry. Japan's fish farms produce fish, shrimp, oysters, and seaweed.

What Natural Resources Exist?

Japan has few natural resources. It imports raw materials like oil, coal, iron ore, copper, aluminum, and wood. Japan spends more money on oil than any other imported product. To reduce its need for imported oil, Japan has developed nuclear power. Its 55 nuclear plants provide 30 percent of the country's electricity.

Japan must import nearly all the raw materials it uses in manufacturing. Japan has invested money in resource-rich countries such as Russia, Indonesia, and Australia.

Robotics

Using robots or machines to do factory work

Reading Strategy: Summarizing

What are some of Japan's important industries?

What Are Some Important Industries?

Japan is a world leader in technology. It has created industries for many different kinds of electronics. It is a major producer of computers, televisions, cameras, and audio equipment. It also makes electronic semiconductors. Semiconductors are used in computers, DVD players, cell phones, household appliances, and video games. However, cars are Japan's biggest industry and most important export. Japan also manufactures steel, ships, machinery, electrical equipment, and chemicals. Almost 25 percent of Japanese workers are in manufacturing jobs. But about 68 percent of Japanese have jobs in service industries.

Why Is Japan's Economy So Strong?

There are many reasons that Japan has a strong economy. The workforce is large, hardworking, and skilled. Japanese schools are among the best in the world. The government offers money and technology to help industries develop. The government also encourages the export of Japanese products and limits foreign imports. Companies apply new technology, such as **robotics.** Robotics uses robots or machines to do factory work. More than half of the industrial robots in the world are in Japan.

What Environmental Problems Exist?

The growth of industry after World War II led to air and water pollution in Japan. Cars cause air pollution. Burning fuel releases sulfur into the air. Japan's mountains block the winds that might blow the air pollution away. The government has spent lots of money to reduce pollution, which has helped.

What happens in nearby countries also affects Japan. Oil tankers in the Sea of Japan have spilled oil. The spills caused water pollution in Japan.

Another problem is too much garbage. Japan has few places to bury their garbage, so much of it is burned. Burning garbage causes air pollution.

Japan is one of the world leaders in recycling. It is creating new land with the recycled waste. They close off areas of the sea and drain the water. Then they fill the area with waste, and cover it with soil.

Japan's dependence on nuclear power is an environmental concern. Many people worry that it is dangerous for a country with so many earthquakes to have so many nuclear plants. Nuclear accidents can cause death, and are always a concern. Nuclear power also produces dangerous waste. Disposing of the waste safely is also a problem.

This family is fishing near Mihama Nuclear Power Plant in Japan.

Lesson 4 Review On a sheet of paper, write the letter of the answer that correctly completes each sentence.

1. The only country with an economy larger than Japan's is _____ *B* _____.

   A Russia   **C** Germany
   B the United States   **D** China

2. Today, about _____ *A* _____ percent of Japanese are farmers.

   A 2   **B** 50   **C** 68   **D** 33

3. Using machines to do factory work is called _____ *C* _____.

   A trade   **C** robotics
   B nuclear power   **D** free market

4. _____ *D* _____ are Japan's most important export.

   A Electronics   **C** Chemicals
   B Machinery   **D** Cars

5. Nearly 68 percent of Japanese workers work in _____ *B* _____ industries.

   A fishing   **B** service   **C** manufacturing   **D** automobile

What do you think ?

What do you think would happen to Japan's economy if the country were to become isolated like it was in the past?

Close Quarters

My name is Aito. I am 12 years old, and I live in Tokyo, Japan. I have two brothers and one sister. I am the third oldest.

We live in an apartment in our crowded city. Apartments here are labeled by the number of straw mats (*tatami*) that a sleeping room holds. Each rectangular *tatami* mat is numbered as a *jo*. Our apartment has a 6-*jo* sleeping room. Some apartments have rooms that are 12-*jo*, or even larger.

In very small apartments, the living room doubles as the sleeping room. Not mine, though. We have a separate living room. Each of us kids has a study desk and chair in the living room. They take up most of the space.

For each person in my family, we have a light-weight mattress called a futon. At night, we take our futons out of the sleeping room closet. We lay the futons on top of the *tatami* mats. I am used to the noises that my family makes at night. I think I might miss the noises if I were to sleep alone in a room. In the morning, we put the futons back into the closet. The *tatami* mats stay on the floor.

We keep this room uncluttered so it is easy to switch back and forth. There is a single small table in the center of the room. We sit around this table for dinner and conversation. Like most Japanese households, we do not have central heating.

So in the winter, we use a special table that has a heater. We place our legs under the table and cover them with a blanket. It is cozy to gather around the table like this.

My cousins do not have this kind of winter table. They use a kerosene heater instead. It works as a stove, too. They often boil water for green tea on it. I like visiting their apartment. Their sleeping room is warm and humid from the boiling water.

My family likes to have other families over for meals or for tea. It gets very crowded, but I love it. We never ask anyone to spend the night, however. I'm not sure where we'd put them!

Wrap-Up

1. What is a futon?

2. Why do most Japanese families keep only a small table in the sleeping room during the day?

Chapter 22 SUMMARY

- Japan is an east Asian country made up of four large islands and many small ones. Japan's nearest neighbors are South Korea and China.

- Mountains are the most important physical feature of Japan. Japan's other main landform is a coastal plain on which most of its people live.

- The rivers of Japan are short, swift streams. They provide water for irrigation and hydroelectric power. The seas provide fish, which is a staple of the Japanese diet. Many of Japan's lakes are located in the mountains.

- Northern Japan has a humid continental climate. Southern Japan has a humid subtropical climate.

- Because of mountains, people only live on about 20 percent of Japan's land. This has forced the Japanese to become dependent on one another and to value the group and harmony.

- Isolation helped shape Japanese culture. Most Japanese belong to the same ethnic group.

- Shinto and Buddhism are the main religions of Japan. Shinto is a way of living one's life.

- Nearly everyone who lives in Japan speaks Japanese.

- Much of Japan's population is crowded into a few cities along the coast. Many of Japan's cities have more than a million people.

- One of Japan's biggest social problems is its aging population.

- Japan has few natural resources. To reduce its need for imported oil, Japan has developed nuclear power.

- Japan has an export economy. Cars are its biggest industry and most important export. It is a world leader in technology and produces consumer electronics.

- Japan's main environmental problems are air and water pollution, too much garbage, and nuclear waste.

Chapter 22 REVIEW

Word Bank

exports

group

islands

Mount Fuji

robotics

On a sheet of paper, use the words from the Word Bank to complete each sentence correctly.

1. Japan is a country made up of many _____.

2. The Japanese think of themselves as members of a _____ and not as individuals.

3. Japan's most famous landmark and highest peak is _____.

4. The technology that uses machines for factory work is _____.

5. The economy of Japan depends heavily on _____.

On a sheet of paper, write the letter of the answer that correctly completes each sentence.

6. Most people in Japan live on the island of _____.

   A Shikoku   **C** Hokkaido
   B Kyushu   **D** Honshu

7. The most common physical feature of Japan is _____.

   A mountains   **C** plains
   B deserts   **D** many islands

8. The two main religions of Japan are Buddhism and _____.

   A Christianity   **C** Islam
   B Shinto   **D** Hinduism

9. Nearly everyone in Japan speaks _c__.

   A Hokkaido   **C** Japanese
   B Korean   **D** Ainu

10. The cities of __b__ and Yokohama form a megalopolis.

   A Kyoto   **C** Kobe
   B Tokyo   **D** Osaka

On a sheet of paper, write the answer to each question. Use complete sentences.

11. What are three environmental problems that Japan faces?

12. What is the climate like in Japan?

Critical Thinking On a sheet of paper, write your response to each question. Use complete sentences.

13. What was the most important factor in shaping the culture of Japan? Explain your answer.

14. Why do you think Japanese industry has been so successful?

15. The United States stresses the ability to think for oneself. Why do you think this is not as important to the Japanese people?

Applying the Five Themes of Geography

Interaction

Japan is the world's leading producer of pearls. Oysters produce natural pearls. Only a few oysters, however, produce pearls. A Japanese man named Kokichi Mikimoto invented a process to create almost perfect pearls from every oyster. How does this show the theme of interaction?

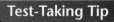

Test-Taking Tip

When taking a multiple-choice test, read every choice before you answer a question. Put a line through choices you know are wrong. Then choose the best answer from the remaining choices.

23

The Koreas

The Koreas have great modern cities with high-rise buildings. They also have beautiful mountain areas with few people. War has separated Korea into two parts, North Korea and South Korea. South Korea has a strong economy. However, North Korea is one of the most isolated countries in the world. Its economy is poorly developed and it suffers from food shortages.

Goals for Learning

◆ To describe where the Koreas are located

◆ To identify their most important features and climate

◆ To describe the culture of the Koreas and how and where most Korean people live

◆ To describe the economies of North and South Korea and the environmental challenges they face

Geo-Stats   The Koreas

Nation: South Korea or Republic of Korea

Population: 48,847,000

Area: 38,023 square miles

Major Cities: Seoul (capital), Pusan, Inch'ŏn, Taegu

Major Languages: Korean

Major Religions: Buddhism, Christianity

Life Expectancy: 77

Literacy: 98%

Number of Telephones: 62 million (land and cellular)

Nation: North Korea or Democratic People's Republic of Korea

Population: 23,113,000

Area: 46,541 square miles

Major Cities: Pyongyang (capital), Nampo

Major Languages: Korean

Major Religions: Buddhism, Confucianism

Life Expectancy: 71

Literacy: 98%

Number of Telephones: 1.1 million (cell phones are banned)

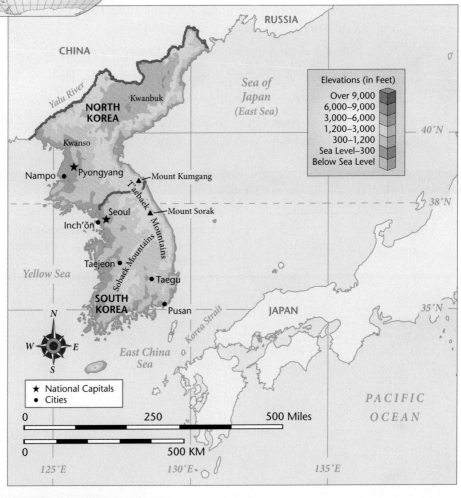

RUSSIA

CHINA

Yalu River

Sea of Japan (East Sea)

NORTH KOREA

Kwanbuk

Kwanso

40°N

Elevations (in Feet)
Over 9,000
6,000–9,000
3,000–6,000
1,200–3,000
300–1,200
Sea Level–300
Below Sea Level

Nampo ● ★Pyongyang ▲—Mount Kumgang

Taebaek

38°N

Seoul ★ —Mount Sorak

Inch'ŏn ●★

Mountains

Taejeon ● Sobaek Mountains

Yellow Sea

● Taegu

SOUTH KOREA

● Pusan

JAPAN

35°N

Korea Strait

N

W E

S

East China Sea

★ National Capitals
● Cities

0   250   500 Miles

0   500 KM

125°E   130°E   135°E

PACIFIC OCEAN

Map Skills

Korea is a peninsula, surrounded by water on three sides. It is located in eastern Asia between the Yellow Sea and the Sea of Japan. The peninsula is about 600 miles long and 105 miles wide. There are two countries on the peninsula: North Korea and South Korea. The Korean Peninsula is located about 125 miles from the coast of Japan.

Study the map and answer the following questions:

1. Where are the tallest mountains on the Korean peninsula?

2. What is the capital of North Korea? South Korea?

3. What river forms North Korea's border with China?

4. What body of water separates the Korean Peninsula from Japan?

5. How might Korea's nearness to China affect its politics and culture?

Reading Strategy:
Questioning

Asking yourself questions as you read may help you become a better reader. It will make you think about what you are reading. As you read this chapter, ask yourself:

◆ What do the photos have to do with life in Korea?

◆ What in this chapter is like something in my life?

◆ How can I remember what I am reading?

◆ After reading the chapter, ask yourself, "Can I summarize what I have read in this chapter?"

Key Vocabulary Words

Lesson 1	*Lesson 4*
Parallel A line of latitude	**Transboundary pollution** Pollution from one country that affects a different country

Objectives

◆ To know where Korea is located

◆ To describe how geography shaped the region's history

◆ To understand why there are two Koreas

◆ To identify the regions of Korea

Where Are the Koreas Located?

North and South Korea share a peninsula on the eastern edge of Asia. The peninsula is west of Japan. The Yalu River forms the border between North Korea and China. A small part of Korea borders Russia. The Yellow Sea borders the Koreas to the west. The Sea of Japan, or the East Sea, is to the east. The Korea Strait separates it from Japan. North and South Korea are divided by a line that lies near the latitude of 38 degrees north.

How Did Geography Shape History?

The Koreas' nearest neighbors are Japan and China. Over 2,000 years ago, the Chinese came to Korea. The Chinese introduced their religions and the Chinese written language. The Chinese influenced the Korean culture.

Many times in its history, Japan invaded Korea. Japan's influence on Korea grew after Japan defeated China in 1895. In 1910, Japan made Korea a Japanese colony. The Japanese forced Koreans to learn Japanese. They forced Koreans to adopt Japanese names and to follow the Shinto religion. Between 1939 and 1945, Japan moved thousands of Korean workers to Japan to work in their factories. It was not until the end of World War II in 1945 that Korea regained its independence.

Why Are There Two Koreas?

During World War II, troops from the Soviet Union and the United States drove the Japanese out of Korea. Soviet troops came in from the north. The United States soldiers came from the south. The two armies met at 38 degrees north latitude.

When the war ended, the Soviet Union wanted Korea to become a Communist state. The United States wanted it to be a democracy. Because neither side was willing to give in, Korea was divided into two separate countries in 1948. One was North Korea, or the Democratic People's Republic of Korea. The other was South Korea, or the Republic of Korea. The 38th line of latitude marks the approximate border between the two.

**Reading Strategy:
Questioning**

Can you think of a United States event that was similar to what happened in the Koreas?

Parallel

A line of latitude

Reading Strategy:
Questioning

What do you know about the Korean War?

In 1950, North Korea invaded South Korea. The United Nations sent troops to defend South Korea. Most of the troops were from the United States. Communist China sent in troops to help the North Koreans. The Korean War lasted three years. More than 5 million people died. In 1953, both sides agreed to stop fighting. The border between North and South Korea stayed near the 38th line of latitude, or the 38th **parallel**.

What Regions Exist in Korea?

North Korea is divided into two geographical regions. The Kwanso region is in the northwest and the Kwanbuk region is in the northeast. The Kwanso region is an area of land that is more flat and is the main farming area of North Korea. The Kwanbuk region is very mountainous. Mining and forestry are its major economic activities. Pyongyang, North Korea's biggest city and capital, is in the Kwanso region.

Reading Strategy:
Questioning

Can you see the mountains on the map on page 527?

South Korea has a broad coastal plain in the west. This is where most of its major cities are located and where most of the people live. The plain is the major farming region of South Korea. The rest of the country is covered with hills and low mountains. Korea has no active volcanoes. South Korea has about 3,000 islands located off the west and south coasts. A few islands in the Sea of Japan are important to Korea's large fishing industry.

Lesson 1 Review On a sheet of paper, write the word in parenthesis that makes each statement true.

1. North and South Korea are located on (a peninsula, an island) on the eastern edge of Asia.

2. The (Yalu, Huang) River separates North Korea from China.

3. The Korea Strait separates Korea from (China, Japan).

4. The 38th parallel separates South Korea from (China, North Korea).

5. (China, Japan) made Korea a colony in 1910.

What do you think ?

Why do you think Korea may have a love/hate relationship with China and Japan?

- To describe the physical features of Korea
- To identify its major rivers
- To describe Korea's climates

What Are the Physical Features of Korea?

Korea is made up mostly of mountains and hills. Mountains cover more than 70 percent of Korea. The highest mountains are to the east and north. About 80 percent of North Korea is covered with mountains. People can farm only about 16 percent of the land. The highest mountain peaks on the Korean Peninsula are in the Sobaek and T'aebaek ranges.

The eastern part of the Korean peninsula is mountainous and has only a very small coastal plain. South Korea is not as mountainous as North Korea. Its highest mountains are about 5,000 feet high. The western area of South Korea bordering the Yellow Sea is a broad coastal plain. Despite being densely populated, much of Korea is covered with forests.

What Are the Bodies of Water?

The rivers of Korea are short. Most of the rivers of North Korea flow west and empty into the Yellow Sea. The longest river is the Yalu River. The Tumen River flows into the Sea of Japan. The Taedong River flows through Pyongyang, North Korea's capital. The Han River flows through Seoul, the capital of South Korea. The rivers formed large alluvial plains of rich farmland.

This village is on the East Sea coast of South Korea.

Many of Korea's natural lakes are located in the mountains. The lakes are small. South Korea has several lakes made by damming rivers. The Koreans use many foods that come from the sea. In coastal regions, people eat fish, shellfish and seaweed. In mountainous regions, they eat salted or dried fish.

What Are the Climates of the Koreas?

Korea has several climates. The climate is influenced by Korea's closeness to the Asian landmass. This causes weather extremes. In the north, the climate is humid continental. Summers are very hot; winters are very cold. South Korea has a milder climate with four seasons. Winters are usually long, cold, and dry. Summers are short, hot, and humid. The weather is also affected by the monsoons. Most rain falls during June, July, and August. Some parts of the south have an almost subtropical climate. South Korea has from one to three typhoons per year. Typhoons usually pass over South Korea in August.

How Does the Environment Affect the People?

Because Korea is so mountainous, people living in one valley or mountain range were cut off from those living somewhere else. They developed different cultures. The customs of the people, the way they dressed, and even their languages were different.

The two Koreas have developed very differently since they became separate in 1948. North Korea is still a Communist state. It has few dealings with other countries. Most people cannot travel either into or out of the country. We know little about North Korea. South Korea is a democracy with a free market economy. South Koreans enjoy a high standard of living. It is much richer than North Korea.

Lesson 2 Review On a sheet of paper, use the words from the Word Bank to complete each sentence correctly.

1. The main physical feature of Korea is _____.

2. One mountain range in Korea is the _____ range.

3. Northern Korea has a humid _____ climate.

4. North Korea has a _____ form of government.

5. South Korea is a _____.

What do you think

Why do you think the two Koreas developed so differently?

Objectives

◆ To describe the culture of Korea

◆ To know the language they speak and the religions they practice

◆ To describe some of Korea's social problems

What Cultures Exist in This Region?

Korea has little cultural diversity. Korea's culture and civilization are unique and quite distinct from both the Chinese and the Japanese. Foreigners, including Westerners, Chinese, and Japanese, make up a small percentage of the population.

What Language Do the People Speak?

The language of the Korean people is Korean. The Korean language is related to Turkish, Hungarian, and Finnish. However, it uses some Chinese characters and has the same sentence structure as Japanese. People in different mountain regions speak their own dialects. They also eat different foods, dress differently, and have different types of homes.

For over 2,000 years, Koreans spoke Chinese and Korean. This was during the long periods when China controlled Korea. For a long time, only male rulers learned to read and write. They used Chinese ideograms. Most Koreans could not read or write.

King Sejong invented a new Korean alphabet in 1444. He created the new form of writing because the Korean language was different from Chinese. Chinese ideograms were hard for common people to learn. The Korean alphabet has 24 letters. Today, about 73 million people speak Korean.

What Religions Do the People Practice?

Buddhism has played an important role in the art, architecture, literature, and the performing arts of Korea. Many Koreans are Buddhists. The Buddha's birthday is observed as a national holiday. Many people visit and pray at Buddhist temples.

Reading Strategy:
Questioning

What do you remember about Confucius from the chapter on China?

The teachings of Confucius influenced Koreans. His teachings influenced their educational system and their government. Today, traditional Confucian ideas still affect how Koreans act toward one another. They believe in respect between father and son, order between old and young, and trust between friends.

Geography in Your Life

Shamanism

Have you ever heard of a shaman? A shaman is a religious person who uses magic to cure the sick, find hidden things, or to control events. An early religion in the Koreas was shamanism. A shamanist believes that there are invisible forces or spirits that affect people. The role of the shaman is to protect people from these spirits. Shamanism remains an important force in Korean society today. Some well-educated business people hold ceremonies with offerings of wine and food in hopes that their new business will be successful. Families sometimes seek the services of a shaman when they face a serious illness.

Korea is different from many other Asian countries in that many people are Christians. The Catholic religion was introduced to Korea by missionaries in the 1600s. Many Protestant religions also sent missionaries. Since the 1950s, there has been a huge growth in Protestant churches. Almost 25 percent of all Koreans are Christians.

What Problems Do the People Face?

In the 1950s, half of Korea's people were farmers. Many Koreans lived in isolated villages and never traveled far from them. In those days, sons traditionally did not leave home when they married. Instead, they brought their wives into the household. In the past, a typical Korean home sometimes had extended families living together.

As Korea became more industrialized, people began moving to the cities. The pattern of family living changed. There was not enough room for large families to live together. Single adults often had their own apartments. Young couples lived apart from their parents.

This wall was built in the 1700s. It was built to protect the village of Suwon, South Korea. Suwon has grown into a large city.

Today, one quarter of South Korea's people live in the capital city of Seoul. Nearly half the South Korean people live in Seoul and its suburbs combined. At the end of World War II in 1945, Seoul had less than 1 million people. It has grown to be one of the world's megacities with a population of over 20 million. It is the center of South Korea's government, economy, education, and culture. With growth came many urban problems. Many people live in poor housing. Some are homeless. Traffic jams have made Seoul one of the world's most congested cities.

A second problem is the growing gap between the rich and the poor. Some South Koreans have become very rich. But the number of poor people is also growing.

However, the biggest problem facing Korea may be a political one. North Korea is Communist. Its economy is based on farming, and it is isolated. The people of South Korea are much freer. They live in an industrial nation and seek closer ties with other countries. Most Koreans hope that one day the two Korean republics will be united again.

Lesson 3 Review On a sheet of paper, write the answer to each question. Use complete sentences.

1. What language do Koreans speak?
2. What religions do Koreans practice?
3. Who brought the Protestant religions to Korea?
4. What percentage of Koreans are Christians?
5. What are three problems facing the people of Korea?

What do you think ?

Do you think that North and South Korea should be reunited? Explain your answer.

Saving the Dolphins

Dolphins often swim where tuna swim. People who fish follow the dolphins to help them find tuna. Some fishers use drift nets. These nets are hard to see and drift over a huge area of ocean—as much as 40 miles. The nets catch everything in their path. That can include dolphins and other animals. This kills all the animals. As much as 40 to 50 percent of the catch in drift nets is wasted. Since 1959, drift nets have killed about 7 million dolphins.

In the 1970s, some people began to campaign to stop drift-net fishing. Today, many tuna fish cans have dolphin-safe labels. That means that no dolphins were killed to catch the tuna. Instead, fishers used a different method of fishing.

People who fish in Korea, along with those from Japan and Taiwan, have been known for using drift nets. In 1992, the United Nations agreed to ban drift nets that are longer than 1½ miles. In 1997, the Republic of Korea agreed to cut its use of drift nets by half. More and more, countries are finding that the decisions they make affect the entire world.

Wrap-Up

1. Why do people who fish follow dolphins to catch tuna?

2. Why do you think Korea agreed to reduce its use of drift nets?

Make a Difference

Not all tuna is dolphin safe. Go to your local grocery store. Check for dolphin-safe labels. Report back to your class about what you find.

- ◆ To describe the economies of North and South Korea
- ◆ To identify their natural resources
- ◆ To describe the environmental problems the countries face

These North Korean workers are sewing pieces of clothing. Some South Korean industries want to move their factories to North Korea. The people in North Korea work for much less money than they do in South Korea or China.

What Is the Economy Like?

The economies of North and South Korea are very different. South Korea has a strong economy. It produces a wide variety of goods. South Korea is the fifth largest car maker in the world. About 40 percent of the labor force is involved in manufacturing.

North Korea is one of the world's poorest countries. The country's industrial production and power output have dropped. Factories mostly make supplies for North Korea's large army. It is the fifth largest army in the world. Few factories produce consumer goods. Many North Koreans must rely on imported second-hand items from China and Japan. Food shortages are common, and many people would starve without the aid given by other countries.

South Korea's economy is strong for many reasons. It has a large, hard-working, and skilled workforce. Following the Japanese example, government and business have developed close ties. South Korea has many family-owned business groups. These businesses have played a major role in the South Korean economy since the 1960s. Many businesses get money from the government. Some family-owned businesses have well-known, international brand names.

Like Japan, South Korea is an export economy. It is a major trading nation. It exports textiles, clothing, electronic and electrical equipment, footwear, machinery, and fish products. It manufactures many consumer products such as microwave ovens, toasters, televisions, stereo equipment, and computers. South Korea is the largest builder of ships in the world. It is an important steel maker.

South Korea is moving some manufacturing to countries where labor costs are less. It is building factories in other countries such as China and Indonesia. Agriculture is still important. Today, there are still many rice farms along the coastal plain.

What Natural Resources Exist?

Korea is not rich in natural resources. Pyongyang, the capital of North Korea, is located near deposits of coal and iron ore. North Korea also has some deposits of lead, tungsten, zinc, graphite, copper, gold, salt, and fluorspar. It is using its rivers to develop hydroelectric power. South Korea has many of the same resources. It has deposits of coal, tungsten, graphite, and lead.

Because it has so few natural resources, South Korea must import much of its energy. It also depends heavily on nuclear power for its energy needs. Nuclear power provides about 40 percent of the country's electricity.

North Korea needs electrical power. Many parts of the country are completely dark at night because of shortages. It wants to build nuclear power plants to produce electricity. This worries many people in the world. Because North Korea is closed to foreigners, they could be developing nuclear power either for electricity or for nuclear bombs.

What Environmental Problems Exist?

The growth of industry in South Korea has led to serious air and water pollution. Cars, diesel buses, and trucks cause air pollution. Coal is also a common fuel. Burning coal causes air pollution. South Korea is working hard to cut down on levels of pollution.

Since pollution does not stop at a country's border, Korea is affected by pollution from its neighbors. This is called **transboundary pollution**. Industrial pollution from China's factories affects the air in Korea. South Korean steel mills cause air problems in Taiwan and Japan. The governments of China, Japan, and South Korea are working together to deal with pollution problems, but progress has been slow.

Water quality is also a problem. It is so bad that few people drink tap water. Some people are moving because pollution in their communities is at dangerous levels. Both North and South Korea have very high pollution levels.

These Korean women are sorting fish to dry.

Lesson 4 Review On a sheet of paper, write the letter of the answer that correctly completes each sentence.

1. Factories in North Korea mostly make supplies for _____.

    A consumers   **C** the army

    B business   **D** foreign investors

2. South Korea has many _____ business groups.

    A family-owned   **C** government

    B nuclear   **D** second-hand

3. South Korea is the world's largest builder of _____.

    A electronics   **B** ships   **C** chemicals   **D** cars

4. No one knows if North Korea is developing _____ power for electricity or for bombs.

    A electronic   **C** manufacturing

    B nuclear   **D** construction

5. Some of Korea's air quality problems are caused by pollution from _____.

    A Taiwan   **B** Russia   **C** Japan   **D** China

What do you think ?

What do you think the United States should do about North Korea's possible nuclear weapon program?

Rules for Children

In North Korea, the government tightly controls the people. Their rights are secondary to the rights of the state and the ruling party. That party, the KWP (Korean Workers' Party) makes the rules for teenagers.

On weekdays, teenagers get up at around 6 A.M. They get ready for school and help their parents with light housework. Most North Korean students walk to school. However, since students are not allowed to arrive at school alone, they meet at a place they have chosen. From there, they march to school in rows.

Once at school, members of the student government body inspect the students' uniforms and hair. Both must be tidy. In addition, students must wear a pin with a picture of the late North Korean president on it. Classes meet for 50 minutes with 10-minute breaks. School goes until 3 or 4 P.M. There is one 30-minute period for exercise.

North Korean students must go to certain extra-curricular activities. These activities are planned and taught by the Kim Il Sun Socialist Youth League. Sometimes they are political lectures or lessons. They might be trips to museums, monuments, or historical sites of the Korean Revolution. Sessions on poetry, science presentations, and debate contests are also common. All of the activities are designed to enforce North Korean unity and pride.

Teenagers rarely skip school. Those who miss school once without notice or leave early three times in a month are punished—their food for one day is taken away. Students usually behave well at school. If they misbehave, a KWP worker at the school will probably contact the parent's boss at work. The boss then blames the parent for not following the party's rules at home.

About the age of 16 or 17, most city girls go to work on farms or in factories. Boys of the same age are required to begin their eight years of military service. There are schools for children of special talent: dance, music, the arts, science, foreign language, and athletics. But, students in these schools, too, are subject to strict government control.

Wrap-Up

1. What is the role of the student government body as students arrive at school?

2. Why do North Korean teens rarely miss or act up in school?

- North and South Korea share a peninsula on the eastern edge of Asia, directly west of Japan.

- Its closeness to Japan and China influenced Korea's history and culture. Buddhism and the teachings of Confucius were introduced from China. In 1910, Japan made Korea a Japanese colony. After World War II, Korea was divided into two countries, North and South Korea.

- The northern part of the Korean peninsula has two geographical regions: the Kwanso region in the northwest and the Kwanbuk region in the northeast. South Korea has a broad coastal plain in the west. The rest of the country covered with hills and low mountains.

- Mountains are the most important physical feature of Korea. The rivers of Korea are short. The Yalu River divides Korea from China. The Korean rivers formed large alluvial plains of rich farmland.

- The northern part of Korea has a humid continental climate. Parts of the south have a humid subtropical climate.

- Korea's culture has little diversity. People living in mountain valleys developed a somewhat different culture.

- Most Koreans identify themselves as Buddhists. However, nearly 25 percent are Christians.

- Nearly everyone living in Korea speaks Korean.

- Urbanization, a growing gap between the rich and the poor, and the political problem of reuniting the two Koreas are the major problems.

- North Korea is one of the world's poorest countries. Food shortages are common.

- South Korea has an export economy. It is a major trading nation. It has a high-tech economy. It manufactures many consumer products.

- Korea is not rich in natural resources. North Korea has coal and iron ore and a few other minerals. South Korea has many of the same resources. South Korea relies on nuclear energy for much of its energy needs. North Korea would like to develop nuclear power. But it may also be developing a nuclear weapons program.

- Korea's main environmental problems are air and water pollution, and transboundary pollution. Both countries rank low in air and water quality.

Chapter 23 REVIEW

Word Bank

exports
Japan
parallel
peninsula
Strait

On a sheet of paper, use the words from the Word Bank to complete each sentence correctly.

1. Korea is on a _____ on the eastern edge of Asia.

2. The Korean _____ divides Korea from Japan.

3. _____ made Korea a colony in 1910.

4. The 38th _____ divides North Korea from South Korea.

5. The economy of South Korea depends heavily on _____.

On a sheet of paper, write the letter of the answer that correctly completes each sentence.

6. Korean culture has been influenced by its neighbors, _____.

   A Russia and China
   B Japan and Indonesia
   C India and Russia
   D Japan and China

7. The most common physical feature of Korea is _____.

   A mountains   **C** plains
   B deserts   **D** many islands

8. Most Koreans are followers of the _____ religion.

   A Christian   **C** Islamic
   B Buddhist   **D** Hindu

9. North Korea has a _____ form of government.

   A religious   **C** Communist
   B economic   **D** democratic

10. The Korean city of _____ and its suburbs has a population of over 20 million people.

    A Seoul   **C** Tokyo
    B Pyongyang   **D** Beijing

On a sheet of paper, write the answer to each question. Use complete sentences.

11. Why are there two Koreas?

12. How does Korea's closeness to the huge Asian landmass affect its climate?

Critical Thinking On a sheet of paper, write your response to each question. Use complete sentences.

13. How is pollution from other countries a problem for most of the world's countries? Explain your answer.

14. Why do you think South Korea's economy is so much more developed than North Korea's?

15. Do you think the Koreas will become one country again? Why or why not?

Applying the Five Themes of Geography

Region

Korea is usually viewed as one region. Make a case for including South Korea in the same economic region as Japan.

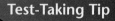

Test-Taking Tip

When a test item asks you to write a paragraph, make a plan first. Jot down the main idea of your paragraph. List supporting details you want to include. Then write your paragraph.

The War in Vietnam

Vietnam was once part of France's colonial empire in Southeast Asia. During World War II, Japanese forces took control. When the war ended, France tried to regain control. However, some Vietnamese did not want France to rule them any longer. They declared Vietnam independent. They fought a war against the French.

In 1954, a treaty granted independence to Laos and Cambodia. This same treaty divided Vietnam into North Vietnam and South Vietnam. Communist forces controlled North Vietnam; non-Communist forces governed South Vietnam. The United States supported the government of South Vietnam because it was not Communist. The U.S. government was afraid that North Vietnam and its Communist supporters in the south would make all of Southeast Asia Communist.

In 1964, the United States began sending thousands of soldiers to help South Vietnam. By 1968, more than 500,000 Americans were fighting there. The fighting lasted nine years. The United States and the Communists dropped thousands of bombs on both parts of Vietnam. About 2 million Vietnamese were killed, 4 million wounded, and 6 million made homeless. Nearly 58,000 U.S. soldiers died.

During the war, the United States greatly damaged Vietnam's environment. U.S. planes dropped a chemical called Agent Orange on the thick vegetation of the jungles. This chemical killed about one fifth of Vietnam's forests.

Agent Orange also poisoned the water and the soil. It destroyed the crops. People and animals who were accidentally sprayed often got sick.

Vietnam is slowly recovering from the war. However, it is a poor country with limited resources. Visitors to Vietnam today still see reminders of a terrible war that ended more than 35 years ago. Signs like the one below warn people about the dangers of land mines.

Wrap-Up

1. What country controlled Vietnam before World War II?

2. Why did the United States support the government of South Vietnam?

3. How many Vietnamese people and how many U.S. soldiers died in the war?

4. What was Agent Orange?

5. Why has Vietnam not yet recovered from a war that took place more than 35 years ago?

- China is the fourth largest country in the world. Japan is made up of four large islands and many small ones. Korea occupies a peninsula across the Sea of Japan.

- Mountains are the most important physical feature of China, Japan, and Korea. For centuries, these mountains and the sea isolated these nations. This isolation shaped their cultures.

- The three most important Chinese rivers are the Huang He, the Yangtze, and the Xi. They are highways into the middle of China. Japanese and Korean rivers are short, swift streams that provide water for irrigation and hydroelectric power.

- Over 90 percent of Chinese people are Han Chinese. The remaining people belong to several minority groups. Most Japanese belong to the same ethnic group. Korea's culture has little diversity.

- Many Chinese people still follow their ancient beliefs. Several Chinese minorities practice Islam. The main religions in Japan are Shinto and Buddhism. Most Koreans are Buddhists, but nearly 25 percent are Christians.

- Most Chinese speak Mandarin Chinese. Most of China's large minority groups speak their own language. Nearly everyone living in Japan speaks Japanese. Koreans speak Korean.

- China has more people than any other country. Most Chinese people work the land. Because of mountains, people can only live on about 20 percent of Japan. About half of them live on Honshu, Japan's largest island.

- Japan has a strong economy. Cars are its biggest industry and most important export. Consumer electronics is a big industry in South Korea. Both South Korea and Japan depend on imported raw materials. Both Japan and South Korea have export economies. Most Chinese people farm for a living. China's economy is one of the fastest growing in the world. More people are moving to urban areas to work in factories.

- Japan's main problems are the change in population balance, air and water population, and too much garbage. Korea's biggest problem is reuniting the two republics. Among China's problems are population growth, its relationship with Taiwan, deforestation, and water shortages.

The Pacific World

The Pacific World is a huge area that includes much of the south Pacific Ocean. It includes two large island nations—Australia and New Zealand. Australia is famous for its Great Barrier Reef. This underwater photo shows some of the colorful fish that live near the reef.

The Pacific World also includes thousands of small islands in the Pacific Ocean. People live on about 800 of them. Tourists like to visit them for their beauty and for their warm weather.

Antarctica is the coldest, windiest place on Earth. It has an Arctic climate. Most of the people who live there are scientists who are doing research.

Chapters in Unit 10

24 Australia and New Zealand

Australia and New Zealand have much in common. Both were colonies of Great Britain and most of their people speak English. Europe has strongly influenced their cultures. However, their future is closely linked with Japan, China, Southeast Asia, and other nations that rim the Pacific Ocean.

Goals for Learning

◆ To describe where Australia and New Zealand are located

◆ To identify their important physical features and their climates

◆ To describe their cultures and how and where most of the people live

◆ To describe their economies and the environmental challenges they face

Geo-Stats   Australia and New Zealand

Nation: Australia
Population: 20,264,000
Area: 2,969,978 square miles
Major Cities: Canberra (capital), Sydney, Melbourne, Brisbane, Perth, Adelaide
Major Religion: Christianity
Major Language: English

Nation: New Zealand
Population: 4,076,000
Area: 103,883 square miles
Major Cities: Wellington (capital), Auckland
Major Religion: Christianity
Major Languages: English and Maori

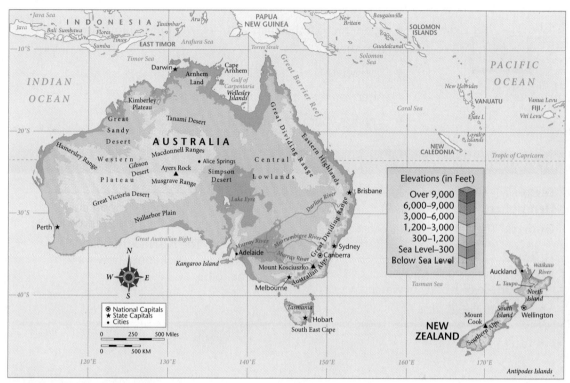

Map Skills

Australia and New Zealand are the two largest countries in the Pacific World. In fact, Australia is a continent. It is the sixth largest country in the world. Australia has many large deserts and mountain ranges. New Zealand is made up of two large islands and many smaller ones.

Study the map and answer the following questions:

1. What ocean is west of Australia? What ocean is east of Australia?

2. What is the name of Australia's eastern mountain range?

3. What are the national capitals of Australia and New Zealand?

4. What are Australia's major deserts?

5. How would you describe the land of Australia based on what you see on this map?

Reading Strategy:
Predicting

If you predict as you are reading, it prepares you for what you are about to read. Predicting will help you learn new information. As you read:

◆ Look through the chapter to see what new information is in there.

◆ Use what you know to predict what is new.

◆ After you read a section, check your prediction.

◆ Change your prediction as needed.

Key Vocabulary Words

Lesson 1 ──────────────
Hemisphere One half of Earth

Outback The hot, dry land in Australia

Lesson 2 ──────────────
Reef A string of rock, sand, or coral close to the surface of a body of water

Magma Hot liquid rock

Lesson 3 ──────────────
Boomerang A wooden weapon curved so that it returns to the person throwing it

Dreamtime The native Australian Aborigines' belief about how they came to be

Objectives

◆ To know where
Australia and
New Zealand
are located

◆ To describe how
geography shaped
the history of
Australia and
New Zealand

Hemisphere

One half of Earth

Outback

The hot, dry land
in Australia

Remember, a
meridian is an
imaginary line that
circles Earth and runs
through the North
and South Poles.

Reading Strategy:
Predicting

Can you look at the
map on page 549
and predict what
regions exist?

Where Are Australia and New Zealand?

Australia and New Zealand are in the Southern **Hemisphere**.
A hemisphere is one half of Earth. Geographers divide Earth
into northern and southern hemispheres at the equator. The
continent of Australia lies between the latitudes of 11 degrees
south and 40 degrees south. New Zealand is about 1,000 miles
southeast of Australia. Most of it lies between latitudes 35 and
47 degrees south.

Geographers also divide Earth into the eastern and western
hemispheres. The prime meridian and the international date
line divide these hemispheres. Australia and New Zealand are
in the Eastern Hemisphere.

Australia extends both north and south of the Tropic of
Capricorn. The Coral Sea and Pacific Ocean are to the east;
the Arafura Sea and the Timor Sea are to the north; the Indian
Ocean is to the west and south; and the Tasman Sea is to the
southeast.

What Regions Exist?

Australia has three regions—the Western Plateau, the Eastern
Highlands, and the Central Lowlands. The Western Plateau
covers the western two-thirds of Australia. It is a huge, dry area
with few trees. The middle of the plateau is desert. The desert
area has sand and sand dunes. The areas that are not desert are
used to raise livestock. The region's biggest cities are Adelaide
and Perth. Both cities are on a coast. On the southern edge
of the Western Plateau lies the flat Nullarbor Plain. Nullarbor
means *no trees*. The plain is desert with few plants.

Australia's second major region is the Central Lowlands. This
is also a very flat region. In the south, people grow wheat, but
most of the land is not suited for farming. Central Australia,
including parts of the Western Plateau and the Central
Lowlands, is a hot, dry area called the **outback**.

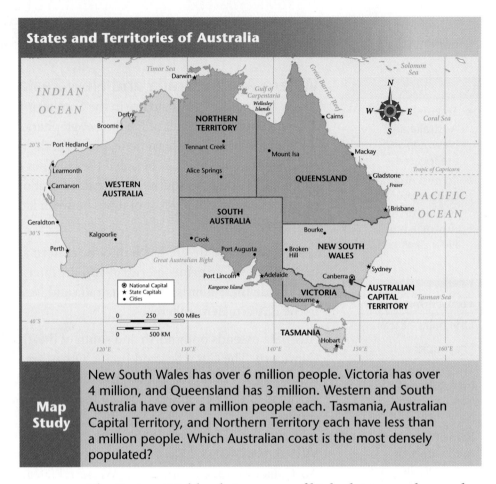

States and Territories of Australia

INDIAN OCEAN

Timor Sea

Darwin ★

Gulf of Carpentaria

Wellesley Islands

Solomon Sea

Derby ●

Broome ●

NORTHERN TERRITORY

Cairns ●

Coral Sea

20°S — Port Hedland ●

Tennant Creek ●

Mount Isa ●

Mackay ●

Learmonth ●

Alice Springs ●

Tropic of Capricorn

Carnarvon ●

WESTERN AUSTRALIA

QUEENSLAND

Gladstone ●

Fraser ●

PACIFIC OCEAN

Geraldton ●

30°S

Kalgoorlie ●

SOUTH AUSTRALIA

Brisbane ★ ●

Perth ★

● Cook

Bourke ●

Port Augusta ●

● Broken Hill

NEW SOUTH WALES

Great Australian Bight

Port Lincoln ●

Adelaide ★

Canberra ⊕

Sydney ★

⊕ National Capital
★ State Capitals
● Cities

Kangaroo Island

VICTORIA

Melbourne ★

AUSTRALIAN CAPITAL TERRITORY

Tasman Sea

0   250   500 Miles

0   500 KM

TASMANIA

Hobart ★

40°S

120°E   130°E   140°E   150°E   160°E

Map Study
New South Wales has over 6 million people. Victoria has over 4 million, and Queensland has 3 million. Western and South Australia have over a million people each. Tasmania, Australian Capital Territory, and Northern Territory each have less than a million people. Which Australian coast is the most densely populated?

The Eastern Highlands is an area of high plateaus and rugged hills. Most of it is covered with grasses or forest. The Great Dividing Range separates this region from the Central Lowlands. The mountains cause a lot of rain to fall on the east side of the mountains. The mountains block rain from reaching the interior of Australia. Most Australians live in the southern part of this region. Most of Australia's largest cities are located there.

New Zealand is very different from Australia. Unlike Australia, the entire country gets plenty of rain. New Zealand is covered with tall mountains and hills. South Island has the highest mountains. Some have glaciers. North Island is smaller, but is where most New Zealanders live. Most of North Island has rolling hills and plains. There are active volcanoes and a volcanic plateau.

People can raise cattle in the huge, dry outback of Australia.

Reading Strategy:
Predicting

What have you read so far that would help you predict how geography shaped history in Australia or New Zealand?

How Did Geography Shape History?

Australia and New Zealand are far from other parts of the world. Sydney is Australia's largest city. From Sydney to Tokyo, Japan, is 5,000 miles. From Sydney to Singapore is 3,900 miles; and from Sydney to Honolulu, Hawaii, is 5,100 miles. Europe and North America are even farther. In the past, few settlers wanted to make the long and hard trip to this region.

Great Britain founded Sydney in the late 1780s. They sent their prisoners to Australia. Most of Australia's first European settlers were people from Britain's jails.

Lesson 1 Review On a sheet of paper, write the word in parenthesis that makes each statement true.

1. Australia and New Zealand are in the (Northern, Southern) Hemisphere.

2. New Zealand is 1,000 miles (northwest, southeast) of Australia.

3. The (Western, Eastern) Plateau covers two-thirds of Australia.

4. The (Eastern Highlands, Western Plateau) is an area of highlands and rugged hills.

5. (Great Britain, New Zealand) founded the city of Sydney.

What do you think ❓

Why do you think most people in Australia live along the eastern coast?

- To describe the main physical features of Australia and New Zealand
- To identify the main bodies of water
- To describe the climates of the region

Reef

A string of rock, sand, or coral close to the surface of a body of water

Magma

Hot liquid rock

Uluru, or Ayers Rock, is a landmark in Australia.

What Are the Main Physical Features?

Australia is the flattest continent. Most of it is not more than 900 feet above sea level. It is one of Earth's oldest landmasses. One mountain range, the Great Dividing Range, runs along Australia's east coast. The tallest mountain is Mount Kosciuszko, which is only 7,310 feet tall. The Australian Alps rise at the south end of the range.

Near the center of Australia's outback is Uluru, or Ayers Rock. This red rock is six miles around and about 1,100 feet high. The huge sandstone rock formation contains iron oxide, which gives the rock its orange-red color.

Another physical feature of Australia is the Great Barrier Reef. A **reef** is a string of rock, sand, or coral close to the surface of a body of water. Skeletons of sea animals that have died form the islands. The Great Barrier Reef is a group of coral islands. It follows the northeastern coastline of Australia for about 1,250 miles. More than 1,000 different types of fish live among the coral of the Great Barrier Reef. Many tourists come to see it.

New Zealand has a very different geography. Its two main islands are located along the border of the Australian and Pacific tectonic plates. Because of this, New Zealand has many earthquakes and volcanoes. However, most of these volcanoes no longer erupt. Beneath the surface of these volcanoes, hot liquid rock called **magma** heats underground water. Geysers shoot hot water and steam into the air. Pools of boiling mud, geysers, and hot-water springs are found south of Lake Taupo on North Island.

Reading Strategy:
Predicting

Could you have predicted what the physical features of Australia and New Zealand were by looking at the physical map?

Writing About Geography

Imagine you are trying to interest people in traveling to Australia or New Zealand. Write an article describing the things in either Australia or New Zealand that might attract tourists.

Reading Strategy:
Predicting

Can you predict what the climates might be like from what you have read so far?

Mountains cover much of New Zealand. The main feature of South Island geography is a mountain range called the Southern Alps. Mount Cook is New Zealand's highest mountain. It is over 12,000 feet high. Glaciers wore down New Zealand's mountains and carved out valleys and fjords. Tasman Glacier is the largest glacier at 18 miles long.

What Are the Main Bodies of Water?

Australia is hot and dry with few rivers and lakes. Most of Australia's rivers flow eastward from the Great Dividing Range. Australia's biggest cities are located on the east coast along these rivers. Sydney is located on the Parramatta River. Melbourne is near the Yarra River. The Murray River is the longest river in Australia. The Darling and Murrumbigee Rivers are its two most important tributaries. The Murray-Darling system captures the rainfall off the western slopes of the Great Dividing Range and carries it inland. These waters are used for irrigation.

Australia's largest lake is Lake Eyre. It is a large salt lake in the lowest point of Australia. Lake Eyre is normally dry. It fills completely on average only twice a century. When filled, the lake takes about two years to dry up again.

New Zealand has many short, fast-moving rivers that provide hydroelectric power. The longest river is the Waikato on North Island. New Zealand also has many small lakes. A huge volcanic explosion created Lake Taupo. It is the largest in New Zealand.

What Is the Climate Like?

Australia and New Zealand are in the Southern Hemisphere. So, their seasons are opposite those of the Northern Hemisphere. The hottest summer months in Australia and New Zealand are December through February. Winter is June through August.

Australia has several climates. Northern Australia has a tropical savanna climate with high temperatures all year long. The summer months receive the most rain. Tropical cyclones may occur. The dry season is from May to October. Most of Australia has a desert climate with hot days and cool nights. The southeastern corner of Australia has a Mediterranean climate with mild, wet winters and warm, dry summers. The eastern coastal areas have a humid subtropical climate.

Sydney Opera House is a famous landmark in Sydney, Australia.

High mountains and its closeness to the sea affect New Zealand's weather. The southwest coast of South Island is one of the wettest areas in the world. This is because western winds bring wet air from the sea. Most of New Zealand has a marine West Coast climate with mild temperatures.

How Does the Environment Affect the People?

Few people live in the hot desert climate of Australia's outback. About 80 percent of Australians live along the southeastern and eastern coasts, within 100 miles of the ocean. These areas have enough rain and the mildest temperatures.

In New Zealand, most people live in areas with the mildest climate. About 75 percent of the population lives on North Island. About 80 percent of the people live in cities. Auckland, a city of over a million people, is the largest city. It is located on the east coast of North Island.

Lesson 2 Review On a sheet of paper, write the answer to each question. Use complete sentences.

1. Where is Australia's mountain range located?

2. What is the name of Australia's famous red rock?

3. What creates the Great Barrier Reef?

4. Where would tourists find geysers and pools of boiling mud?

5. What are the summer months in Australia and New Zealand?

What do you think ?

The Great Barrier Reef draws many tourists. Along with the tourists come powerboats, hotels, and other services that cause harm to the reef. What do you think is the best way to protect the Great Barrier Reef?

Objectives

◆ To describe the cultures of Australia and New Zealand
◆ To identify the main religions
◆ To understand their problems

Boomerang

A wooden weapon curved so that it returns to the person throwing it

What Cultures Are in Australia?

Before Europeans arrived, between 300,000 and a million Aborigines lived in Australia. Aborigines, or Kooris as they call themselves, were the original people of Australia. They lived by hunting and gathering. They did not settle in one place but were nomadic people. Their main weapons were a spear and a wooden **boomerang**. A boomerang is curved so that it returns to the person throwing it. The Aborigines lived in groups scattered across Australia. They spoke many languages, but had no writing. They passed along their knowledge by talking.

In 1787, the first Europeans arrived in Australia from England. Soon the Europeans took the Aborigines' land. The Europeans killed thousands of Aborigines who refused to leave their land. Many thousands died from the diseases the Europeans brought. Today, fewer than 400,000 Aborigines remain. They make up only about 2 percent of the population.

The first European settlers in Australia were prisoners from England. The prisoners had filled the jails in England, so the British decided to ship them to Australia. When their prison terms were up, the prisoners were set free and given land. The government also gave land to army officers.

Aborigines used spears and boomerangs as weapons to kill animals.

By 1850, there were almost a million Europeans in Australia. Many Australians have European ancestors. After World War II, many immigrants came to Australia from Greece and Italy.

In recent years, immigrants have come to Australia from Malaysia, Hong Kong, Singapore, Vietnam, Laos, and Cambodia. Australia has one of the highest percentages of immigrants in the world. Over 24 percent, or almost 5 million, of its people were born in another country.

Dreamtime

The native Australian
Aborigines' belief
about how they
came to be

*About 15 percent of
New Zealanders are
Maori. This man is
wearing an authentic
costume of the Maori.*

Reading Strategy:
Predicting

Now that you have
read about the
cultures, can you
predict what religions
people practice?

Many immigrants come to Australia in hopes of improving
their standard of living. Wages are higher in Australia than they
are in the countries from which the immigrants come. The
immigrant workers have helped build up Australia's labor force.

What Cultures Are in New Zealand?

The Maori are New Zealand's native people. Geographers
believe that most of the Maori arrived from Polynesia in the
1400s. They lived in small villages and fished, hunted, and grew
vegetables. They created beautiful carvings with stone tools.
Then the Europeans came and introduced diseases and guns.

The first Europeans in New Zealand were traders, whale
hunters, and missionaries. In 1840, England made New Zealand
a British colony. It promised the Maori they could keep their
land. But soon European settlers started taking Maori lands.

Today, the Maori make up about 15 percent of New Zealand's
population. Some continue to live in traditional ways. Most,
however, live in New Zealand's urban areas.

Most New Zealanders came from the British Isles. Later
immigrants came from Germany, France, Scandinavia,
southern Europe, and Australia.

New Zealand has been more willing than most other countries
to accept refugees. After World War II, a number of Europeans
came. After the Vietnam War, about 7,000 refugees settled in
the country. Since the 1980s, other Asian immigrants have
come from Hong Kong, China, Taiwan, and South Korea.

What Religions Do the People Practice?

Most Australians and New Zealanders are Christians.
However, because of Asian immigration, other religions such
as Buddhism, Hinduism, and Islam are growing.

The Aborigines practice a religion called **Dreamtime**. It is a
belief about how they came to be. The idea is that the past,
present, and future are all part of the present. Aborigines
believe that nature has powerful spirits. They also believe that
the spirits of their ancestors live in nature. Some Aborigines are
Christians, but many still follow their ancient religion.

What Languages Do the People Speak?

English is the official language of Australia. Australian English is a little different than the English spoken in other countries. Some Aboriginal words have become part of the language, as have some American-English words. Other immigrants have brought their own languages with them. The big cities have newspapers in Italian, Greek, Arabic, Chinese, and English.

New Zealand has two official languages, English and Maori. Maori, however, is only spoken by one in four Maori.

What Are the Population Trends?

Reading Strategy:
Predicting

What do you think you will learn about in this paragraph?

Since World War II, the birthrate in Australia and New Zealand has risen, and the death rate has fallen. Australia's population growth rate is one of the highest in the developed world. There are many immigrants. Australia's population has grown from about 6 million in 1930 to over 20 million in 2006.

Another trend is the movement to big cities. Fewer than 15 percent of Australians live in rural areas. Most Australians and New Zealanders live in large cities. The Auckland area is home to nearly one-third of all New Zealanders. About two-thirds of Australia's people live in the biggest cities of Sydney, Melbourne, Brisbane, Adelaide, and Perth.

What Problems Do the People Face?

Australia and New Zealand are members of the British Commonwealth of Nations. This group of nations was once part of the British Empire. Now the countries are independent but choose to work together. Both Australia and New Zealand must decide whether to remain in the Commonwealth.

A second problem in Australia and New Zealand is their treatment of the native peoples. In the past, European settlers treated these people badly. They gave them little education, medical care, or housing. Both nations have passed laws promising rights to the native people. For example, the Australian government gave the Aborigines special rights to Uluru because it is sacred to them.

Cathy Freeman: 1973–

In 1997, Cathy Freeman, an Aborigine sprinter, won the world championship for the 400-meter event. Afterward, many people cheered and clapped, but others booed because she ran around the track carrying two flags. One flag represented her Australian citizenship; the other flag represented her Aborigine background.

Freeman is the leading track star of Australia. In 1990, at 16, she won the gold medal at the Commonwealth Games. That same year she was named Young Australian of the Year. Then, in 1996, she won a silver medal at the Olympic Games in Atlanta. In 2000, she won a gold medal at the Olympic Games in Sydney, Australia.

Lesson 3 Review On a sheet of paper, write the letter of the answer that correctly completes each sentence.

1. The original people of Australia are ___C___.

   A Indians   **B** Maori   **C** Aborigines   **D** Ainu

2. The first European settlers in Australia were ___B___.

   A farmers   **C** whalers
   B prisoners   **D** missionaries

3. Most Australians and New Zealanders are ___D___.

   A Hindus   **C** Muslims
   B Buddhists   **D** Christians

What do you think ?

How do you think the small number of children living in the outback or remote areas of New Zealand get their schooling?

4. The official language of Australia is ___A___.

   A English   **C** French
   B Polynesian   **D** Japanese

5. Most Australians and New Zealanders live in ___C___.

   A rural areas   **C** large cities
   B small towns   **D** the outback

Objectives

◆ To describe the economies of Australia and New Zealand
◆ To identify their natural resources
◆ To describe the environmental challenges they face

What Is the Economy Like?

Australia and New Zealand have well-developed economies. Their people enjoy a high standard of living. The largest number of people in both Australia and New Zealand work in service industries. They are the fastest growing part of the economy. Service industries include construction, trade, banking, communications, education, business services, and tourism. Tourism is the fastest growing and largest part of the service industry.

Originally, agriculture was a big part of the economy. Farming is less important in both Australia and New Zealand now.

New Zealand is slowly making the change from farming to industry. About 15 percent of New Zealanders work in manufacturing. In Australia, the percentage is a little higher. Most manufacturing companies are small. They are located around the major cities.

Tourism is important to the economies of both Australia and New Zealand. Tourists come because of the good weather and the beautiful scenery. Tourism adds billions of dollars per year to the economy. Nearly a half million people work in tourism. Many people work in hotels and restaurants. Local artists earn a living by selling their work to tourists.

How Does Trade Affect the Economy?

Reading Strategy: Predicting

How do you think Australia's location would affect its economy?

Both Australia and New Zealand have large export markets. Because their populations are small, trade with other countries is important. New Zealand is the world's largest exporter of lamb and mutton, the meat of full-grown sheep. New Zealand is the third largest exporter of wool, which comes from a sheep's fur. It also is an important fruit producer. It ships apples and its native kiwi fruit around the world. Dairy products like butter and cheese, fish, shrimp, and wood and wood products are also important exports.

Reading Strategy:
Predicting

Was your prediction about the economy of Australia correct, or do you need to change it?

Australia exports both agricultural and mineral resources. Its main agricultural exports are wheat, barley, beef, and mutton. Its mineral exports include coal, gold, bauxite, iron ore, natural gas, and uranium. Japan and China are Australia's main trade partners. Coal and iron ore make up two-thirds of Australia's exports to China.

Australia and New Zealand have close economic ties. There is free trade between the two countries.

What Natural Resources Exist?

Australia has many natural resources, including coal, bauxite, iron ore, natural gas, and oil. It also has rich deposits of lead, zinc, copper, nickel, and silver. Australia produces gemstones, such as diamonds, sapphires, and pearls. It mines 60 percent of the world's natural opals, used in jewelry.

New Zealand's mineral resources include natural gas, iron ore, and coal. However, other natural resources are more important. Its coastal waters provide seafood. Its fast-flowing rivers provide two-thirds of New Zealand's electricity.

What Are Some Major Industries?

Both Australia and New Zealand raise many sheep for food and wool. However, modern fibers have forced down the price of wool, so it is now of less importance to the economy. Australians raise cattle on the hot, dry grasslands of the outback. Food processing and wood and paper products are the leading manufacturing industries of New Zealand.

Australia has a wide range of industries. Mining is probably the biggest industry and the most important part of the economy. Manufacturing industries include chemicals, electronics, food processing, clothing, and wine. Construction of cars and ships, oil refining, paper products, and steel products are others.

Tourism is important to both countries. People come to see animals and birds that are found only in these countries. Kangaroos, koalas, platypuses, and wallabies exist only there. There are beautiful beaches for surfing and swimming. The mountains offer beautiful scenery and skiing.

What Environmental Problems Exist?

Australia has many plants and animals that do not exist anywhere else. Protecting them is a problem. Some Australians want to kill kangaroos because they think there are too many of them. People also cut down the trees koalas eat. Then the koalas don't have enough food.

Another problem is animals that Europeans brought to Australia. Australia had no cats, rabbits, or foxes. But Europeans brought these animals to Australia. Cats and foxes hunt and kill the native Australian animals and birds. Rabbits eat anything that grows and destroy pastures and native plants. This causes soil erosion.

Australian land cannot support all the animals that graze on it. The animals eat the plants down to the roots, and the plants die. Then the land becomes a desert. Brush fires are a natural hazard. Lightning causes most of the fires. It also has the problem of irrigation and fertilizers building up salt in the soil.

Because New Zealand gets plenty of rain, it can support more animals. It does not have the brush fires that Australia has.

A concern to both Australia and New Zealand is global warming and climate change. Australia has had years of drought. It is running out of water for irrigation and for animals. In New Zealand, the rising ocean temperature threatens its fisheries.

Koalas eat eucalyptus leaves. When people cut the trees down, koalas do not have enough food to eat.

Geography in Your Life

Park Ranger

Australia has about 500 national parks that cover over 100,000 square miles. Two of the most famous are Great Barrier Reef Marine Park and Kakadu National Park. Kakadu contains prehistoric cave paintings. These provide evidence of human life in Australia some 50,000 years ago.

Park rangers must protect these parks. Rangers also protect people. They may rescue a lost camper or help a rock climber get back to solid ground. They may chase away a wild animal that comes too close to campers. Rangers must know first aid to help injured campers. They must also work to prevent forest fires.

Park rangers are skilled campers themselves. They help campers understand the relationship between plants, animals, and the environment. They teach people to respect this environment.

Word Bank

China 3

European 5

mutton 2

opals 4

service 1

Lesson 4 Review On a sheet of paper, use the words from the Word Bank to complete each sentence correctly.

1. The largest number of people in both Australia and New Zealand work in _____ industries.

2. New Zealand is the world's largest exporter of lamb and _____.

3. Australia's biggest trade partners are Japan and _____.

4. Australia produces gemstones such as _____.

5. _____ settlers brought animals to Australia that killed native animals.

What do you think ?

What is good and what is bad about tourism in Australia and New Zealand?

Geography in Today's World

Protecting the Coral Reefs

The Great Barrier Reef may be over 5 million years old. In the past few decades, though, people have put it in great danger.

Fishing, tourism, and mining put the reef at risk. One type of fishing, bottom trawling, scrapes the life off the bottom of the ocean. Tourism, with its fast boats and pollution, is another problem. In the 1960s, people wanted to drill for oil near the reef. This was one reason why Australians first decided to guard this unique place.

In 1981, the United Nations added the Great Barrier Reef to its World Heritage List. Australia is working to protect the reef. It has banned mining and spear fishing with scuba gear. It has banned people from some areas of the reef. Australia has good reasons to protect the reef. It is protecting an $8 billion-a-year tourist industry. It is also preserving a world treasure.

Wrap-Up

1. Why is the Great Barrier Reef more in danger now than before?

2. Do you think that people are the biggest threat to the reef? Why or why not?

Make a Difference

There are places worth protecting near where you live. Find out from a local conservation group or on the Internet what natural areas are in danger. Choose one of these areas to help protect. Then ask what you can do to make a difference.

Learning the Lingo

My name is Jack. I am 16 years old, and I live in New Zealand. My cousin from the United States is coming for a visit. I haven't seen him in yonks. Yonks—that's our way of saying a long time. My Mum says I should e-mail and tell him some things about New Zealand before he gets here. She says he'd be dead chuffed—er, pleased—to know some of our lingo before he gets here. Here goes!

Dear Cuz,

Here are some talking tips for your trip!

If you're hungry, you can always find tinned goods in the cupboard. You can make yourself a sarnie, what you Americans call a sandwich. Or order take-away, what you would call take out.

If someone tells you he is brassed off at you, he's disappointed. If someone tells you he'll have your guts for garters, that means you're in big trouble. If someone says bugger off, she's telling you to get lost. But if she says she's buggered, she's just exhausted. Big difference, there.

If someone asks you to bust a gut, give it your best effort. Otherwise, he'll call you a piker for giving up too easily.

If someone tells you the food is dodgy, don't eat it. It's probably spoiled. Oh, and stand back if someone says she's about to chunder because she's going to vomit!

The footpath is the sidewalk, not a path in the woods. But if someone tells you to get off the grass, they think you're pulling their leg.

If you fancy a girl, don't tell her she's quite nice. Here, that's what you say when you can't think of anything better! If a girl says she'd like you to give her a ring, don't panic. That just means she wants you to call her, not marry her!

If my Mum says we have to stay home one day, it's probably because the rellies are coming over. Rellies are relatives or family members.

For the beach, pack your jandals, what you Americans call flip-flops. Bring a jersey (sweater) for cool nights. And whatever you do, don't forget your knickers—underpants!

I think that's enough for now, Mate. You'll have to suss out the rest when you get here!

Cheerio! Jack

Wrap-Up

1. What is the word for "a long time"?

2. If the food is dodgy, would you want to eat it? Why or why not?

Chapter 24 SUMMARY

- Australia and New Zealand are located in the Southern Hemisphere. The continent of Australia is a huge island. New Zealand has two large islands and many small ones. Australia is divided into three regions—the Western Plateau, the Eastern Highlands, and the Central Lowlands.

- Australia is flat and low. One mountain range, the Great Dividing Range, runs along Australia's east coast. New Zealand has mountains and hills.

- The most important physical features of Australia are its Western Plateau, Uluru or Ayers Rock, and the Great Barrier Reef. Earthquakes, geysers, and mountains are important features of New Zealand.

- Australia is hot and dry with few rivers and lakes. Most of Australia's rivers flow eastward from the Great Dividing Range. Australia's biggest cities are located on the east coast along these rivers. New Zealand's fast-moving rivers provide hydroelectric power.

- Australia has several climates: tropical savanna in the north, desert in the outback, Mediterranean in the southeast, and humid subtropical in the eastern coastal areas. Most of New Zealand has a marine West Coast climate with mild temperatures.

- The original people of Australia are the Aborigines. The original people of New Zealand are the Maori. When Europeans arrived, many of the native people lost their land.

- The main language of Australia is English. New Zealand has two official languages, English and Maori.

- Most Australians and New Zealanders are Christians. The native people practice their own religion.

- Australia and New Zealand have well-developed economies. Their people enjoy a high standard of living. The largest numbers of people work in service industries. Tourism is important to the economies of both Australia and New Zealand. Tourists come to enjoy animals, beautiful scenery, and pleasant weather.

- The main environmental problems are protecting the unique animals who live there, stopping deforestation and soil erosion, and protecting the environment from tourism.

Chapter 24 REVIEW

Word Bank

Ayers Rock 2

desert 1

Dividing 4

flat 3

geysers 5

On a sheet of paper, use the words from the Word Bank to complete each sentence correctly.

1. Few people live in Australia's outback because of its _____ climate.

2. The large red rock formation in Australia is called Uluru, or _____.

3. New Zealand is mountainous, but most of Australia is _____.

4. Most of Australia's rivers flow eastward from the Great _____ Range.

5. Magma causes _____ to shoot hot water and steam into the air.

On a sheet of paper, write the letter of the answer that correctly completes each sentence.

6. Australia and New Zealand are located in the __B__ Hemisphere.

   A Northern   **C** Western
   B Southern   **D** Arctic

7. A large __c__ covers more than two-thirds of Australia.

   A forest   **C** plateau
   B rock   **D** glacier

8. Sydney and Melbourne are among the largest cities of __A__.

   A Australia   **C** New Zealand
   B Hawaii   **D** Fiji

9. The Aborigines and the Maori are the __C__ of Australia and New Zealand.

   A immigrants   **C** native peoples
   B prisoners   **D** physical features

10. Both Australia and New Zealand have large _____B_____ markets.

   A import   **C** zoo

   B export   **D** agriculture

On a sheet of paper, write the answer to each question. Use complete sentences.

11. What are the main physical features of Australia?

12. What are the main physical features of New Zealand?

13. What are the chief natural resources of Australia and New Zealand?

Critical Thinking On a sheet of paper, write your response to each question. Use complete sentences.

14. How are Australians similar to or different from people living in the United States? Explain your answer.

15. Why are Australia and New Zealand more dependent on foreign trade than countries like the United States, China, and India?

Applying the Five Themes of Geography

Location

Why is the location of Australia and New Zealand important to their history?

Test-Taking Tip

If you are asked to compare and contrast things, be sure to tell how they are alike (compare) and how they are different (contrast).

Pacific Islands and Antarctica

People live on about 800 of the more than 20,000 Pacific Islands. Some are independent island nations. Some are territories of other countries. All are near the equator, and they enjoy warm climates.

Antarctica is a continent covered with ice. Most of the people who live there are scientists who study Earth.

Goals for Learning

◆ To describe where the Pacific Islands and Antarctica are located, their physical features, and climates

◆ To describe the cultures, people, economies, and environments

Geo-Stats Key Pacific Islands

Nation: Papua New Guinea
Population: 5,670,000
Area: 178,704 square miles
Capital: Port Moresby

Nation: Solomon Islands
Population: 552,200
Area: 10,985 square miles
Capital: Honiara

Nation: Fiji
Population: 906,000
Area: 7,054 square miles
Capital: Suva

Nation: Federated States of Micronesia
Population: 108,000
Area: 271 square miles
Capital: Palikir

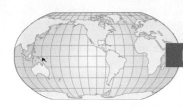

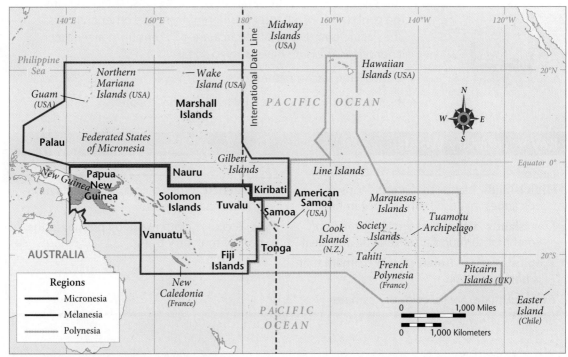

Map Skills

The Pacific Islands cover a large part of the Pacific World. The islands are usually divided into three regions: Micronesia, Melanesia, and Polynesia. There are also some islands outside these regions. The Pacific Islands include almost 800 islands on which people can live. All of the islands are near the equator.

Study the map and answer the following questions:

1. In what region on the map is Papua New Guinea located?

2. What United States state is in the Polynesia region?

3. Near what line of longitude is the international date line?

4. What island nation is closest to Australia?

5. After looking at the map, what do you think the cultures of the islands may be like?

Reading Strategy:
Text Structure

When you preview this chapter, you may notice it is different from other chapters in this book. Most chapters have had four lessons. This chapter is different; it has only two lessons. That is because the content of the chapter is different from the other chapters. The Pacific Islands and Antarctica are different from any other landmasses that you have studied so far.

◆ Read the lesson names.

◆ Read the Reading Strategy notes in this chapter.

Key Vocabulary Words

Lesson 1 —————————————————

High islands Islands that are the tops of volcanoes that rise from the ocean floor

Low islands Islands that are atolls made of coral that surround a sunken volcanic peak

Tropical marine climate A rainy climate that is hot year-round

Arctic climate A very cold, dry climate

Lesson 2 —————————————————

Trade deficit When a country imports more goods than it exports

Tapa A coarse cloth made by pounding the bark of mulberry trees

---

Reading Strategy:
Text Structure

Notice how each of the three Pacific Island regions has its own paragraph.

Where Are the Pacific Islands?

The Pacific Ocean covers nearly one-third of the surface of Earth. It contains thousands of islands. Geographers sometimes call the region Oceania because the Pacific Islands are scattered throughout the Pacific Ocean.

The Pacific Islands have three regions. Melanesia is a region that is south of the equator, and north and northeast of Australia. It stretches from Papua New Guinea to the international date line. The Melanesian islands include Papua New Guinea, the Solomon Islands, Vanuatu, New Caledonia, and the islands of Tuvalu and Fiji.

Micronesia means *little islands.* It lies in the Pacific, north of the equator between Hawaii and the Philippine Islands. It is north of Melanesia and east of the Philippine Islands. The water area of Micronesia is as large as the United States. However, its land area is smaller than the state of Rhode Island. The islands of Micronesia include the Federated States of Micronesia, Palau, Kiribati, the Northern Mariana Islands, Guam, the Marshall Islands, and Nauru.

Polynesia is east of Micronesia and Melanesia. Its islands include American Samoa, the Cook Islands, French Polynesia, the Pitcairn Islands, Samoa, Tonga, and Tahiti. The state of Hawaii is part of the United States and in Polynesia.

Some Polynesian islands have great land for growing crops.

Where Is Antarctica?

Antarctica is the southernmost continent on Earth. It includes the South Pole, which is the most southern point on Earth. It is surrounded by oceans and seas. It is divided by the Transantarctic Mountains. Antarctica is the coldest, driest, and windiest continent. Ice covers 98 percent of it. Antarctica receives almost no rain or snow, so it is sometimes called the world's largest desert. Most people who live in Antarctica are scientists who live there for short periods of time.

How Were the Pacific Islands Formed?

There are two types of islands in the Pacific. **High islands** are the tops of huge underground volcanoes that rise from the ocean floor. High islands receive lots of rain. They have rich soil, which is good for farming. Many high islands are covered with forests. Many have fresh water. As an example, the Hawaiian Islands are high islands.

Ice covers 98 percent of Antarctica. It is the coldest, driest continent on Earth.

Low islands are atolls made of coral. These low coral islands surround a sunken volcanic peak. They are often circle-shaped with a shallow pond in the center. They are usually only 10 or 20 feet above sea level. They have few trees. Because low islands have no mountains, they have no streams or rivers. Fresh water is limited. They can only support a small number of people.

How Did the Geography Shape History?

Oceania is far from most places in the world. It is a huge area, but the areas where people can live are very limited. Many of the cultures developed with little contact from other people. But in December of 1941, the Japanese forces attacked Pearl Harbor in Hawaii. This brought World War II into the Pacific. Japan started to take control of the Pacific Islands.

Japan took over much of the Pacific, and threatened Australia. But in June of 1942, the United States and its allies stopped Japan. After the Battle of Midway, Japan no longer controlled the Pacific.

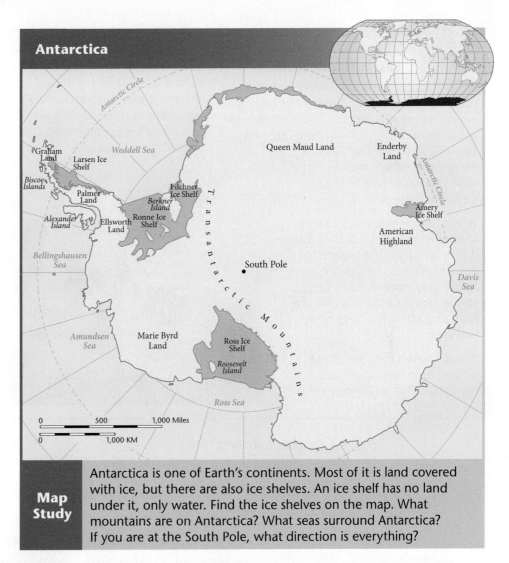

Antarctica

Antarctic Circle

Weddell Sea

Graham Land
Larsen Ice Shelf
Biscoe Islands
Palmer Land
Filchner Ice Shelf
Berkner Island
Alexander Island
Ronne Ice Shelf
Ellsworth Land

Queen Maud Land

Enderby Land

Amery Ice Shelf

American Highland

T r a n s a n t a r c t i c   M o u n t a i n s

South Pole

Bellingshausen Sea

Davis Sea

Amundsen Sea

Marie Byrd Land

Ross Ice Shelf

Roosevelt Island

Antarctic Circle

Ross Sea

0   500   1,000 Miles
0   1,000 KM

Map Study

Antarctica is one of Earth's continents. Most of it is land covered with ice, but there are also ice shelves. An ice shelf has no land under it, only water. Find the ice shelves on the map. What mountains are on Antarctica? What seas surround Antarctica? If you are at the South Pole, what direction is everything?

Tropical marine climate

A rainy climate that is hot year-round

Arctic climate

A very cold, dry climate

What Are the Climates of This Region Like?

The Pacific Islands have a **tropical marine climate**. The weather is hot most of the year. There is little difference between the highest temperature of the year and the lowest. There are only two seasons. One is rainy; the other is rainier.

Antarctica has an **arctic climate**. It is the coldest place on Earth. It is a frozen desert with little precipitation. The coldest temperature ever recorded on Earth was -128°F at the South Pole. The summer temperature along the coast might be about 50°F. The mountain areas of Antarctica are the coldest.

Geography in Your Life

Easter Island Statues

Easter Island is a volcanic island in the south Pacific. It is over 2,000 miles from the nearest population center. That makes it one of the most isolated places on Earth. Few people live on it today. Admiral Roggeveen, who came upon the island on Easter Day in 1722, named it Easter Island.

When Roggeveen and his crew arrived at Easter Island, they found a stunning sight. All around the edge of the volcanic island stand huge, gray stone statues. Each statue looks like the top half of a human. Each statue is 15 to 40 feet high.

People carved the statues out of the stone from a volcanic mountain. But, this mountain is in the middle of the island. No one is certain how the statues were moved down from the mountain. Each statue is a single stone weighing as much as 50 tons. The statues on the island's edge may mark burial places and probably had a religious purpose.

Lesson 1 Review On a sheet of paper, write the word in parenthesis that makes each statement true.

1. The Pacific Ocean covers nearly (one-half, one-third) of the surface of Earth.

2. Papua New Guinea, the largest of the Pacific Island countries, is part of (Polynesia, Melanesia).

3. (Volcanic, Coral) islands are high, and have lots of fresh water and rich soil.

4. (Polynesia, Antarctica) is the coldest, driest, and windiest continent.

5. (Few, Many) people live on the Pacific Islands.

What do you think ?

How do you think global warming will affect the people of Oceania?

Objectives

◆ To describe the cultures, religions, and languages of Oceania

◆ To describe the economy, environment, and the problems the people face

What Cultures Are in Oceania?

The original people of Melanesia are likely to be the ancestors of the people who live there now. These people are Papuans. They came from New Guinea where they lived for thousands of years. The Papuans were among the first people to develop a system of farming. Another group of people came from Southeast Asia about 3,500 years ago. On most Melanesian islands, people live in small villages. Since they live in traditional ways, they have little contact with outsiders.

People from Southeast Asia settled Micronesia more than 3,000 years ago. Micronesia's people are very diverse. They have many different cultures and languages. There are about 20 different languages spoken in Micronesia.

The first Polynesians lived in Tonga and Samoa. They were excellent sailors. They sailed to many other islands.

Reading Strategy:
Text Structure

Use the map at the beginning of the chapter to help you understand this paragraph.

As you can see from the map on page 571, other nations own or control many of the Pacific Islands. Guam, the Northern Mariana Islands, American Samoa, the Midway Islands, and Wake Island are colonies or territories of the United States. France or the United Kingdom control many other islands.

What Religions Do the People Practice?

The diverse people of the Pacific Islands had their own native religions. In the late 1600s, Christian missionaries arrived. They introduced Christianity to Oceania. In the 1900s, Christianity became popular in the region. Today, churches are often the center of village life. Protestant churches are especially common. But in recent years, there has been growing interest in traditional religions. Other world religions are present in very small numbers.

Trade deficit

When a country imports more goods than they export

What Languages Do the People Speak?

It is not surprising that in an area as large as Oceania, people speak many different languages. Although the region is home to only 0.1 percent of the world's population, Oceania contains one-third of the world's languages. Papua New Guinea may have as many as 1,000 different languages. Many of the languages belong to a group called Papuan languages. The languages of the Pacific Islands are closely related to one another. Some of the languages of the region have as few as several hundred or several thousand speakers.

On the larger islands, European languages are common. For example, some islands that share the French colonial history speak French. People speak English on Guam, American Samoa, the Pitcairn Islands, and the Northern Mariana Islands. These and other islands are either part of the United States or controlled by Great Britain, Australia, or New Zealand. Hawaii is part of the United States, and the people speak English. Some Hawaiians speak both English and Japanese.

Reading Strategy:
Text Structure

Notice that the words *trade deficit* are bold in the paragraph about problems. This means the definition is above, and in the paragraph itself.

What Problems Do the People Face?

One of the problems facing the islands is population growth. Land is very scarce and can only support a limited number of people. Yet, the population is growing fast. This tropical paradise may soon have great problems. There may be more people than the land can support. Many people are unemployed and poor.

Another problem is a **trade deficit**. This means that countries import more than they export. The islanders want many of the same things that people everywhere want. Televisions, bicycles, computers, and music players have to be imported. Even food is imported. This adds to the trade deficit. Importing food has led to less traditional subsistence farming.

Maintaining traditional cultures is another problem. Outside people influence the islanders. Computers and television expose them to new ideas that are not traditional beliefs and cultures.

Reading Strategy:
Text Structure

You can tell from the question what this paragraph will be about.

Who Lives on Antarctica?

Antarctica is land covered by an ice sheet that is about a mile thick. It is cold, icy, and empty. About 45 countries in the world claim land on Antarctica. These countries agree that they will use the land for scientific purposes only. Almost everyone who lives in Antarctica is a scientist.

One of the places where scientists live is the Amundsen-Scott South Pole Station. It is named after Robert F. Scott and Roald Amundsen. They were the first two explorers to reach the South Pole in 1911–1912. Antarctica's cold, clear air, its high altitude, and its six months of darkness allow scientists to do research there that they could do nowhere else.

Scientists at the station do many kinds of research. They have discovered that Antarctica has the cleanest air in the world. This clear air allows them to use powerful telescopes. With these, they detect heat that cannot get through the atmosphere anywhere else on Earth. Using technology, scientists track changes in carbon dioxide. They release balloons into the air above Antarctica. The instruments in the balloons measure the amount of ozone there. They are doing research on global warming at one of the coldest places on Earth.

Scientists on Antarctica release balloons to measure ozone in the atmosphere.

This is an example of a decorated tapa cloth. Tapa cloth is made from the bark of mulberry trees.

What Is the Economy Like?

The economy of most of the Pacific Islands is based on tourism. Tourists come because of the tropical climate, sandy beaches, beautiful scenery, and the relaxed way of life. Many people come to the islands to swim and to explore the coral reefs from under water. Tourism provides many service jobs.

Local artists earn a living by selling their work to tourists. Artists in Oceania make beautifully decorated masks. They also weave baskets and make carvings out of wood. Another traditional art is the painting of **tapa** cloth. People make this cloth from the bark of mulberry trees. The bark is soaked in water and pounded to make a thin sheet. Then, one or more artists draw designs on the cloth.

Agriculture is the basis of many of the economies of smaller Pacific Islands. The commercial crops grown are coconuts, coffee, sugarcane, cassavas, fruits, and vegetables. Coconuts are especially important. Coconut oil is used in cooking oil, soap, suntan lotion, brake fluid, and many other products.

On some of the larger islands such as Hawaii, pineapples, bananas, cacao, sugarcane, ginger, and vanilla are cash crops. Fewer people make their living by farming. In some cases, people have lost their jobs to machines and cheaper foreign competition. Land that used to be farmland now has hotels, golf courses, and other tourist attractions.

Fishing is a key industry. Some islanders fish mainly as a way to feed their families. However, some work for large commercial fish traders. Islanders sell live fish to people in China.

What Natural Resources Exist?

Some volcanic islands have minerals. Coral islands are made of coral, so they have no mineral resources. Papua New Guinea has deposits of gold, copper, oil, and natural gas. New Caledonia has nickel, chrome, iron, manganese, cobalt, gold, and silver. Phosphate, a chemical used in fertilizer, is found in Nauru. Except for Papua New Guinea, trade in mineral resources is limited because of the great distance between these islands and foreign markets.

Do you think the
people of Oceania
would be better off
if they formed one
unified country? Why
or why not? Write a
paragraph explaining
your opinion.

What Environmental Problems Exist?

The biggest environmental problem facing Oceania is protecting the fragile coral reefs. One of the threats to the coral is from sunken ships. During World War II, over 3,000 ships sank in this region. Tourists like to dive among the wrecks. However, many of these ships are rusting and starting to leak oil. The oil not only threatens the coral, but also the huge tourist industry. Tourists won't come to fish or swim at beaches that are ruined by oil.

Some fishing also threatens the coral. The reefs are places where fish go to lay eggs or to give birth. Some fishers use explosives near the coral. The explosions stun the fish and make them easier to catch. Fishers catch adult fish before they lay eggs or give birth. The explosives also damage the reefs.

Antarctica is also threatened. Some scientists who lived there were careless about getting rid of trash and sewage. People either burned or threw garbage into the oceans. Some bases are now using wind to generate electricity. However, Antarctica has strong winds that often damage the windmills. Then there are useless windmills around. There are also tourists visiting, which can affect the environment. So, areas have been set up where no vehicles or tourists can go. Many of the people who serve as guides are becoming better educated about the environment and how to protect it.

Lesson 2 Review On a sheet of paper, write the answer to each question. Use complete sentences.

1. Who were the Papuans and where did they come from?
2. Why do people speak so many different languages in Oceania?
3. Who lives in Antarctica?
4. What is the economy of the islands based on?
5. What two things threaten the coral reefs?

What do
you think

What is good and
what is bad about
tourism in the Pacific
Islands?

Island Eating

My name is Kaula, and I am 14 years old. I live on the island of Tahiti. One of my favorite things is my family's Sunday meal. On Sundays my mother cooks in the traditional way, using a large outdoor pit oven.

A pit oven is not your ordinary oven but a hole in the ground. Ours has been in the backyard as long as I can remember. First, we use fire to heat rocks in the hole. Then we wrap the food in banana leaves and place it on the hot stones. We cover everything with dirt to keep in the heat. Food usually takes 3 to 4 hours to cook.

My favorite Sunday meal is chicken with coconut milk and *fafa*, a type of spinach. I also like raw fish soaked in lime juice. My mother serves this in a salad. Sweet potatoes are always part of our meal. For dessert, we often have papaya puree, or mashed papayas. Papaya is a fruit that grows in tropical climates like ours. My mother covers the papayas with sugar and coconut milk, bakes them, and serves them warm. Delicious!

We never use a table on Sundays. Instead, we lay the food out in baskets and bowls on a carpet of banana leaves.

My mother likes to invite friends and family to our Sunday meals. When she does, my job is to decorate with flowers. They are everywhere in Tahiti, so my task is not too difficult. I find gardenias, hibiscus, and *tiares*, a type of gardenia that is our national flower. I arrange the flowers into bouquets, which I place all around, inside and outside. Mother ties banana leaves and coconut tree leaves around the balcony.

When we have guests, my mother wears one of her beautiful hand-made dresses. They are brightly colored floral-print garments. She never lets us eat until our guests are finished. In this way, she makes sure they have been well fed. Once a plate is empty, she rushes to refill it. Our friends now know to leave a little on their plate when they are finished.

The rest of the week seems dull compared to Sunday. Too bad today is only Tuesday!

Wrap-Up

1. How do Tahitians use pit ovens?

2. What is the Tahitian national flower?

- The Pacific Islands and Antarctica cover the largest part of the Pacific World. The Pacific Ocean covers nearly one-third of the surface of Earth. It contains thousands of islands. Geographers sometimes call the region Oceania because the Pacific Islands are scattered throughout the Pacific Ocean.

- Geographers divide the area into four regions: Micronesia, Melanesia, Polynesia, and Antarctica. Antarctica is the southernmost continent on Earth. It includes the South Pole, the most southern point on Earth.

- There are two types of islands in the Pacific. High islands are the tops of huge underground volcanoes. Low islands are atolls made of coral.

- Oceania has a tropical marine climate. Antarctica is an arctic desert.

- The original people of Melanesia most likely came from New Guinea. They were called Papuans. People from Southeast Asia settled in Micronesia more than 3,000 years ago. Some islands are colonies of European countries or controlled by the United States.

- Most of the people of Oceania are Christians, although some still practice native religions.

- Oceania contains one-third of the world's languages. Many are native languages, but some people also speak English and French.

- The three major problems the people of the region face are population growth, a trade deficit, and maintaining traditional culture.

- The economy of most of the Pacific Islands is based on tourism. Many of the economies of smaller Pacific islands are based on agriculture. The commercial crops grown are coconuts, coffee, sugarcane, cassavas, and other fruits and vegetables. Fishing is a key industry.

- Only volcanic islands have mineral resources. Papua New Guinea has the most mineral resources in the region.

- The biggest environmental problem facing Oceania is protecting the fragile coral reefs.

Chapter 25 REVIEW

Word Bank

Antarctica

high islands

low islands

thousands

tropical

On a sheet of paper, use the words from the Word Bank to complete each sentence correctly.

1. The Pacific Ocean contains _____ of islands.

2. The southernmost continent is _____.

3. Islands that are the tops of underwater volcanoes are _____.

4. Islands that are atolls made of coral that surround sunken volcanic peaks are _____.

5. Oceania has a _____ marine climate.

On a sheet of paper, write the letter of the answer that correctly completes each sentence.

6. Oceania is located mostly in the _____ Hemisphere.

  A Northern   **C** Western

  B Southern   **D** Arctic

7. The population of Oceania is _____.

  A growing   **C** staying the same

  B shrinking   **D** changing

8. _____ is the coldest, driest, and windiest continent.

  A Micronesia   **C** Polynesia

  B Melanesia   **D** Antarctica

9. Most people living in Antarctica are _____.

  A Aleuts   **C** fishers

  B Polynesians   **D** scientists

10. Minerals can be found on _____.

  A all islands   **C** volcanic islands

  B coral islands   **D** low islands

On a sheet of paper, write the answer to each question. Use complete sentences.

11. What are the main physical features of the Pacific Islands?

12. What is the climate of Oceania?

13. What is the main activity on Antarctica?

Critical Thinking On a sheet of paper, write your response to each question. Use complete sentences.

14. If oil is found in the waters near Antarctica, should drilling be allowed? Explain your answer.

15. How would you protect the coral reefs? How would that affect the people who live there?

Applying the Five Themes of Geography

Location

How does the location of Antarctica affect what happens there?

Test-Taking Tip

When you reread a written answer, imagine that you are someone reading it for the first time. Ask yourself if the ideas and information make sense. Revise your answer to make it clearer and more organized.

Viewing Aerial Photographs

Have you ever looked down on Earth from an airplane? Have you ever seen pictures of the land taken from high above? If so, you probably gained a better understanding of the area's geography after seeing things from above. Geographers use photos from airplanes or outer space to study an area's physical geography. They call these aerial photographs. These photographs tell many things about the land, the people, and patterns around the world.

Just what can be seen from above? Geographers can study such things as vegetation, population, land use, weather, and other important details. Colors can show how land is divided. An aerial photograph taken at night can show population patterns by pointing out where human-made lights appear. Two aerial photographs of the same place taken years apart can show how land has changed over time. Aerial photographs are taken from high up. Because of this, geographers can study many things that would not have been clear from on land.

The aerial photo on this page shows the Swan River in Australia. The Swan River is in western Australia and flows through the city of Perth. The land looks different in this photo from how you would see it if you stood on Earth. This way of looking at Earth can answer many questions about the geography of our planet.

Wrap-Up

1. What does the aerial photograph on this page tell you about the Swan River in Australia?

2. How might this aerial photograph help geographers?

3. Why are aerial photographs helpful?

4. What things can geographers discover from aerial photographs?

5. What would you want to learn about Earth from an aerial photograph?

- The Pacific World is located in the Southern Hemisphere. Australia and New Zealand are its two largest countries. The Pacific Islands and Antarctica cover the largest part of the Pacific World. Antarctica is the southernmost continent on Earth. It includes the South Pole, the most southern point on Earth.

- The original people of Australia are the Aborigines. The original people of New Zealand are the Maori. Papuans settled in Melanesia, and Southeast Asians settled in Micronesia.

- English is the main language of Australia and New Zealand. The Pacific Islands have thousands of languages.

- Most Australians and New Zealanders are Christians. The native people practice their own religion. Most people of Oceania are Christians, although some still practice native religions.

- Oceania has a tropical marine climate. Antarctica is an arctic desert. Australia has several climates, but is mostly desert.

- Fewer people are farming in both Australia and New Zealand where industry is growing. The economy of most of the Pacific Islands is based on tourism.

- Australia and New Zealand are rich in natural resources. Most of Oceania is not.

- The biggest environmental problem facing Oceania is protecting the fragile coral reefs. Australia's main environmental problems are deforestation, overgrazing, soil erosion, and destruction of the Great Barrier Reef. Australia and New Zealand have the problem of trying to treat the native people fairly.

Glossary

A

Absolute (ab´ sə lüt) The exact spot or area of a place (p. 27)

Adobe (ə dō´ bē) A sun-dried brick made from mud and straw (p. 491)

Agribusiness (ag´ rə biz´ nis) The business of farming on large farms with many machines and chemicals (p. 175)

Alluvial (ə lü´ vē əl) Fertile soil left behind by a river after a flood (p. 426)

Altitude (al´ tə tüd) How high above sea level a place is (p. 124)

Ancestor worship (an´ ses´ tər wėr´ ship) Worshipping members of one's family who lived long ago (p. 333)

Animist (an´ ə mist) A person who believes that things in nature contain a spirit and who worships ancestors (p. 333)

Apartheid (ə pärt´ hāt) A system that set blacks and other non-white South Africans apart from whites (p. 360)

Aquifer (ak´ wə fər) An underground water source (p. 310)

Archipelago (är´ kə pel´ ə gō) A chain of islands (p. 141)

Arctic (ärk´ tik) The cold area at the most northern part of Earth (p. 190)

Arctic Circle (ärk´ tik sėr´ kəl) The area of latitude about 66.5 degrees north of the equator (p. 99)

Arctic climate (ärk´ tik klī´ mit) A very cold, dry climate (p. 575)

Atheist (ā´ thē i st) A person who does not believe in God (p. 287)

Atoll (at´ ol) A chain of islands made up of coral (p. 145)

B

Balkanization (bôl´ kə nīz ā´ shən) The breaking up of a geographical area or a group of people into smaller political groups; these smaller groups often fight with one another (p. 260)

Basin (bā´ sn) A low area of land surrounded by higher land, often mountains (p. 71)

Bedrock (bed´ rok´) The solid rock under the soil of Earth's surface (p. 93)

Bilingual (bī ling´ gwəl) Speaking two languages (p. 102)

Bog (bog) A low-lying swampy area that is covered by water for long periods of time (p. 193)

Boomerang (bü´ mə rang´) A wooden weapon curved so that it returns to the person throwing it (p. 557)

Buddhism (bü´ diz əm) A religion based on the teachings of the Buddha and practiced mainly in central and eastern Asia (p. 474)

C

Capitalism (kap´ ə tə liz´ əm) An economic system in which people own their own businesses; also called a market economy (p. 477)

Cash crop (kash krop) A crop raised to be sold by those who grow it (p. 143)

Caste (kast) A Hindu social group (p. 431)

Catholic *See* Roman Catholic

Chinook (shə nůk´) A hot, dry wind along the eastern slopes of the Rocky Mountains (p. 99)

Christian (kris´ chən) A person who accepts the teaching of Jesus (p. 76)

Christianity (kris´ chē an´ ə tē) The religion of Christians (p. 76)

Civil unrest (siv´ əl un rest´) A situation in which people fight the government because they are unhappy with the conditions in their country (p. 360)

Civil war (siv´ əl wôr) A war fought between people from the same country (p. 150)

Clan (klan) A large group of related families (p. 25)

Clear cutting (klir´ kut´ ing) Cutting down and removing every tree in an area (p. 106)

Climate (klī´ mit) The average weather conditions over a period of time (p. 31)

Command economy (kə mand´ i kon´ ə mē) An economy in which the government makes the key economic decisions (p. 292)

Communism (kom´ yə niz´ əm) A government system in which there is no private property; the government owns and controls the land and goods (p. 151)

Consumer (kən sü´ mər) A person who buys and uses goods and services (p. 201)

Continent (kon´ tə nənt) One of the seven large areas of land on Earth (p. 67)

Continental climate (kon´ tə nən´ tl klī´ mit) The climate in landlocked areas far from oceans; a climate of short, warm summers and long winters (p. 99)

Continental Divide (kon´ tə nən´ tl də vīd´) Highest mountain peaks in the Rockies that divide the rivers flowing to the east and to the west (p. 71)

Continental drift (kon´ tə nən´ tl drift) The theory that only one huge piece of land was once in Earth's ocean and that the land then drifted apart into seven continents (p. 163)

Cottage industry (kot´ ij in´ də strē) The making of a product at home (p. 435)

Coup (kü) A sudden, usually violent, overthrow of a government (p. 336)

Crater (krā´ tər) A bowl-shaped hole (p. 71); the bowl-shaped opening at the top of a volcano (p. 512)

Creole (krē´ ōl) A mixture of French and African languages (p. 149)

Cultural crossroads (kul´ chər əl krôs´ rōd) A place where different cultures come into contact with one another (p. 266)

Cultural diffusion (kul´ chər əl di fyü´ zhən) The borrowing of language, customs, and religion from other cultures (p. 76)

Culture (kul´ chər) The languages, religions, customs, art, and dress of a people (p. 24)

Currency (kėr´ ən sē) A system of money (p. 223)

Custom (kus´ təm) Something people do out of habit (p. 26)

Cyclone (sī´ klōn) A storm system with strong winds that spin in a circular motion (p. 428)

Czar (zär) A ruler or king (p. 282)

D

Death rate (deth´ rāt) The number of deaths over a given period of time (p. 172)

Deforestation (dē fôr´ ist ā´ shən) The clearing or destruction of forests (p. 106)

Delta (del´ tə) An area of rich land at the end of a river; new land formed by dirt carried downstream by a river (p. 72)

Descendant (di sen´ dənt) A person who is related to a certain group of people (p. 125)

a	hat	e	let	ī	ice	ô	order	ú	put	sh	she		a	in about
ā	age	ē	equal	o	hot	oi	oil	ü	rule	th	thin	ə {	e	in taken
ä	far	ėr	term	ō	open	ou	out	ch	child	ᵺ	then		i	in pencil
â	care	i	it	ò	saw	u	cup	ng	long	zh	measure		o	in lemon
													u	in circus

Desertification (di zėrt´ ə fə kā´ shən) The change from land that produces crops to desert land (p. 326)

Developed country (di vel´ əp ed kun´ trē) A country that has money to provide services for its people (p. 44)

Developing country (di vel´ əp ing kun´ trē) A country in which people are poor and earn their living mostly by farming (p. 44)

Dharma (där´ mə) One's duty (p. 431)

Dialect (dī´ ə lekt) A form of a language (p. 220)

Dike (dīk) A wall that prevents flooding and keeps back the sea (p. 216)

Diversity (də vėr´ sə tē) A variety of people; differences (p. 103)

Dormant (dôr´ mənt) Not active, such as a volcano that is not likely to erupt (p. 144)

Dreamtime (drēm´ tīm) The native Australian Aborigines' belief about how they came to be (p. 558)

Drought (drout) A long period of weather with little rain (p. 99)

Dune (dün) Hill made of shifting sand (p. 309)

E

Earthquake (ėrth´ kwāk´) The shaking of Earth's surface from plate movement (p. 120)

Economics (ə kə nom´ iks) Everything to do with work or money (p. 31)

Economy (i kon´ ə mē) A system of building, using, and distributing wealth and resources (p. 52)

Elevation (el ə vā´ shən) The height above sea level (p. 74)

Enclave (en´ klāv) A part of a country that is separated from the main part (p. 408)

Enlightenment (en līt´ n mənt) A state of perfect freedom from desire and suffering (p. 474)

Environment (en vī´ rən mənt) The natural world in which a person lives (p. 21)

Equator (i kwā´ tər) An imaginary line that goes around the middle of Earth; it lies half way between the North Pole and the South Pole (p. 27)

Erosion (i rō´ zhən) The process by which running water, wind, or ice break down rock or soil (p. 23)

Escarpment (e skärp´ mənt) A line of cliffs or slopes from a plateau to the plains or sea below (p. 328)

Estuary (es´ chü er ē) A flooded river valley at the mouth of a river where salt water from a sea mixes with freshwater from a river (p. 168)

Ethnic group (eth´ nik grüp) A group of people who have a common language, culture, and set of values (p. 266)

Eurasia (yúr ā´ zhə) The world's largest land mass; the continents of Europe and Asia together (p. 216)

Export (ek´ spôrt) Something sent to another country; to sell something to another country (p. 52)

Export economy (ek´ spôrt i kon´ ə mē) An economy in which a country depends on exports for growth (p. 519)

Extended family (ek stend´ ed fam´ ə lē) A mother, father, children, aunts, uncles, cousins, and grandparents (p. 24)

F

Fault (fôlt) A break in Earth's crust where earthquakes usually happen (p. 352)

Fertile crescent (fėr´ tl kres´ nt) The rich farmland between the Tigris and Euphrates Rivers in Iraq and along the Jordan River in Israel and Jordan (p. 379)

Finance (fī´ nans) The use and management of money by banks and businesses (p. 102)

Fjord (fyôrd) A long, deep, narrow, U-shaped valley formed by glaciers that begins far inland and reaches the sea (p. 193)

Floodplain (flud´ plān) A level area of land built up by flood deposits (p. 490)

Foothill (fut´ hil) A low hill at the base of higher hills or a mountain range (p. 166)

Foreign aid (fôr´ ən ād´) Money, medicine, tools, or machinery given by one country to help another country (p. 55)

Free-market economy (frē mär´ kit i kon´ ə mē) An economy in which the makers of products compete for the buyers of products (p. 201)

Free trade (frē trād´) Trade between countries without taxes or other limits (p. 54)

G

Gale (gāl) A strong wind (p. 195)

Geography (jē og´ rə fē) The study of planet Earth and its people (p. 21)

Geologist (jē ol´ ə jist) A person who studies Earth's physical features and their history (p. 97)

Geothermal (jē ō thėr´ məl) Heat from inside Earth (p. 145)

Geyser (gi´ zər) A hot spring that throws jets of water and steam into the air (p. 193)

Glacier (glā´ shər) A large, slow-moving sheet of ice (p. 22)

Globalization (glō bə lī zā´ shən) The steady bringing together of all the world's economies into one (p. 54)

Global village (glō´ bəl vil´ ij) The sharing of ideas, cultures, and customs around the world (p. 39)

Global warming (glō´ bəl wôrm´ ing) The heating up of Earth from burning oil and gas (p. 42)

Government (guv´ ərn mənt) Laws and customs people live by (p. 25)

H

Harmony (här´ mə nē) The ability to work together and to blend in (p. 513)

Heavy industry (hev´ ē in´ də strē) Heavy machinery, steel, and other industries (p. 201)

Hemisphere (hem´ ə sfir) One half of Earth (p. 551)

High islands (hī ī´ lənds) Islands that are the tops of volcanoes that rise from the ocean floor (p. 574)

Highland climate (hī´ lənd klī´ mit) The varying climate of a mountainous area (p. 74)

Hinduism (hin´ dü iz əm) A religion and way of life practiced by most people in India (p. 430)

Human geography (hyü´ mən jē og´ rə fē) The study of how people live on Earth (p. 24)

Human rights (hyü´ mən rīts´) Freedoms that all people enjoy, no matter where they live or who they are (p. 48)

Humid (hyü´ mid) Very moist or wet (p. 74)

Humid continental climate (hyü´ mid kon tə nən´ tl klī´ mit) A climate with long, cold winters and hot, wet summers; a climate with four different seasons (p. 74)

a	hat	e	let	ī	ice	ȯ	order	u̇	put	sh	she		a	in about
ā	age	ē	equal	o	hot	oi	oil	ü	rule	th	thin	ə	e	in taken
ä	far	ėr	term	ō	open	ou	out	ch	child	ᴴ	then		i	in pencil
â	care	i	it	ȯ	saw	u	cup	ng	long	zh	measure		o	in lemon
													u	in circus

Hurricane (hėr´ ə kän) A tropical storm with strong winds, heavy rainfall, and huge waves (p. 147)

Hydroelectric (hī´ drō i lek´ trik) Power created by running water (p. 72)

I

Ideogram (id´ ē ə gram) A picture, symbol, or mark that stands for a thing or an idea in the Chinese language; a character (p. 494)

Immigrant (im´ ə grənt) A person who leaves one country to live in another (p. 77)

Import (im´ pōrt) A product from another country; to bring a product from another country into one's own country (p. 52)

Industrial Revolution (in dus´ trē əl rev ə lü´ shən) A nonviolent change in the late 1700s that included a great increase in the use of iron, steel, and machines (p. 192)

Industry (in´ də strē) Any form of business, trade, or making things by machines (p. 67)

Interaction (in tər ak´ shən) How people settle, use, live on, and change the land (p. 28)

Intercropping (in´ tər krop ping) Planting different crops in the same field (p. 338)

International date line (in tər nash´ ə nəl dāt līn) A line of longitude that is 180 degrees both east and west of the prime meridian (p. 28)

International trade (in ter nash´ ə nəl trād) The buying and selling of goods and services among people in different countries (p. 223)

Inuit (in´ ü it) The native people of Canada (p. 95)

Irrigate (ir´ ə gāt) To bring water to farmland by pipes or channels (p. 43)

Islam (is´ ləm) The religion of Muslims, who follow the teachings of their holy book, the Koran (p. 267)

Isthmus (is´ məs) A narrow strip of land connecting two larger land areas (p. 119)

J

Jainism (jī´ niz´ əm) A religion that began as a protest to the caste system (p. 431)

Jewish (jü´ ish) The followers of Judaism (p. 267)

Judaism (jü dē´ iz əm) The religion of the Jewish people who believe in one God as the creator of the universe (p. 267)

Jungle (jung´ gəl) A thick growth of trees and vines (p. 121)

K

Karma (kär´ mə) The force created by a person's actions that helps determine that person's future (p. 431)

L

Lagoon (lə gün´) A shallow body of water separated from the sea (p. 328)

Landlocked (land´ lokt´) Surrounded by land and far from oceans (p. 99)

Landslide (land´ slīd´) The rapid sliding of earth, rocks, or mud down a slope (p. 471)

Latitude (lat´ ə tüd) How far north or south of the equator a place is (p. 27)

Lava (lä´ və) Hot, liquid rock (p. 120)

Leeward (lē´ wərd) The side away from the wind (p. 74)

Levant (lə vant´) The coastal farming region of Syria, Lebanon, and Israel (p. 379)

Life expectancy (līf ek spek´ tən sē) The number of years an average person usually lives (p. 335)

Light industry (līt in´ də strē) The making of products that people use every day (p. 500)

Location (lō kā´ shən) The place on Earth that something is (p. 27)

Loess (lō´ is) A fine and fertile soil that the wind deposits on the ground (p. 166)

Longitude (lon´ jə tüd) How far east or west a place is from the prime meridian (p. 27)

Low islands (lō ī´ lənds) Islands that are atolls made of coral that surround a sunken volcanic peak (p. 574)

M

Magma (mag´ mə) Hot liquid rock (p. 554)

Mainland (mān´ land´) A large area of land that is not an island (p. 141)

Manual labor (man´ yü əl lā´ bər) Physical work that requires little skill (p. 514)

Marine West Coast climate (mə rēn´ west kōst klī´ mit) A climate from Southeast Alaska to California that has mild, cloudy summers and wet winters (p. 74)

Maritime (mar´ ə tīm) Bordering on or being near the sea (p. 94)

Market economy (mär´ kit i kon´ ə mē) A system in which people, not the government, own businesses—also called capitalism (p. 271)

Mediterranean climate (med ə tə rā´ nē ən klī´ mit) A climate like that of countries near the Mediterranean Sea: mild, wet winters and hot, dry summers (p. 74)

Megacity *See* Megalopolis

Megalopolis (meg ə lop´ ə lis) A vast city made up of many cities, one right next to another (p. 78)

Meridian *See* Prime meridian

Mestizo (me stē´ zō) A person who has both native and European ancestors (p. 125)

Metropolitan (met rə pol´ ə tən) A city and its suburbs (p. 78)

Microstate (mī´ krō stāt) A very small country (p. 235)

Migration (mī grā´ shən) A large movement of people from one place to another (p. 29)

Missionary (mish´ ə ner ē) A member of a church who travels to spread religious beliefs (p. 333)

Monastery (mon´ ə ster ē) A place where people who have taken religious vows or promises lives (p. 474)

Monk (mungk) A person who has made a religious promise and lives in a monastery (p. 474)

Monotheism (mä´ nə thē i zəm) A belief in only one God (p. 386)

Monsoon (mon sün´) Winds that change direction according to the time of year and bring heavy rains in the summer (p. 428)

Moor (mur) A rolling plain covered with grasses and low shrubs (p. 193)

Movement (müv´ mənt) How people, ideas, and products move between places (p. 29)

Mulatto (mə lat´ ō) A person whose ancestors are African and European (p. 148)

Multiculturalism (mul ti kul´ chər ə liz əm) A blend of many cultures (p. 76)

Multinational (mul ti nash´ ə nəl) Companies that do business in many countries (p. 54)

Muslim (muz´ ləm) The followers of the Islam religion (p. 267)

a	hat	e	let	ī	ice	ȯ	order	u̇	put	sh	she		a	in about
ā	age	ē	equal	o	hot	oi	oil	ü	rule	th	thin	ə	e	in taken
ä	far	ėr	term	ō	open	ou	out	ch	child	ᴛʜ	then		i	in pencil
â	care	i	it	ȯ	saw	u	cup	ng	long	zh	measure		o	in lemon
													u	in circus

N

Narrows (nar´ ōs) A place where a river becomes narrow; a strait that connects two bodies of water (p. 264)

Natural resource (nach´ ər əl ri sôrs´) A raw material from the earth (p. 44)

Navigable (nav´ ə gə bəl) A body of water that is deep and wide enough for ships to sail on (p. 146)

Nomad (nō´ mad) A person who moves from place to place (p. 316)

North Atlantic Drift (nôrth at lan´ tik drift) A warm ocean current that begins in the western Caribbean Sea and travels northward through the Atlantic Ocean (p. 195)

Nuclear family (nü´ klē ər fam´ ə lē) A mother, father, and their children (p. 24)

Nuclear waste (nü´ klē ər wāst´) The waste produced by atomic power plants (p. 295)

O

Oasis (ō ā´ sis) An area in the desert with enough freshwater to grow crops or sustain life (p. 310)

Offshore (ôf´ shôr´) Off or away from land in water (p. 130)

Outback (out´ bak´) The hot, dry land in Australia (p. 551)

Overdevelopment (ō vər di vel´ əp ment) Building an area too quickly, without paying attention to the harmful effects (p. 155)

P

Paddy (pad´ ē) A wet field in which people grow rice (p. 477)

Pangaea (pan jē´ ə) The one huge piece of land that once was in Earth's ocean (p. 163)

Parallel (par´ ə lel) A line of latitude (p. 530)

Pass (pas) An opening in a mountain range (p. 216)

Pastoralism (pas´ tər əl i zəm) Combining farming crops and animals (p. 316)

Peak (pēk) The highest point of a mountain (p. 216)

Peat (pēt) Plants that have died and rotted; material burned for heat (p. 193)

Peninsula (pə nin´ sə lə) A strip of land surrounded on three sides by water (p. 121)

Per capita income (pėr kap´ ə tə in´ kum) A way to measure how rich a country is by dividing total income by the number of people (p. 201)

Permafrost (pėr´ mə frost) Ground that is always frozen (p. 99)

Permanent agriculture (pėr´ mə nənt ag´ rə kul chər) Farmers use chemicals on the same field each year (p. 316)

Physical geography (fiz´ ə kəl jē og´ rə fē) The study of Earth itself; the study of the land, water, air, plants, and animals of the natural world (p. 22)

Place (plās) The physical and human features that make an area special (p. 28)

Plain (plān) A flat stretch of land (p. 23)

Plateau (pla tō´) An area of level highland (p. 23)

Plate tectonics (plāt tek ton´ iks) The belief that there is slow movement of Earth's plates (p. 119)

Pogrom (pō grom´) An organized killing of groups of people, especially Jewish people (p. 288)

Polar climate (pō´ lər klī´ mit) A climate with long, cold winters and short, warm summers (p. 285)

Polder (pōl´ dər) A piece of land that was once part of the sea (p. 216)

Political (pə lit′ ə kəl) Having to do with the government—laws and customs people live by (p. 25)

Pollution (pə lü′ shən) Something dirty, impure, or unhealthy (p. 42)

Population density (pop yə lā′ shən den′ sə tē) The average number of people living in each square mile of an area (p. 49)

Precipitation (pri sip ə tā′ shən) Rain or snow that falls from the sky (p. 74)

Prevailing winds (pri vāl′ ing wind) Winds that usually blow from the same direction (p. 355)

Prime meridian (prīm mə rid′ ē ən) A fixed point that is 0 degrees longitude and runs through Greenwich, England (p. 28)

Producer (prə dü′ sər) A company or farmer who makes a product to sell (p. 201)

Protestant (prot′ ə stənt) A Christian who does not belong to the Roman Catholic branch of Christianity (p. 76)

R

Radical (rad′ ə kəl) Using extreme measures or force to get a result (p. 407)

Rain forest (rān′ fôr′ ist) A thick area of trees in the Tropics where a great deal of rain falls (p. 122)

Reef (rēf) A string of rock, sand, or coral close to the surface of a body of water (p. 554)

Reform (rē fôrm′) A change in how people do something to make things better (p. 498)

Region (rē′ jən) An area on Earth's surface that geographers define by certain similar characteristics (p. 24)

Regionalism (rē′ jə nə liz′ əm) Feeling more loyal to one part of a country than to the whole country (p. 243)

Reincarnation (rē in kär nā′ shən) The belief that every living creature is reborn as another living creature (p. 431)

Relative (rel′ ə tiv) How one place compares to another place (p. 27)

Religion (ri lij′ ən) A set of spiritual beliefs or practices about a god or gods (p. 25)

Renewable resource (ri nü′ ə bəl ri sôrs′) A raw material that can be replaced as it is used up (p. 81)

Reservoir (rez′ ər vwär) A place where water is collected and stored, usually created by damming a river (p. 404)

Resource (ri sôrs′) A thing of value, often found in nature, that we can use to do or make something (p. 21)

Rift (rift) A break in Earth's crust (p. 350)

Rimland (rim′ land′) The land, often islands and coastal plains, around the edge of an area (p. 142)

River system (riv′ ər sis′ təm) A group of rivers that join together (p. 71)

Robotics (rō bot′ iks) Using robots or machines to do factory work (p. 520)

Roman Catholic (rō′ mən kath′ ə lik) A Christian who is part of the largest branch of Christianity, led by the pope (p. 76)

Romance language (rō′ mans lang′ gwij) A language that comes from Latin (p. 220)

a	hat	e	let	ī	ice	ô	order	ů	put	sh	she	ə	a	in about
ā	age	ē	equal	o	hot	oi	oil	ü	rule	th	thin		e	in taken
ä	far	ėr	term	ō	open	ou	out	ch	child	ŦH	then		i	in pencil
â	care	i	it	ȯ	saw	u	cup	ng	long	zh	measure		o	in lemon
													u	in circus

Runoff (run´ ôf´) Material mixed with water that washes into rivers and lakes after it rains (p. 367)

Rural (rür´ əl) An area away from cities, such as a farm (p. 49)

S

Sahel (sä hel´) A belt of semiarid land that stretches across Africa from Senegal on the west coast to the highlands of Ethiopia in the east (p. 326)

Sandbar (sand´ bär´) A ridge of sand built up by ocean waves (p. 328)

Sandstorm (sand´ storm´) A wind storm that blows sand through the air (p. 447)

Savanna (sə van´ ə) A flat, grassy plain in the Tropics with few trees (p. 326)

Savanna climate (sə van´ ə klī´ mit) A hot climate that has a very wet season and a very dry season (p. 169)

Scandinavia (skan də nā´ vē ə) The five countries of northern Europe: Norway, Sweden, Finland, Denmark, and Iceland (p. 190)

Sea level (sē lev´ əl) The level at the surface of the ocean (p. 71)

Service industry (sėr´ vis in´ də strē) A business that does not make a product (p. 53)

Shifting agriculture (shift ing ag´ rə kul´ chər) Farmers use a field for a few years, then move to a different field (p. 316)

Shinto (shin´ tō) A Japanese religion in which followers worship spirits in nature (p. 516)

Shogun (shō´ gun) A powerful Japanese military leader (p. 510)

Shortage (shôr´ tij) Not having enough of something (p. 268)

Sikhism (sē´ kiz´ əm) A religion that combines parts of the Islam religion with Hinduism (p. 431)

Silt (silt) The rich soil carried by river water (p. 310)

Sirocco (sə rok´ ō) A hot, dusty, summer wind that sweeps northward from the Sahara (p. 311)

Slave (slāv) A person who is held against his or her will and forced to work for free (p. 148)

Slavic (slä´ vik) Having to do with people from central Asia who settled in eastern Europe (p. 266)

Slum (slum) A rundown, poor, overcrowded part of a city (p. 50)

Society (sə sī´ ə tē) A group of people living together who have common ideas, beliefs, activities, or interests (p. 21)

Specialize (spesh´ ə līz) To work on what one does the best (p. 52)

Staple crop (stā´ pəl krop) A food that people eat most often (p. 338)

Steppe climate (step klī´ mit) A climate with very hot summers and very cold winters, with little precipitation (p. 74)

Stilts (stilts) Heavy poles used to hold up houses (p. 472)

Strait (strāt) A narrow passage of water between two larger bodies of water (p. 235)

Subarctic climate (sub ärk´ tik klī´ mit) The cold climate that is just outside the Arctic Circle (p. 99)

Subcontinent (sub kon´ tə nənt) A large landmass that is smaller than a continent (p. 425)

Subsistence farming (səb sis´ təns farm´ ing) Growing crops mainly to meet the needs of one family (p. 153)

Subtropical climate (sub trop´ ə kəl klī´ mit) A climate with hot and humid summers and mild winters (p. 74)

Suburb (sub´ ėrb) An area next to a city (p. 78)

T

Taiga (tī´ gə) A swampy, evergreen forest bordering on the arctic tundra (p. 284)

Taliban (tal´ ə bən) A religious group that believes in a strict form of Islam (p. 451)

Tapa (tä´ pə) A coarse cloth made by pounding the bark of mulberry trees (p. 580)

Tariff (tar´ if) A tax that countries put on goods they import (p. 223)

Technology (tek nol´ ə jē) The use of science and machines to improve ways of doing things (p. 39)

Tectonic *See* **Plate tectonics**

Temperate climate (tem´ pər it klī´ mit) A climate that is neither very hot nor very cold and has warm and cool seasons (p. 169)

Terrace (ter´ is) A flat field that people create on a hillside (p. 477)

Territory (ter´ ə tôr´ ē) An area of land that is part of a country, but is not officially a province or a state of a country (p. 94)

Terrorism (ter´ ə riz əm) The use of fear and power to control people (p. 451)

Tide (tīd) The regular daily rise and fall of ocean waters (p. 224)

Tierra caliente (tyär´ ə kol yen´ tā) An area of land at a low altitude with a hot average temperature (p. 124)

Tierra fría (tyär´ ə frē´ yä) An area of land at a high altitude with a cold average temperature (p. 124)

Tierra templada (tyär´ ə tem plä´ dä) An area of land that is neither too hot nor too cold (p. 124)

Trade barrier (trād´ bar´ ē ər) A law or act that limits imports or puts special taxes on them (p. 131)

Trade deficit (trād´ def´ ə sit) When a country imports more goods than it exports (p. 578)

Trade imbalance (trād´ im bal´ əns) When a country is paying more for imports than what it receives from its exports (p. 340)

Tradition (trə dish´ ən) An idea, belief, or custom that people pass down to their descendants (p. 39)

Transboundary pollution (trans boun´ dər ē pə lü´ shən) Pollution from one country that affects a different country (p. 538)

Tribe (trīb) A group of people sharing the same habits, language, and ancestors (p. 25)

Tributary (trib´ yə ter ē) A smaller river that flows into a larger one (p. 71)

Tropic of Cancer (trop´ ik uv kan´ sər) An imaginary line that lies 23.5 degrees north of the equator (p. 73)

Tropic of Capricorn (trop´ ik uv kap´ rə kôrn) An imaginary line that lies 23.5 degrees south of the equator (p. 73)

Tropical marine climate (trop´ ə kəl mə rēn´ klī´ mit) A rainy climate that is hot year-round (p. 575)

a	hat	e	let	ī	ice	ô	order	ù	put	sh	she		a	in about
ā	age	ē	equal	o	hot	oi	oil	ü	rule	th	thin	ə	e	in taken
ä	far	ėr	term	ō	open	ou	out	ch	child	ᵺ	then		i	in pencil
â	care	i	it	ȯ	saw	u	cup	ng	long	zh	measure		o	in lemon
													u	in circus

Tropical savanna climate (trop′ ə kəl sə van′ ə klī′ mit) A climate that is hot year-round and has a wet and dry season (p. 123)

Tropics (trop′ iks) The area between the Tropic of Cancer and the Tropic of Capricorn (p. 73)

Tsunami (sü nä′ mē) A huge ocean wave caused by an underwater earthquake (p. 475)

Tundra (tun′ drə) A plain with no trees located in a cold climate (p. 93)

Typhoon (tī fün′) A tropical wind and rain storm that forms over the ocean; also called a hurricane (p. 471)

U

Underemployment (un′ dər em ploi′ mənt) When a person trained for one job must accept another job that often pays less and requires fewer skills (p. 315)

Unemployment (un em ploi′ mənt) The condition of people not being able to find jobs (p. 245)

Urban (ėr′ bən) Having to do with a city (p. 49)

Urbanization (ėr bə nī zā′ shən) Developing more cities or having more people moving into cities (p. 50)

V

Valley (val′ ē) A stretch of lowlands between mountains (p. 119)

Veld (velt) A grassy plain in southern Africa (p. 350)

Volcano (vol kā′ nō) A mountain formed when hot liquid rock comes from deep within Earth to its surface (p. 120)

Voodoo (vü′ dü) A religion that believes good and evil spirits influence a person's daily life (p. 149)

W

Water table (wô′ tər tā′ bəl) The level of underground water (p. 501)

Wetland (wet′ land′) Land covered with water some or most of the time, but where plants continue to grow (p. 106)

Windward (wind′ wərd) The side from which the wind is blowing (p. 74)

Y

Yurt (yůrt) A tent with a wooden frame covered with rolls of wool (p. 408)

Index

Photo Credits

Every effort has been made to secure permission and provide appropriate credit for photographic material. The publisher deeply regrets any omission and pledges to correct errors called to its attention in subsequent editions.

Cover images (background) © Cedric Crucke/Shutterstock; (center left) © Getty Images; (center) © Lenice Harms/Shutterstock; (bottom left) © Vishal Shah/Shutterstock; (bottom right) Courtesy of Katie Colón; pages iii, v, vi, vii, ix, x © Getty Images; page xviii © Blend Images/SuperStock; page xxii © Andres Rodriguez/Shutterstock; page 16 © The Stocktrek Corp/Jupiter Images; page 23 NOAA; page 24 (left) © Corbis; (right) © Photodisc/Punchstock; page 29 © Vova Pomortzeff/Shutterstock; page 41 © Image 100/Jupiter Images; pages 42, 43 © Getty Images; page 45 © Jeff Greenberg/PhotoEdit; page 46 © Hisom Silviu/Shutterstock; page 49 © AP Images; page 50 NASA/Photo Researchers, Inc.; page 53 © Art Wolfe/Danita Delimont, Agent; page 54 © Horizon International Images Limited/Alamy Images; page 56 © Getty Images; page 60 © Li Wa/Shutterstock; page 62 © Steve Allen/Brand X Pictures/Jupiter Images; page 68 © Robert Brenner/PhotoEdit; pages 69, 70 © Getty Images; page 75 © Will and Demi McIntyre/Photo Researchers, Inc.; page 77 © Tom Bean/Corbis; page 78 © Getty Images; page 79 © Purestock/SuperStock; page 80 © AP Images; page 81 © Bryan Busovicki/Shutterstock; page 83 © Getty Images; page 85 © Don Ryan/AP Images; page 86 © Jeff Greenberg/PhotoEdit; page 94 © Cosmo Condina/Jupiter Images; pages 95, 101 © B. & C. Alexander/Photo Researchers, Inc.; page 103 © Nik Wheeler/Danita Delimont, Agent; page 104 © Howard Sandler/Shutterstock; page 107 © Getty Images; page 108 © Lori Adamski Peek/Getty Images; page 112 © Dennis MacDonald/PhotoEdit; page 114 © Mike von Bergen/Shutterstock; page 122 © Imelda Medina/EPA/Corbis; page 123 © Corbis; page 126 Courtesy of Katie Colón; page 129 © Charles & Josette Lenars/Bettman/Corbis; pages 133, 134 © A. Ramey/PhotoEdit; page 142 © Lorne Resnick/AGE Fotostock; page 144 © Ron Niebrugge/Alamy Images; page 145 © Danny Lehman/Corbis; page 151 © Mark Breck/Shutterstock; page 154 © Allen Furmanski/Shutterstock; page 156 © Reuters/Corbis; page 165 © Mark Breck/Shutterstock; page 170 © Natalia Bratslavsky/Shutterstock; page 171 © Tim Holt/Photo Researchers, Inc.; page 173 © Victor Rojas/AFP/Getty Images; page 174 © Getty Images; page 176 © Dario Lopez-Mills/AP Images; page 178 © Mike von Bergen/Shutterstock; page 182 © Fernando Llano/AP Images; page 184 © Nick Martucci/Shutterstock; page 191 © Colin and Linda McKie/Shutterstock; page 195 © Stelian Ion/Shutterstock; page 196 © Peter Baxter/Shutterstock; page 197 © PhotoAlto/SuperStock; page 199 © Topix/Alamy; page 200 © Macduff Everton/Corbis; page 201 © Richard Sheppard/Alamy; page 202 © Galina Barskaya/Shutterstock; page 203 © Comstock/SuperStock; page 205 © Peter Forsberg/Alamy Images; page 206 © David Sanger Photography/Alamy Images; page 213 © Carsten Medom Madsen/Shutterstock; page 215 © Cesair/Shutterstock; page 219 © Gregor M. Schmid/Corbis; page 220 © Michael Mattox/Shutterstock; page 221 © Jan Kranendonk/Shutterstock; page 222 © Albo/Shutterstock; page 226 © Elpis Ioannidis/Shutterstock; page 227 © Egmont Strigl/Imagebroker/Alamy; page 228 © Eddie Linssen/Alamy Images; page 236 © Paul Vorwerk/Shutterstock; page 239 © Svetlana/Shutterstock; page 242 © Bartlomiej K. Kwieciszewski/Shutterstock; page 244 © Doug Pensinger/Getty Images; page 246 © Bettmann/Corbis; page 248 © David Cleaves/Alamy Images; page 252 © Don McKinnell/Cephas Picture Library/Alamy Images; page 254 © Cloki/Shutterstock; page 259 © Dino Ablakovic/Shutterstock; page 261 © Boyer/Roger Viollet/Getty Images; page 267 © Marek Slusarczyk/Shutterstock; page 269 © INTERFOTO Pressebildagentur/Alamy Images; page 270 © John Novis/Photofusion Picture Library/Alamy Images; page 274 © Justus de Cuveland/Imagebroker/Alamy; page 283 © OlgaLis/Shutterstock; page 286 © Zastavkin/Shutterstock; page 288 © Martyn Vickery/Alamy Images; page 289 © ITAR-TASS/AP Images; page 290 © Zastavkin/Shutterstock; page 296 © Bryan & Cherry Alexander Photography/Alamy Images; page 300 © INTERFOTO Pressebildagentur/Alamy Images; page 302 © Fernando Rodrigues/Shutterstock; page 307 © Jose Antonio Sanchez/Shutterstock; page 309 © Jose Fuente/Shutterstock; page 310 © Trans-World Photos/SuperStock/Jupiter Images; page 312 © Oliver Gerhard/Alamy Images; page 313 © Brakefield Photo/

Staff Credits